Patronage and Politics
in Scotland

Patronage and Politics in Scotland, 1707–1832

RONALD M. SUNTER

Department of History
University of Guelph

JOHN DONALD PUBLISHERS LTD
EDINBURGH

ISBN 0 85976 132 0

Exclusive distribution in the United States of
America and Canada by Humanities Press
Inc., Atlantic Highlands, NJ 07716, USA.

The publisher acknowledges the financial
assistance of the Scottish Arts Council in the
publication of this volume.

Phototypeset by Quorn Selective Repro,
Loughborough.
Printed in Great Britain by Bell & Bain Ltd.,
Glasgow.

Acknowledgements

Like any author of a work on Scottish history based upon manuscript sources, I am principally indebted to the helpful staffs of the Scottish Record Office and the manuscript division of the National Library of Scotland, and I have much pleasure in acknowledging their unfailing courtesy. My gratitude is also due to the owners of manuscript collections deposited in the Scottish Record Office whose contribution is warmly appreciated.

The following institutions and their staffs also contributed to this work: the North Riding Record Office, the National Maritime Museum, the India Office Library, Edinburgh University Library, Edinburgh Central Library, and the University of Guelph Library. I am also obliged to the Navy Record Society, whose valuable publications have made naval history so much more accessible.

The Social Sciences and Humanities Research Council of Canada contributed to this work in two ways, first, by awarding research grants to support travel to Scotland, and secondly, by their support of the Scottish collection in the University of Guelph Library.

I must also thank Dr. William Ferguson for permission to make use of his thesis and for his encouragement, and Mr. John Tuckwell, of John Donald Limited, for his patience in dealing with an overseas author who is such a poor correspondent.

Finally, as is customary, I affirm that any errors which remain are my own.

Ronald M. Sunter
University of Guelph

Contents

Part I
Patronage

1

Patronage, Politicians and Voters

Eighteenth-century politics have long had an unsavoury reputation, and although in the case of Scotland much of that reputation can be traced to the persuasive, but not strictly accurate, writings of Henry Cockburn and other Whig reformers of the early nineteenth century, it must be conceded at the outset that there is something to be said for the received account. The Whig reformers had their own political views in mind when they described the typical Scottish politician as a man whose position was secured by extensive bribery of a small venal electorate concerned only with individual advantage, or, alternatively, by the politician ignoring the true electorate and placing reliance upon nominal and fictitious voters who had been added to the freeholders rolls in the counties. In their zeal for a long overdue expansion of the tiny electorate, the critics, however, fail to offer a convincing explanation of how any opposition candidates managed to secure election if the whole system was so totally corrupt, for the argument that certain constituencies were blessed with unusually pure and honest voters is not one which carries much conviction.

It would be difficult to seriously question the received account in relation to the royal burghs, for corruption was rampant in most, if not in all, of them. Politicians who hoped to secure the representation of a burgh district were unlikely to succeed, or, if by some aberration a victory could be obtained, to retain the seat, without satisfying the demands of the burgh oligarchies, whose ambitions were rarely modest. On the other hand, if Scottish political life in the counties is assumed to be explained by the suggestion that bribery was all in all, this would be a misleading impression, for many freeholders were less in the pocket of a political manager than the managers themselves would have liked to think, or conventional accounts would suggest.

Small electorates can be managed by politicians, and when the typical county might number forty to sixty freeholders in its electoral roll, while even one of the more extensive lists would rarely exceed 150 voters, many of whom would be nominally qualified, there was clearly opportunity for manipulation. The art of management, however, was more than the successful bribery of fifty per cent plus one, if for no other reason than the fact that there was never enough of the articles of bribery to employ it on such a scale, even if the voters had been willing to be so bought. The creation of nominal and fictitious votes was by far the greatest abuse to disfigure Scottish politics in the eighteenth century, but that was a form of political corruption which long survived even the Reform Act of 1832,[1] and the only abuse which was truly confined to the period under consideration was that which attempted to capitalise upon the opportunities for manipulating the voters, through a judicious application of patronage, which the small number of voters appeared to invite. The freeholder voting upon a nominal qualification was unquestionably a perversion of the constitution, but the appearance of such voters is also a tacit admission by their creators that they were unable to manipulate the genuine freeholders by corrupt means. Eighteenth-century voters were greedy for patronage, but their openness to bribery was normally limited by their sense of their own position in society. County voters, like their counterparts in the burghs, could be managed, and some of the politicians acquired considerable reputations for their skill in swaying voters, but does that justify the interpretation so sedulously propagated by early nineteenth-century reformers? Was Scotland, in fact, an abyss of political corruption before the country was rescued by the Whigs in 1832?

Political management in a county setting was conducted by different methods from the outright bribery which was so significant a tool of burgh politicians. County freeholders, often indiscriminately styled 'barons', as indeed some of them were, whose estates had been erected into free baronies by a crown charter, were gentlemen landowners of the shire, the direct vassals of the crown, and most of them were fully conscious of holding a social position which demanded that they should not be seen to be in any man's pocket. Such gentlemen freeholders could be manipulated, but they rarely considered themselves the hired retainers of a politician, whose support the latter could take for granted. Patronage was a vital tool of management, but it was never more than a tool, and it was one which was not generally employed in the form of direct bribery. Effective management of a county interest required the politician to do more than strike a bargain in which a vote, or votes, was the return for immediate patronage.

When a politician assisted a freeholder with a gift of a patronage appointment, he would almost always give it in the guise of an act of friendship, and it was the friendly relationship which was the truly significant factor. The intent of the politician was of course to create a feeling of obligation, which he undoubtedly hoped would stand him in good stead at the next election, but such feelings were all the stronger because the shrewd political manager never breathed a word about a bargain or the anticipated political return. Acts of seemingly disinterested friendship, reinforced by regular social contacts, were in fact the only sound approach to building a powerful county interest. On the other hand, even if the politician demonstrated his ability to provide a great deal of patronage, if he did not follow it up with effective social contact, he would be laying a poor foundation for a political interest, and the gratitude of the freeholders under those circumstances could be short-lived. Having laid the groundwork of his interest, the politician had to be ready when election time rolled around again, and at that point an incumbent who could re-apply to constituents whom he had frequent occasion to meet, and ask them for a continuation of their friendship, without suggesting for a moment that any of them had a duty to support him in recognition of an implied bargain for past favours, was in a far stronger position than a man whose only contacts with his constituents took the form of patronage letters.

Patronage was necessary, because it was expected that the member of parliament should be able to obtain it, a fact which goes a long way towards explaining the close links between so many Scots members of parliament and administration. The politician's dilemma has never been better stated than by George Dempster in a letter which he wrote to Sir Adam Fergusson in 1783:

> It is expected that we Members of Parliament should be independent men and men of influence at the same time. That we should be ready to serve our country by opposing bad measures, and our constituents, by supporting every ministerial measure, and that we should disregard the frowns and yet court the favour of our rulers ... The only way I can settle the matter in my brain is to ask little favours of any group of ministers that I stand nearest to, just as I should do a pin or a pinch of snuff, and let the higher duties of my station be as little affected by the one as the other. But this is not very correct, for 1mo. your little favour is perhaps a great one to the person for whom it is obtained and the person who grants it may not agree with you in the justness of the epithet of little. 2o. By our nature we are susceptible of great impressions from small causes. The manner in which the most trifling favour is granted often stamps a great value on it ... 3to. When you ask a minister to do a favour for you or your friend it founds an expectation that you will in return confer a favour upon him. True indeed, the favour granted and expected are somewhat incommensurate. And one would be justified for laughing at a minister who should wonder at your refusing him 20 millions to carry on a foolish war, because at your request he had granted Andrew Blackburn a place in the Customs worth 15£ a year ... [2]

Unfortunately, when a minister with a firm grip on government patronage was involved, a refusal to offer such a return would effectively deprive the member of parliament of further opportunities to aid his own constituents.

In a contested election, however, it was impossible to do much with direct patronage, even if such were available, for there was never enough to do more than grease the palms of a handful of venal men, most of whom were to be found in the burgh councils. There are examples of bribery to be found in the documentation relating to county elections, with votes being purchased outright by timely patronage, but such examples are rare. In 1734, for example, when Campbell of Ardkinglas was faced with a contest in Stirlingshire, this government politician attempted to secure the support of some of the freeholders who were normally to be found in the interest of the Duke of Montrose. One of these gentlemen, Buchanan of Balfunning, who had not yet offered his vote to any candidate, was quite open about his ambitions for, as Ardkinglas remarked, 'he declairs ... he is ready to vote for me providing ther is any thing done for John Buchanan his son'.[3] The laird of Balfunning wanted a tide waiter's place for his son, but Buchanan was clearly not prepared to settle for promises, for he 'insists that he may see his son's commision before the election'. An open sale of a vote, such as this, was quite unusual, however, and Buchanan of Balfunning appears to have been particularly unscrupulous, even on Ardkinglas's own showing, for the latter suggested that if Buchanan could see a commission for his son, 'we have him, if not Montrose has him, to whom he ows many obligations'.[4] As it turned out, the government moved too slowly, for Campbell of Ardkinglas was unable to obtain a revenue office in sufficient time, and the laird of Balfunning voted with the Montrose party in the election of 1734.[5]

The same election provides a further example of bribery, once again involving a Buchanan laird, Moses Buchanan of Glins, whose price for supporting Ardkinglas was the consent of government to his son's succession to John McCure's office of keeper of the register of sasines of Renfrew. In order to secure Moses Buchanan's vote, Sir James Campbell of Ardkinglas was induced to give a bond of £140 Sterling, to be forfeited if the candidate failed to obtain the desired office upon McCure's death. That bill was given, as Ardkinglas explained, 'at the very time the Bell was Ringing for the Election, by which I carryed my Election by two Votes'.[6] Unfortunately for the member of parliament, however, when he approached Lord Ilay to secure the desired permission for young Buchanan to succeed to the office of keeper, his request was denied on the ground that this would be enough to make the post hereditary. Ilay did offer to make good Sir James Campbell's financial loss, but the latter had still not obtained a settlement for the £140 forfeited to Moses Buchanan even in 1739.[7] Beyond question, Moses Buchanan and his son bargained for their votes on the actual day of election, and indeed as Sir James acknowledges, it was their votes which carried his election. In all probability there were always a few freeholders in any county who could be prevailed upon in this way to swing their votes behind a candidate who offered a guarantee of advantage. Nevertheless, the fact remains, these are exceptional cases, and it is worth remarking that even in the two cases cited, the freeholders concerned had not come under any previous commitment to a rival candidate. To switch a vote which had been promised was a still rarer occurrence, and such conduct was seen for what it was, ungentlemanly and unacceptable in persons of the social rank of freeholder. In contrast, in the cruder world of burgh politics, similar conduct was common enough to scarcely elicit comment. In the counties, however, at any period in the eighteenth century, the open sale of a freeholder's vote to the highest bidder was apt to attract censure.

Social attitudes demanded that the politician who aspired to a county interest should handle his constituents with greater care than merely bargaining for votes. Most politicians themselves saw matters in this light, and could harshly rebuff freeholders and their relatives who believed otherwise. David Scott, for example, told one of his Angus constituents in the last years of the eighteenth century, when refusing his request for patronage, that he was

> the last person on earth who would promise you service in return for your brother's vote . . . and therefore, whether these assertions were ever made [by friends] or not, it would be highly unbecoming in me to assist you in the manner you wish, even if in my power. I served your brother when I had not the most distant idea of my ever having use for his services, and if upon the same principle I ever serve you, it must be when publickly known that I neither can benefit by the services of you or him . . . [8]

David Scott was not one of the more successful county politicians, and perhaps his attitude is a little too pure for the real world of eighteenth-century politics, but it represents, even if in an exaggerated form, the general political maxim that the politician performs friendly services for his friends without haggling over a bargain, or even implying that an understanding existed which might suggest that a vote was given for services rendered, or as in this case, for services which might be performed at a future date.

Almost all freeholders would have taken strong exception to the suggestion that their support had been purchased, and this was as true of those gentlemen who had recently obtained posts for themselves or their sons as it was for those who had been less fortunate. When a general election took place, the limited amount of disposable patronage was stretched very thinly, and in Scotland most of what was available would be swallowed by the burgh politicians, where a crucial vote or two might carry the election of a delegate without alienating others. Indeed, in a burgh contest, a well publicised appointment could provide the necessary evidence to the members of council that one of the potential members of parliament had the ear of government. The ability to obtain some patronage during an election contest was often essential to success, for it was not uncommon for every candidate in a crowded field to claim to be a friend of the administration in power. Councillors, most of whom firmly believed that their representative should have close ties with the ministers of the crown, found in a candidate's ability to place friends in local revenue offices and other patronage appointments, and equally, his ability to move political enemies out of such places in the district towns, an effective means of evaluating a candidate's qualification for membership in the House of Commons. In the Scottish burghs bribery and corruption was a way of life for the civic leaders, and direct bribery was rarely absent, but in the counties the employment of patronage would be much more subtle.

It would be wrong to suggest that any segment of an eighteenth-century electorate was truly independent, and a number of ties joined the freeholders to the party, or interest, of a local politician. In this period few lairds could really afford the luxury of complete freedom of action in their politics, for the only means of avoiding ties of obligation, which were nonetheless real for being unspoken, was to refuse to accept any favour. No doubt George Dempster was correct when he wrote that 'the true spirit of our constitution ought to make it criminal in a member of Parliament to offer any constituent the smallest personal favour',[9] but such an opinion was at variance with the facts of eighteenth and early nineteenth-century life. In an age in which almost every worthwhile appointment likely to attract a gentleman could be obtained only through political interest, true independence was a luxury for a few wealthy bachelors without close kin, and politicians were expected to satisfy their constituents' needs. Two bribe-hungry burgesses of North Berwick explained matters quite plainly in a letter which they wrote to Henry Erskine when the latter became Lord Advocate of Scotland in 1806. They advised

> that his Lordship should seize the chief or entire management of all Scots affairs, in the same way that Dundass formerly did, whereby he would become popular in the country, when he could turn out the Dundass party, and put in their places his own friends and well-wishers. His Lordship has a large scale to go on. He has the church, excise, custom-house, post-office, and many other lucrative situations in his power.[10]

Henry Erskine's correspondents could have added to their list several other varieties of revenue officer, judicial appointments, university chairs, first appointments in the army or the navy, and where these could be obtained without purchase, advancement in rank in these services, Indian and colonial patronage, and much more. In any branch of government, civil or military, promotion always came easier to a man who could add political interest to ability, and on occasion the active support of a great man could more than compensate for very limited abilities. Independence, in so far as this entailed freedom from obligation to a politician, was thus restricted to men with independent wealth and few dependents, but for most freeholders the friendship of a politician was a necessity at some point in their lives. The need to start younger members of a family upon a career frequently brought a freeholder to seek the aid of a politician, and this was one of the major elements in interest building. Accordingly, it is necessary to define what should be considered as bribery in the context of the period, rather than as it might be regarded in the twentieth century. To contemporaries, as their private letters demonstrate, the term was effectively restricted to the sale of a vote in return for money, an offer of employment, or other reward during an actual election contest. In other words, contemporaries viewed bribery as a bargain in which a vote was exchanged for something tangible at a time of election, but quite apart from the general distaste for such transactions, there was insufficient patronage available to permit its lavish use, and there was certainly never enough money.

Political power in a county, nonetheless, did demand that the politician make efficient use of patronage to help his friends. No politician, whether a great magnate intent on retaining a traditional dominance in his region, a minister of the crown seeking favourable returns for his administration, or a landowner merely wishing to make a good figure in his own county, could manage without access to patronage with which to reward his friends' loyalty by helping them in their times of need. To most voters patronage appointments were an economic necessity, and for much of the eighteenth century the relative poverty of so many of the Scottish gentry in comparison to their social counterparts in England eased the task of the politician who sought to manipulate them.

If a freeholder stood in no immediate need of a government office for himself, he would normally have sons or other relatives to provide for, and what other outlets were open to younger sons or brothers without capital save patronage appointments? Government offices were obtained through the intervention of a great man, a man of influence, and a job-seeker without such connections had virtually no chance of success in his quest. In 1720, for example, the Duke of Montrose remarked to a Scottish friend, that he had been advised by an official of the Treasury that a presentation to the office of land waiter of the customs at Port Glasgow had been submitted by the commissioners of customs in Scotland. The response of the Treasury official upon receiving the nomination, according to the duke, was to 'put the presentation in his pocket, desiring me rather to name somebody that might be useful for my interest, for nobody knows this Achterlonie'.[11] The salary of the post to which the unlucky Mr Achterlonie aspired was a mere twenty pounds per annum, but Montrose did not disdain it, conscious that 'triffling as such a post is it may effectuallie oblidge some body who may be reddie to repay such a favor upon ane other occasion'.[12] Such favours were the cement of county politics, creating and maintaining political influence, for the Scottish gentry had long memories, both for kindness and injury, and if the latter was rarely, if ever, forgiven, neither was a favour forgotten. If the recipient acted true to type, a sense of obligation could affect voting behaviour many years after the favour had been conferred. Arguably, this is another kind of corruption, but it was in general a very long-range bribery, and it was invariably offered in the guise of friendship.

Under normal circumstances the bulk of government patronage in Scotland would be distributed through the agency of ministers familiar with local politics, and it was this which gave the crown its commanding influence in the country. On the other hand, even efficient 'managers', such as Lord Ilay or Henry Dundas, could never claim absolute mastery of Scotland in fact, whatever they may have alleged to their colleagues, for no manager ever possessed a monopoly of desirable patronage, some of which always remained in private hands. Prior to the abolition of the heritable jurisdictions in 1747, those nobles who possessed extensive judicial rights controlled their own patronage. Such lords could provide for a number of gentlemen in their direct service, appointing to offices ranging from bailies and sheriffs-depute, procurators-fiscal, and clerks to such minor posts as regality officers and keepers of prisons. But even the lowliest appointment might oblige a freeholder who in turn desired to serve some obscure relative or other dependent, while in those appointments which demanded legal training, young advocates could establish their reputation as jurists, which in turn might attract business to their law practices in Edinburgh. James Haldane, when seeking the office of bailie of the regality of Lennox from the Duke of Montrose, hoped by that means to 'occasion . . . partys to imploy him at Edinburgh',[13] and doubtless he was not alone in seeing this connection. The greater landowners would also employ other gentlemen servants in the management of their estates in the early eighteenth century, some of whom might be freeholders, and all of whom would have connections with the voting freeholders, and while it is true that some of these appointments were poorly paid, one has to bear in mind the comparative poverty of so many of the Scottish gentry in terms of money income. As the Duke of Montrose remarked, even if the salary were small, 'a small thing to one that has little is still of value'.[14] Naturally, with the increasing prosperity of Scotland in the course of the eighteenth century, the value of minor private patronage diminished, but it could be replaced on occasion by alternatives, and at no time did the agents of administration control all available employment.

Some Scottish politicians were major stockholders or directors of the East India Company, and important patronage was attached to the office of director. Some directors were of course friends of administration, and used their powers of patronage as far as possible to supplement the efforts of government, but others, and notably the Elphinstone family, used their Indian patronage to sustain an opposition to Henry Dundas in Scotland. First appointments in India were in the gift of the directors of the East India Company. When the number of new writerships, cadetships and surgeoncies which would be required became known each year, the total was divided as evenly as possible into thirty shares. The chairman and deputy-chairman took two shares each, and the remaining directors one share each, and they were free to use these nominations as they saw fit, within certain broad guidelines established by parliament.[15] All of these appointments could be used to help friends and thus to sustain a political interest.

County freeholders and burgh magistrates alike found Indian patronage attractive, for an Indian appointment opened up a career to a poor gentleman as none of the alternatives then available could do. In India, army officers in the Company's service were advanced by time promotion, mitigated in some degree by considerations of evident merit, and commissions were not openly bought and sold as they were in the British army. The lucky recipient of an Indian cadetship had at least the prospect of returning home as a wealthy senior officer, assuming of course that he survived the very real hazards of life in the East. Not surprisingly gentlemen with poor prospects at home clamoured for Indian appointments, and a large proportion of the successful applicants were in fact Scots. To a politician there was no better means of building and preserving a political interest than a demonstrated ability to secure some of the Indian patronage. On the other hand, however much it might be in demand, Indian patronage was never plentiful, for it fluctuated from one year to the next in accordance with Indian needs rather than the wishes of the Scottish politician. In the period 1821–1825, for example, the number of new appointments each year ranged from a low of 237 to a high of 494, but even in one of the better years such a total divided into thirty shares was not going to permit even the best supplied politician to buy his election.[16] Used carefully, however, over an extended period, Indian patronage could permit a politician to capitalise upon feelings of gratitude aroused by acts of seemingly disinterested friendship several years earlier, acts which would in fact be quietly brought to mind by a shrewd politician's regular enquiries about the activities of his young friend in India.

Some freeholders were just as keen as was the average burgh councillor to retain close ties with the government ministers. Lawyers with a keen sense of the value of good political connections for their own professional careers were often very ready to fly in the direction of the politicians who were seen to have power. Henry Erskine once remarked of a Scottish judge and freeholder that 'he was first my enemy, when I came into power he was my great friend, when I went out he turned cool again & left off cultivating me, in that state we now remain, but I make no doubts were I in again, I should have him back again'.[17] Other freeholders, however, were less career-motivated, and often showed considerable loyalty to a particular political interest over an extended period of time, and as a generalisation it might be suggested that they were less likely to jump from one interest to another than were the lawyers with judicial preferment in mind. Without patronage, however, political interests withered in time, for the needs of the voters would drive them to look for aid elsewhere if there did not seem a reasonable probability that their present connections might recover their lost influence in London.

The scarcity of employment suitable for the sons of a gentleman provided the man who could meet that need with very real influence in his region, and a favour of considerable value to a freeholder need not involve any major place in government service. In 1749, for example, Lord Panmure was asked to obtain a small revenue post of tide waiter for a brother of one of the Angus freeholders. The laird who sought the politician's aid had found himself in an embarrassing predicament when a brother had unexpectedly returned to the family estate after many years spent at sea. As the laird described his situation, his brother

> was not pinched in his education would he apply'd ... he was bred to the sea way of life, rov'd & stray'd thro' almost this universe, with regrate I write his ambition never exceeded that of walking before [the] mast, and after had broken a good constitution to return back upon his Bror. without either money or cloaths, the injury he has done being wholly to himself pleads compassion. My children are two boys & four girles, and ... my Bro[the]r William, which he is whithr. I will or not, having brot home so much of the ruffness and unguarded stile of expression that I cannot shew my young flock such a copy, otherwise he would not be denyed necessary at my house ... [18]

Clearly, a member of parliament who could take the foul-mouthed uncle William far from the laird of Craigie's children might legitimately expect the memory of such a favour to persist for an election or two. Under normal circumstances small favours of this type could be obtained by a politician with government connections, and it was only circumstances of a temporary nature which made job provision difficult for Scots politicians, such as the effective block which appeared in 1737 following the lynching of an officer of the City Guard of Edinburgh, when as a writer remarked, the hanging of Captain Porteous 'sticks vastly in his majesties stomach and has been a great detriment to our countray-men in getting any thing done'.[19] The more normal situation, however, was that indicated by a correspondent of a Berwickshire member of parliament, who remarked that 'a Member of a County who has served materially ... ought to have full credit 'wt a minister to the extent in view'.[20]

Good connections with a minister would be advantageous to any political interest, for freeholders and councillors often requested assistance which only government could provide. This was particularly true when the request did not involve employment, for the successful conferment of a small charitable favour was in fact more likely to be long remembered than the award of a place. On occasion a member of parliament might be asked to obtain a sinecure, a nominal place which would provide income without the necessity of having to do anything to earn it. John Wallace, one of the magistrates of the burgh of Arbroath, explained his reasons for seeking a sinecure appointment worth £50 or so for his son, by emphasising his fear that 'the lad will turn out but indifferently qualified for business otherways I should not give so much trouble in asking something for him ... I'm doubtfull he's but unfitt for anything requires attendance'. [21] Pensions might also be requested for those whose finances had become disordered, and shrewd politicians, like Mungo Graeme of Gorthie, the manager of the Duke of Montrose's interest in Scotland, knew that time spent asking a pension in the charity roll for the sister of a laird might produce a political return for many years. The lady in question was married to a lawyer who, in spite of being a writer to the signet, must have been singularly incompetent, for, as Gorthie remarked, 'he's a senseless fellow that can make no shift for her and a great many children they have'.[22] The laird, however, would have a short memory indeed if he did not feel a deep sense of gratitude to the man who could remove the spectre of this large indigent family becoming a charge upon his estate.

Councillors and freeholders involved in business activity, particularly manufacturing, might also seek commercial favours through their member of parliament, such as the award of a contract. In 1789, for example, an unsigned letter received by Sir Thomas Dundas advised the member of parliament that a Mr. Glen, a freeholder of Stirlingshire, would be greatly obliged if he could obtain introductions to colonels of regiments who might be induced to give the enterprising Mr. Glen the clothing contracts for their units.[23] A land lease was another kind of commercial favour which recurs, and this too could form a useful and persuasive means of keeping a voter's loyalty, as in the attempt to augment the Argyll interest in the burgh of Stirling in 1756 by giving a tack of land in Argyllshire to Robert Campbell, a brother of the laird of Barcaldine, who was one of the merchants of the town.[24] A politician might even be asked for land grants in the colonies, as Henry Dundas was, on one occasion by Provost John Buchan of Stirling, who requested the favour for one of the former magistrates who intended to settle in Canada.[25]

Occasionally the pressure for favours from a voter who felt that the obligation was on the other side, because of the applicant's voting record, could be excessive, and it might be pushed far beyond what the politician would consider reasonable. A freeholder named John MacLachlan exerted considerable pressure upon Lord Milton, the manager of the Argyll interest, after MacLachlan had supported that interest in the politics of his county. MacLachlan successfully obtained through Milton's aid a delay in a foreclosure by the Royal Bank, and the freeholder hoped to persuade the politician to continue to stand between him and his creditors because of the value of his vote to the Argyll interest, arguing that

> My behaviour in the lat[e] Election got me so many enemies, who have been at pains to stir up all my creditors agst me, which puts me under a necessity of selling the lands by which I have my vote, or to borrow money. My oyr. lands I cannt think of selling as they answer so well for my bussiness of breeding and fattening cattle and have good woods and sclate quarys upon them ... [26]

Just in case Lord Milton failed to appreciate his value, MacLachlan stressed that he had been approached by the rival interest in the county and had been offered sufficient to make him easy for life, and accordingly implied that Milton had an obligation to aid him with his creditors and enable him to arrange further loans. MacLachlan, moreover, was not averse to seeking further advantages for himself, for while acknowledging Milton's assistance in getting him a tack of two farms in Morvern for nineteen years, which would scarcely appear to be a short lease, he complained that he had been informed that other tenants had obtained tacks of three times the length of that which he had from the Duke of Argyll, urging that he could 'be as usefull as any in that Countrey by introduceing a cheap method of improvement and otherwise'.[27]

Many Scottish freeholders were involved in colonial trade and the plantation economy of the West Indies and, as might be expected, they saw their member of parliament's influence in London as a route to obtaining the advantages which they desired in the colonies. In 1795–6, for example, the member of parliament for the county of Angus found himself much concerned with the fate of a piece of crown land which happened to be situated within the plantation lands in the island of St Vincent belonging to Patrick Cruickshank of Stracathro, one of the Angus freeholders. The laird of Stracathro, from the urgency of his correspondence, was clearly in terror that the land in question might be granted to another, for he was not attempting to secure a gift of the land but offering to pay full market value for it.[28]

Voters who themselves got into a brush with the law, or whose friends had done so, were also among those seeking a politician's intervention. In 1746, for example, William Grant, who in spite of his seemingly humble occupation of carpenter was the son of an Inverness-shire laird, chose a particularly inconvenient moment to take leave from the service of the Hudson's Bay Company and return to Scotland, for he was promptly committed to prison on suspicion of treason when he reached Scotland during the turmoil occasioned by the Jacobite Rising. William Grant, however, was described as 'a very honest man & sincere friend to the present happy establishment', a claim which was being made in the aftermath of the Jacobite defeat for many Scots.[29] In the circumstances, any aid which a politician could offer was a very material favour which would long be remembered by the friends of the individual in difficulties.

In addition to the services of every kind asked by the voters, effective management would also involve the politician in substantial expenses, for any major political figure owed it to his position in society to give generously for any public concern. Sir Thomas Dundas, the member of parliament for Stirlingshire, was asked to contribute the not inconsiderable sum of £850 sterling towards the cost of the bridge of Frew.[30] Sir Thomas's father, Sir Lawrence Dundas, when active in the politics of the city of Edinburgh, was a notable supporter of charities and other good causes, contributing on one occasion as much as £1,000 for the raising of nine companies of Royal Edinburgh Volunteers for service in the American War of Independence, a contribution exceeded only by the city itself, which gave £1,050.[31] Politicians with a burgh interest regularly made contributions to the cost of public works in the communities with which they concerned themselves, as Lord Panmure did in 1761, when he subscribed for the construction of a new town hall in Montrose.[32]

Those who attempted to manage the political affairs of a county or district of burghs had not only to contribute towards any public project in their area, they were expected to be the leading subscribers, and it mattered little whether or not they agreed with the project in view. In 1739, for example, the Duke of Montrose was advised that the gentlemen of Stirlingshire had determined to enliven the normal Michaelmas proceedings with an assembly and race meeting, a project whose promoters were not among the duke's political friends. Montrose, however, understood that although he had not been consulted and

> it be perhapes beginning a foolish & expensive scene, since the Gentlemen in general apear to give into it and have allreddie begun to subscribe some for one and some for two guineas ... considering my estate in that shire, and that L[or]d George has offer'd his service [as member of parliament] it will no doubt be expected that the whole family should subscribe. Upon such occasions even trifles become matters of consequence and must not be neglected ... Certain it is we must be the highest subscribers for that will be expected, the quantum to be subscribed by each must be regulated by what is done by others ... L[or]d Graham & L[or]d George to be equall, whatever L[or]d Rothes or L[or]d Erskine give, my two sons must be higher by a guinea each, and I one guinea higher than either of my sons ...[33]

Charitable donations, however, did nothing to enhance a political interest, even if a lack of charity could seriously harm it, for a substantial contribution from a major political figure was no more than was expected by the gentlemen of a county or the magistrates of a burgh. The major tool of management was always employment, for it was only through interest that anything worthwhile could be obtained, for even appointments in mercantile houses at home or abroad could often only be obtained through interest, while all appointments in government service were patronage appointments, in fact if not always in theory.

The most desirable form of employment for many Scots in the eighteenth century was that provided by the East India Company, and a politician with access to this commodity was normally a man of strong interest in his region. Burgh councillors were particularly enthusiastic about the opportunities which a career in India might offer to their sons. They were indeed too enthusiastic, for the demands of several burgh councils could prove too much for the resources of even the best-endowed East India Company director. David Scott, for example, complained that he got so many requests for Indian patronage from the council of St. Andrews that if the remaining burghs in his district were to seek aid in proportion to the size of their communities it 'would require more patronage than the whole East India Direction have in their gift'.[34] Admittedly, a hard-pressed politician could occasionally borrow a cadetship or other appointment from another director, promising to repay the loan in a future year, but the small size of the Indian official class meant that such a practice of burdening oneself for the future could be hazardous. The small number of Indian places was, however, one of its attractions and certainly raised its value in the eyes of the applicants. In the 1830s the total number of European military officers serving in India amounted to only 4,487, of whom 752 were serving in the royal army, as opposed to the regiments in the Company's employ, thus reducing the total to a mere 3,735. The Indian civil administration was even smaller, numbering only 857, with 32 on average required annually to maintain the strength of the service. Of the remaining places of interest to freeholders and other voters, the medical service employed 542 officers, while the Indian Marine, the naval service of the Company, provided places for only 12 captains, 14 commanders, 46 lieutenants and 71 officers of lesser rank in its warships and dockyards. [35]

A place in the small Indian establishment offered the successful applicant a career which could bring great responsibilities at an early age and at what was nominally a junior rank, and perhaps more importantly, it was well rewarded. The best appointments upon entry were those of writer, the junior civil rank, for such civilians, it was claimed in the course of a debate in the East India House,

> lived most sumptuously, kept a number of servants, horses and carriages. After ten years service, they could by means of a civil fund as it was called, proceed to England, for three years on leave of absence, with a salary of 500£ per annum; and after 22 years of service they retired permanently with a pension of 1,000£ a year. [36]

The Company's military officers, if less well paid than their civilian brethren, were yet infinitely better placed than their counterparts in the military service of the crown. Rank for rank, East India Company officers received double the pay of an officer of a royal regiment, while serving in a country with a much lower cost of living. After twenty-two years' service, an officer of the Company's armies was entitled to retire with a pension equal in value to the full pay of a royal officer or equivalent rank. The cash value to be placed upon a first appointment as writer or cadet is uncertain, for it obviously depended upon the number of years in which a candidate would draw the salary, but contemporaries no doubt took the possibility of an early death from disease into account when they spoke of a value of £1,000. [37] Accordingly, it is evident that a gift of such significance could have been of no small value to a freeholder or councillor who would otherwise have found difficulty in endowing a relative so generously at the commencement of his career.

The one major restriction upon the usefulness of Indian patronage to the manager of a political interest was the fact that it was restricted to the young. There were strict age limits for entry to the training establishment maintained by the Company to train its recruits, for cadets and writers had to enter within the ages of fifteen and twenty-two, and there was thus great anxiety to secure a place in a director's list which would ensure that an appointment could be secured before age excluded the candidate for ever. Directors would normally maintain such lists of candidates in order of the date of receipt of the applications, but this apparent fairness had occasionally to be circumvented in case of urgent necessity by borrowing from another director with a less crowded list in the case of an older candidate, for it was often not feasible to advance a candidate over the heads of others in a list for fear of giving lasting offence. The keen demand made patronage a double-edged weapon for the politician, who could find himself making enemies as readily as friends unless he proceeded with the utmost caution in everything he attempted.

Indian patronage was further divided by the intended destination in India, for military cadets were not appointed for service in India at large, but to a particular presidency, each of which maintained its own army. Of the three divisions, Bengal ranked first, followed by Madras and lastly by Bombay, in an order determined by the potential opportunities in each location. A politician who could offer a friend's relative one of the better appointments could consider that he had rendered a signal service, which he was rarely slow to point out. 'I have got an appointment for young Walker for Madras instead of Bombay which I am sure will please his friends',[38] David Scott told his agent in St. Andrews, on one occasion. William Elphinstone, another East India Company director, advised his friend, the Glasgow merchant Peter Spiers, that he could

> easily get your son changed from Bengal to Bombay, but I cannot advise it. Bengal is certainly the best appointment, and I intended that your son should have the best. I do not wonder that he should wish to be with Graham ... I have regretted ever since I knew Graham's very superior ability that he is gone to Bombay. Bengal is head quarters and there he must have got on much better, and higher than at Bombay, there is a greater field for him to act in ... [39]

If the military and civil branches of the East India Company's service were the most attractive forms of Indian patronage, the appointment of surgeon, either in India itself or on board an East Indiaman, one of the privately owned merchant vessels which carried Indian trade, was considered a desirable place by many Scots with the necessary professional training. Of the less well known Indian appointments, a place in the Indian Marine also attracted a number of Scots even though it was based at unpopular Bombay, for it was a service which promoted by seniority, and death from wounds or disease could allow the rapid elevation of a healthy midshipman to a position of command. The attraction of such a place was enhanced by the prize money paid in time of war to officers of the Indian Marine as to those of the Royal Navy, but the time promotion was unique to the Indian service, virtually guaranteeing advancement in rank.[40]

Cargoes taken to and from the East were carried in specially built ships, which were among the largest contemporary merchantmen, the East Indiamen, and the officers' places in these ships were an additional source of private patronage for those politicians who enjoyed influence with the owners of the ships, for it was the owners, not the Company, who appointed the commander and mates of East Indiamen. Ships sailing to India which were not directly owned or managed by the Company were considered to be permanently chartered to the Company, but the value of the charter to the vessel's owners and officers was determined by the port to which it was sent, and that was a decision made by the Company. Accordingly, this power to name destinations gave the senior officers of the East India Company considerable influence over shipowners and they could, in turn, make use of such influence to aid their own political interest.

East Indiamen, being large vessels with correspondingly large crews, were run on a lavish scale reflecting the profits generated by Indian voyages, with one of the smaller ships manned by about sixty men and a larger vessel carrying a crew of as many as 130. The crew would in turn be commanded by an unusually large number of officers for a merchant ship, for, in addition to the commander, the ship might carry six mates, a surgeon, a purser, five midshipmen and a surgeon's mate, [41] any one of whose places would be of value to a politician seeking to build up an interest. The value of an officer's place in an East Indiaman did not lie in the salary, which was only marginally more attractive than that paid to other ship's officers. The great advantage which officers of East Indiamen possessed over their counterparts in less favoured ships was their customary right to own a certain proportion of the cargo carried, and to sell that share at the end of the voyage for their own profit. Cargo shares were of course proportioned to rank, but for the more senior officers it could almost guarantee wealth. The commander of an East Indiamen might bring home with him 38 tons of cargo, his chief mate was allowed eight tons, the second officer six tons, and the remaining officers in decreasing proportion, but for all of them it was an important part of their remuneration. The commander of a ship, however, had additional perquisites which added to the value of his appointment, for it has been claimed that he could make as much as £1,500 in a single voyage from the fares paid by passengers, while he even had the right to sell for his own profit at the end of the voyage the dunnage, that is the bamboos and rattans employed to keep the cargo from shifting. In short, the command of an East Indiaman was a very profitable situation, and accordingly the award of a good voyage was said to be

> the greatest thing in the power of a director, or rather of the chairman—for a Bombay or China voyage to a large ship is . . . generally supposed nearer £10,000 profit than £5,000. In my own private opinion I should calculate on the £10,000 being the most probable sum . . . [42]

Even if a Bombay or China voyage was as profitable as David Scott suggested, a vessel with excellent accommodation for passengers was likely to bring a greater reward to its commander if it went to Bengal, for the centre of government was the destination of many of the wealthier travellers. Unfortunately, however, a good many East Indiamen were unable to enter the Bay of Bengal, which was effectively restricted to vessels whose bottoms had been plated with copper to prevent damage from marine worms. Accordingly, for many ships without such protection, Bombay was the desired port of destination, and getting a suitable voyage was one of the primary concerns of members of parliament with East Indian connections who included among their constituents captains of East Indiamen. The commander of the East Indiaman *Woodcott*, Captain Ninian Lowis, married the daughter of a prominent Stirlingshire freeholder, John Monro of Auchenbowie, and thereafter the voyages of Auchenbowie's son-in-law were of no small concern to the county member, Sir Thomas Dundas.[43] Such examples can easily be multiplied without going beyond the bounds of the county of Stirling, The Honourable William Elphinstone, a gentleman active in the politics of both Dunbartonshire and Stirlingshire, was three times chairman of the East India Company and always maintained close relations with the shipping interest, having himself commanded the East Indiaman *Tryton* before becoming a director, while the Haldanes of Airthrey, significant in the political life of Perth, Dunbarton and Stirlingshire, had similar connections with the Indian shipping interest. Indeed, Captain Ninian Lowis, of the *Woodcott*, like many another officer of the Indian fleet with Scottish connections, became a freeholder in his home county. Moreover, through the agency of these men, many Scottish gentlemen found places as midshipmen on board East Indiamen and, with experience gained in that rank, could be advanced in the hierarchy of ship's officers, although it must be conceded that an appointment as midshipman, or fifth or sixth officer of an Indiaman was not to be compared to the value of a writership or cadetship in the Company's own service.

The principal difficulty with an officer's place in an East Indiaman was its insecurity and the difficulty of obtaining advancement in rank. The system of private ownership, and the profits which were made by the captains, made it very probable that the command would go to a friend of the owner, or, since many of the ships were owned by partnerships, to one of the actual proprietors of the vessel. The captain and the chief and second mates received cargo allotments of value, but officers of junior rank were unlikely to make very substantial profits, even if they were not forced to share their allocation of cargo space with the commander in order to obtain a place at all. The profit from private trading, which was the chief attraction of service in an East Indiaman, was really a monopoly of the senior officers, and considerations of nepotism and private interest ensured that there was a considerable element of uncertainty in an officer's career in this service. In contrast, those lucky enough to obtain a place in the East India Company's own service could anticipate a reasonable career without the necessity of further patronage, even though, without question, a servant of the Company whose career was watched by a great man would rise more rapidly. A sea officer, however, who was without significant influence, was likely to find himself regularly passed over for promotion by friends of the owners being groomed for command. Indeed, to secure an officer's place at all for an Indian voyage was something only obtainable by interest. A commander might be so well pleased with an officer that he might wish to retain his services for another voyage, and if a part-owner might be able to insist upon it, but appointments normally went by interest. Competition could be fierce, as a young Dundee officer discovered when even the influence of the powerful David Scott failed to secure him a place for the voyage of 1801 because

the application I fear came too late. My solicitations have been to Mr. Bonham as owner of the *Belvedere,* to Mr. D. Hunter, owner of the *Lord Hawkesbury,* and lastly to Mr. Palmer, owner of the *Boddam.* Each of the Second Mate's berths were filled up just before my application . . . Such things should be applied for previous some months to the taking up of ships as otherwise they are filled & generally with others to succeed in case of vacancy . . . [44]

The member of parliament did not give up his efforts to find a place for the young officer, but the close connection between parliamentary politics and placement was made abundantly clear by Scott's insistence to his correspondent that the young man's father, a Dundee councillor, would first have to make clear 'whether he is to be friendly' to the politician. 'You know the bad consequence of my laying myself under unnecessary obligation, and you will therefore take care that I only do it for real Friends that I can depend upon,' the member of parliament warned.[45]

Accelerated promotion in an East Indiaman was only to be obtained through political or family interest, such as that exerted by the Earl of Findlater upon James Oswald of Dunnikier. Lord Findlater wrote in favour of a young man named Robert Ross, who had returned to Britain after completing two voyages as midshipman in Captain Haldane of Airthrey's ship, the *Duke of Gloucester*. The next step in rank for a man of Ross's experience would be fifth mate, but Lord Findlater, who insisted that young Ross had been 'much commended', attempted to secure a fourth mate's place for his friend. Once again the motive was political. 'You know my connection with this brothers,' wrote the earl, 'and I believe he is a very fine lad.'[46] Without such interest an officer was likely to remain in a junior post for many years, whatever experience he might accumulate. Some such unfortunates ultimately abandoned the East Indiamen for a place in the pilot service in India, after they had acquired sufficient influence with important passengers to secure such an appointment, while others might take a place as an officer of one of the so-called country ships, which operated only in the East and did not return to Europe.

In the world of the eighteenth century almost everything went easier with the patronage of a great man, a fact which is as true of non-governmental posts as it is of those in the service of the crown. It would be a rare individual who was able to make use of a political connection who failed to do so, for the advantages were well known. Letters of recommendation were often requested by those about to sail for India or another overseas possession, and such letters were even sought by those already serving in India when they appreciated that the interest of a man of influence would accelerate their own advancement. In the service of the East India Company experience was an asset, and merit was expected in those promoted, but interest united to merit was always a much stronger argument than merit alone. Thomas Cockburn, a young Berwickshire man serving at Madras, requested his freeholder father to approach his member of parliament to seek letters of recommendation to the governor, Lord Macartney, for as the father pointed out, 'every thing goes by interest, and he is very anxious to have Letters of Weight'.[47]

It was the scarcity of Indian appointments, coveted by so many applicants, which gave such great influence to those politicians able to produce some of them for their friends. At the same time, however, the politician's inevitable inability to satisfy all of his friends demanded great management skills to mollify the disappointed. Failure to secure an appointment, particularly when that failure could be linked to an appearance of neglect, would produce lasting enmity more certainly than the gift of patronage could ensure permanent friendship. The ability of the politician to provide patronage, of whatever nature, was never more than a tool of management, and however useful it might be to the man who could supply it, patronage in itself did not remove the need for active and continuous management of the voters included within the interest. Social contacts had to be preserved, and ties flowing from feelings of friendship remained indispensable. A member of parliament unable to gratify a constituent's wish for a cadetship for his son had to explain that failure, and if age did not intervene as a barrier to future prospects, the politician would be expected to indicate when a successful outcome might be anticipated.

Politicians, however, were quite capable of making any assistance look somewhat larger than life and thus attempt to reap the last ounce of voter gratitude for their services. An appointment of fairly uncertain prospects could be described in such glowing terms that a possibility of prosperity could be turned into an appearance of certain advancement to high rank. David Scott managed this effectively in one of his communications with Patrick Rigg, the principal figure in the burgh of Cupar, to whom he offered an appointment as clerk in the India House for a young man favoured by the burgh council. The clerkship was in fact virtually unpaid for three years, during which the juniors were paid only £20, and had to live in London in the style of gentlemen. However, as Rigg was advised,

> At the expiration of three years they come to £70 per annum and rise by seniority to the heads of the respective offices provided they have ability and character. You'll be surprised at such low paid offices being so highly in request until I acquaint you that the heads of our different departments have most liberal allowances, £500, 700, 1000, 1200, 1500, and as far as £2,000 per annum, some of the heads of offices have including perquisites. I give you this little history ... so that our friends of Cupar may know that we don't do things by halves ... [48]

As David Scott described it, a low-paid clerkship, which would necessitate payment of a living allowance by the clerk's friends, was miraculously translated into a certain path to riches and a special compliment to the civic leaders of the town of Cupar. Interest was needed to obtain any office, but all too often it was also required to rise in rank thereafter, and something more than the 'ability and character' mentioned by Scott would be needed to take the junior clerk to the headship of a department. Superior qualifications were, indeed, by no means a guarantee of preferment, on the testimony of David Scott himself, who admitted on another occasion that 'there was some altercation about the superior qualifications of the other candidates, but on my shewing the chairman the anxiety I had to provide for your friend, with his assistance I carried it'.[49] The desire to satisfy friends could, on occasion, prove embarrassing to a patron if the manifest incapacity of their candidate was disclosed. David Scott, when strongly pressing the candidacy of Abram Robinson for a surveyor's post in the East India Company's service, encountered one of the occupational hazards of a politician in this period, when he found that his candidate was totally lacking in any manner of qualification for such a situation. Scott complained bitterly to the gentleman who had recommended Robinson that

> You can have no conception how I was hurt at finding that the poor man had not the least education not even so far as to write his own name. Of course he was rejected, but it threw me into a most awkward situation indeed to recommend such an illiterate person for such an office. My Friend you should have informed me on this

head. Had you known how it subjects a person in my situation to exposition recommending improperly I am sure you would have given me the fullest information. I never had an idea he could not write until I took him into a private room to try him in writing . . . [50]

If politicians were normally able to manipulate freeholders and councillors by judicious use of their patronage powers, it is equally clear that they were on occasion themselves manipulated, and for all David Scott's obvious embarrassment over the Robinson affair, it is evident that he felt unable to show much resentment towards the man who had led him into that predicament. The necessary appearance of friendship had to be maintained at all times, and patronage continued to flow in the direction of the town of Perth from which the unfortunate Mr. Robinson came. Indian patronage and the prospect of such patronage was the cement of David Scott's political interest in the Dundee district of burghs. A following based upon the prospect of future advancement and the ability to secure employment for new candidates for office was always much easier for politicians who, like David Scott, were favoured by Administration, for there were so many ways in which Government could afford to help politicians without the age barriers which limited the free employment of Indian patronage. Nowhere was it easier for an administration politician to provide help than in questions relating to military and naval preferment, but for a politician in opposition it was much more difficult, though not impossible, to help or hinder a career.

NOTES

1. William Ferguson, 'The Reform Act (Scotland) of 1832: Intention and effect,' *SHR* 45 (1966), 105–114.

2. James Fergusson *Letters of George Dempster to Sir Adam Fergusson, 1756–1813*, 120–121 (London, 1934), 22 Sept., 1783.

3. NLS Saltoun, MS.16555, Sir James Campbell of Ardkinglas to Lord Milton, 15 May, 1734.

4. Ibid.

5. SRO. Minutes of the Freeholders of Stirlingshire, SC67/59/1/83, 30 May, 1734.

6. NLS. Saltoun MS.16555, Sir James Campbell of Ardkinglas to Milton, 3 Jun., 1734.

7. NLS. Saltoun MS.16576, Sir James Campbell of Ardkinglas to Milton, 8 Nov., 1739.

8. India Office Home Misc. 728/147, Letter Books of David Scott, David Scott to David Ferguson, 9 Jan., 1796.

9. James Fergusson *Letters of George Dempster to Sir Adam Fergusson*, 121.

10. Alexander Fergusson, *The Hon. Henry Erskine, with notices of his kinsfolk and of his times* (Edinburgh, 1882), 438–9.

11. SRO. Montrose, GD220/5/832, Duke of Montrose to Mungo Graeme of Gorthie, 12 May, 1720.

12. Ibid.

13. SRO. Montrose, GD220/5/811, Mungo Graeme of Gorthie to Montrose, 5 Sep., 1714.

14. SRO. Montrose, GD220/5/812, Duke of Montrose to Mungo Graeme of Gorthie, 18 Dec., 1714.

15. R. Montgomery Martin, *East Indies*, vol. 2 (London, 1837), 122–3.

16. *The Oriental Herald,* Jul., 1827, 'Debate at the India House on the patronage of

Directors, 20 Jun., 1827'.

17. SRO. Scott of Harden, GD157/2880/1, Francis Scott to Hugh Scott, 21 Feb., 1789.

18. SRO. Dalhousie, GD45/14/432, James Guthrie to Lord Panmure, 9 Aug., 1749.

19. SRO. Scott of Ancrum, GD259/4/2, Henry Balfour to Sir John Scott of Ancrum, 1 Apr., 1737.

20. SRO. Scott of Harden, GD157/2943/12, Thomas Cockburn of Rowchester to Hugh Scott, 7 Jun., 1783.

21. SRO. Dalhousie, GD 45/14/432, John Wallace to Lord Panmure, 17 Mar., 1751.

22. SRO. Montrose, GD220/5/816, Mungo Graeme of Gorthie to Montrose, Sept., 1715.

23. North Riding Record Office, Zetland Papers, ZNK/X/2, Anonymous to Sir Thomas Dundas, 29 Nov. 1789.

24. NLS. Saltoun, MS.16695, Mrs. Mary Campbell to Milton, Mar., 1756.

25. SRO. Melville Castle, GD51/6/2113, Provost John Buchan to the Lord Advocate.

26. NLS. Saltoun, MS.16696, John MacLachlan to Lord Milton, 26 Jan., 1756.

27. Ibid.

28. India Office Home Misc. 728/209-211 and 507-8, and SRO. Melville Castle, GD/51/1/198/2/18-19 refer to this matter.

29. NLS. Saltoun, MS.16646, John Grant to Lord Milton, 9 Mar., 1747.

30. North Riding Record Office. Zetland Papers, ZNK/X/2, Note on Bridge of Frew payment.

31. *Scots Magazine* 42, Appendix, 712 (1780).

32. SRO. Dalhousie, GD45/12/431, Receipt issued by William Speid, town clerk of Montrose, 1 Oct., 1761.

33. SRO. Montrose, GD220/5/905, Duke of Montrose to Mungo Graeme of Gorthie, 17 Sept., 1739.

34. India Office Home Misc. 729/3, David Scott to Alexander Duncan, 13 Nov., 1796.

35. R. Montgomery Martin, *East Indies*, Vol.2, 102-4.

36. *The Oriental Herald*, Jul., 1827, 194.

37. *Ibid.*

38. India Office Home Misc. 729/75, David Scott to Alexander Duncan, 26 Mar., 1797.

39. SRO. Cunninghame-Graham, GD22/1/327, William Elphinstone to Peter Spiers, 1823.

40. India Office Home Misc. 729/70, David Scott to John Leighton, 17 Apr., 1797.

41. C. Northcote Parkinson, *Trade in the Eastern Seas, 1793-1813* (Cambridge, 1937).

42. C.H. Phillips (ed.), *Correspondence of David Scott, Director and Chairman of the East India Company* (London, 1951), i, 92-3, David Scott to Sir William Nairne, 2 Dec., 1796.

43. North Riding Record Office. Zetland Papers, ZNK/X/2, John Monro of Auchenbowie to Sir Thomas Dundas, 22 Mar., 1789.

44. India Office Home Misc. 729-731/507, David Scott to William Chalmers, 25 Nov., 1800.

45. Ibid.

46. *Memorials of the Public Life and Character of the Right Hon. James Oswald of Dunnikier* (1825), 203-4, The Earl of Findlater and Seafield to James Oswald, 22 Aug., 1766.

47. SRO. Scott of Harden GD157/2943/7, Thomas Cockburn to Hugh Scott, 21 Dec., 1781.

48. India Office Home Misc. 729/41, David Scott to Patrick Rigg, 16 Feb., 1797.

49. India Office Home Misc. 729-731/492, David Scott to Patrick Stirling, 18 Oct., 1800.

50. Ibid.

2
Revenue Appointments and Political Management

Of all the varieties of patronage at the disposal of Scottish politicians, the most useful were those connected with taxation, for, quite apart from the undeniable opportunities for profit which might accrue to an official charged with the collection of public revenues, through his possession of such monies between the time of collection and the time of accounting for the receipts, the ability to increase or moderate one's zeal was in itself a valuable asset for officers who were themselves often intimately involved in the political and social life of their communities. The regular salaries attached to the more important posts in the customs and excise administration, for example, were in themselves attractive to many voters in Scottish constituencies, and were the objects of a great deal of political negotiation, for this kind of appointment was the normal currency of management for the politician able to procure it, and the links between parliamentary politics and the disposal of such offices made the nominal right of appointment possessed by the boards of commissioners in Edinburgh somewhat illusory. In theory, customs and excise appointments were made by the boards of commissioners in Edinburgh, but the fact that the commissioners' recommendations had subsequently to be confirmed by the Treasury in London allowed plenty of opportunity for political intervention. Indeed, the appointment of customs commissioners and the various patent officers at the head of the establishment, such as comptroller-general, receiver-general, secretary and solicitor, were themselves items of crown patronage of the most valuable kind. The general supervisor of the Scottish interests of the Duke of Montrose, Mungo Graeme of Gorthie, received a reward for his political zeal on behalf of his chief in the form of the post of receiver-general of customs in the 1720s, an appointment which carried the not insignificant salary of £300 per annum, together with a supplementary allowance of £230 for payment of clerks.[1] Important or insignificant, customs appointments were, however, obtainable only by those who could expect a political favour, and many of the officers were in fact the nominees of a member of parliament and often the active partisans of that politician.

The customs establishment was one of the more extensive branches of the eighteenth-century bureaucracy, and the fact that its officers were necessarily widely dispersed enhanced the attraction of the service for freeholders, burgh councillors and their friends, for an appointment in their home district was not an unreasonable objective. A port of some significance was staffed by a group of customs officials — headed by a collector, who would be assisted by a varying number of additional supervisory officers and a body of tidesmen and boatmen. The value of the various ranks in the service was not, however, a uniform one, for the rewards varied in accordance with the importance of the trade passing through the port, and the differences in salary were substantial. In 1728, for example, while Alexander Legrand, the collector of Leith, enjoyed a place worth £100 per annum, William Gordon, the officer holding the same rank at Aberdeen, was paid £50, while Hugh Baillie, the collector of Orkney, had to make do with a mere £30 per annum. Port Glasgow and Leith, the main centres of trade, were the ports with the best-paid officers, but equally, they would also require the greatest amount of work from the incumbents, who would be much more under the eye of the supervisory staff based at Edinburgh, which might well make a less well-paid, but remote, port more attractive to the more independent officers. The junior supervisory rank in the service, the landwaiters, were paid a uniform salary of £25, but the ordinary gaugers, or tidesmen, were paid as irregularly as their supervisors, with salaries which ranged from £20 to £12.[2] Not surprisingly the variations in salary made transfers almost as common an object of solicitation as first appointments and promotions, but requests for a change of post might, however, be occasioned by more significant matters than the possibility of attracting a few additional pounds in salary.

Political correspondence often includes some pretty broad hints of the kind of recompense which local revenue officers may have expected from their offices. A request which Sir Ludovick Grant of Grant received from one of his friends for the removal of a revenue officer to another port stated the case quite frankly:

> Would you be so good as to get John Brown removed from Ardersier to Garmath, or to Chanonry, that Nathy Litch might be stationed at Ardersier, for as Nathy Litch keeps a publick house at Ardersier, and has laid out money in building and furnishing it, the poor man will be ruined if he is not stationed there, and obliged to go to a distant place, and neglect the business of his house.[3]

Reading between the lines, it would appear that the inconvenient placement of John Brown at Ardersier, and the unwillingness of the supervisor to station Mr. Leitch in his home town, may have been prompted by the suspicion of a conflict of interest between the duties of an officer charged with the prevention of smuggling and the keeper of an inn. Conflict of interest is rarely emphasised in the eighteenth century, however, and there can be little doubt that many customs officers held their posts for sound business reasons which had little to do with the remuneration offered by the crown. When Mr. Leitch established his public house in the village of Ardersier, so conveniently placed to catch the military traffic from Fort George, he wisely retained his seat in the council of the royal burgh of Nairn, and for a valuable parliamentary elector a mere transfer to the desired post was very little for a member of parliament to arrange. Customs officers, moreover, might be located on a particular station as a favour to burgh councillors, some of whom were not infrequently deeply involved in smuggling, and there is a suspicious insistence in some of the correspondence upon the placing of an individual in a very specific place, particularly in those districts distant from Edinburgh. Why, for example, would a politician with the wide-ranging interests of Lord Fife lay such pointed emphasis upon the placing of such a minor official as a tide waiter, writing that he wished William King to be appointed at Macduff *Down Creek*, as opposed to any other location in that district? [4]

The connection between smuggling, parliamentary politics and the conduct of customs officials was brought out strongly in the election for Wigtown in 1761, when that town was the returning burgh of a district of four towns, for the position of the customs officers of Wigtown was thought likely to topple the dominant interest of Lord Galloway and his son Lord Garlies.[5] Wigtown and Whithorn were normally controlled by the Earl of Galloway, with the Earl of Stair, who dominated the burgh of Stranraer, as the chief rival. The Dalrymples of Stair, with the backing of the Duke of Argyll, were contesting Galloway's control of this district, [6] and the misconduct of the local customs officials for a time appeared to offer the Argyll interest an unusual opportunity to make a political breakthrough in the south-west.

One of the leading members of the council of Wigtown, Bailie Hooks, was the owner of a ship sailing from the Swedish port of Gothenburg, which brought into Whithorn Bay a large quantity of smuggled tea and iron. It appears that the tea was intercepted after having been successfully landed, but during the ensuing enquiry it transpired that the bailie had also imported a considerable quantity of Swedish iron in excess of what had been found suitable by the Wigtown customs officers.[7] Finding himself in some difficulties, with his ship seized by order of the customs commissioners in Edinburgh, Bailie Hooks offered to try to carry the burgh of Wigtown for the candidate favoured by the Duke of Argyll in return for some ready cash and the expectation of assistance with the Court of Exchequer. As Argyll was informed,

> whoever His Grace shou'd name wou'd be agreeable and Mr. H[ooks] wou'd chearfully give his assistance in bringing matters to success in Wigton ... Mr. H. thinks that £700 may be necessary or a sum not exceeding £1,000, besides the necessary application to the C[ustom] House Officers & Post Master ... [8]

Apart from the strong suspicion that the revenue officers of Wigtown were rather too closely associated with smuggling, their failure to determine at their first survey the proper quantity of dutiable iron imported by Bailie Hooks suggested a method of changing the composition of the town council when the vital election of a delegate to represent the burgh at the ensuing parliamentary election was to be held.[9] Two members of the Wigtown council could not vote in a parliamentary election without voiding the election, for the Earl of Galloway and his eldest son Lord Garlies were both members. If Argyll could count on the friendship of the Earl of Selkirk, who had friends on the burgh council, the Galloway interest might prove to be less impregnable than was commonly believed, for two of the councillors were 'considerable tenants to Lord Selkirk whose leases are near expir'd'.[10] More importantly, however, David Agnew, the collector of Wigtown, McCulloch of Torhouse, the controller of customs, Gordon of Drumbeg, the surveyor, and a tide waiter named McKeen, were also councillors, and all of them were in some danger of losing their posts for incompetence if nothing worse. The suggestion made to the Argyll interest was that an order from the Board of Customs should be sent to Wigtown demanding the attendance of these officers in Edinburgh on the day of election, whereby it was hoped that a party of Lord Galloway's enemies might carry the day. As it turned out, the plan of Bailie Hooks was too optimistic and Lord Galloway retained control of the council of his town, but the incident affords a clear illustration of the close links between parliamentary and municipal politics and the holding of official appointments in the period, and indeed the officers in question were placed in their situations through the political influence of the Galloway family.

The close connection between politics and revenue patronage made it difficult for superiors to discipline officers who stepped out of line, and even when an officer was actually dismissed he could, and did, fight to secure his reinstatement by pulling political strings. Robert Carrick, the collector of excise at Inverness, is a case in point. Carrick reached that rank after twenty years' service which included considerable experience in the intermediate rank of supervisor of excise at Forfar before being advanced to his collectorship. Unfortunately for Carrick he was quickly reduced to the rank of a 'common gauger'[11] when an anonymous letter was received by the Board of Commissioners advising them that all of the excise supervisors in Scotland systematically maintained false diaries allegedly recording their activities. According to Carrick's admittedly biassed complaint, the anonymous correspondent must have been an ambitious junior officer, for 'there is no body of Men so full of plot and envy as the Excise'.[12] The removal of Carrick, and a number of other officers, clearly would open the way to promotion for others, but the charge that Carrick had claimed in an official record to have been in places which he had not in fact visited was not denied by the complainant. On the other hand it was a very swift descent from the heights of a collectorship to the rank of a common gauger for a man who had friends among the voting freeholders, and some of those friends at once moved to his aid, their resolve strengthened by Carrick's complaint that while five supervisors were dismissed, the other four were quickly reinstated in their rank and only he remained reduced, while, according to Carrick, at least one of the lucky men had been guilty of far more serious omissions than himself. The other four supervisors, however, had one advantage over Mr. Carrick: they were all political friends of Lord Melville, and for that reason their removal could only be a temporary demotion.[13]

The unlucky Robert Carrick did not despair, however, for he found his own method of bringing political pressure into play, for he was the brother-in-law of Mr. Glassford of Tillicoultry, a Glasgow merchant, whose votes would determine the outcome of the parliamentary election for Clackmannanshire in 1806. The small county of Clackmannan was closely divided between two candidates, the honourable George Abercromby and Major Robert Dundas, the conflict in fact being between Lord Dundas and the Abercromby family. The political situation could not have been more evenly divided, as a document in the Zetland papers[14] makes clear:

For		Against	
Mr. Erskine of Mar	1	Sir Rob[ert] Abercromby	1
Mr. Bruce of Kennet	1	Rev. Mr. Cathcart	1
Mr. Erskine junior	1	Mr. G. Abercromby	1
Mr. Glassford say (but not		Mr. John do.	1
more than)	2	Mr. James do.	1
Honble. Law[rence] Dundas	1	Mr. Cameron	1
Major Robert [Dundas]	1	Kippendavie yo[unge]r	1
	—	Mr. C[rawford] Tait	1
	7		8

But if Easter and Wester
K[ennet] be added   2
                                                  9

The political state made it clear that Robert Dundas would win his election if two additional nominal voters could be placed upon the roll, but the whole scheme would of course come to nothing should he lose any of his voters, or if Mr. Glassford would not also divide his valuation and make a second vote.

Lord Dundas was fully aware of Glassford's importance to his political interest in Clackmannan, and had taken steps to try to oblige him in a matter relating to his West Indian business interests, but Glassford was also conscious of his position in the political sphere, and fully intended to use it to secure his brother-in-law's reinstatement. Glassford had declared his intention of supporting Lord Dundas's interest in the election, but when he was visited by Alexander Bruce of Kennet, who was managing the election for Lord Dundas, 'we really found all not so right'.[15] Glassford, in short, would do nothing unless Carrick was restored to his place:

> he mentioned his charters were out & superiorities divided, but that he wou'd not move a step till his request was complied with, and hinted of being indifferent whether it was now done or not, as he cou'd afford to settle three hundred pr.ann. on Mr. Carrick and continue in friendship with his neighbour Mr. Abercromby.[16]

One month later Glassford was reported to be completing the work of preparing nominal votes, and in this his lawyer, who lacked experience in such matters, was being helped by the agent of Lord Dundas, who clearly considered him still an ally, but on August 6th, Glassford removed such illusions by making it quite plain that he meant what he had said about his price for support, and denied that he was in any way pledged to Lord Dundas:

> What he wanted, & what he expected to have been done, was to get his brother-in-law Carrick, who was reduced to the situation of an excise officer, reinstated in his former situation of a Collector of Excise ... Till it was *done he would make no votes*.[17]

Charles Innes, an experienced lawyer who advised Lord Dundas in political matters, had no doubt about the desirability of acting to meet Glassford's wishes, pointing out that Carrick had not been dismissed for malversation, which would have made reinstatement a difficult matter, but for 'some piece of neglect or inattention',[18] and in fact another of Dundas's correspondents appeared to get closer to the heart of the difficulty when he met with Glassford, reporting that

> It was obvious from his conversation that Mr. G[lassford] & A[bercromby] often meet & hunt together, have become gracious, and that his voting agt him is rather uphill work with him -- at the same time if his Brother in law is reinstated in his former situation we think he will still go with us ... [19]

The surviving correspondence does not make clear what happened to Mr. Carrick, but as Glassford had by the time of election three votes prepared and George Abercromby defeated Major Dundas, it may be surmised that Lord Dundas's failure to secure the reinstatement of the collector of Inverness was seen by Glassford as a neglect which justified his remaining friendly with Abercromby.

Political connections were often the principal criterion suggested to justify the promotion of an officer of excise, and some of them were quite ready to employ their own votes to advance their careers so long as this was permitted by Parliament. In 1756, for example, John Drummond, supervisor of excise at Paisley, and a freeholder of Perthshire, mustered all of his connections to aid his bid for advancement to the office of general supervisor at Glasgow. Mrs. Mary Campbell of Boquhan, a lady with important political connections in the town of Stirling, sent Drummond with her letter of recommendation to call on Lord Milton, the intermediary through whom much of the Duke of Argyll's patronage was distributed. Drummond also took with him several other letters of recommendation, but as Mrs. Mary pointed out, his chief claim to advancement was that

> Mr. Drummond is a voter in Perth Shire and stands by L[ord] John Murray, he really is well recommended by all ranks for an active good officer, but vastly tender so wants to be where he may have less fatigue ... [20]

Drummond also, presumably, was not averse to the larger salary which was attached to the superior rank, and his tenderness did not stop him from making the journey to Perth to vote for Argyll's candidate, when John Murray carried the crucial vote for preses of the Michaelmas head court by a single vote. On his journey back to Paisley, Drummond did not neglect to stop at Boquhan and call upon Mrs. Mary Campbell, who in turn advised her cousin Lord Milton that Drummond 'said he wou'd a road a hunder miles to serve our intrest & while he lives you may command him in any manner in his power'.[21]

Having ensured that Argyll's deputy had been made aware of his wishes and of his loyalty to the duke's interest, Drummond did not neglect to advise Lord Milton that he had been approached by Captain Haldane, another candidate seeking the votes of the freeholders of Perthshire. Haldane, according to Drummond, had assured him that he might 'depend on all his interest in order to make me happy in every opportunity, in the event on my giveing him my vote & intrest'.[22] Drummond, however, assured Milton that he had made no reply to this request, but the implication was left quite clear, though unstated. As the election approached in the spring of 1761, and it became certain that there would be a close contest in Perthshire, even a single vote could be of material importance, and Drummond was well aware of the strength of his own position. Promotions in government service were likely to go to those officers who were able to make themselves useful politically, and if the connection between advancement and political activity was blatant in the case of Drummond, it was a link which long persisted, for even when revenue officers were deprived of the franchise, this did not materially alter the connection between holders of a revenue office and the politicians whose solicitations remained the usual route to advancement. Throughout the eighteenth century and well into the following one, politicians could aid or hinder the career of a revenue officer, and they did not hesitate to employ that ability for their own ends. To help a friend, such as John Drummond, would always, as Mrs. Campbell remarked, 'gain us more friends in his way who have votes and show we don't drop or forget a man who dos to the outmost of their power to serve our interest'.[23] Even in 1789, long after revenue officers ceased to personally exercise the right of voting, and were rarely active in county politics, their promotions were still determined by their connection to voters. In Lord Dundas's patronage book, for example, an entry states that one of Dundas's political friends, Colonel Erskine, wished Mr. McVay, the officer of excise at Denny in Stirlingshire, to be advanced in rank, citing as the reason for seeking such promotion that the man was the son-in-law of Napier of Craigannet, a freeholder of the county. [24]

When Scotland was under the management of a powerful politician, such as the Earl of Ilay or Henry Dundas, almost all worthwhile patronage was channeled through the manager's hands. Experience alone most certainly did not secure an officer advancement in the customs administration and political interest was essential, as a letter received by Lord Panmure in 1739 made clear. The applicant, who was strongly connected to the voters of Angus, sought Panmure's assistance to obtain a post of inspector of customs for his son, Robert Fullerton, who had served for five years as clerk of the customs and had acted as inspector when some of these officers were under suspension. There was a vacancy for a permanent inspector, for one of them had been promoted to be solicitor of customs, and Robert Fullerton was considered satisfactory by the customs commissioners. The problem, however, was that although efficiency demanded that an inspector be experienced and the commissioners, Fullerton believed, would appoint his son if they were permitted, 'they are actuated in all these matters by the influence of the Earle of Isla, who often fills up these employments at London without any presentments'.[25] Perhaps wisely, Robert Fullerton did not insist on that particular post, and offered the politician an easier alternative, though one considerably inferior in value to that of an inspector of customs, by suggesting that a lieutenancy of marines might be had through political interest. At the end of the eighteenth century the situation was essentially unchanged, for we find the private secretary to Henry Dundas writing to a customs commissioner virtually ordering the placement of 'Mr. John Findlay, Excise Officer at Montrose ... upon the Examiners list, if found to be properly qualified'. [26] Vacancies were normally filled by the commissioners' presentation by the end of the century, but that presentation could be a formality and their autonomy restricted to the rejection of manifestly unqualified candidates.

The links between politics and patronage cannot have been beneficial to the efficiency of the customs service as a revenue-collecting agency, for all too often strong political interests could secure an important post for a man with little or no experience who was placed over the head of men far better qualified than himself, and presumably resentful of their own failure to secure advancement. Even Port Glasgow, the centre of the Chesapeake tobacco trade, and as such the port with the largest customs establishment in Scotland, could have an unqualified officer placed in a position of responsibility. In the admittedly biassed complaint sent to the Duke of Montrose by Mungo Graeme of Gorthie in 1716, Gorthie's brother, John Graeme, does appear more likely to have proven an effective revenue officer than the man whom Campbell interest placed in the post of land surveyor:

> This Mr. Cochran is a son of Ochiltry's, who by the character I have had of him has been allways Jacobite, and ye may guess who recommends him ... I must add this that the post of Land Surveyor at Port Glasgow is a post of very great importance to the revenue being the place where all tobaccos are imported, which necessarily requires besides honesty, a good deall of experience, which my brother has had and Mr. Cochran knows nothing of, never haveing been yet imployed in the Customs.[27]

In 1721 there was another vacancy for a land surveyor at Port Glasgow, and this time the strongest solicitation was made by George Smollett, whose father was one of the major political figures in the Glasgow district of burghs through his control of the town council of Dumbarton. Smollett gently reminded the Duke of Montrose of his own political value and then sought the duke's interest to secure the post for one Lauchlane McLauchlane. The young man was claimed to be 'abundantly capable of the office',[28] but if he had any experience which might justify his placement in a supervisory post, it was not mentioned. McLauchlane, however, had one significant qualification: he had married a granddaughter of the elder Smollett, and the town of Dumbarton's vote might hang on his success.

Many burgh councillors and freeholders were happy enough to see one of their numerous sons placed in even the humblest post in the excise administration. On the other hand, it was sometimes difficult to be certain of this, for there were some lairds who took a very unfavourable view of such officers, and there was a danger that a politician who desired to win a friend might make a mortal enemy. Lord Milton, for example, came close to doing that while he was attempting to strengthen the position of Sir James Campbell of Ardkinglas as the Administration's candidate for the representation of Stirlingshire. Milton had written a letter to one of the Stirlingshire lairds, assuring him of his friendship and advising him that one of the laird's sons had been given a post as a salt officer. Unfortunately that gesture was not appreciated, for, as Ardkinglas pointed out,

> a Salt officer heir in the country is an approbrious name, and all dispise it, but with submission, if on[e] of his sons could be a land waiter, it would sound better, and as

to this I only venture, that if one[e] of Powfouls sons was made a land waiter it might take, and I know ther are land waiters posts the salary whereof is not above tuinty five pound a year as for example Borrowstonness, wher there is on[e] John Lyon who has been ther nine or ten years with great approbation of his superiors, if he could be provided better, and on[e] of the sons provided heir near home it might be a bait ... [29]

If a misjudgment could offend, equally it was possible to gratify a voter by an offer, even when that offer was refused. In the troubled politics of the city of Edinburgh in 1761, Ilay and Milton made an easy friendship by offering, through the convener of trades, a post in the customs administration to one of the council deacons. The post offered, that of general inspector of tobaccos, was a good one, and the intended recipient, Deacon Murray, was well pleased, although he declined to accept. Murray was reported to have said

it was a genteeler office than he could have expected; But that as it required constant attending and writeing in the custom house, which could not suit the business he carrys on, as a wool merchant, and that he would rather wait till something should cast up, that would answer better with his business.[30]

In the meantime, of course, the Administration could dispose of the general inspector's office to another party while being sure of the political interest of Deacon Murray, a result which in all probability was anticipated by the astute Milton.

In the middle of the eighteenth century, customs and excise officers had a particularly high profile in the politics of seaport burghs, where many of them were themselves trades voters with a voice in the election of deacons who would sit in the burgh councils. Such officers were clearly vulnerable to pressure from their superiors in the service, or from those able to exert influence upon such superiors. The situation in the burgh of Inverkeithing was made plain by the provost, John Cunningham, who sought the intervention of Lord Milton in 1746 with the supervisory officer in charge of that port. One of the Inverkeithing officers, the tide waiter, was 'threatened to be removed or broke' if he joined Provost Cunningham in the burgh elections, a sad state of affairs, when, as Cunningham complained, 'your Lordship knows what I do is from no other view than to serve the D[uke] of A[rgyl]e & your lordship's interest, and have his grace's order for doing so'.[31] In the case of the remaining officer at Inverkeithing, the situation was reversed, for John Main, a wright and watchman of excise, was 'most inveterate ag[ains]t us'. Milton, the provost believed, should write to the collector of customs to have him tell the threatened tide waiter that he was in no danger, and at the same time secure an order for Main to cross to West Lothian for a few days, around the time of the burgh elections, in order to get him out of the way, for the election of the deacon of the wrights would turn on this single vote.[32]

The vulnerability of minor revenue officials to demotion or removal made it imperative for them to remain on good terms with men of influence able to mar their careers, and shortly after his clash with the provost of Inverkeithing Main made his peace with the Cunningham family. Adherence to the interest of Provost Cunningham, however, inevitably brought the officer into conflict with those interests which might challenge the Cunningham power in the burgh. Employment was more easily lost than obtained in the eighteenth century, for supervisors with power of removal over their subordinates rarely had much inclination to investigate the accuracy of an accusation against one of their officers, if that charge was brought with the support of a man of political influence who might harm his own career if thwarted. When conflicting political interests were involved, the supervisor would be forced, however reluctantly, to choose between them. No doubt this was the choice which prompted the removal of a land waiter from Inverness in 1734, for the politics of that burgh were then particularly troubled. Lord Lovat attempted, without success, to replace one of his clansmen in his office of land waiter after he had been removed by the commissioners, without investigation, following a complaint that he had spoken disrespectfully of a supervisor.[33] Equally, in the case of John Main at Inverkeithing, he and his two fellow excisemen were threatened with the board's displeasure in 1752, when the collector of Bo'ness accepted, without any enquiry into the facts, an allegation that they had been guilty of excessive drinking and had thereby neglected their duties.[34] Whether the men had truly neglected their duties is unknown, though in view of the social norms of the period the drinking must have been heavy indeed to have been called 'excessive ', but employment in government service, even when obtained, was never easy to retain, and the chance of doing so was greatly enhanced by a wise choice of political friends.

Loss of employment as the result of an uninvestigated charge of neglect of duty or malversation was not the only threat hanging over the head of an officer of the revenue. For some men promotion was eagerly desired, but even a promotion in rank could be distinctly harmful, as John Main discovered when he was drawn into another political conflict in 1752. The member of parliament for the district of burghs which included Inverkeithing, Colonel Haldane, was no friend of the Cunningham family, and in 1752 he began to try to overturn that interest in the council of Inverkeithing. The charge of neglect of duty levelled against the exciseman in September of that year appears to have emanated from the Haldane party, and a further complication appeared soon after the burgh election, in which Provost Cunningham and his friends again prevailed, for John Main was promoted. Main was removed from his place as salt watchman and advanced to the rank of tidesman, a strange development when linked to a charge of neglect of duty. Surprisingly, perhaps, at least at first glance, this promotion was secured by Colonel Haldane's interest with the commissioners, for John Main had been firmly attached to the Cunningham interest in burgh politics. A salt watchman was paid a salary of £15 per annum, while a tidesman was paid £20, so on the face of it Main seemed to have little cause for complaint. However, as Captain Robert Cunningham pointed out, as watchman Main was actually paid his £15, while in his promoted post he had not been appointed to any port and held an appointment as tidesman at large, which meant that he was only paid when he was actually employed,[35] and Haldane interest with the commissioners would make his tours of

duty few and far between unless he experienced a timely political conversion. Cunningham rightly remarked that with this appointment Main was placed 'intirely in the power of his superior officers upon the coast, and if he should happen not to be favoured by them, his employment is not worth one shilling'.[36]
The aggrieved Main, in short, sought either an appointment as tidesman in a particular port, which would carry a regular salary, or failing that even a restoration to his former post of watchman, and naturally he attempted to secure his livelihood through his political friends, the Cunninghams.

There are two sides to every story, of course, and obviously no supervisory officer was likely to admit that he had participated in an attack upon the position of burgh politicians known to be in the interest of the Administration. The official version of John Main's transformation from watchman to tidesman was that this was a great favour to Main and would be a temporary appointment until he could again be reappointed to his duties as watchman at Inverkeithing. Colin Campbell, to whom Lord Milton directed his inquiry about the removal of Main, insisted that the watchman could be returned to his former station, and that his temporary appointment as a tidesman was not a punishment, but a favour. As Campbell described it,

> John Main who Cunninghame makes such a rout about is only ane extraordinary salt watchman, and the Duke of Hamilton's salt works where he was employed being now silent for want of coal this Main was of course discontinued, but then as the Collector thought [Main] a good one, wee directed him to employ Main as a tidesman: this was doing him a great favour, and whenever the salt works are set a going Main will be reponed to his former station.[37]

Provost John Cunningham admitted that Main had not possessed a commission as watchman and was indeed an extraordinary officer employed only when there was work for him to perform, but there seems little reason to doubt that Main's removal was intended to serve the political interest of the Haldanes, for his removal was not an isolated case, and, moreover, when the Hamilton salt works resumed operations the excise supervisors did not in fact restore Main to his old post, but appointed an individual named Cunnan to the vacancy.[38]
Main was not the only excise officer resident in Inverkeithing, and the Cunningham party, while continuing to press for Main's reinstatement, did not neglect the remainder of the excise establishment. They were well placed to exert political pressure, for in 1753 Captain Robert Cunningham was the candidate for the parliamentary seat for this district, avowedly standing as a friend of the Duke of Argyll. Political power was signified to the inhabitants of a burgh by the ability of a dominant faction to place its friends in the local revenue offices, and equally, by their ability to obtain the removal of their enemies among the office holders. Accordingly, the battle over the excisemen of Inverkeithing was intensified, for the rival Haldane party had no intention of giving way, and they too had friends able to influence the placement of excise officers.
If the first round went to the Haldanes through their removal of that active member of the hammermen's trade, John Main, the Cunningham party quickly

retaliated by securing, through the agency of the member of parliament for Stirlingshire, Captain James Campbell, the removal of a tidesman stationed at Inverkeithing named Morris, who was an active Haldane partisan. At the same time, with the assistance of Lord Milton, the vacant post of tidesman was given to Colin Sharp, a surgeon and member of the Inverkeithing burgh council, who was, needless to say, a Cunningham man.[39] Shortly thereafter, however, the Haldane party struck back, by securing the return of Morris to the Inverkeithing station and the transfer of Sharp to distant Ayr, where his ability to participate in burgh politics would be somewhat restricted. The Haldane partisan, Morris, moreover, said openly that he defied Captain Cunningham and all his friends and supporters to remove him again from the town. In the circumstances James Cunningham felt that Captain Robert Cunningham's election hopes would be considerably strengthened if Morris were proven wrong, and accordingly advised Lord Milton that

> if your Lordship would be pleased to get him removed to another station & orders not to return him to Innerkiething, it will be doing great service to Captain Cuninghame's cause, & would be the severest stroke that Colonel Haldane's friends at Innerkiething & Dunfermling could meet with, as they confidently give out that now he is to be continued, & Mr. Sharp [whom Captn. Cuninghame got placed as Tydesman at Innerkiething & is a steady friend] turned out & that all Captn. Cuninghame's friends in these burrows who have posts from the Government will soon lose them . . . [40]

The last sentence in Captain James Cunningham's statement gets to the heart of the matter, for burgh influence depended above all on evident good relations with the men of power who dispensed patronage. Failure to keep their friends in office would rapidly doom the Cunningham interest in these burghs to extinction, as councillors and trades voters started to reconsider their former loyalties and to listen to the argument of the Haldane partisans that the colonel had the ear of government. The proof of a close connection with men of power was provided in burgh politics by a politician's ability to determine the fate of minor resident officials, and the Cunningham party was clearly being outmanoeuvred by the Haldanes in this matter.

Provost John Cuningham, as leader of his party in the council of Inverkeithing, was well aware of political realities and accordingly pressed strongly for some support from his patrons, particularly in the case of the well-known John Main. If, as the provost pointed out, two watchmen were now required at Inverkeithing, how should Cunnan have a place and Cunningham's friend be left essentially unemployed? It was a good question, and suggested strongly that the Argyll interest was less powerful than it was believed to be by the community at large. The provost noted, moreover, that Cunnan was named by the commissioners in Edinburgh, among whom Haldane's influence lay, and the effect was extremely damaging to both the Cunningham and the Argyll interests in the district. Main's removal at the instigation of Cunningham's enemies, and the appointment shortly thereafter of Cunnan to act in his place, had, as Provost Cunningham remarked, made 'a very great noise',[41] and by providing this evidence of their influence, the Haldane party could argue plausibly that all of the partisans of the Cunningham faction then in office would not retain their places for much longer.

Naturally, in view of the political interest of Lord Milton and the Duke of Argyll, John Main was not left to languish in the state of promoted unemployment to which Colonel Haldane's enmity had consigned him, but although they were able to secure a port appointment for Main which brought him a regular salary, it was at Bo'ness, on the Lothian shore of the river Forth and directly under they eye of Haldane's ally, Collector Middleton, who sent the unfortunate Main 'on every drudgery piece of business to different places to put him to all the expence & trouble the Collector can devise'.[42] The influence of Argyll and Milton clearly had proved insufficient to turn matters around in the excise establishment at Inverkeithing where it would have done most good.

Burgh politics could be a hard game for little people, for they could be badly injured by those against whom they acted. John Main was a very minor figure in the politics of Inverkeithing, for he was not a councillor, but Main was influential in the hammermen's trade, and in a contested election for deacon of the hammermen John Main's vote carried the contest for Cunningham's friend. Colonel Haldane, with considerable vindictiveness, though undoubtedly to make an example to deter others from doing the like, set out to ruin him, and removed him from the place which gave him his living on grounds of redundancy, and replaced him with one of his own friends. The fate of a watchman became a major element in burgh politics in this district, for although Captain James Cunningham was clearly sympathetic to John Main on personal grounds, there was more at stake than the solvency of a single family. Main had been promised by the Cunningham party that he would regain his place, yet it had not been done. Captain James Cunningham remarked that

> it gives me vast pain to have brought this poor man & his family to misery in this way; you know that you told me & wrote me long ago that you would get him replaced at Innerkiething & get him a warrand from the treasury ... I told the man & his friends that he might depend on it, but it has train'd so long, that I am ashamed to see them; they came to me last time I was over all in tears lamenting their miserable fate; and besides the loss to the poor man & family, I do assure you these things do great harm to your interest, & makes people believe that Haldane can do every thing, & you must own there is some reason to think so, since he turns out your friends & gets in his own ... for my part I cannot have the face to go near the town again till this poor man gets justice done him ... [43]

With a parliamentary election campaign now in full swing, the failure of the Cunningham party to demonstrate sufficient political interest to keep their friends in their places was immensely damaging. As the candidate, Captain Robert Cunningham pointed out to Lord Milton, John Main's fate made others hesitate. 'His being so ill used for being my friend, makes a great outcry against me, and will certainly contribute largely to make my other friends shy in appearing for me.'[44] The effects were felt beyond Inverkeithing, for the manager of the Cunningham interest in the eastern burghs of the district, Captain James Cunningham, was clear that it was essential to have John Main and Colin Sharp back in their places before the election and Haldane's friends removed, as 'it not only does harm in that one town, but in all the rest; Haldane's interest is cryed up, & the Haldanes can do every thing is the general talk ... '[45]

In the burgh of Inverkeithing the effect would have been disastrous had not Captain Robert Cunningham's money been lavishly dispensed among the councillors and magistrates, for as was to be expected, it had not been in Cunningham's power to convince anyone in the town that he was under the protection of the Duke of Argyll. Cunningham explained that

> Appearances are certainly against me, which is the reason that all my assertions are discredited. Every man of the town in employment is exerting himself for Colonel Haldane ... if it is thought desirable that the burrow should be secured for the future to the Duke of Argyll's interest, (and you may be assured it shall always be at his Grace's disposal whilst it remains in our family) an example should be made of some person in employment ... [46]

To nobody's surprise Colonel George Haldane secured his election for the Dunfermline district of burghs in 1754, in spite of the enmity of the Duke of Argyll, and it must be conceded that the colonel's ability to remove office holders made a substantial contribution to his victory. On the other hand, Colonel Haldane did not succeed in winning the vote of the burgh of Inverkeithing itself, a failure which may perhaps be linked to the lasting hostility of the burgesses occasioned by his own quick temper two years earlier, for in 1752 he had given Provost John Cunningham a black eye when he had encountered the chief magistrate on the steps of the tolbooth, an error of judgement which served to undo much of the Haldane party's work in that town, and indeed ran the colonel some risk of being mobbed.[47] A political interest, however, as Colonel Haldane demonstrated could overcome the opposition of powerful politicians, and the chief casualties were often the little people, like the unfortunate John Main, caught in the battle of interests. But for government officials stationed in the royal burghs neutrality was rarely a viable option, for all of these posts were patronage appointments obtained through political interest, and their retention demanded the continuing friendship of a politician. The difficult part was picking the correct patron.

Political patronage within the burghs might, however, relate to matters other than the employment of revenue officers, for even the location of an excise office could be a political question. If a magistrate or other influential figure in a town was the owner of a building in which an excise office was then located, he too was vulnerable to pressure should he waver in his loyalty to the political interest which had given him this tenant. In October 1734, for example, Captain Charles Campbell, the manager of Lord Ilay's interest in the town of Stirling, attempted to overthrow the existing majority in the burgh council. Campbell believed he could strengthen his hand by making an example of a council member in order to demonstrate where power lay. As Captain Campbell wrote to Lord Milton:

> If I can but keep our folks in the same spirrit they are in I make no doubt but we shall gaine ground; the Excise office is keept here in one Henderson's who is our grate eneemy, all my friends beggs it may be removed to one David Napier's ... [48]

In case Lord Milton missed the importance of making this change, Campbell took the trouble of repeating the request three days after first suggesting it, which was clearly long before the judge could have hoped to arrange such an alteration.[49] The rental of such an office could not have been great, but it was little things which often had a quite disproportionate impact upon burgh councillors, for such a move would give tangible proof that the party which could arrange it had the ear of government and could thus effect other, and perhaps more far-reaching, changes. Councillors had an understandable reluctance to commit themselves to a political course which would deprive them of access to patronage, and it was for this reason that it was necessary for politicians to provide demonstrations of power. Minor revenue posts, and as in this case, even the location of rented office space, were one of the more effective methods of impressing the members of a town council with what could be done for them, or to them.

Many men who obtained small posts as excisemen were not themselves members of a burgh council, but it would be unusual to find revenue officers in Scottish towns without close political links with men who mattered in the politics of burgh or county. Even when a small office was given almost as an act of charity, there would usually be a political motive in the background. In 1747, for example, Mrs. Mary Campbell of Boquhan sought the patronage of her kinsman, Lord Milton, for a resident of Stirling whose already precarious circumstances had been rendered still more unstable by an unexpectedly large addition to his family, his wife having been 'brought to bed of three children who are alive and well'.[50] Mrs. Campbell hoped that a tide waiter's post might be found for the man, but there was more to it than charity, for, as she advised her cousin, William Anderson's brother was a rich baker who had lately filled the office of deacon convener of trades in Stirling, and 'as he has a near connection with severalls in the present management I wish if possible you could fall on a way to get this small thing for him, it wou'd make a noise amongest the folks to see that we are at pains to do for them'.[51] As in the counties, the effective manager of a political interest in a burgh would distribute favours in an effort to create feelings of obligation, and if management in the towns could take a much cruder form than would be commonly acceptable among the freeholders, that similarity should not be lost sight of, for as Mrs. Mary Campbell suggested, if such small favours were given, 'in greatetud they should serve those who get favours done them'.[52]

In the counties likewise, members of parliament were continually bombarded with requests for small offices in the customs for friends of voting freeholders, though the practice of leaving the small posts in the seaports to the burgh members restricted the supply to the provision of officers to towns which were not royal burghs. The correspondence of members of parliament was filled with information on the state of health of incumbents in order that timely application might be made for the posts should they die or retire from service. 'There is one

Mr. Milne, officer at Oldcambus, a very old man quite worn out & unfitt for that station & is expected that he can't live much longer', an eager applicant for a place advised Hugh Scott, the member of parliament of Berwickshire.[53] A few weeks earlier that same candidate had drawn the member of parliament's attention to 'one David Denholm an old worn out officer at Thorntonloch nigh Dunglass in East Lothian who is about being supperannuated'.[54] In the case of this applicant, he would have been happy to have obtained any place in the service, for he hoped to arrange thereafter for a transfer to the stations which he really desired, Coldingham or Eyemouth, where he had business interests.

When a voter who had an interest in securing a revenue place for a friend learned of an opportunity, he would invariably press the member of parliament strongly to obtain it. Vacancies were not the only occasions for such pressure, for there were on occasion officers functioning without a treasury warrant, and should this fact become known, pressure would be exerted to secure their removal in order to create a vacancy for a man with friends among the freeholders or councillors. In 1762, for example, Lord Panmure was advised by one of the Angus voters that upon the death of a tide waiter at Montrose, a replacement had been sent there from Alloa or some other place on the Firth of Forth. The writer remarked that he had 'never doubted but that he had succeeded in his place by a commission from the Treasury untill of late that I discovered that he only officiated by orders and an interim warrand from the Commissioners of Customs'.[55] Panmure's constituent left the member of parliament in no doubt about his expectation that the appointment would be transferred to one of his own friends, and in fact it was very difficult for a politician to evade such requests without disobliging a voter. On the other hand, if the member of parliament was induced to solicit for the removal of an acting officer, any failure to arrange the question satisfactorily would be taken in his constituency as a failure of political interest in London and evidence of a lack of effective power, which again could prove damaging at the next general election.

When a member of parliament was considered to be in a position to influence senior officers' careers, he might, however, find himself offered minor patronage posts to use as he saw fit, without having to do much to seek them. This was the situation in which James Oswald of Dunnikier found himself in 1751, when a chain of patronage was drawn back to him. A senior officer advised Oswald that

> An application having just been made to me by one of our officers stationed at Edinburgh, in a genteel post, desiring my recommendation of a young spark to him for a clerk, at a salary of £35 per annum. I have accepted the compliment, and laid my finger upon it; and recollecting, from my own experience of elections, the desire you may probably have to introduce the younger son or nephew of a gentleman, who is one of your electors, into business, I imagine it may not be impertinent to offer it to you at this juncture ... [56]

More senior posts were employed as tools of patronage at a higher level, for they might be the object of the ambition of a substantial freeholder with his own political interest, whose support might be of value to the Administration directly.

Sir Robert Dalyell of the Binns clearly saw himself in that light when, in 1760, he approached Lord Milton to inform him of his wish to be of use to Milton's politics in West Lothian. Dalyell did not pitch his ambitions at too lowly a level, telling the deputy of the Duke of Argyll that

> the being the representative of a family formerly in some repute has made me desirous of raising myself to taste the *Douceurs* of our mild Government; please allow me therefore to beg that your Lordship would procure me to be appointed Inspector General of the Salt, and if that office is already disposed of, to humbly pray that your Lordship will have me in your eye when another proper employment becomes vacant. The being established on a proper footing ... will make me have greater weight in our politicks, and encourage others to join me ... [57]

Sir Robert's luck was not in on this occasion, however, for Milton had already promised the desired appointment to Cockburn of Clerkington to induce him to lead the opposition in East Lothian to Sir Hew Dalrymple of North Berwick, in order to secure the seat for Andrew Fletcher, younger of Saltoun.[58] Something more than a vote was expected in return for the major posts, but essentially they too were employed to aid the development of a political interest. An ordinary member of parliament who attempted to gratify constituents by pressing for a senior appointment was likely to be put firmly in his place by the Treasury, for this happened even to the well-connected David Scott, when representing the Dundee burghs in 1796. The provost and council of St. Andrews, who were never slow to seek patronage of any type, had asked Scott to obtain the placement of a supervisor in the list of candidates for a collectorship. However much the excise supervisor may have been appreciated by the councillors of St. Andrews, he was regarded with less enthusiasm at the Treasury, and the member of parliament was told bluntly that if any office about St. Andrews fell vacant, which was usually left to the recommendation of the Burgh Member, he should have the nomination, and as Scott advised the provost, 'they hoped that from reasons which must naturally occur to myself, I would be satisfied with the propriety of their answer'.[59] The office in question was not minor patronage, for as Scott remarked, it had a value of from £300 to £1,800 per annum, and for that reason it was unlikely to be given to gratify a town council.

The connection between parliamentary politics and the filling of revenue posts was continuous throughout the eighteenth and early nineteenth centuries. The newer taxes, such as that upon windows, were no different from the more traditional revenues. In 1782, when Roderick McLeod, the surveyor of window lights for Berwickshire, died, there was considerable competition for the succession, during which it emerged that the method of filling such appointments involved the county member of parliament. These officers held a commission from the Treasury, which was awarded upon the recommendation of the Barons of Exchequer in Edinburgh, supported by the member of parliament for the county.[60]

Postal appointments were equally subject to the demands of politics. Local post masters were invariably associated with the political life of their communities and were unlikely to retain their posts without strong political interest. In 1747 the postmaster of Stirling was one of the magistrates, Bailie Maiben, and it was made clear enough that his job was at stake in the political contest of that year, for Sir Peter Halkett of Pitfirrane, one of the candidates seeking to represent the district in parliament, complained to Lord Milton that the bailie

> came to me in a fright and told me, that Mr. Haldane had been there for two days, that he had been threatened with being turned out of his bread if he did not vote for Captain Haldane, and that they had given him as post master a letter for Captain Haldane to be forwarded in which they desired him to speak to Sir Everard Falkoner, Post Master General, that he might keep in this man or turn him out as he should vote upon this occasion . . . [61]

The bailie apparently also read the correspondence which passed through his hands, perhaps as part of his own political activities, or he would not have learned of the contents of the letter in question, but in any event his adherence to the Duke of Argyll's friend, Sir Peter Halkett, did him no harm and he was still postmaster of Stirling in 1755, when his ill-health and reported nearness to death induced Lord John Murray to seek the post, in the event of Maiben's death, for a Stirling surgeon who was a son of James Graham of Bowhaple, a Perthshire freeholder.[62] Politically, the office of postmaster had additional value, for much of the minor patronage was filled by the Treasury upon the first significant application, and here timely notification of a death, or a serious illness, was essential. Postmasters could, and did, ensure that priority was given to the letter advising of these developments which was intended for their own particular political friend in London, and that his enemies' letters would be delayed until the next post.

Revenue patronage was of course normally restricted to those Scottish politicians friendly to the current administration, but even here there was something in private hands, although its importance was of diminishing value as the country became more prosperous. In 1718, for example, the Duke of Montrose, as chancellor of the University of Glasgow, was seeking a gentleman to collect the teinds of Drymen, which were payable to the university. The duke immediately saw an opportunity to improve relations with the powerful Buchanan family, none of whose members were of great wealth, but several of whom were freeholders in Dunbartonshire and Stirlingshire. The duke and his close associates saw this small office as 'some mean to treat those folks who Club together and are disposed to believe that I'm incompatible wt them'.[63] The post of collector was shortly thereafter settled upon Buchanan of Balfunning,[64] one of the freeholders of that name who was in urgent need of remunerative employment, and in this regard, any collection, however small the salary, gave the collector temporary custody of the funds, which could, in all probability, be employed to advantage in the period between collection and transmittal.

NOTES

1. Anon., *The Present State of Scotland,* 'The Customs Establishment' (Edinburgh, 1728).

2. *Ibid.*

3. SRO. Seafield, GD248/97/7/11, Alexander Brodie to Sir Ludovick Grant, 6 Jan., 1755.

4. SRO. Seafield, GD248/63/3, Lord Fife to Sir James Grant, 11 Jan., 1791.

5. NLS. Saltoun MS 17533/91-2, 'Memorial for the Borough of Wigton', 1761.

6. Sir Lewis Namier and John Brooke [eds.], *The History of Parliament: the House of Commons, 1754-90*, ii, 512.

7. 'Memorial for the Borough of Wigton ', op. cit.

8. NLS. Saltoun MS 17533/93, 'Offer of Wigton, 1761 '.

9. NLS. Saltoun MS. 17533/95, 'Memorandum about the Galloway Burrows, 26 Mar. 1761'.

10. 'Memorial for the Borough of Wigton ', op. cit.

11. North Riding Record Office. Zetland papers, 1794-1806, MS. ZNK/x/2, 'Case of Mr. Carrick, former Collector of Excise'.

12. Ibid.

13. North Riding Record Office. Zetland MS. ZNK/X/2, Alexander Bruce of Kennet to Lord Dundas, 5 Jul., 1806.

14. North Riding Record Office. Zetland MS. ZNK/X/2, William Handyside to Alexander Bruce of Kennet, 7 Jul., 1806.

15. North Riding Record Office. Zetland MS. ZNK/X/2, Alexander Bruce of Kennet, 5 Jul., 1806.

16. Ibid.

17. North Riding Record Office. Zetland MS. ZNK/X/2, William Handyside to Lord Dundas, 6 Aug., 1806.

18. North Riding Record Office. Zetland MS. ZNK/X/2, Charles Innes to Lord Dundas, 7 Aug., 1806.

19. North Riding Record Office. Zetland MS. ZNK/X/2, William Handyside to Lord Dundas, 6 Aug., 1806.

20. NLS. Saltoun MS. 16695, Mary Campbell to Lord Milton, 18 Oct., 1756.

21. NLS. Saltoun MS. 16714, Mary Campbell to Lord Milton, 30 Oct., 1760.

22. NLS. Saltoun MS. 16714, John Drummond to Andrew Fletcher, 3 Nov., 1760.

23. NLS. Saltoun MS. 16715, Mary Campbell to Milton, 30 Oct., 1760.

24. North Riding Record Office, 'Lord Dundas's Patronage Book'.

25. SRO. Dalhousie MS. GD45/14/432, Robert Fullerton to Lord Panmure, 1 and 31 Dec., 1739.

26. India Office Home Misc. Letter Books of David Scott, 728/140, W. Gartshore to Robert Graham of Fintry, 9 Dec., 1795.

27. SRO. Montrose, GD220/5/819, Mungo Graeme of Gorthie to Montrose, 18 May, 1716.

28. SRO. Montrose, GD220/5/837, George Smollett to Montrose, 11 Nov., 1721.

29. NLS. Saltoun MS. 16555, Sir James Campbell of Ardkinglas to Milton, 20 May, 1734.

30. NLS. Saltoun MS. 16718, William Alston to Milton, 25 Mar., 1761.

31. NLS. Saltoun MS. 16618, John Cunningham to Milton, 19 Sept., 1746.

32. NLS. Saltoun MS. 16618, John Cunningham to Milton, 20 Sept., 1745.

33. SRO. Seafield, GD248/97/1, Lord Lovat to Sir James Grant, 5 Oct., 1734.

34. NLS. Saltoun MS. 16679, Robert Midleton to David Rankine, 25 Sept., 1752.

35. NLS. Saltoun MS. 16678, Robert Cunningham to Milton, 10 Nov., 1752.

36. Ibid.

37. NLS. Saltoun MS. 16678, Colin Campbell to Milton, 19 Dec., 1752.

38. NLS. Saltoun MS. 16882, Robert Cunningham to Milton, 25 Jul., 1753.

39. NLS. Saltoun MS. 16682, James Cunningham to Milton, 14 Nov., 1753, with document marked 'Memo Cunningham 53'.

40. Ibid.

41. NLS. Saltoun MS. 16682, John Cunningham to Capt. James Cunningham, 18 Jul., 1753.

42. NLS. Saltoun MS. 16682, James Cunningham to Robert Cunningham, 19 Jul., 1753.

43. Ibid.

44. NLS. Saltoun MS. 16682, Robert Cunningham to Lord Milton, 25 July., 1753.

45. NLS. Saltoun MS. 16682, James Cunningham to Robert Cunningham, 19 Jul., 1753.

46. NLS. Saltoun MS. 16682, Robert Cunningham to Milton, 28 Sept., 1753.

47. NSL. Saltoun MS. 16678, Robert Cunningham to Milton, 4 Oct., 1752.

48. NLS. Saltoun MS. 16555, Charles Campbell to Milton, 25 Oct., 1734.

49. NLS. Saltoun MS. 16555, Charles Campbell to Milton, 28 Oct., 1734.

50. NLS. Saltoun MS. 16642, Mary Campbell to Milton, 18 Jun., 1747.

51. Ibid.

52. Ibid.

53. SRO. Scott of Harden, GD157/ 2952/3, Robert Cossar to Hugh Scott, 8 Apr., 1783.

54. SRO. Scott of Harden, GD 157/2952/2, Robert Cossar to Hugh Scott, 9 Feb., 1783.

55. SRO. Dalhousie, GD45/14/432, David Doig to Lord Panmure, 16 Mar., 1762.

56. *Memorials of the Public Life and Character of the Right Hon. James Oswald of Dunnikier* [Edinburgh, 1825], 220-222, Corbyn Morris to James Oswald, 24 Dec., 1751.

57. NLS. Saltoun MS. 16714, Sir Robert Dalyell to Milton, 15 Mar., 1760.

58. *Memorials of the Public Life etc ... of James Oswald, op. cit.,* 308–311.

59. India Office Home Misc. 729/17, David Scott to the Council of St. Andrews, 23 Nov., 1796.

60. SRO. Scott of Harden, GD157/2950/2, George Home of Branxton to Hugh Scott, 15 Mar., 1782.

61. NLS. Saltoun MS. 16647, Sir Peter Halkett to Milton, 25 Jun., 1747.

62. NLS. Saltoun MS. 16693, Lord John Murray to Milton, 14 Feb., 1755.

63. SRO. Montrose, GD220/5/823, Duke of Montrose to Mungo Graeme of Gorthie, 18 Dec., 1717.

64. SRO. Montrose, GD220/5/824, Duke of Montrose to Mungo Graeme of Gorthie, 27 Jan., 1718.

3

Military and Naval Patronage

Many Scots were attracted by the possibility of earning their living with their swords, in spite of the fact that this was not a particularly attractive career in an age when advancement in rank was frequently purchased and promotion hard to obtain without both private means and interest. Family tradition attracted many Scots into the army who might have been better advised to look elsewhere, but in time of war there was always the hope that disease or wounds would carry off enough military superiors to create vacancies without purchase and permit advancement in rank. First commissions could be obtained through political interest, and this would appear to have been the situation of Philip Hay, whom Admiral Lord Keith managed to place in the 11th Foot as an ensign on the strength of imaginary past service, though his patron remarked that 'if his father cannot get at old General Grant or Lady Sutherland he may not be confirmed. I wrote that he was a volunteer at Ollionles etc. not a word true, but that is nothing'.[1] An ensign, however, might find the next step a little harder, while command of a company was rarely to be had without the ability to purchase the commission of a holder of a captaincy or very strong political interest to secure the place in an expanding army in a new battalion. The regular army was never a good career for a poor gentleman, for its strength fluctuated too greatly, with new units created in an emergency and as quickly disbanded with the return of peace. An officer with private income might find the half-pay given to those no longer employed in active units an agreeable augmentation of his resources, which he might be content to draw for the remainder of his life. On the other hand, if the half-pay officer was trying to maintain an impoverished existence as an unwanted guest in the home of a brother, he (and the brother) could become very anxious to secure a place for him in an active formation, in spite of the poor pay and poorer prospects. Necessity sometimes drove half-pay officers to seek a commission in an active battalion even when they had attained such an advanced age that any chance of a successful military career was long over. The Duke of Montrose wrote in 1733:

> This last Letter of yours incloses a memoriall from Ensign Graham. I should be loath to do the poor gentlemen such an injury as to apply at this time of day for an ensigncy to him who was an ensign between five and six and twenty year ago, by which he'd come to be commanded in the army by severall unborn when he was made an officer . . . he is infinitely happier with his half pay than he possibly cou'd be if he came into the army after having been so long out of it . . . [2]

The army was an unsatisfactory occupation for a man who lacked the money to purchase promotion, for he was likely to be in the situation of the Master of Elphinstone, who complained in 1715 that 'I have served as Capt[ain] this nine years which I have the vanity to believe intitelis me to something better than a company of foot '.[3] War and the resulting expansion of the army, together with the military traditions of the Scottish gentry, invariably, however, brought a flood of Scottish officers into the army, in spite of the poverty of many of them, and that in turn provided politicians with the necessary connections with a useful way of winning friends cheaply. During the American War of Independence General James Grant of Ballindalloch, the member of parliament for Sutherland, found the attractions of a military life to be a great help to his political interest, asserting to a correspondent that 'if this business continues I could provide for all the Sutherlands in the country. A commission is an easier business than a tyde waiter or a land waiter'.[4]

Commissions in an expanding army might be made available without purchase, either to support the interest of Administration politicians or to stimulate recruiting and sometimes both, but rarely could they serve an opposition politician directly, although the fact that military commissions were not immediately under the control of the Government manager for Scotland permitted some indirect approaches by opposition members and their friends. An alternative way into the commissioned ranks of the regular army was by going on war service with a battalion as a volunteer, hoping to be chosen by the commanding officer to fill a vacancy in the field. Once again, however, the volunteer with powerful friends to reinforce his claims for advancement was in a much stronger position than a volunteer without influence. Even opportunities to serve, without rank or pay, as a volunteer, could be elusive, and even previous military experience was of little assistance, as Lieutenant Callander discovered when he attempted to rejoin the army as a volunteer in a regiment about to embark for India. The Lieutenant's friends were advised that the only way of getting to India, short of enlisting as a private soldier, was to travel as an officer's servant, though with the prospect of becoming a recognised volunteer upon arrival. Such a passage was not an attractive prospect, for the Lieutenant would be obliged to pay £25 towards the cost of his accommodation, yet he would have to 'be a servant in fact as well as nominally, that is he must eat and live with the servants of the officers of the ship and those of the passengers, no verry desirable berth for a gentleman'.[5]

It was not impossible for a poor gentleman to rise in the army, even without political connections, but for those lacking the interest of a great man promotion depended upon opportunities to demonstrate outstanding gallantry and leadership qualities. Scots in this position, however, might hope during their service to encounter a senior officer of the same name, which might induce the latter to act as patron without the normal ulterior motives. General James Grant, for example, in spite of his political preoccupations, found

> a very genteel accomplished young man, serving with great credit as a Corporal of Marines at Boston, he had an opportunity of distinguishing himself at different times in action, and tho' a stranger & unknown to be a gentleman, he was much respected in his low station & warmly recommended to me by the officers with whom he served, in consequence of which I procured him a commission in a young corps & afterwards got him into the 64th Regt. I gave him money to fit him out like a gentleman. He

deserved the notice I took of him, he behaved well and died poor man of a wound he received at Brandywine . . . [6]

The young corporal, it should perhaps be pointed out, was also a Grant, but indeed with the recommendation of his own officers he was to a great degree responsible for his own advancement to commissioned rank, and this kind of promotion for gallantry was by no means an isolated example, for a considerable number of non-commissioned officers of suitable education, many of them Scots, reached the junior commissioned ranks. Further advancement, however, was slow indeed for those officers who were unable to purchase a step in rank in their turn.

Although recent research appears to raise some uncertainty about the purchase of commissions in the artillery and engineers, [7] purchase certainly had a less prominent place in the promotions in the technical corps. On the other hand, entry into commissioned rank in those corps was hard to obtain without significant political interest. Admiral Lord Keith encountered difficulty with an important freeholder who had requested, through an intermediary, that a young man named Maitland might be admitted as a cadet into the college at Woolwich. The letter had not been answered, and the Laird of Gartmore took offence, declaring 'that if he did not get such trifles to oblige his friends that they might depend upon his going against them'.[8] The appointment, however, was impossible to obtain, because it depended upon the Master General of the Ordnance, Lord Mulgrave, with whom Lord Keith had no influence. Moreover, it was a scarcely a trifle or a thing easy to get, for Mulgrave's predecessor in office, Lord Chatham, had a list of 165 candidates with vacancies for only sixteen or seventeen a year.[9] Entry into the artillery or engineer branches through Woolwich demanded early action, for a candidate had to be placed on the list at eleven years old, in order to hope to secure a place before the age limit of fifteen had been passed. It was an appointment, as William Adam pointed out, which 'often follows at a great distance of time after the application & entring on the list'. [10] It followed, therefore, that most of the military appointments to which Scottish freeholders and burgh councillors aspired were in the line infantry and to a lesser degree the cavalry, augmented during the wars with France at the turn of the century with numerous local military units of a temporary nature.

Permission to sell a commission or permission to purchase one was again something which might involve the intervention of a politician. Occasionally the politician was unable to help. In 1728, for example, Lord Milton, in spite of his involvement in the political management of Scotland, failed to secure permission for David Stewart of Ballachallan to purchase the commission of Lieutenant Graham of the Royal Regiment of North British Fusiliers, because the King had prohibited buying, selling or resigning commissions.[11] It should perhaps be added that Stewart was not attempting to enter the service at a higher than normal rank, for fusilier regiments did not employ the rank of ensign, the equivalent rank being that of second lieutenant, which was what was sought. In 1717, Captain Ferguson, with the support of Brigadier Preston, wrote to the Duke of Montrose to seek his 'help to his merit in purchasing from Major James Lauson his post as Major'.[12]

Captain Ferguson, however, was not the senior in his rank, but the other captains were unable to make the purchase. Even then, though, the intervention of a great man was believed to be necessary, and ability to pay was not alone sufficient. Indeed, the influence of the duke was sought at Court in order to secure the King's permission, and Brigadier Preston argued in support of the transaction that

> Major Lauson bought his majority and has been often wounded in former occasions, and those he received in the late affair att Preston are soe severe now upon him that he thinks it impossible for him ever to be fitt for service. His numerous family may have some credit with your Grace to plead with his Majesty to allow him to dispose in favours of your humble servant Captain Fergusone . . . [13]

Political intervention was often the only means of securing permission for the sale of a commission to another. In 1753, for example, Provost William Christie of Stirling sought Lord Milton's intervention with Lord Loudoun on behalf of his son-in-law, Ensign Gunning, who wished to purchase from Charles Elphinstone his commission as Lieutenant of Stirling Castle, or if that was not permitted, the commission of the Ensign of the Castle. [14] Political intervention was advisable even when an applicant had the necessary financial strength to make a purchase, and if a gift of a commission was a greater compliment, permission to purchase was nonetheless gratefully accepted.

Shrewd military gentlemen were always aware of political realities, and upon entry some already had promotion in mind. John Rose, for example, a son of the laird of Kilravock, was commissioned ensign in Lord Semple's Regiment in 1741, but, upon receiving his choice of the company to which he would be attached, fixed upon that of Captain Campbell of Carrick 'because the Lieutenant of that Company is a very pretty fellow & will probably be soon made a Capt. which (with Interest) will make room for John's own preferment'. [15] On occasion, strong political interest could push a young man forward much more rapidly than could have been for the good of the service. In 1739 Lieutenant Alexander Stewart, of Captain Monro of Culcairn's Highland independent company, died, and Lord Lovat strongly urged that the place should go to Francis Grant, one of the sons of Sir James Grant of Grant. The appointment, as Lovat advised, 'would give him the rank of Lieut. & you could easily afterwards get him out of our companys to a marching reg[imen]t either as lieut[enant] or captain'. [16] The Laird of Grant duly approached Government, through the Earl of Ilay, and secured the commission. It might be supposed, however, that Francis Grant, as a newcomer to military life, should have entered as an ensign rather than as second-in-command of the company in question. Lovat, however, had no doubts, insisting that Ensign McDonald should be passed over, alleging that the unfortunate man

> is a perfect ideot and sot, not capable to do the duty of a Lieut. nay not of any post, but it is charity to keep him as he is, & it would be wronging of the company not to make Frank lieut[enant] for I know that my young favourite would take pleasure to dreel the company & keep them in order . . . [17]

In all probability, however, Ensign McDonald's major failing was that he was neither a Fraser nor a Grant, and in that region dominated by family interests, his political connections were insufficient to secure his advancement.

The relatively plentiful supply of physicians in Scotland and the attraction of the university medical schools for sons of the gentry made the medical officers' appointments in the army and navy almost as attractive as the similar appointments in the service of the East India Company. Those places in army units were invariably awarded through political interest, though admittedly rarely in so blatant a manner as that adopted by Sir David Cunynghame, a West Lothian politician, when disposing of the junior medical officer's place in his regiment in 1760. Sir David advised his friend, Sir Robert Dalyell, that the post of surgeon's mate was worth three shillings and sixpence per day, and requested that his correspondent would oblige by

> pointing out some of the friends of our party to whom I might give it. If its not worth the acceptance of any of our own side of the question, I shall willingly bestow it upon any of the other side & beg you will do me the favour to accept of the nomination ... This I hope will convince both friends & foes that I have at least an inclination to serve the gentlemens familys of this country ... [18]

In certain regiments, however, qualifications beyond the strictly medical were demanded of the surgeons, for in Highland regiments knowledge of the Gaelic language appears to have been more seriously demanded of medical officers than of the combatant officers. Malcolm Macqueen, a nephew of an Inverness laird, and recommended by Norman Macleod of Macleod to General Simon Fraser as surgeon of his regiment, had studied medicine at Edinburgh university and had recommendations from his professors, but Macqueen's qualifications were rounded off by his ability to speak Gaelic 'in its purity, which is necessary for a surgeon of a Highland regiment'.[19] This too was the strongest argument offered in favour of one Sandy Forbes, who hoped for the office of surgeon's mate of the Sutherland Fencibles in 1779, though in his case he clearly intended to be an officer in name only for he intended to apply for leave to complete his degree at Edinburgh University and to sail for India as an officer of an East Indiaman at the first suitable opportunity.[20] Medical appointments in military units were believed to provide useful experience to recent graduates or students, and were much in demand.

Politicians were often able to arrange matters to the satisfaction of their constituents in other questions broadly relating to the military profession. In 1716, for example, the Duke of Montrose was hard pressed to maintain his political dominance of Glasgow when he was approached by a member of the university on behalf of a recently promoted lieutenant of Brigadier Preston's regiment, one of the senior corps of the army. The lieutenant believed 'it will be a long time before he can expect to be advanced to be captain in so old a corps. Theirfor would gladly by y[ou]r Gr[ace's] interest be promoted either to be a captain of foot, or a lieut[enant] of dragoons in the new levies'.[21] Conversely, when a war was being concluded and there was a prospect of reductions in the size of the army, many officers of the younger regiments attempted to avoid reduction to half-pay by trying their interest with a politician, but the practice of transferring to a new regiment to accelerate promotion, and then regaining a place in an old one while retaining the rank already gained, demanded very good political connections. Those with political value, however, could demand and often get what they wanted in the army, and if the expected advancement was delayed too long they could show anger quite openly. In 1790, when the county of Cromarty was being contested, one of the freeholders serving in the army demanded, as the price of his support for the candidate favoured by Henry Dundas, that he should be given a company in a regiment stationed in Britain. As Dundas's correspondent advised, the young officer had begun to write letters

> expressive of much impatience, I used my best endeavours to keep him quiet, in a reliance on your promises, from which he might rest assured of a company, and soon, either that in the 48th or some other as good … He has … left Edinburgh in great dudgeon, and express'd no small share of anger … there can be no great reliance had on him, unless soon provided for.[22]

Solicitations for military promotion could become quite pointed if the politician did not act quickly, as the Earl of Marchmont discovered when he failed to secure a promotion for Lieutenant James Wedderburn, whose uncle complained was

> still a leutenant in the Fusiliers, others have advanced who have neither served so longe nor are so far forward in the rank of leutenants nor have the interest I shud think he has trough your Lop. & the Register. What gives me most concern is least he gete a stepe by some other interest & that wd. be vastly inconvenient … [23]

A polite but clear piece of blackmail to a politician who dominated, but was not in absolute control of, the writer's county politics. Military commissions were in demand in Scotland, and Scottish politicians were expected to be able to satisfy their friends, and with an almost constant 25 per cent of the officer corps drawn from Scotland they clearly succeeded to an astonishing degree in obtaining positions for their countrymen.[24] The politician who could provide them won friends. 'If people of small fortunes are carried of by C[ommission]'s can I wonder at it?' asked the Duke of Montrose. 'I see what influence such baits have over their betters.' [25]

Politicians who were able to offer such attractions did not hesitate to make good use of their powers to win votes. In 1723, for example, Colonel John Campbell wrote to a Dunbartonshire laird to warn him that

> The Duke of Argyll was lately very much surprised at hearing your Son was the chief person who went round the shire of Dumbarton with Mr. Colhoune to make interest against my father at a time when he had actually given me orders to write to offer to bring him a Quarter Master in his owne Regt. till he had a vacancy to make him an officer. This put a stope to the offer … Now what I have to offer as a sincere friendly

advise is that upon this occasion you will write to His grace (if you think proper) to offer your vote and interest for the next elections ... [26]

The permanent military garrisons in Scotland provided a number of minor posts which featured prominently in burgh politics, particularly in Stirling, where the Christie family influence in council over an extended period ensured that much of the small change of military patronage came their way. In 1721, for example, Provost Christie approached the Duke of Montrose for his interest to secure the post of armourer of Stirling Castle for his son-in-law, James Graham. The Duke, aware that the incumbent armourer was dead, used his interest with the Board of Ordnance, pointing out that 'it might serve my interest in the town of Stirling'.[27] The Duke passed on this information to his agent among the burgh politicians, instructing that he should 'take that opportunity of fixing, as much as is possible, Christie'.[28] Unfortunately the post of armourer was not granted to James Graham, but the need to placate Provost Christie still produced action at the Board of Ordnance which transferred the Master Gunner of Stirling Castle to Portsmouth and commissioned the provost's son-in-law to succeed to the Stirling post.[29]

James Christie, in addition to his civic duties, was a clothier and merchant, and he did not miss the opportunity to translate political connections into contracts. He ranged widely, soliciting in 1741 the office of sutler of Stirling Castle, believed to be profitable, and at the same time the contract to clothe Lord Loudoun's independent company permanently stationed in the castle.[30] In the same year, 1741, Christie was also pressing Lord Milton to exert his influence with the colonel of the Highland Regiment 'to give me the Cloathing of that Regiment for the incouradgement of our Scots manufactorys ... this jobb wou'd employ many poor familys in the country ... '[31] It was not Christie alone who saw the connections between peripheral military patronage and profit, and offers of minor posts about the Castle of Stirling were often considered worth making by politicians soliciting the town's vote. When the Haldanes challenged the Campbell influence in Stirling, they promised Deacon Ellise of the hammermen that he should be made smith of the Castle and that a member of the tailor's trade should replace the castle storeman.[32] In that instance they were unsuccessful, for the interest of Lord Milton and the Earl of Ilay was considerably stronger than that of the Haldanes, but the more attractive posts in the permanent garrison were always in demand from tradesmen in the town. In this regard it might be added that the permanent garrison included many soldiers who practised trades in the community when they were not on duty, and the smith and storeman were presumably in this category. Town and fortress were closely connected, and indeed the burgh of Stirling not infrequently had a battalion of infantry in the town itself as well as the permanent garrison. That situation lent itself to a kind of reverse patronage if the town annoyed the Administration, and the advice sent to Lord Milton in 1734 when the Stirling people were 'very insolent ' and 'were Drinking at the Cross disappointment to L[ord] I[lay] and all his Designs' was that the bulk of the troops should be removed, together with much of the community's business, as a preliminary to an attack on the town council. Milton was advised that this 'will be a means to make most of the Trades fly against the present sett. I am laying a scheme to get them all turned out against Michaelmas '.[33]

Some of the burgh politicians were themselves military officers. In the first years of the nineteenth century the town of Inverkeithing was controlled by an officer of the Royal Marines named David Ballingall, and Colonel Ballingall left the Lord Advocate in no doubt that he was most unhappy with his removal from an appointment as an inspecting field officer. For this reason, the Colonel pointed out, he could not 'consistent with my wounded feelings support his Lordship's friend at the late General Election ... '[34] Patronage was always a double-edged weapon for the politicians. If its distribution won them friends, a loss of employment was readily blamed on the same men who assumed credit for the award of patronage, and frequently credit was assumed but blame apportioned when the politician's responsibility was unclear. Certainly from what Ballingall wrote, it is clear that Lord Melville to whom he had written had shown the letter to the Commandant of Royal Marines, Lieutenant-General John Campbell. Unfortunately that was insufficient to keep Ballingall employed, for the General was not on good terms with Ballingall, and clearly did not feel compelled to serve Lord Melville, and it was the latter whom Ballingall chose to blame for his misfortunes, complaining of the injustice of this treatment when 'Lord Melville never had a more staunch friend, nor strinuous supporter in the district of these Boroughs'.[35]

In the early eighteenth century poverty was partially responsible for the many applications for military rank, for in the first half of the century even a commission in a new regiment, and the near certainty of half-pay at the conclusion of the war emergency, was attractive. James Graham of Airth, for example, urged the Duke of Montrose to provide for Graham of Drynie, one of his relatives, in a new regiment, for 'it would be a seasonable relief for a numorous and very poor family'.[36] On the other hand, some of the freeholders seeking patronage demurred at the price expected. Lord Panmure was solicited by a Forfarshire freeholder in 1739 for a place in the new levies of Royal Marines for his son, for which the laird offered to 'pay such an allowance ... as was reasonable. And believing the price might be much moderated by your Lordship's intercession ... '[37] The laird was startled to learn, however, that the lieutenancy of Marines would cost £300, and shrewdly wondered if there was not a better opportunity afforded by the expansion of the army and the removal from the infantry regiments of many subalterns to fill captaincies in the Marines. Panmure's constituent concluded that 'subaltern commissions would fall much in their price. And as your Lordship is so good as to talk to some of the Agents that deal that way I shall be exceedingly obliged ... if any thing can be done'.[38]

Scottish gentlemen followed military careers in the service of the United Provinces of the Netherlands as well as in that of their own country, and political influence extended over the North Sea to include the Scots-Dutch regiments. In 1741, for example, political control of the Dunfermline district of burghs turned on the vote of the town of Inverkeithing. That burgh was controlled by Provost

John Cunningham, whose son was an officer of the Dutch army, and the provost made his wishes quite clear to one of the candidates who solicited the town's vote whom he believed might have friends in the Netherlands. In short, the town of Inverkeithing was determined by the arrival of a letter from Count Nassau promising that Lieutenant Cuningham should obtain the next company of infantry which fell vacant, and at the same time requesting support for one of the candidates for the parliamentary election.[39] The other side of the coin was the pressure which could be exerted upon such foreign soldiers if they attempted to come home to vote in an election in opposition to a man of influence. In the same election, though in a different constituency, as that in which Lieutenant Cunningham secured his captaincy, an impoverished Berwickshire gentleman named Brown, who was serving as a private soldier in Holland, though a son of the late Sir Alexander Brown of Bassenden, returned to Scotland to cast his vote as a freeholder of Berwickshire. Unfortunately Brown intended to oppose the interest of Lord Home who was himself a soldier serving in the Netherlands and with many powerful friends there. Lord Home ordered his agents in Scotland to seize Brown as soon as he landed and to impress upon him 'what is very trew that if he oppose me he will dissoblige Prince Waldeck and all his officers',[40] and thus presumably ruin any chance which he might have of advancement. Influence with senior officers and ministers was also employed for arranging the attendance or absence of military freeholders or councillors. Friends found leave to attend an election easily obtained, while enemies of the powerful would find their services in great demand with their regiments, at least until a vital election had taken place.

The army absorbed most of the Scottish gentry who hoped to make their living from the sword, but there were also many Scots in the Royal Navy and Royal Marines, and those who entered the senior service appear to have been attracted by the substantial advantages which the navy had over the army for a gentleman of limited means. As a political tool naval patronage was rather less in the control of Administration than was military patronage, for although the Board of Admiralty retained all home patronage, there were many flag officers commanding squadrons in distant waters who enjoyed the right to make necessary promotions in their ships. At least one of the Scots of flag rank, Admiral Lord Keith, was no friend of the Administration, and he employed his own patronage to augment the Indian patronage distributed by his brother, William Elphinstone, in order to sustain an opposition political interest.

Naval officers required a patron at three times in their career, and it was useful to have powerful friends at all times in order to secure seagoing appointments. The first need for patronage was to facilitate entry; secondly, it could ease the promotion of midshipmen to the rank of lieutenant; and thirdly, it would aid the advancement of a lieutenant to the rank of commander of a small warship or captain of a larger one. At the conclusion of a war there were invariably far too many officers for the reduced number of ships retained in commission, and interest was a great help in securing a place in one of them. On the other hand, naval appointments demanded, in addition, evidence of competence. Promotion required successful completion of an examination, and no captain would willingly saddle himself with an incompetent watchkeeping officer when that officer's negligence could lead to the loss of the ship and the captain's inevitable court-martial. Patronage in effect chose from among the qualified candidates those whose rise would be accelerated, and its advantages in easing the movement upwards on a rapidly narrowing ladder is evident.

Even at the point of entry there was overcrowding, and in 1786 an officer pointed out to a correspondent that 'the ship is allowed but two midshipmen, and we have sixteen gentlemen on board who are rated able seamen & captain's servants '.[41] Obviously it would be much easier to leave the ranks of the captain's servants if a candidate had the support of a powerful political interest, though no doubt sheer professional ability might win the assistance of superiors. All too typical, however, was Lord Keith's remark in 1799 that he had given a lieutenant's commission to 'the Duchess of Atholle's friend Glen Geary . . . a heavy dog too',[42] while passing over a brighter but less well-connected midshipman. To do the navy justice, however, it must again be emphasised that powerful interest could rarely secure promotion for the unqualified, and in the naval service some ability was a prerequisite for advancement. There are examples of officers whose promotion was clearly desired by their superiors who yet could not be advanced. One of the minor problems of a fleet commander involved in politics was the well-connected incompetent. Lord Keith encountered this difficulty in the person of a Midshipman Mayers, who told the admiral that he was qualified for promotion to lieutenant. Keith, accordingly, had a commission made out, but, as the admiral complained, 'behold he had not passed, I ordered three captains to examine him, he declined to go, consequently I was obliged to tear the commission '.[43] Even an admiral's good wishes could not dispense with the ability to pass a professional examination.

Incompetent candidates with friends valuable to Keith's political interest could try his patience sorely. Such was Midshipman Adam Ross, whom Keith after several years of effort finally pushed into commissioned rank. The first reference to the young gentleman is found in Lord Keith's private correspondence in October 1797, when the admiral complained to his sister that he was 'plagued with Adam Ross. He has no intellect and does not improve a bit: I wish he was in the army'.[44] Keith was at that time second-in-command of the Mediterranean fleet, and his superior, Lord St. Vincent, no doubt familiar with Keith's political needs, was willing to assist, but some midshipmen were not promotable. 'Lord St. V[incent] offers Ross a commission, but I dare not mention his passing, it is vexatious.'[45] But the longer Ross remained unpromoted, the more offended his friends would become, especially when they saw the sons of other freeholders advanced in rank. 'Fintry's son is returned well. I have put him into the *London* to act as lieutenant,' the admiral reported. 'I had kept it open for Ross as long as I could.'[46] In 1799, however, things took a turn for the better, for a number of prizes captured from the enemy and retained with the fleet created an acute shortage of officers to command them. It would seem that this occasioned a relaxation of promotional standards, for Admiral Keith finally disposed of his problem by this addition of two captured corvettes and a frigate to his fleet. 'Mr. Ross goes lieutenant into one of them if he can pass his examination on the morrow',[47] Keith informed his sister, and it would seem that the examining board were duly impressed by their admiral's anxiety, for they took a chance on this doubtful candidate. 'Ross, I thank God, is off my hands, sent into *El Teresa*, a Spanish frigate, 3rd lieutenant.'[48] Ability alone was clearly not the only factor influencing the promotion of naval officers, and it is not surprising that some of those promoted did not successfully fill their new posts. There were officers like Lieutenant Moncrieff, promoted by Lord Keith at the Cape of Good Hope in 1795 in order to oblige Scottish friends. 'Will you write Charles Napier that I made his man Moncrieff a lieutenant,' Keith wrote, 'and I am now obliged to invalid him to prevent his being dismissed by a court martial. He is a filthy drunken beast . . . '[49] A naval officer could rise in rank quite rapidly if he had the friendship of the commander-in-chief of a distant station. The honourable George H.L. Dundas, admittedly an officer of considerable merit, as well as the son of Lord Dundas, an important Whig politician, served in the Mediterranean under Lord Keith's command. Here politics and local interest coincided, for the father of the young officer was an important landowner in the area of Scotland in which the Elphinstone interest was being upheld by Lord Keith, and indeed, before acquiring his peerage, Lord Dundas had represented Stirlingshire in the House of Commons. George Dundas went to the Mediterranean as a lieutenant in Lord Keith's flagship, the *Queen Charlotte*, and when that vessel was lost by fire he was immediately appointed in the same rank to the newly commissioned *Guillaume Tell*, a ship-of-the-line taken from France, on 11th April 1800. Eighteen days later Lord Keith saw another opportunity to help Mr. Dundas, for a number of new appointments were made in consequence of the commissioning of another captured French vessel, the *Carmine*, and George Dundas found himself Flag Lieutenant in the *Minotaur* in place of John Stewart who had been appointed acting commander of another vessel, whose commander in turn had assumed command of the newly commissioned ship. Within a few months George Dundas was himself commander of the *Lutine*, and on 2nd November transferred in this rank to the sloop *Calpe*, again newly commissioned, and with this record of command his career was firmly established and his subsequent rise rapid, for in this case Keith had made no mistake in patronising a friend. Finally, on 17th August 1801, Commander Dundas was appointed acting captain of the newly commissioned *San Antonio*, having completed the transition from junior lieutenant to post-captain in just over one year.[50]

Naval patronage was regularly used, within the limits imposed by regulation, to sustain a political interest, and even if the powers of a flag officer in the field of promotion were restricted in Europe, an officer in command of a ship, or in a position to influence that commander, could still place boys on the first rung of the promotional ladder by securing for them appointments as midshipmen or, failing that, captain's servants. The Royal Navy became a popular career for Scots in the eighteenth century, from about the period of the American Revolution onwards, and it was a particularly apt choice for a gentleman of small means for it was a less expensive profession than that of an army officer. In 1778, when an English captain could remark that 'more than two-thirds of my quarter deck are Scotch',[51] the proportion of Scots among the officers of a vessel commanded by one of their own countrymen would be substantial.

In theory, the captain of a ship was entitled to take into his ship as midshipmen, volunteers, or captain's servants any of the sons of his friends who hoped for a naval career, but in practice even this form of entrance patronage was limited and largely in the hands of flag-officers, for it would be a captain with a liking for half-pay who would refuse the requests of an influential admiral. The limitations of a captain's powers of patronage are illustrated by a letter written to William Graham of Airth, a Stirlingshire freeholder, in 1785:

> I assure you uncle every way has been tried to get Thomas on board some of H.M. ships, but all in vain ... my last hope ... rested with my friend Captn. Hood, who was commissioned some days ago for a Cutter Built Sloop of War ... but the day he was commissioned for her, he received a letter from his uncle Lord Hood, who got him appointed, beging, or rather desiring, that he would not take a Midshipman, or young gentleman till he saw him, as he had some particular friends that he must beg him to take on board. This Brig is only allowed a Mate & two Midshipmen, and do as they will Captn. Hood tells me he cannot stow above six, four of whom will get no pay; and had he room the Adm[ira]l has twice that number for him ... [52]

Admirals, and those with influence over such officers, were in a position to patronise persons recommended by their friends. If an admiral commanded on a distant station, he had considerable patronage at his disposal. He could make mates and midshipmen into lieutenants, and he could advance some lucky lieutenants to the rank of commander or captain. At home, where an admiral's powers were much more restricted, and even the most favoured officers could expect to have to wait for their promotion until the end of the admiral's period of command, when it was customary to make him the compliment of a few promotions on striking his flag, it was still possible to introduce new entrants to a seagoing life. Promotions were always more difficult to arrange than first appointments, for there were always far more qualified candidates for promoted posts than there were places to be filled, but it is clear, from the complaints of those who deplored the favouritism implied by the intervention of political interests, that this was a common route to advancement. Earl St. Vincent, for example, writing in 1801, remarked that 'the list of lieutenants abounds with improper persons who have obtained promotions by influence'.[53]

First appointments, on occasion, could be a matter of considerable urgency to a freeholder or a burgh magistrate, and that kind of favour was not particularly difficult to arrange, if a politician had taken the precaution of developing connections with influential navy men. Sometimes a midshipman's place was sheer necessity, as in the case of a son of an Angus freeholder named David Lyell who found himself involuntarily a member of the Royal Navy. David Lyell had been returning to Britain from Carolina as a member of the crew of a merchant vessel when his ship was intercepted by a cruiser and he was impressed for service in an undermanned warship. The young man's brother wrote to Lord Panmure to see if David could make the best of the situation in which he found himself by obtaining a midshipman's place. The brother carefully laid the groundwork for his request to the politician at the outset, pointing out that he had now received his charter and was qualified as a voter and promising that 'you may stedfastly rely I will serve your Lordship on all occasions to the outmost of my power'.[54] To a man of Panmure's connections this was not a particularly difficult matter in time of war, even with the qualification which the Lyells made to their request, that ships about to sail for the West Indies were not acceptable, but it was clearly a very material favour to the family concerned. The pressing of a gentleman, though no doubt a poor gentleman in wordly goods, was not uncommon, and in 1741 Lord Panmure got a very similar request from another of his constituents on behalf of Mr. Charles Duncan, 'a son of Ardownie's, who's now a foremasthand aboard the *Royal Sovereign* his Majesty's Ship lying at Chatham ... '[55] The press-gang gave politicians an effective method of giving a very real service to the parties more directly concerned, and it was one which should have created a lasting sense of obligation, for life before the mast in one of His Majesty's ships was not likely to be easily forgotten. Officers of merchant ships were particularly vulnerable if they did not have in their possession a written protection from impressment issued by the Admiralty, and David Scott was enabled to oblige both Provost Watt of Forfar and several influential merchants of Dundee by securing the freedom of Peter Brown, the mate of the ship *John and Nancy* of Dundee, though in this case the Dundee magistrates had to provide an able seaman as a replacement for Brown before he was freed from the pressing tender. [56] To a politician the ability to do this kind of service was vital, and it was even more urgent if a political contest was in progress, lest the opposition perform the service. Captain Charles Campbell, the Government agent in the burgh of Stirling in 1734, wrote to Lord Milton to desire the freedom of a Stirling man named Kier who had been pressed by Captain Oliphant of the *Terrible*, a cruiser stationed in the Forth. The problem was that Kier had friends in the town council and, as Campbell pointed out, 'my eneemys here have wrote to My Lord Grange; if the man is sett at liberty I begg it may be by y[ou]r interest, and that you'll be so good as write me so, for it will do me service in this place'.[57]

Requests for a place as midshipman, or if that was impossible, as a captain's servant with prospects of future advancement to that rank or that of master's mate, another stepping stone to commissioned rank in the Royal Navy, were much more frequent than requests for aid in freeing a man from the press. It is clear from the surviving correspondence that a naval career had become attractive to the Scottish gentry by the middle of the eighteenth century, perhaps because expenses at sea were much lower than those incurred in an army officer's mess, while not the least of the attractions of a naval career in time of war was the possibility of prize money. Pressure for places in the navy was so great that it could prove a difficult tool for politicians able to supply such appointments, for there was never enough to meet all the demands for it, and the obligement of one could offend other freeholders less fortunate. The difficulty of using this form of patronage whose scarcity could give offence to those who were unlucky is illustrated by the difficulties of the Duke of Montrose and his son, Lord George Graham, in 1739-40, when Lord George, who hoped to combine a career as a naval officer with membership in the House of Commons, first obtained command of a ship, and was thus enabled to offer places in the line of command to the sons of freeholders in the area of Montrose influence in central Scotland. Unfortunately, Lord George's first command was a vessel with an extremely small crew of only 45 men, including officers, which left little room for many aspirants to commissioned rank.[58] Lord George did not long remain in command of such a small vessel, however, and no sooner did he attain a more substantial command than the Duke of Montrose sent orders for the sons of the lairds of Auchenbowie and Balfunning to be sent to London with a view to joining Lord George. It is clear from the tone of the Duke's letter that these were staunch political friends, and in the case of one of them Montrose was even prepared to help to equip the son for his new life at sea, remarking,

> my neighbour I know is not rich, and my intention allways was, if he sent a son to sea, to be kind to him so as to save his being a weight upon him, this is in a good measure dew to his firmity and the obligations I have had to him on that acct … [59]

Before Lord George obtained this command, however, his inability to render the services expected of him by some of the family's political friends was a liability, and was seen as such by Montrose, who wrote with some anxiety to deny allegations that the son of another gentleman of the region was serving in Lord George's ship, but was on board the flagship of the admiral. The Duke insisted that 'its fitt it be understood … for it might give umbrage to Achinbowie and Balfunning', and he was very clear that the gentleman in question, the son of Glengyle, should not, under any circumstances, join Lord George's ship.[60]

Given the significance of patronage in securing a promotion, or in placing an officer in a situation where he might have an opportunity to distinguish himself, and thus strengthen his claims to advancement, there was a good incentive to arrange for a transfer to another ship where favour might be expected. The loss of an efficient officer, however, was not to be accepted without protest by the captain who lost his services, and Captain Robert Digby, for example, protested in strong terms the impending transfer of Midshipman Callender from his ship to Captain Keith Stewart's *Berwick* in 1778, pointing out that 'this Mr. Callender I made a midshipman myself upon finding Sir Lawrence Dundas was his friend' and complained of 'Scotch captains being allowed to pick the quarterdecks of other ships without the captain's consent … '[61]

Midshipman Callender's friends no doubt were aware that efficiency united to interest was the strongest claim to promotion in the navy, and Lord Keith's correspondence abounds in references to interest being a motive in bringing a man forward in the service: 'I have made McKenzie a lieutenant into the *Rattlesnake*; he was a friend of Mr. Dunsmuress and recommended by Lord Elphinstone to me, so I am glad to have served him',[62] a comment which suggests that the admiral was influenced by something more than Mr. McKenzie's personal abilities. Equally, when it came to promotion to captain in the

Mediterranean fleet, interest was obviously a strong influence upon the admiral, for he remarks in July 1799 that 'Adam Drummond came to me yesterday. I wish I could give him a post, but I could not pass Lord Bute's son with decency'.[63] It would be improbable that men totally unqualified for their rank would be placed in a fleet commanded by the patron whose own career might be damaged by inefficiency, but given the situation in the fleet, of far more qualified applicants than available places, the choice was likely to fall upon a friend of a friend. For the man without interest, the opportunity to distinguish himself in action, and thus by securing mentions in despatches to attract the attention of the Admiralty, was a harder road to advancement. Many political debts were paid with a word in the right ear at an appropriate moment, and the friends of naval officers were never slow to ask the aid of their member of parliament or another politician with reason to maintain good relations with them. On occasion the requests were intended to push a candidate forward much more rapidly than was normal. Such a request was made to Thomas Dundas by four of the councillors of Dunfermline who pressed him to use his interest with Lord Sandwich to get Midshipman Ebenezer Fish serving on board the *Warwick* a place as a lieutenant of marines, since the marine officers were not required to have the years of sea-service demanded of naval lieutenants.[64]

Freeholders who were disappointed in their expectation of aid from the political interest which they had supported were ripe for an attack by another interest, and some of the freeholders in this situation did not scruple to state their position quite bluntly. In the autumn of 1751, for example, Alexander Hume Campbell, the brother of the Earl of Marchmont, and member of parliament for Berwickshire, wrote to Lord Anson, the First Lord of the Admiralty, telling him how important it was to his interest that Lieutenant James Home should be made a post-captain, and reminding Lord Anson that this favour had already been promised to Lord Marchmont during a conversation in the House of Lords.[65] Early in January 1758, however, Lieutenant Home's brother, David Home of Wedderburn, complained that the promise had not been kept and that the lieutenant had been ordered to join a fireship at Spithead which was being prepared for foreign service. 'This,' complained Wedderburn, 'gives him vast uneasiness, for if he is ordered abroad before he gets his Post he dispairs of it for some time.'[66] Lord Anson, bombarded as he was from all directions by demands for favours, was hard to move towards action, and Lieutenant Home no doubt felt it would be a case of out of sight out of mind. As Wedderburn pointed out, 'tho' he has Lo[rd] Anson's promise to do for him he relies little on it unless your Lo[rdshi]p & the Register intirfire for he will find a readie excuse, he was abroad or he wd have been provided'. [67] Marchmont himself was forced to admit that 'Lord Anson's promises are so long in the performing that I reckon none of us will build sudden expectations upon them'.[68]

The member for Berwickshire went immediately to the head of the Administration and 'desired the D[uke] of Newcastle to refresh his Lordship's memory', but Lord Anson was a master of diplomatic procrastination, never refusing an important supporter of Government, yet delaying performance of his undertakings. Marchmont was driven to complain that Anson had been ready enough to promise that he would 'do it the first moment it was possible', and had already been strongly urged to promote Lieutenant Home by the Duke of Newcastle, but yet had done nothing.[69] The delay and the excuses clearly angered the Laird of Wedderburn, for he responded to Lord Marchmont's letter with an implied threat combined with a reminder of past loyalty. The message was clearly stated nonetheless, and it must have been an alarming one to Marchmont and his brother, for Wedderburn was an important freeholder with many connections in the country:

> Your Lo[rdshi]p may remember I mentioned a letter to you which I had from an acquaintance in London (whom I know is intimat with Mr. Elliot & likewise converses with others of the Com[misione]rs of Admiralty) about the time James was put in to the *Pluto*, which amongst other things said that if we wd think of changing sides he could with authority say the Leutenant wd be a Captain in a verie shorte time. I know not by what authority he reckoned us on anie side for we never had anetered so deepe on the subject as to declair anie thing about it . . . & when Mr. Elliot came to the Board the second time, applieing to Lord Minto & writeing to Mr. Elliot was proposed to me, but as we did not care to come under obligations that way neither of these were done . . . as we knew your Lo[rdshi]p's sincerity. I only mention these things that your Lo[rdshi]p may make what use you think proper of them.[70]

The delay in securing the desired promotion appears to suggest that the Marchmont interest, however influential in Berwickshire, was not particularly effective in London, and there were Scottish politicians who showed themselves better able to redeem promises that had a political importance. James Christie, one of the leading figures in the town council of Stirling, had a son in the navy named Francis Christie, who had served six years as a midshipman in the West Indies, and had confidence in his ability to pass the examination for lieutenant. Interest, however, was required to secure an appointment in this rank, for the alternative was an unwanted retiral to Stirling on half-pay. Christie, so adept at getting the aid of Administration for his own business, knew exactly where to look for help, and approached Lord Ilay through his deputy, Lord Milton, and without any attempt to bargain simply asked for an appointment for his son, promising that it would 'forever laye me under the deepest obligationes'.[71] Since Christie had the vote of the burgh of Stirling at his disposal after the Michaelmas elections of 1740, when the friends of James Erskine of Grange were turned out of council by Christie's party, Ilay and Milton showed their appreciation of the magistrate's friendship by ensuring that Sir Robert Walpole recommended Mr. Christie to Sir Charles Wager to such effect that the admiral named Christie to the highly desirable post of lieutenant in a new frigate, with all the prospects of prize money which such an appointment entailed.[72]

Among the senior naval officers with Scottish political interests some were in opposition to the Administration, and one at least, Admiral Lord Keith, because of the importance of the commands which he held, was able to utilise naval patronage to sustain the political interest of the Elphinstone family of which he was a member. Lord Keith was followed in the navy by his nephew, Admiral Fleming of Cumbernauld, who was even further estranged from the Administration by his support of parliamentary reform. A senior officer, when employed, was able to place young men in the line of command by securing their entry as midshipmen, an appointment which became increasingly in demand with the expansion of the navy during the wars against France at the end of the eighteenth and opening of the nineteenth centuries. Junior naval officers were nominally ratings, for a midshipman was a warrant officer in contrast to the army equivalents, the ensign of foot or cornet of cavalry, who enjoyed commissioned rank, but it was for that reason that the Admiralty did not monopolise first appointments in the fleet, only interesting themselves in appointments at the rank of lieutenant or above.

Lord Keith's career, in which he held important commands in distant waters, particularly at the Cape of Good Hope and in the Mediterranean, gave him further opportunities to strengthen his political interest by advancing his friends in the service. Both commands were theatres of war in which many prizes were taken, some of which were added to the fleet and consequently required officers to command them. Keith was able to appoint officers even to the coveted rank of captain, which was in that period for all practical purposes the ultimate promotion, since admirals were drawn automatically from the more senior members of the captains' list. But if naval patronage did prove to be of considerable value to the Elphinstone family interest, reinforcing the impact of the Indian patronage distributed by Keith's brother, William Elphinstone, the fleet could only provide patronage for those officers fortunate enough to be employed in a command in a suitable station far from Great Britain. Officers employed in northern Europe, where much of the navy was inevitably disposed, had little patronage at their disposal, and what they got was obtained only after a battle with the Board of Admiralty. Lord Keith, however, employed his powers of patronage effectively to make the Elphinstone interest powerful enough to defy even Henry Dundas's dominance of Scottish politics. Much of the remaining employment suitable for gentlemen, however, was more fully in the hands of the Administration and its delegates, and that in itself affords sufficient explanation of the strength of government in Scottish political life.

NOTES

1. National Maritime Museum. Keith Papers, Kei/128, Lord Keith to his sister, 21 Sept., 1793.

2. SRO. Montrose, GD220/5/883, Montrose to Mungo Graeme of Gorthie, 22 Feb., 1793.

3. SRO. Montrose, GD220/5/530, Charles, Master of Elphinstone to Montrose, 26 Jul., 1715.

4. Sir William Fraser, *Memorials of the Family of Wemyss of Wemyss* (Edinburgh, 1888), iii, 247, General James Grant to the Hon. James Wemyss of Wemyss, 1 Dec., 1775.

5. NLS. Airth, Acc.3012/xxvii/F2, Henry Graham to William Graham of Airth, 5 Feb., 1786.

6. SRO. Seafield, GD248/57/3/51, General James Grant to Sir James Grant of Grant, 2 Mar., 1780.

7. *Journal of the Society for Army Historical Research*, Winter 1982, p. 252.

8. SRO. Cunninghame-Graham, GD22/1/326, Peter Spiers to Lord Keith, 28 Jul., 1811.

9. SRO. Cunninghame-Graham, GD22/ 1/326, Lord Keith to Peter Spiers, 2 Aug., 1811.

10. SRO. CunninghameGraham, GD22/1/326, William Adam to W.C.C. Graham, 5 Aug., 1811.

11. NLS. Saltoun MS.16539, Sir James Wood to Lord Milton, 15 Feb., 1728.

12. SRO. Montrose, GD220/5/726, Brigadier Preston to Montrose, 16 May, 1717.

13. Ibid.

14. NLS. Saltoun MS.16682, Mary Campbell of Boquhan to Milton, 5 Feb., 1753.

15. SRO. Rose of Kilravock, GD125/26, Hugh Rose, younger of Kilravock to Lady Kilravock, 10 Apr., 1741.

16. SRO. Seafield, GD248/97/4/3, Lord Lovat to Sir James Grant, 3 Feb., 1739.

17. SRO. Seafield, GD248/97/4/11, Lord Lovat to Sir James Grant, 9 Mar., 1739.

18. NLS. Saltoun MS. 16174, Sir David Cunynghame to Sir Robert Dalyell, 20 Jul., 1760.

19. HMC Laing MSS, ii, 483, Norman Macleod of Macleod to General Simon Fraser, 13 Nov., 1775.

20. SRO. Seafield, GD248/56/2/13, Rev. James Grant to Sir James Grant, 13 Apr., 1779.

21. SRO. Montrose, GD220/5/819, Mungo Graeme of Gorthie to Montrose, 15 Feb., 1716.

22. SRO. Melville Castle, GD51/1/198/6/2, Alexander Shaw to Henry Dundas, 12 Apr., 1790.

23. SRO. Home of Wedderburn, GD267/16/10, David Home of Wedderburn to the Earl of Marchmont.

24. James Hayes, 'Scottish Officers in the British Army, 1714–63', *SHR*, April, 1958, 23–33.

25. SRO. Montrose, GD220/5/909, Montrose to Mungo Graeme of Gorthie, 11 Apr., 1741.

26. SRO. Ross Estate, GD47/501, Col. John Campbell to Buchanan of Drumakill, 30 Jun., 1723.

27. SRO. Montrose, GD220/5/835, Montrose to Mungo Graeme, 20 Jul., 1721.

28. Ibid.

29. SRO. Montrose, GD220/5/838, Montrose to Mungo Graeme, 27 Jan., 1722.

30. NLS. Saltoun MS.16584, James Christie to Lord Milton, 31 Oct., 1741.

31. NLS. Saltoun MS.16584, James Christie to Lord Milton, 16 Jan., 1741.

32. NLS. Saltoun MS.16645, John Finlayson to Milton, 23 Dec., 1747.

33. NLS. Saltoun MS.16555, Capt. Charles Campbell to Milton, 10 Jun., 1734.

34. SRO. Melville Castle, GD51/1/198/26/12, Col. David Ballingall to Robert Dundas, 24 Sep., 1807.

35. Ibid.

36. SRO. Montrose, GD220/5/563, James Graham of Airth to Montrose, 28 Jul., 1715.

37. SRO. Dalhousie, GD45/14/432, Robert Fullerton to Lord Panmure, 18 Dec., 1739.

38. SRO. Dalhousie, GD45/14/432, Robert Fullerton to Lord Panmure, 10 Jan., 1740.

39. NLS. Saltoun MSS.16643, Major Cochrane to Milton, 14 Jul., 1747; 16647, Sir Peter Halkett to Milton, 19 Jul., 1747.

40. NLS. Saltoun MS.16648. Lord Home to Milton, 17 Jul., 1747.

41. NLS. Airth MS.3012/xxvii/F2, Lieut. David McDowall to William Graham of Airth, 22 May, 1786.

42. National Maritime Museum. Keith Papers, Kei/128, Lord Keith to his sister, 13 Jul., 1797.

43. Ibid.

44. National Maritime Museum. Keith Papers, Kei/128, 27 Oct., 1797.
45. National Maritime Museum. Keith Papers, Kei/128, 18 Dec., 1798.
46. National Maritime Museum. Keith Papers, Kei/128, 7 Feb., 1799.
47. National Maritime Museum. Keith Papers, Kei/128, 5 Mar., 1799.
48. National Maritime Museum. Keith Papers, Kei/128, 8 Mar., 1799.
49. National Maritime Museum. Keith Papers, Kei/128, 10 Nov., 1795.
50. National Maritime Museum. Keith Papers, Kei/L/37, 'List of Appointments and Removals of Commissioned Officers by the Right Hon. Lord Keith, Commander-in-Chief etc., in the Mediterranean', and 'List of Acting Commissions granted by the Right Hon. Lord Keith . . . '
51. G.R. Barnes and J.H. Owen [eds.], *The Sandwich Papers, 1771–81* (London, 1932), i, 262–3, Captain Robert Digby to the Earl of Sandwich, 17 Jan., 1788.
52. NLS. Airth MS.3012/xxvii/F2, Lieut. David McDowall to William Graham of Airth, 15 May, 1785.
53. Edward Pelham Brenton, *Life and Correspondence of John, Earl of St. Vincent* (London, 1838), ii, 72, St. Vincent to Viscount Bulkeley, 18 Jun., 1801.
54. SRO. Dalhousie, GD45/14/432, Thomas Lyell, junior, to Lord Panmure, 20 Mar., 1740.
55. SRO. Dalhousie, GD45/14/432, Alexander Hunter to Panmure, 23 Apr., 1741.
56. India Office, Home Misc. 729–731/221 and 222, David Scott's Letter Books, David Scott to Provost Watt, 8 Aug., 1798 and Evan Nepean to David Scott, 8 Aug., 1798.
57. NLS. Saltoun MS.16555, Capt. Charles Campbell to Milton, 24 Apr., 1734.
58. SRO. Montrose, GD220/5/1481, Lord George Graham to Mungo Graeme of Gorthie, 10 Jul., 1739.
59. SRO. Montrose, GD220/5/906, Duke of Montrose to Mungo Graeme of Gorthie, 21 Mar., 1740.
60. SRO. Montrose, GD220/5/905, Montrose to Mungo Graeme of Gorthie, 18 Aug., 1739.
61. *The Sandwich Papers, op. cit.,* i, 262–3.
62. National Maritime Museum. Keith Papers, Kei/128, Lord Keith to his sister, 15 Apr., 1795.
63. National Maritime Museum. Keith Papers, Kei/128, 13 Jul., 1795.
64. Patronage note included in the Zetland papers, North Riding Record Office, ZNK/X/2.
65. SRO. Home of Wedderburn, GD267/16/10, Alexander Hume Campbell to Lord Anson, 26 Sept., 1757.
66. SRO. Home of Wedderburn, GD267/16/10, David Home of Wedderburn to the Earl of Marchmont, 20 Jan., 1758.
67. Ibid.
68. SRO. Home of Wedderburn, GD267/16/10, Lord Marchmont to Wedderburn, 28 Jan., 1758.
69. Ibid.
70. SRO. Home of Wedderburn, GD267/16/10, David Home of Wedderburn to the Earl of Marchmont, 6 Feb., 1758.
71. NLS. Saltoun MS.16581, James Christie to Lord Milton, 2 Apr., 1740.
72. NLS. Saltoun MS.16584, James Christie to Milton, 16 Jan., 1741.

4

Legal, Church and University Patronage

The link between judicial appointments and parliamentary politics has been one of the most durable connections, and it is therefore scarcely surprising that in the eighteenth century an appointment to the bench was not to be had without considerable political interest, and that this culmination of the career of a lawyer-freeholder was the reward of lengthy association with the great men of the period. But if appointment as a lord of session was major patronage at any period in Scotland's history, there was in the eighteenth century considerable demand for any post which could make use of legal education, for there is some reason to believe that the country was oversupplied with lawyers in view of the desperate efforts which some of them made to obtain a salaried post, no matter how minor. Equally, in this period, the chances of becoming a beneficed clergyman were greatly enhanced if political interest was exerted on the candidate's behalf in the case of crown patronages, while no politician-nobleman, with his own ecclesiastical patronage available, would be likely to ignore political considerations when placing a minister. The Administration, moreover, while having the greatest influence in both judicial and church appointments, had sole control over a number of academic posts, which were also attractive to some of the freeholders, several of whom succeeded in obtaining university chairs.

The abolition of the heritable jurisdictions in 1747 substantially increased the influence of the Government over the Scottish voters by effectively restricting judicial patronage to the Crown. Prior to that date, however, some of the greater landowners, as lords of regality, maintained private courts which gave them opportunities to attract lawyer-freeholders to their service and hence to their political interest. Regalian jurisdiction could be extensive, as for example that of the Duke of Montrose, whose bailie officiated within the baronies of Mugdock, Dundaff, Fintry, Buchanan, Kincardine and Aberuthven, and the lands of Kilpont, Eliston, Pumpherston, Clifton and Cliftonhall.[1] Montrose also appointed a second bailie to hold his courts in the regality of Tarbolton,[2] which was considered too detached from the main body of the duke's superiorities to be handled by the same judge, and, in addition, the duke was himself bailie of the regality of Glasgow with power to appoint a deputy to act in his place. Taking all of these courts and their personnel, bailies, clerks and procurators-fiscal, a great landowner like the Duke of Montrose was able to oblige a considerable number of his friends with offices which owed nothing to the Government. Many of the sheriffships were also heritable offices, which again conferred powers of private patronage upon their holders where this had not been specifically reserved to the Crown, and a great magnate who had inherited a small empire of such judicial rights had considerable powers of influence in his region, both from the offices themselves and the opportunities which they gave to oblige friends, and from the powers of the courts, for regalian jurisdiction was extended over the possessions of landowners who held their estates as the vassals of the magnate. The connection between patronage of this type and parliamentary politics could not be stated more clearly than in a letter which John Graham of Dougalston wrote to Mungo Graeme of Gorthie in 1741, saying that he had made an arrangement with the Laird of Glinns, one of the Stirlingshire voters:

> I have got Glinns and his friend Moses Buchanan at last to be perfectly weel pleased to accept of the Clerkship for the Regalities of Mugdock & Lennox, but they still want that commission should be granted by his Grace, so I thought it would not be a misse to send up the commission to be subscrived by the Duke, for Glinns is to make Mr. Buchanan a Barron in Stirlingshire, tho' that will not answer for nixt elections ... [3]

In 1714, the laird of Gleneagles solicited the post of bailie of the regality of Lennox for his son James Haldane, an advocate who 'not haveing reccommendation or interest enought to bring him quickly into business ... thought this might contribute some thing to it',[4] but the Duke of Montrose kept such appointments firmly in the hands of Graham gentlemen who looked upon him as their chief. Private court patronage was not just a reserve of employment for members of a political interest, however, for there was danger in it for the patron. A bad choice could arouse discontent which would more than offset the value of an appointment in attaching an individual voter to an interest, and it was wise to take abilities and honesty into account when disposing of the posts.

When the Duke of Montrose arranged for his own appointment as bailie of the regality of Glasgow in the winter of 1714/15, in order to prevent the office from being obtained by his rival the Duke of Argyll,[5] the object was not to make money out of the profits of the court but to increase the duke's influence in the city of Glasgow. In a town where the politics of two great interests clashed, it was essential to make the best possible use of any means of influence and to have a deputy functioning in the regality court in a way which would make friends for the duke's interest rather than enemies. The incumbent bailie-depute, a man named Sproull, was not acceptable, for in his other capacity as commissary, Sproull was making life difficult for some of the duke's friends, notably the duke's 'vassal Dowan, whose son marryed irregularly'.[6] Upon investigation it appeared that the bailie had been acting in a manner which aroused doubts about his honesty, for after a conversation with Dowan, Mungo Graeme of Gorthie informed the duke that

> Sproull has been a constant persecutor of his, he's in another process with him just now, besides the one I mention'd formerly, and besides severalls that he has been forced to compone ... I wish I had written to y[ou]r Gr[ace] in time to have kept him out of the commission of the justices of peace, for he's troublesome and terrible to his poor neighbours in all capacitys ... [7]

A deputy of Sproull's reputation, officiating in the regality court, would be certain to make enemies for the politician who appointed him, and Gorthie strongly advised the duke to get rid of the bailie-depute immediately. Sproull, in Gorthie's opinion, was 'the most unacceptable man in the whole earth',[8] and in fact it does appear that the official was chiefly concerned with his own profits, for he had even interfered with the jurisdiction of the Duke of Montrose's regality court of Lennox. 'He has no regard to the decreets of y[ou]r courts, but repells them currently,' the duke was told, and the writer added his own opinion of the intention of the bailie-depute in thus attacking a rival jurisdiction. By rejecting the decreets of the Lennox court, the bailie-depute forced the litigants to incur the charges of an action in the Court of Session, or, alternatively, as Sproull was said to expect, 'by this means to bring them to a composition'.[9] Forcing a litigant to settle with a judge who had usurped jurisdiction, in order to avoid still higher costs in a superior court, was not likely to have enhanced the popularity of the regality court of Glasgow, and, quite apart from the fact that he was himself injured by Sproull's actions, Montrose had little choice but to remove the bailie-depute at the first opportunity.[10] That, however, raised the question of a suitable successor.

The difficulty with a post like that of judge of the regality court of Glasgow was that while it could help or harm a political interest, depending upon the use made of the powers of the court by the appointee, the office itself was not a profitable one if the judge was not trying to bend the laws to his own advantage. As Gorthie pointed out, 'its a post that no honest man can make any profit by, anything near to compense his pains'.[11] The post, in short, was not too easy to give, for it required a suitably qualified candidate who would be willing to serve without any real prospect of personal advantage, and such people are always somewhat scarce. It would, of course, benefit the Montrose interest to see the post in safe and honest hands, for the court had considerable powers in the suburbs of the city of Glasgow. Alternatively, the duke might give the post to someone who would take it in order to oblige the town council of Glasgow, perhaps even a member of that council, or one of the town's lawyers. On the face of it, the last alternative looked the most promising in the circumstances, but unfortunately the principal lawyer employed by the burgh council, Blackhouse, lived in Edinburgh, and was thus unsuitable for a charge which required residence because of the frequency of the court's meetings. The town's procurator-fiscal, a lawyer named Sim, was the only other professionally qualified man in the town's service whom it was thought safe to appoint. According to John Graham, who knew Glasgow well, Sim was 'the only man of our town's set of lawyers that he can think proper to trust it with, ye know the naturall temper of those lawyers of a low class is to be sharpers, and thats what ye would avoid ... '[12] In this case, however, since the post itself was unattractive, it appears that Sim decided against accepting a place which might have necessitated his abandoning his other and more profitable place of procurator-fiscal, for in the end the Duke of Montrose had to give the commission to a member of the burgh council, although subject to recall in the event of any difficulty.

A similar situation in some respects developed over the office of fiscal of the regality court of Lennox, or Mugdock, an appointment which was held by William Weir, the town clerk of the burgh of Rutherglen, a gentleman who also officiated as commissary of Hamilton and Campsie. The combination of duties proved to be more than one man could perform, and Weir, in short, neglected his duties in the regality court and in fact spent most of his time in Rutherglen, where his family resided. The judge of the regality court of Lennox was James Graham, an advocate closely connected to the Montrose family and its interests, but much of the day-to-day business of his court was actually performed by Woodrop, who was Graham's substitute, and Colquhoun, the regality clerk. In 1739 Woodrop and Colquhoun precipitated a minor crisis by refusing to tolerate Weir's absenteeism any longer, and the former in fact greatly alarmed James Graham by threatening to resign. Once again the problem was a lack of suitable replacements should Woodrop go, and Graham indeed considered the bailie-substitute indispensable, for

> he is ane exceeding honest man as weel as creditable in those parts and pretty weel versant and above all cautious so as he never proceeds in any thing the least arduous without adviseing with me . . . he is ane exceeding weel wisher to the interest of your Grace and being by far the most equitable man of his trade in those parts, and that if hee should quit it I really know not one in those parts with whom I could confide the office so as I could answer for it, the writers there haveing all so dwindled away that few are left but sharpers and jackanapes . . . [13]

James Graham's solution was to suggest that the Duke of Montrose dismiss William Weir, but that was easier said than done, for Weir had been appointed in order to oblige one of Montrose's friends,[14] and James Graham had not made a solution any easier to obtain by promising his substitute that Woodrop should have the appointment of procurator-fiscal to give as he chose.

Weir quickly got wind of the plan to remove him and discussed the matter with the bailie, James Graham, and the latter had to agree that there was no blame which could be attached to Weir's conduct beyond his recent irregular attendance, but it was hardly possible for a court to function without a prosecutor, and although Weir was going to have to go, James Graham insisted that 'it should be done in the most decent manner and almost with his own consent'.[15] Weir had been piling one office upon another, and had recently added to his collection that of sheriff-substitute in the Nether-ward of Lanarkshire, although, as his friend Andrew Gardner urgently pointed out to the duke, this was a precarious place which was held only during the pleasure of the sheriff-depute of Lanarkshire,[16] but Weir had undoubtedly taken on too much. Most reluctantly, for he had no wish to offend Andrew Gardner, a good friend, whose wife was William Weir's aunt,[17] the Duke of Montrose agreed to James Graham's proposal for Weir's removal,[18] but this was done only in order to retain the services of a good man in the office of bailie-substitute, for whom no alternative was in sight.

From what we have seen it might be supposed that private judicial patronage was more trouble than it was worth, but the offices were in fact received as a sign of favour by many lawyers, who could of course use them as stepping stones to better things. Perhaps also, a new officer might learn how little his place was actually worth after he had accepted it, although in this regard it must be remembered that even the crown offices were poorly paid. In 1734, for example, Gabriel Napier of Craigannet, the sheriff-depute of Stirlingshire, pressed Lord Ilay to help him add the office of keeper of the register of sasines for Stirling and the stewartry of Menteith to his official holdings, for he found the sheriffship to be more trouble than it was worth. Napier complained that this post had been solicited by friends on his behalf, acting in the belief

> that some profits attended the office, tho' by experience I have found the contrair, and now that I have been eight moneths in it, the emoluments does not amount to eight pound st[e]r[1ing], which my substitute refuses to take for his pains in attending the court, because it deprives him of acting as pro[curato]r by which he could gain double that sum ... [19]

Napier was not the only sheriff to find that there was more honour than reward in his office, for according to the petition submitted by Erskine of Alva, who had been appointed sheriff-depute of Perthshire in 1748, his salary of £250 per annum did not take him very far, for his county,

> being the most disaffected of all the northern counties and infested by many lawless thieves and robbers, the remains and refuse of the rebell army, required the utmost zeal ... To effectuate the service it required the assistance of four substitutes, whose salaries were £110, so that after paying the fees of precepts etc. the shirreff depute received not much above £120 for this painful and dangerous service ... [20]

Gabriel Napier, however, did not neglect to tell Lord Ilay that the failure of his sheriffship to provide adequate compensation for his services was only a partial explanation of his financial embarrassment. The minister was told plainly that 'the election of a member of parliament, and other publick services, has drawn me into a great deall of expence, and no small trouble ... '[21] The return expected for his political friendship was an additional post to augment his salary, and one advantage of a sheriffship was that it could be combined with another small office in the same district. The combined salaries of two or more such offices might keep a government supporter happy, while the sheriffship itself was a stepping stone to an appointment as a baron of exchequer or a lord of session, should the lawyer be well connected and joined to a strong political interest.

The important judicial dignities in Edinburgh attracted a great deal of competitive interest, and men watched the health of the incumbents closely in order to be sure to be first to ask for the vacant place in the event of a death. In 1734, for example, Lord Lovat wrote to Ilay seeking an appointment as a lord of session for Lewis Colquhoun, a son of the Laird of Grant, remarking that

> The Justice Clark by all appearances is near his exit ... and go when he will few Campbells or Frasers have reason to lament or regrate him. If the old tyrann dips as every one that sees him expects, his *depouilles* may make three of your friends & relations happy ... [22]

Lovat ended that appeal by emphasising his belief that it was 'a most wise &

prudent maxim that a man in power should do for those that he is pretty sure will stand & fall with him in all events',[23] and in general that was the major qualification for appointment to the judicial bench in eighteenth-century Scotland.

It was not merely the major items of patronage, such as appointment to the Court of Session, which occasioned deathwatch reports to politicians from the jobhunters, for the health of local officers was as much a matter of careful calculation, and the first to apply was the most likely to be successful when a vacancy occurred. Sir John Stuart, the sheriff-depute of Berwickshire and solicitor of the stamps in Scotland, was, in 1782, failing in health and was unable to 'take his exercise on horseback, which was his life, and is deprived of his ordinary potations by his confinement', reported a Berwickshire freeholder. The writer wanted Hugh Scott, the member of parliament for the county, to secure one of Sir John's places for him, remarking that 'I have had the sheriffship in view at his death, [although] the other place is reckoned more lucrative and is possibly already secured'.[24]

When an energetic Government manager had successfully concentrated much of the available patronage in his hands throughout the country, the chance of obtaining very much without paying active court to the great man was slight. On the other hand, should a change take place in the Administration, opportunities were created for those who were not established in the ministerial waiting list, and pressure could be increased upon the member of parliament to actively solicit preferment for his own constituents. Thomas Cockburn, a Berwickshire freeholder, was an active member of the interest of Hugh Scott, younger of Harden, the member of parliament for the county of Berwick, and he presented Scott with a number of alternatives. Cockburn would prefer appointment as a clerk of session, but failing that

> there is another thing, keeper of the register of hornings etc. in Edinburgh, held at present by John Flockhart a man of no consideration, but that he was clerk to L[or]d Chesterhall and to Lord Loughborough, when he was advocate here. He is old and infirm ... I know such things are bespoke, and it is a good time in the beginning of a ministry. I dare say the L[or]d A[dvocate] had bespoke both places, his attention & industry for his friends was remarkable, but that is over for the present and now is your time ... [25]

Appointments to places in the Court of Session at any level were valuable items of patronage which were employed in general to enhance the political position of the Government. When political considerations took primacy over whether qualifications it is not surprising that some of the appointments were given to candidates ill-suited to the duties they were called upon to perform, such as the Lanarkshire freeholder appointed macer of the Court of Session who, according to James Boswell, 'had a constant hoarseness, so that he could scarcely be heard when he called the causes and the lawyers, and was indeed as unfit for a crier of court as a man could be. I said he had no voice *but at an election* '.[26]

Influence over the machinery of the law could give a politician additional means of gratifying friends and intimidating enemies, for a word in the right place could greatly ease the problems of those who came into conflict with the laws. Two major Jacobite risings, and the plotting which took place on other occasions, were enough to put a considerable number of gentlemen in danger and, indeed, so long as the Jacobite cause retained a substantial following in Scotland it had a further effect upon politics, for the unwillingness of many gentlemen of Jacobite sentiments to take the oaths to Government further limited an already small electorate. It was, however, the politician's ability, if well connected in London, to secure pardon for gentlemen implicated in Jacobite plotting, but who were not obvious leaders which proved a valuable management tool. Obviously a politician able to perform this service conferred a very material favour on the endangered man and his relatives, and such a favour could attach their loyalty to the interest able to save them. Whatever the gentleman in question might feel about the Hanoverian monarchy and the Jacobite cause he could, in the circumstances, hardly refuse to take the oaths to Government and cast his vote for his friend in a subsequent election. It should not be forgotten, moreover, that Jacobite gentlemen had non-Jacobite relatives, and a favour to the kinsman in difficulties with the law was also a favour to lairds who might have good reason to expect the politician's help. Those politicians who were connected with the Administration found that the year 1716 produced a bumper crop of solicitations for the pardon of those implicated in the Rising of the previous year. Typical of the requests reaching government politicians was a letter sent to the Duke of Montrose by John Graham of Killearn, writing on behalf of the Laird of Culcreuch, a Stirlingshire freeholder. Killearn told the duke that the laird intended to write

> anent his brother-in-law Northsyde to see if any thing can be gott don for him in order to his being pardoned for his unhappy rebellion. He was very earnest that I should give your Grace the trouble of a lyne about him which I thought I could not weel decline since I cannot say but I always found Culcreuch very ready on every occasion to advance your Grace's interest in the shyre soe far as he was capable . . . [27]

When a politician with an interest to maintain was a member of the House of Lords, the practice of taking appeals from the Scottish courts to the Upper House of Parliament afforded the politician further opportunities to oblige his friends. Lairds, and even peers, found it worth their while to seek the attention of their friends among the lords of parliament when an appeal in which they were concerned was about to be considered.

In the eighteenth century the scales of justice could be tilted in favour of a relative or friend, or it was feared that this was the case, unless strong interest was made in behalf of a litigant in order to ensure equity. The fear, whether justified or not, undoubtedly enhanced the influence of a politician, for evenhanded justice would therefore appear to be due to his favour. In 1707, for example, when one of the Duke of Montrose's associates found himself in legal difficulties, he begged for his chief's intervention, pointing out that 'my pursuer is laterlie married to a near relative of the Justice Clerks and My Lord Arnistons, which makes it more necessar Your Gr[ace] should interest your self to take it away by arbitratione'.[28] Criminal charges and fines were other matters capable of adjustment by a politician, and again were likely to encourage lasting feelings of gratitude to the man who secured a suspension or remission. A Dunbartonshire gentleman attached to the Duke of Montrose became involved in what he described as 'a foolish ploy [which] happened at Glasgow the first day at the Circuit held ther with some of our friends & Barrowfields, wher we were all fyned'.[29] The Exchequer was now demanding payment of the fines, and the duke was informed that the Earl of Mar, as Secretary of State, had secured a remission of the fine for one of his friends; Montrose's dependent, getting quickly to the point, inquired whether 'your Gr[ace] can without truble tip a wink to any of the Barrounes [of Exchequer] for Wattie and me'.[30] The ability to 'tip a wink' was another of the assets of a political manager which has received less attention than the more obvious ability to secure employment for friends. In burgh politics the habit of taking quarrels to law made the ability to suspend a legal process or to threaten its resumption a regular tool of the Administration's local managers. It was perhaps not accidental that the deputy political manager for the Earl of Ilay, Lord Milton, was the Lord Justice Clerk, for between them the head of the Justiciary Court and the crown law officers controlled the criminal justice system. Typical of many letters was one which Milton received from the provost of one of the royal burghs in 1740, reporting that one of the councillors was wavering in his political loyalty. The provost had confronted the man and had issued a warning, telling him that 'the process before the Judiciary at the Croun's Instance was still hanging over his head & if he transgressed those who assisted to bring him of[f] may also get the affair moved againe, at least for £30 of expenses'.[31] The ability to help or to harm was not the least of the tools in the politician's inventory, and it may indeed have been of greater value than some of the more troublesome varieties of patronage, where a favour for one could easily anger others who were disappointed.

The most hazardous of all forms of patronage for the political manager was the presentation of a minister to a parish, for unless there was general agreement among the heritors and other parishioners, strong feelings were likely to be aroused in a church where patronage was still regarded as an alien intrusion without scriptural authority. The fact remained, however, that the right to present a minister was shared between the Crown, the nobility and some of the major landed gentry, while town ministers were often the appointees of the burgh councils.[32] Accordingly every politician was confronted with the sometimes unpleasant duty of suggesting a suitable replacement for a deceased minister after a delicate balancing of the claims of potential candidates.

Patronage of this type produced a great deal of difficulty for both the church and the politicians, and in 1742 Robert Dundas, lord Arniston, was induced to complain of the

very bad use that hath been made of the Crowns patronages, presentations given sometimes as rewards of corruption to a bailie or councellors brothers etc. sometimes to any body named by a voter or a great man without the least regard either to heritors of a parish or people ... [33]

Lord Arniston's complaint was entirely justified, for church patronage was grossly abused to serve immediate political ends. George Dempster, the member of parliament for Dundee burghs, whose election at St. Andrews would 'certainly turn on a single vote unless I am able to provide a Councillors son in a Kirk',[34] urged nothing more than political consequences when pressing for the settlement of the St. Andrews clergyman, and many presentations were indeed political bribes. In county politics much the same attitude prevailed, for in 1799 Admiral Lord Keith's chief complaint about a presentation made by Lord Elphinstone was that the latter had not seen fit to agree to the wishes of an important laird, remarking that 'I should suppose Lord E. does not recollect that the Gleneagles people have 3 votes in Dumbarton. I know not where he will bestow a kirk to more advantage ... '[35]

The difficulty with kirks, however, was that there was almost always someone, apart from unsuccessful candidates for the post of minister, who was unhappy. In 1719, for example, when Mr. Muir, the minister of Kilbryde, died, the Duke of Montrose, with the support of the Duke of Roxburghe, offered to appoint any man whom Montrose's friends Gorthie and Dougalston would recommend.[36] Naturally, what the duke had in mind was his own political interest, and his managers duly picked a man named Hamilton for the vacant charge, a gentleman whose brother was a bailie of one of the royal burghs in which the Montrose faction took an interest. The presentation, however, was resisted by Lord Selkirk, who had been 'importuned with letters from Scotland which jumble him'.[37] Montrose, however, pressed the candidacy of William Hamilton, chiding his fellow peer for ingratitude and suggesting 'that its ane ill requitall he's likely to give by showeing a backwardness to [a] brother of Baillie Hamilton's who showed some zeall for the service of his bro[the]r at his election. I'le try him again'.[38] The issue clearly was not the merit of William Hamilton as a pastor, and the duke felt that the question turned on the past and future services of the clergyman's brother, the bailie. It might be added that William Hamilton was well supplied with interest to advance his settlement, for he had served Lord Haddington as a page when at college and had continued in Haddington's service as chaplain. [39]

In 1721, when the minister of Inchinnan in Renfrewshire was named to the chair of church history in the University of Edinburgh, thus creating a vacancy for a minister, the right of presentation belonged to the Duke of Montrose. On this occasion the duke was more cautious, asking his friend Gorthie to take care to seek a suitable candidate. 'Pray think of a right man wt out regard to recommendations, which hitherto have not been of great service to me in the like cases,'[40] the duke suggested. Good intentions quickly evaporated, however, when Sir Robert Pollock, a gentleman with whom the duke had no wish to quarrel, suggested a candidate for the vacant charge. Fortunately the man with this powerful patron was popular with the parishioners, but one cannot help suspecting, from Montrose's comments, that this was really a secondary consideration:

Sr Ro[bert] Pollock thinks that his namesake's being placed at Inshennan will do him considerable service and reckons that the hopes of it has gain'd him the Toun of

Pasely's vote, why should not his man have it, since the people are pleased wt him ... [41]

The burgh of Paisley, although not a royal burgh and thus not forming part of one of the parliamentary districts, had a vote in the county elections for Renfrewshire in right of the burgh lands, and it was the burgh vote which provided the candidate with his strongest argument for preferment.

The trouble which a political interest could encounter, however, came when friends of the political interest fell out over a choice of minister, and in a country which took its religion seriously that was all too easy to do, and that in turn opened the road to intrigue by political enemies. The Duke of Montrose ran into this difficulty in 1725 when he obtained a crown presentation for a minister named Smith to serve the parish of Cardross.[42] To give the duke his due, he was suitably cautious, for he advised that the presentation be kept secret 'till things be ripen'd wt the ministers of the presbytery and heretors, and people, as much as possible'.[43] The threat, however, was apparent from the outset, for Montrose's enemies the Campbells had been actively attempting to disappoint the duke's recommendation, and were thus well placed to take full advantage of any subsequent trouble to strengthen Argyll's following and weaken the interest of the family of Montrose. A second note of warning was issued a month later, when Andrew Gardner, a member of the Montrose interest, advised that Smith would meet with much opposition from the heritors,[44] and indeed one of the heritors attempted to bargain with the duke by letting it be known that his attitude towards Mr. Smith might change if the Duke of Montrose allowed the laird to purchase the superiority of some of his lands.[45] On this occasion there was serious difficulty in settling the crown presentee, and the very real danger to the political interest of the duke lay in the fact that the opposition and the rival candidate were set up by some of his own friends.[46] It was this danger which made church presentations so hazardous for the stability of a political interest, for however a presentation was given, almost always there were some who were grievously offended.

The danger of harming an interest to help an individual friend demanded the greatest caution in placing ministers in rural parishes, and after a number of mistakes the Duke of Montrose became very reluctant to present any candidate without a careful sounding of opinion together with an evaluation of the merits of the candidate himself. The duke's attitude is made plain in a letter which he wrote to Mungo Graeme of Gorthie in 1737 when asked to obtain a church for a brother of a Graham laird, who was one of the most active members of the Montrose interest. In spite of that claim to assistance, Montrose told his political manager that he was unwilling to recommend a candidate for presentation to another peer when he was 'intirely ignorant what sort of man he is'. Having been disappointed in some of the ministers whom he had presented, the duke insisted that

Upon his true character must depend my appearing for him or not. If he has parts and some learning (in short if he is a tight fellow ...) to be sure I ought and will continance him as his people have allways been friends and dependers, but if his only merit is being of the name and disburthening his brother of the charge of mentaining him that is not ane argument sufficient for me either to recommend him to my friend L[or]d Dundonald, or to give him a church of which I am patron my self when a vacancy shall happen. You know verie well the trouble there is in placeing ministers, before I embarque in such matters I must be well satisfied of all circumstances and especiallie of the character of the person I apear for ... [47]

Sir James Campbell of Ardkinglas, the member of parliament for Stirlingshire in the Argyll interest, found out the cost of a disputed patronage appointment in 1756, when the church of Gargunnock became vacant. The formidable Mrs. Mary Campbell of Boquhan, a lady with great influence in the affairs of the town of Stirling, and with equally strong views on the choice of a minister for her parish church, demanded that the king's presentation should be obtained for Robert Ure, who was the assistant minister of St. Ninian's parish. Writing to Lord Milton, Mary Campbell told him that Ure was 'the choice of two heritors & your humll. servt. and the whole session with the whole congregation except three heritors'.[48] Unfortunately there was some uncertainty about the right of presentation, for there was some question whether the right to present belonged to Erskine of Carnock, and the latter had given his presentation, at the request of the member of parliament, to a clergyman named Bruce. That was Sir James Campbell's undoing in this section of his county, for he had undertaken to get the presentation for Bruce in order to oblige one of his friends who had accepted a nominal vote from him, but the friend, David Gourlay, was only a small heritor, and the bulk of the landed property in the parish together with the kirk session were firmly attached to Mr. Ure. Mrs. Campbell insisted that Lord Milton should go over Sir James Campbell's head and obtain a crown presentation, for 'if Bruce be our Minister the whole session will demit and a great division will be in the parish'.[49] Milton had no intention of sharing the unpopularity which was attaching itself to Sir James and promptly referred the matter to the Solicitor-General for action, but the end result, as Mrs. Campbell pointed out, was that 'our Member has lost his interest in this parish and really by most of our friends in the shire'.[50] Milton's prompt offer of assistance, however, had deflected the criticism from the Argyll party itself, and Mrs. Mary happily was able to report that those who were once Sir James Campbell's friends 'continues firm in their good wishes to my Chief and Lord Milton, those two healths is often drunk without naming their Member'.[51]

Presentations in the hands of the Crown were normally disposed of by the county member in a manner agreeable to the majority of the heritors, although obviously the wishes of political friends would have the greatest weight, but that in itself could be troublesome, for by the later eighteenth century the Treasury was imposing its own rather rigid rules. In 1783, for example, when a vacancy arose in the parish of Campsie, almost all of the heritors were united with the body of inhabitants of the parish in favour of a Mr. Burns to be their minister, and they requested Sir Thomas Dundas, then the county member, to obtain a presentation. Sir Thomas was quite willing to try, even though 'four gentlemen, two of whom are of another communion',[52] had declined to sign the petition. Unfortunately Lord North saw the question in a different light, for the four dissenting proprietors had asked for the presentation of another candidate. The Minister's choice was based upon an examination of the Registers of Exchequer, by which it appeared 'that the owners of much of the greater part of the property in the district interest themselves for Mr. Lapslie',[53] who accordingly obtained the presentation regardless of the fact that two of Lapslie's supporters were not members of the Church of Scotland. In short, as a presentation changed from a piece of management patronage, it became a right of the major landowners of a parish to present whomsoever they wished, providing a majority of the landed property was favourable.

Earlier in the century there was much less emphasis upon the exact valuation of a heritor's holdings, but there was, equally, little doubt in the minds of freeholder-heritors that they should be the judges of the qualifications of a candidate, and that a presentation should be obtained in accordance with their views. A Nairnshire laird, writing in 1728, strongly discounted any popular opinion, remarking that

> tis hard, I think, to be baffled to please ill meaning parsons, or a senseless rabble who ought to have no vote in choosing of a Minister, tho' the clergy allow of it to serve their own ends, for why should a fellow be allowed to choose a minister, who in a few years nay perhaps in a few months may be for ever turned out of the parich. Tis certainly the heritors who have a right to be judges in those matters . . . [54]

Presentees were, however, not infrequently the objects of popular hostility whether for doctrinal differences, style of preaching or the fact that the people were not sufficiently involved in the choice. In the Highlands it might even be a matter of clanship, for in 1776 Lord Kames declared fugitive five women who had been responsible for assembling a mob which had insulted and attacked Patrick Grant, the new presentee at Boleskine, part of the forfeited Lovat estate, 'in resentment that they were not to get a gentleman of the name of Fraser to be their minister'.[55] The right to present was a doubtful political asset, for although it was a means of obliging some who might be useful upon a future occasion, many more might easily be alienated and mindful of the offence every Sunday.

University posts, however, were an attractive means of obliging friends, and a good deal safer, for popular feeling was rarely aroused and it was relatively easy to escape from an importunate friend by arguing that the place had already been promised. It was, moreover, generally a patronage source for government itself, and no ordinary burgh or county member of parliament would have much concern with it, though George Dempster of Dunnichen, when member of parliament for the Dundee district, thought it worth his while to attempt an approach to Lord Cassillis, who had the right of presentation to the chair of humanity in the University of St. Andrews, to seek that appointment for political advantage. It appeared that one of the bailies of St. Andrews was completely subservient to a Mr. Dick, who was the burgh schoolmaster and the bailie's brother-in-law. The schoolmaster of St. Andrews was ambitious 'and aspires eagerly to the dignity of being professor of humanity in this university'.[56] The member of parliament saw in this ambition an opportunity to strengthen his own interest in the burgh by detaching the schoolmaster's brother-in-law, the bailie, from the opposition party in the council, for the bailie was at that moment firmly attached to that faction by a promise from Dempster's rival that he would procure a kirk for the bailie's son. A letter from Lord Cassillis, on the other hand, would, Dempster believed, 'cancel in a moment the obligation arising from my opponent's promise'.[57]

Most of the chairs, however, were not subject to such private patronage, but they were still employed for political purposes, though usually on a somewhat higher political level than Dempster intended. A politician with sufficient interest, moreover, was not above contemplating forcing out of their posts political enemies holding university appointments, as the Duke of Montrose clearly intended when expressing the hope that 'wee might have ane opportunity of makeing two empty sadles' in the university of Glasgow, namely the professors of law and medicine.[58] Professors, in consequence, were often active politicians, engaging in the politics of the university burghs and sometimes holding freehold qualifications in the shires. The duties attached to some of these appointments were not too arduous, which made them all the more attractive to a landed gentleman with other interests but a great desire for an increased income. This was the situation outlined by that astute political fixer, Lord Milton, in a letter to the Earl of Ilay suggesting a suitable candidate for a vacant post. The vacancy had been occasioned by the untimely departure of James Haldane, the professor of church history at St. Andrews, who had been burned to death in his room after retiring for the night leaving a candle burning. Milton remarked that this chair had hitherto been a sinecure, though it carried a salary of over £100 per annum and would 'serve any gentleman especially a law[y]er '.[59]

The extent to which some university appointments were political spoils in the eighteenth century is suggested by the demand made in 1714 by Murray of Cringletie, an administration candidate for the representation of the county of Peebles, who made it a condition of his coming forward that his brother should be given the vacant chair of church history in the University of Edinburgh. The Marquis of Tweeddale, when reporting Murray's demand to the Duke of Montrose, remarked of the young gentleman who thus intended to begin an academic career that he was 'scearce one & twenty but people think themselves fitt for any post in this countrey'.[60] The late professor, Mr. Cummyn, had received £100 a year for his services, which was clearly the attraction, and the true note of weary cynicism was provided by Mungo Graeme of Gorthie who, while acknowledging the youth of the candidate, suggested that 'a dispensation from the king for him to travell a year or two will make him a very good professor, as good as Cuminyn was'.[61] The professorship in question was seen by the politicians as nothing more than a means of keeping the Laird of Cringletie happy; it was, as Gorthie put it, 'a very good way to answer the Laird's own expectations till once a good occasion offer'.[62]

If professorial patronage was, in general, a perquisite of those at the centre of political power in Scotland, there was another, though much less valuable, form of academic patronage available to some of the politicians. This was the award of scholarships, which once again was a useful means of obliging voters and strengthening an interest by continuing good service to the voters who adhered to it. As chancellor of the University of Glasgow, the Duke of Montrose was solicited for the scholarships in the University's gift tenable at the University of Oxford, known as Snell's exhibitions,[63] while Sir James Grant of Grant was constantly being asked for bursaries for students at the University of St. Andrews.

Typical of many such letters sent to the Laird of Grant was one written by Lord Kinnoull in 1780 seeking such a bursary for John Duff, a son of the minister of Tippermuir. Connections quickly came to the fore in the application, however, for Kinnoull pointed out that the wife of the minister of Tippermuir was a lady 'for whom the Dowager Lady Findlater has a particular regard',[64] and she was herself the niece of Sir James Grant's uncle, Sir William Dunbar. Where else therefore could a small scholarship be more usefully bestowed than in a manner which would, as Kinnoull indicated, 'much oblige Lady Findlater, & many other friends', while conferring a favour upon a grateful man?[65] Perhaps that type of patronage was of small value in comparison with the need to provide employment for friends, but it was all grist to the mill of a politician intent on keeping his interest solidly united, and it was certainly not scorned by those with bursaries in their gift.

NOTES

1. SRO. Montrose, GD220/5/812, Mungo Graeme of Gorthie to the Duke of Montrose, 31 Dec., 1714.

2. Ibid., GD220/5/894, Montrose to Mungo Graeme of Gorthie, 20 Dec., 1735.

3. Ibid., GD220/5/1522, John Graham of Dougalston to Mungo Graeme of Gorthie, 21 Jan., 1741.

4. Ibid., GD220/5/811, Mungo Graeme to Montrose, 5 Sep., 1714.

5. Ibid., Mungo Graeme to Montrose, 19 Nov., 1714.

6. Ibid., GD220/5/812, Mungo Graeme to Montrose, 24 Dec., 1714.

7. Ibid., Mungo Graeme to Montrose, 29 Dec., 1714.

8. Ibid., Mungo Graeme to Montrose, 24 Dec., 1714.

9. Ibid.

10. Ibid., GD220/5/813, Mungo Graeme to Montrose, 17 Jan., 1715.

11. Ibid., GD220/5/812, Mungo Graeme to Montrose, 11 Dec., 1714.

12. Ibid., Mungo Graeme to Montrose, 27 Dec., 1714.

13. Ibid., GD220/5/905, James Graham to Montrose, undated, c. Sep. 1739, enclosed in a letter from Montrose to Mungo Graeme of Gorthie, 8 Oct., 1739.

14. Ibid., the Duke of Montrose to Mungo Graeme, 18 Oct., 1739.

15. Ibid., James Graham to the Duke of Montrose, Sep., 1739.

16. Ibid., Montrose to Mungo Graeme, 18 Oct., 1739.

17. Ibid., GD220/5/1260, Andrew Gardner to Mungo Graeme, 4 Apr., 1733.

18. Ibid., GD220/5/905, Montrose to Mungo Graeme, 22 Oct., 1739.

19. NLS. Saltoun MS.16588, Gabriel Napier to Lord Milton, 30 Dec., 1734.

20. North Riding Record Office. Zetland Papers ZNK/X/2, 'Memorandum relative to Lord Alva for Lord Dundas'.

21. NLS. Saltoun MS.16588, Gabriel Napier to Lord Milton, 30 Dec., 1734.

22. SRO. Seafield, GD248/91/1, Lord Lovat to the Earl of Ilay, 13 Aug., 1734.

23. Ibid.

24. SRO. Scott of Harden, GD157/2916/4, James Dickson of Antonshill to Hugh Scott, 10 Jun., 1782.

25. Ibid., GD157/2943/10, Thomas Cockburn to Hugh Scott, 29 Apr., 1783.

26. Charles Rogers (ed.), *Boswelliana* (London, 1874), cited in *The Private Papers of James Boswell: The Ominous Years, 1774–1776,* ed. Charles Ryscamp and Frederick Pottle (London, 1963), 39.

27. SRO. Montrose, GD220/5/708, John Graham, younger of Killearn, to Montrose, 20 Feb., 1716.

28. Ibid., GD220/5/138, John Graeme of Killearn to Montrose, 23 Dec., 1707.

29. Ibid., GD220/5/449, James Graham to Montrose, 13 Dec., 1714.

30. Ibid.

31. NLS. Saltoun MS.16581, James Christie to Lord Milton, 17 Sep., 1740.

32. Parliamentary Papers, (P.P.) 1834, v, 203, 'Select Committee on Church Patronage (Scotland)', provides a survey of the state of patronage based on documents of 1769.

33. NLS. Yester MS.7046, Robert Dundas of Arniston to the Marquis of Tweeddale, 15 Apr., 1742.

34. SRO. Dalhousie, GD45/14/431, George Dempster of Dunnichen to Lord Panmure, 20 Jun., 1762.

35. National Maritime Museum. Keith Papers, Letters of George K. Elphinstone, 1773–1820, Kei.128, Lord Keith to his sister Mary, 1 May, 1799.

36. SRO. Montrose, GD220/5/829, the Duke of Montrose to Mungo Graeme of Gorthie, 7 Apr., 1719.

37. Ibid., Montrose to Mungo Graeme, 21 Apr., 1719.

38. Ibid.

39. Ibid., Montrose to Mungo Graeme, 16 Apr., 1719.

40. Ibid., GD220/5/835, Montrose to Mungo Graeme, 19 Jul., 1721.

41. Ibid., GD220/5/837, Montrose to Mungo Graeme, 16 Dec., 1721.

42. Ibid., GD220/5/849, Montrose to Mungo Graeme, 19 Jan., 1725.

43. Ibid., Montrose to Mungo Graeme, 28 Jan., 1725.

44. Ibid., GD220/5/1019, Andrew Gardner to Mungo Graeme of Gorthie, 25 Feb., 1725.

45. Ibid., GD220/5/1018, John Graham, younger of Killearn, to Mungo Graeme of Gorthie, 16 Mar., 1725.

46. Ibid., GD220/5/853, Montrose to Mungo Graeme, 20 Dec., 1725.

47. Ibid., GD220/5/898, Montrose to Mungo Graeme, 8 Apr., 1737.

48. NLS. Saltoun MS.16695, Mrs. Mary Campbell to Lord Milton, 20 Apr., 1756.

49. Ibid.

50. Ibid., Mrs Mary Campbell to Lord Milton, 16 Dec., 1756.

51. Ibid.

52. North Riding Record Office. Zetland Papers ZNK/X/2, William Lennox of Woodhead to Sir Thomas Dundas, 15 May, 1783.

53. Ibid., Lord North to Sir Thomas Dundas, 7 Jun., 1783.

54. SRO. John C. Brodie, W.S., GD247/71/42, Alexander Brodie of Lethan 30 Nov., 1783 (Copy).

55. *Scots Magazine,* 28, Sep. 1766, 500–1.

56. James Fergusson (ed), *Letters of George Dempster to Sir Adam Ferguson, 1756–1813* (London, 1934), 52–3, 14 Sep., 1760.

57. Ibid.

58. SRO. Montrose, GD220/5/838, Montrose to Mungo Graeme, 6 Feb., 1722.

59. NLS. Saltoun MS.16535, Lord Milton to the Earl of Ilay, 19 Jan., 1727.

60. SRO. Montrose, GD220/5/429, the Marquis of Tweeddale to Montrose, 16 Dec., 1714.

61. Ibid., GD220/5/812, Mungo Graeme to Montrose, 10 Dec., 1714.

62. Ibid.

63. Ibid., GD220/5/695, John Haldane of Gleneagles to Montrose, 10 Dec., 1716.
64. SRO. Seafield, GD248/58/1, Lord Kinnoull to Sir James Grant of Grant, 30 Sep., 1780.
65. Ibid.

5

Political Interest and the Collectorship of Supply

Of all of the appointments which might easily be held by a resident freeholder, none was more attractive to many gentlemen than the post of collector of supply. The collectorship, however, was not in the gift of even the most influential politician, for it was an elective office, but it was, nonetheless, intimately connected with parliamentary politics. The collector of the land tax, or cess, was chosen by the gentlemen named as commissioners of supply for the county, and although this might often be a wider cross-section of the county gentry than the parliamentary electors, there was sufficient overlap in membership to make this a political decision. Accordingly, on many occasions the choice of a collector became in itself a trial of strength between the political interests in a county, not only because of the intrinsic attractions of the office itself, but because the collector would be involved in the production of the certificates of valuation required as part of the documentation to be produced for claimants seeking admission to the freeholders roll. A friend in the office of collector of supply could greatly speed up the processing of the claims of allies, while at the same time delaying the completion of the titles of opponents.

The office of collector was a valuable one, and it was regarded as an attractive prize by gentlemen in need of an improved cash flow, for temporary custody of tax revenues and the ability to make some use of such funds for short-term personal advantage was one of the great attractions of any kind of government service which brought an individual into contact with money. The salary paid to the collector by the county for his efforts to extract the cess from the taxpayers, moreover, was sufficient to stimulate competition for the post, and the attraction was enough on occasion to cause severe embarrassment to county politicians, who feared that support for one candidate would lead to the permanent alienation of his rivals and their friends. In short, the office of collector of supply was at the same time highly desirable and extremely dangerous to political interests.

When one political interest was dominant in a county, the politician could attempt to carry matters with a high hand, as Colonel John Campbell of Mamore did in 1727, when a dispute arose over the collectorship of Dunbartonshire. On that occasion the member of parliament openly told the meeting of commissioners of supply that 'as he look't on the representing this shire to be hereditary in some measure in their family, soe he look't on the appointing the collector to be a consequentiall priviledge of it, and he would take ill any opposition given to him'.[1] While the Duke of Argyll had indeed a well-established interest in the county, and John Campbell of Mamore had a long tenure of the parliamentary seat, it is hardly to be wondered that some of the gentlemen resented that blunt statement of Campbell power. John Campbell of Mamore, however, had one powerful weapon at his disposal to reinforce his will, for he told the commissioners that for the future 'none but sure friends should be nominate[d]' commissioners of supply, 'and that all others should be razed out'.[2] The nomination of commissioners of supply was normally entrusted to the county member of parliament, who would submit a list of suitable candidates. As the Duke of Montrose commented, 'such a list is properly the business of the representative of the shire, who certainly will look to his own interest in that matter'.[3] On the other hand, even if in Dunbartonshire Campbell influence was too powerful to be shaken by those who were resentful, in a county which was less securely held, and where a powerful opposition was in being, tactics like those of Colonel Campbell would have been an invitation to disaster.

In a county where more than one political interest existed, competition over the post of collector of supply brought many headaches for the politicians, whose desire to support a friendly candidate was tempered by their very real fears of losing the friendship of those who also desired the collectorship. Sometimes a solution could be found in compromise, in which two candidates would join forces to defeat a third and thereafter share the perquisites of office equitably. In 1715, for example, when the collectorship of Stirlingshire was being made an issue by interests unfriendly to the Administration, the friends of the Duke of Montrose, who was then Secretary of State, arranged for John Stirling, a brother of the Laird of Herbertshire, to become collector jointly with the previous holder of the office, Gabriel Napier of Craigannet.[4] The Montrose interest settled the question in this way through political pressure on the two candidates, for John Stirling was less than enthusiastic about sharing his responsibilities with Craigannet, and it was obviously hazardous to be joined in responsibility for accounting for public money with a colleague of whom the Stirling family had 'no good character'.[5] The arrangement, however, was successfully pressed by the friends of the Duke of Montrose, in order, hopefully, to heal the threat of division in the county, lest feelings of dislike be aroused to the point of threatening the stability of the Montrose interest in parliamentary politics.

The joint-collectorship was short-lived, however, and the office was shortly thereafter acquired in the county of Stirling by another freeholder in the Montrose interest, MacFarlane of Kirkton, though not without some difficulties.[6] The annual election of a collector was carried by similar means to those employed to secure the election of a member of parliament. The standard approach was to seek the friendship of the major landowners in the county, particularly the leaders of the dominant political interest, and they in turn approached their own friends. In 1723, for example, the member of parliament for Stirlingshire was John Graham of Killearn, the chamberlain of the Duke of Montrose, a man chiefly remembered for having been relieved of the duke's rents at pistol point by Rob Roy MacGregor. Killearn, in 1723, acted as the intermediary between the duke and the gentlemen of Stirlingshire, informing the duke's local representative of Montrose's wish that his friends should be asked to appear for MacFarlane of Kirkton to be collector of supply.[7] When a politician took a stand on the question of the collectorship, a successful election was essentially a reaffirmation of the strength of the political interest which was then in control of the parliamentary seat, while a defeat in this apparently local question was usually the harbinger of a severe electoral contest when Parliament should be dissolved.

The difficulty facing any county politician in relation to the collectorship of the cess was his inability to please everyone. A staunch friend expected the countenance of the politician to whom he had attached himself, and a failure to actively canvass for a candidate might well be repaid in full by hostility at the next general election. At the same time, if two friends were running in opposition to one another for the same office, aid to one was sure to offend the other. Equally, the office had to be filled by a gentleman who would be acceptable to the majority of the county, and would preferably gain general acceptance, for anything less than that once again raised the spectre of potential hostility at the following parliamentary election.

The year 1726 saw this difficulty emerge in an aggravated form in the county of Stirling, where two candidates came forward to challenge the re-election of MacFarlane of Kirkton, who had enjoyed the endorsement of the Duke of Montrose for several years past. Unfortunately for the peace of mind of the duke, both of the new candidates had the support of influential lairds to whom Montrose was himself obliged. Stirling of Craigbarnet, an impoverished member of an important regional family, was the first to solicit support for his attempt to displace Kirkton, and Craigbarnet and his relatives were friends of the Montrose political interest and therefore dangerous to offend.[8] The incumbent, MacFarlane of Kirkton, was also sure of a substantial body of support among the gentry of the county, while the situation was made even more hazardous when David Cunningham, a brother of the laird of Ballindalloch, a gentleman who could not be ranked among Montrose's friends, also came forward,[9] but with the support of two important lairds, Colonel Blackadder, and Callendar of Craigforth, to both of whom, as Montrose ruefully remarked, he had obligations.[10]

To his increasing embarrassment, Montrose found himself bombarded with solicitations from three directions, which left him in an impossible situation. Montrose, like many politicians of the period, was loyal to those who were loyal to him, and in this case felt he had no choice but to support MacFarlane of Kirkton, for 'Kirkton haveing allways stood by me its impossible in honour to drop him. I think I am oblidged to show him my good will, and to give him my interest upon this occasion'.[11] Clearly, however, the disputed collectorship was creating an unusually good opportunity for the enemies of the Montrose interest to split that interest and thus prepare the way for an attack upon it on a future occasion. If Montrose openly endorsed Kirkton, and carried his re-election, he might gravely offend some of his own friends. At the same time, if by a failure to take a decisive stand Kirkton should be defeated, it would be easy to describe that as a defeat for the Montrose interest to which Kirkton had long been attached.

Stirling of Craigbarnet was in urgent need of remunerative employment, for he was a poor laird whose 'circumstances are realy such as not to have bread'.[12] Even if such remarks are not to be taken literally, Craigbarnet was clearly living in poverty and was burdened with a 'numerous family'. More to the point,

Craigbarnet had the sympathy of prominent members of the Montrose interest, like John Graham of Dougalston, who told Montrose's commissioner that Craigbarnet was entitled to expect aid, for

> Craigbarnett is the representative of ane old family and is in verry great straits, to my certain knowledge, having a verry numerous family, and verry litle to give them. I am fully persuaded that if you knew his circumstances, you would think this an act of charity. He is indeed a Jacobite, [but I think charity, for I can give it no other name] should be extended to all. They were allways servants to my Lord duke's family, this man's Grandfather was killed at Philliphaugh, and his father taken prisoner ... [13]

Memories were long in Scotland, and a gentleman whose forefathers had fought and died with the Marquis of Montrose in the wars against the Covenanter Government in the previous century could still feel entitled to expect assistance from the current chief of that family, and more importantly there were others in the county who thought likewise.

In all probability Craigbarnet did not really expect to displace Kirkton as collector, for as one of his friends put it, 'if your grace be not alrady ingaged it would be a great act of charity, but if you are he is willing to joyn him self wt any on[e] your Grace will name'.[14] The sharing of the collector's salary was really what appears to have been in the thoughts of Craigbarnet and his friends, for Dougalston too returned to this point in his letter to Montrose's commissioner, telling him that Craigbarnet's friends had given him to understand that they would support Kirkton's re-election, 'with the same sellary that he now has if he would give Craigbarnett fifteen or twentie pound sterling yearly out of it'.[15] The land tax was not intended to be a pension fund, but it is evident that it could, and occasionally did, serve as such, for joint-collectorships were common.

Montrose, however, finding himself in such an impasse, and with the prospect of recurring battles before him, for the collector held office for only a single year before having to seek re-election, had his own solution to the difficulties which the office entailed for such as himself. In his view the only way of preventing the disputes was to make the office less attractive, and the best means of doing that was to lower the salary. Early in February 1726 Montrose instructed his commissioner in Scotland to organise his friends to support the plan of a reduction in emoluments for the collector, believing that this would discourage the new candidates and ensure Kirkton's re-election, for the duke was determined 'to stand by him upon the above terms, I mean of a smaller sellary for the future'.[16] In the duke's opinion, successfully lowering the salary would effectively 'remove the eternal lure of division'. [17]

The friends of Montrose who supported the various candidates were very troublesome, for political management required careful and friendly replies, and it was clear that they could not all be given the answers they expected or hoped to receive. The friends of David Cunningham, such as Colonel Blackadder, had to be put off with a clear refusal, and a request to persuade Cunningham to withdraw,[18] while at the same time every effort had to be made to engage all those gentlemen who had not committed themselves to a candidate to rally to Kirkton.[19] At first glance the easiest solution to the difficulty which the eager candidates for the collectorship had created would appear to have been to take the advice which was being so strongly urged, and install Craigbarnet to share the office with Kirkton, for Craigbarnet would certainly have been willing to accept even a small fraction of the emoluments in his desperate need. Such a solution would without question have pleased many of the gentry, but it was impossible for Montrose to agree to it. 'Craigbarnet I know is poor and the interest of his friends might be of service,' the duke remarked, 'but do you know that he was att Sheriff Moor, how would that sound here?'[20] If Philiphaugh was a mark in Craigbarnet's favour with the Montrose interest, and his ancestor's service with the Great Marquis deserved reward, his own participation in the 1715 Rising and his continuing Jacobitism made him an undesirable ally for a Whig politician like Montrose. It was, moreover, a particularly inconvenient time to create any appearance of associating with Jacobitism, for the election of a member of parliament in the Montrose interest, Graham of Killearn, was in dispute, and it would be a bad bargain to lose a parliamentary seat in return for securing the collection of supply to a Jacobite, however needy.

There was no taint of Jacobitism about the other challenger. David Cunningham was ensign of the garrison company of Stirling Castle, and was son-in-law of Callander of Craigforth, an influential laird, and brother of another freeholder, but Montrose's arranged reduction of the salary of the collector appears to have reconciled Mr. Cunningham to his military duties, and MacFarlane of Kirkton retained the post for another year. Craigbarnet was not so easily disposed of, however, and by the winter of 1726-7 the Montrose interest had hit on another scheme designed to satisfy the needy Jacobite laird with the influential friends.

Obviously it was no more sensible for a politician to compromise his own position at court by allowing enemies to point to a connection between his politics and Jacobitism than it had been in the previous year, yet Craigbarnet's plight was serious and a failure to help him would offend many. The man's Jacobitism clearly prevented him from securing any alternative office, and the division of the collectorship had to be resurrected. The means of providing for Craigbarnet was provided by another candidate, Michael Elphinstone of Quarrel, a relative of Lord Elphinstone, who, in December 1726, announced his own candidacy. The Laird of Quarrel did not have the slightest intention of sharing the spoils of office with Craigbarnet,[21] but he was unlikely to get anywhere near the office without strong interest, and those upon whom he relied were ready to see the wisdom of returning to the old practice of sharing the office. It did not prove difficult for John Graham of Dougalston, the sheriff-depute of Stirlingshire, and one of the commissioners of the Duke of Montrose, to arrange a compromise, whereby the commission of collector would run in the name of Michael Elphinstone, but the office would in reality be divided with Craigbarnet, who would receive almost half of the salary.[22]

It was 1747 before trouble was again encountered over the question of the collectorship, and at that time the office had been held without dispute for several years by Michael Elphinstone of Quarrel, whose election had been secured by an alliance of the Duke of Montrose and Lord Elphinstone. By 1747, however, the first Duke of Montrose was dead and his successor was much less actively involved in politics, while the Jacobite rising of 1745-6 effectively removed Stirling of Craigbarnet from the field. Accordingly, with the collector's salary no longer burdened with a kind of pension to a colleague, Elphinstone of Quarrel was challenged by Buchanan of Aucheneen, apparently with the support of friends of the second Duke of Montrose.

According to Lord Elphinstone, the candidacy of Buchanan of Aucheneen was being pressed by Dundas of Lethem, one of Montrose's friends, a gentleman who does not seem to have hesitated to make use of the duke's name in the course of his canvass for Aucheneen. The laird of Lethem's motive, as interpreted by Lord Elphinstone, was to serve his own interest, for it appeared that Aucheneen was 'a bankrupt maltman who broke sixty pounds in Mr. Dundas's debt, & by getting Mr. Buchanan chosen collector of the cess he expects to opperate his payment'.[23] Needless to say Lord Elphinstone did not hesitate to respond to the challenge and rallied his friends, while at the same time pointedly expressing his hope, when writing to the duke, that 'neither my friend or I have done any thing to deserve your Grace's withdrawing your friendship, interest & protection'. [24] Elphinstone also reminded his fellow peer that he had always 'endeavoured to support & strengthen' Montrose's interest in Stirlingshire, and the implication, though unstated, was certainly clear to the duke. The situation which had developed in 1747 was in fact identical with that of 1726, with one friend in opposition to another, and the politician being asked to choose between them.

Montrose was hard pressed to draft a reply to Lord Elphinstone, and in fact the duke took refuge in a claim of ill-health to excuse his failure to solicit his friend's attendance at the meeting of the commissioners of supply on 17th May, 1747. Lord Elphinstone had to content himself with the duke's assurance that he 'would mention to those who mannage my affairs my being honoured with a letter from your Lordship & recommend unanimity upon this occasion ... which I hope will be an inducement to the commissioners of supply to settle without varience'.[25] Montrose was much more open when writing to his friend Mungo Graeme of Gorthie, however, to whom he also sent a copy of Lord Elphinstone's letter. 'You see I plead want of health,' the duke remarked,

> that is that my letter may be the greater compliment, & that I might get better of from writeing any other letters on the subject. I know not what he means, unless that he wants his relation should not now pay to any other, what he did to Craigbarnet; but as I wish not to disoblige him, and that I do not incline to displeas Mr. Dundas, you see I keep as much as possible on generals, besides I don't incline to show that I take part in county matters when I am ignorant of the state of the case, & the gentlemen of the county's sentiments, but at the same time know he would have been displeased had he not heard from me ... [26]

The energetic Mungo Graeme of Gorthie was soon at work among the commissioners of supply, trying to prevent any difference among them over the collectorship,[27] and succeeded, through the mediation of Robert Graham of

Killearn, in persuading Buchanan of Aucheneen to make no opposition to Michael Elphinstone's re-election.[28] The two episodes, however, plainly show the danger to a political interest in any contest for the collectorship, particularly when the candidates are both political friends. An avowed enemy could of course be opposed with propriety, but if sufficient effort was not made to put victory beyond dispute, there was always some danger of humiliation, and, since there were inevitably many gentlemen who loved a winner, there would be some to see such a defeat as a sign to reconsider their political friendships. Craigbarnet had been supported, at considerable inconvenience, by the Montrose interest, mainly in order to please the head of the Stirling family, Stirling of Keir, who was a relative of the Duke of Montrose,[29] but no sooner was Craigbarnet out of the running than another potentially explosive dispute arose which might well have set the Duke of Montrose at variance with Lord Elphinstone or another valuable ally, Dundas of Lethem. The collectorship of supply, as Montrose remarked on another occasion, was 'an affair that too often divides neighbours',[30] and he might have added, it also divided political interests.

The link with parliamentary politics was effective in both directions, however, and a collector who openly opposed the political interest of the politician in control of the parliamentary seat was unlikely to retain his own position beyond the next meeting of the commission of supply, unless of course the political interest in power was about to be destroyed. In 1739, for example, when Lord Panmure held the Angus parliamentary seat, it began to appear likely that the Earl of Strathmore was contemplating a challenge to Panmure's position in the county. One of the freeholders whose continuing friendship to Panmure appeared uncertain was Erskine of Dun, one of the lords of session, but a relative of Lord Dun was then the collector of supply for Angus. Accordingly, some of Panmure's friends were reported to 'have been so free with Mr. Erskine as to tell him that if L[or]d Dunn should appear against' the Panmure interest, then Erskine would certainly lose his collectorship.[31]

The office of collector of supply was one which held its value over time, for the salary appears to have increased at a rate which more than compensated the holder for the ravages of inflation. It was a valuable office in the early eighteenth century, and it was still so at the beginning of the next century. In fact, the collectorship of Aberdeenshire, formerly worth about £70 per annum to the holder, was considered to have increased in value to between £800 and £1,000 by 1800.[32] Equally, the office could never be separated from parliamentary politics, and the frequent elections for the office provided a ready means to measure the strength of political interests.

The significance of the election of the collector of supply for parliamentary politics is emphasised over and over again by the politicians in their correspondence. In 1743, for example, when a number of the friends of Lord Panmure solicited his intervention in support of the candidacy of James Milne for the collectorship of Angus, Panmure was provided with a marked list of commissioners of supply, with those whom Panmure and his brother might be expected to influence carefully pointed out for personal solicitation. The group of gentlemen who prepared the list and signed the covering letter to Panmure, however, emphasised that unless Panmure wrote the letters in favour of James Milne which they had requested, then their friend would withdraw '& let your declared oposers run away with what they could not, were you either present or your intrest heartily interposed'.[33] In these circumstances an election campaign was to be waged with the same zeal which would otherwise be reserved for a parliamentary election.

Getting out the vote was a perennial problem in any kind of election, for many lairds could find plenty of excuses to avoid a tedious journey to the shire town. In the case of the commissioners of supply, there were many gentlemen who accepted that appointment not out of any great and compelling interest in aiding the collection of the land tax but in recognition of their social rank in their county. It was such men who had to be galvanised into action by a pressing personal letter from the leader of the political interest to which they adhered, and, as Panmure was advised, it was 'getting such good friends to take a troublesome jaunt on them' which would 'save a sett of friends from being either affronted or over run'.[34] The office of collector, however, was not like other forms of employment in the period, an asset to a politician able to obtain it. Win or lose, in a contest over a collectorship the office was a liability to a politician, more apt to cost him friends than to lead to anything useful for his interest. The contests, however, were almost impossible to avoid, and they could occasionally be pushed to the extremity of a prolonged election, likely to embitter all concerned in the losing cause. In such contests everyone concerned was fully aware that there was much more at stake than an annual office. David Graeme of Orchill, when describing the contest for the collector of the cess for Perthshire in 1738, which terminated in an election lasting two days, saw his party's victory as one by which 'some peoples management of this shire is interrupted'.[35] However much a politician might desire to avoid involvement in the collectorship contests, it was virtually impossible to escape being drawn in if the friends were involved. Were those friends to suffer humiliation, it would be seen as a defeat for the political interest to which they belonged, and if the politician had attempted to avoid a commitment, that abstention would merely add the resentment of his friends to the consequences of the defeat. In effect, therefore, the collectorship of supply became a gauge of party strength in a county, and unlike the parliamentary elections, the election of a friend only provided security for a single year. The office was, however, ideally suited for a gentleman of ancient lineage, who, for whatever reason, had determined to live upon his own estate, and was experiencing difficulty maintaining his social rank and providing for his family. For such people the office of collector of the cess was eminently attractive, and for that reason the strongest solicitations were made to those who might assist in securing the place. Sir James Grant, for example, was asked in the most pressing terms to assist Mr. Maxton of Tulloquhey, a relation, to secure the collectorship of the cess for Perthshire in 1779. Grant was not himself a landowner in Perthshire, but he was believed to have influence with those who were, and his correspondent insisted that it will be a very particular obligation done to an old friend of your Mother's, who looks upon you & all your family with strong *atatchments*. Mr. Maxton is a very old Baron in the County, has a wife & nine children & a tenth will appear soon. They have a very small income not £200 a year; & these children all to educat & set out in the world in the way of business; that can't be done on little, and this would be a great help, if he gets it ... [36]

The office of collector attracted that type of candidate, and throughout the century it remained in high demand, occasioning many notable political battles in the counties.

NOTES

1. SRO. Montrose, GD220/5/1055, William Colquhoun of Garscadden to Mungo Graeme of Gorthie, 11 Dec., 1727.
2. Ibid.
3. Ibid., GD220/5/862, Montrose to Gorthie, 24 Feb., 1728.
4. Ibid., GD220/5/815, Gorthie to Montrose, 29 Jul., 1715.
5. Ibid., GD220/5/814, Gorthie to Montrose, 9 Jun., 1715.
6. Ibid., GD220/5/828, from Montrose, 31 Mar., 1719.
7. Ibid., GD220/5/1000, John Graham of Killearn to Gorthie, 16 Mar., 1723.
8. Ibid., GD220/5/853, from Lady Kier, Jan., 1726.
9. Ibid., GD220/5/853, from Henry McFarlane of Kirkton, 10 Jan., 1726.
10. Ibid., GD220/5/853, from Montrose, 25 Jan., 1726.
11. Ibid.
12. Ibid., from Lady Kier, Jan., 1726.
13. Ibid., GD220/5/1027, John Graham of Dougalston to Gorthie, 21 Jan., 1726.
14. Ibid., GD220/5/ 853, from Lady Kier, Jan., 1726.
15. Ibid., GD220/5/1027, from John Graham of Dougalston, 21 Jan., 1726.
16. Ibid., GD220/5/853, Montrose to Gorthie, 1 Feb., 1726.
17. Ibid., from Montrose, 6 Feb., 1726.
18. Ibid., from Montrose, 21 Jan., 1726.
19. Ibid.
20. Ibid., from Montrose, 19 Feb., 1726.
21. Ibid., GD220/5/1027, John Graham of Dougalston to Mungo Graeme of Gorthie, 9 Dec., 1726.
22. Ibid., GD220/5/1053, John Graham of Dougalston to Gorthie, 11 Apr., 1727.
23. Ibid., GD220/5/931, Lord Elphinstone to Montrose, 7 Apr., 1747.
24. Ibid.
25. Ibid., GD220/ 5/931, Montrose to Elphinstone, 16 Apr., 1747.
26. Ibid., Montrose to Gorthie, 16 Apr., 1747.
27. Ibid., Montrose to Gorthie, 13 May, 1747.
28. Ibid., GD220/5/1660, Robert Graham of Killearn to Gorthie, 29 Apr., 1747.
29. Ibid., GD220/5/883, Montrose to Gorthie, 6 Jan., 1733.
30. Ibid., GD220/5/931, Montrose to Lord Elphinstone, 16 Apr., 1747.
31. SRO. Dalhousie, GD45/14/431, from Charles Stratton to Lord Panmure, 1 Mar., 1739.
32. SRO. Melville Castle, GD51/1/198/1/10, from James Durno, 10 Jun., 1800.
33. SRO. Dalhousie, GD45/14/432, Archibald Scott, John Fullerton and John Scott to Panmure, 4 Feb., 1743.
34. Ibid.

35. SRO. Montrose, GD220/5/1418. David Graeme of Orchill to Gorthie, 30 May, 1738.

36. SRO. Seafield, GD248/56/4, Lady Christine Grant to Sir James Grant, 20 Jul., 1779.

Part II
Managing an Interest in a Scottish County

6

The Management of the Interest of Sir Thomas Dundas

The politician who could arrange close ties with Government and an intimate connection with those ministers who had the disposal of patronage greatly eased his own task of management. The eighteenth-century freeholders normally saw the duty of their member of parliament as the furtherance of the interests of his county in general and of his constituents in particular, and both of these functions were more easily accomplished when good relations existed between the member of parliament and the Administration. Henry Dundas of Melville, the best known of Scotland's political managers, built his entire career upon his proven readiness to serve his friends, and through them their friends, in a chain of influence which eventually gave the minister considerable power in every corner of the land, and those who were his associates were certainly well placed to manage their constituencies. On the other hand, it was nonetheless possible, even in the days of Henry Dundas's power, for a family which was in opposition to retain a county seat.

Sir Thomas Dundas, the member of parliament for Stirlingshire from 1768 until his elevation to the peerage in 1794, was a landowner much more closely connected with Opposition than with Administration, having married a niece of the Marquis of Rockingham and being a close associate of the Prince of Wales and his circle. Although Sir Thomas was a distant relative of Henry Dundas, there was no friendship between the two branches of the family, but Sir Thomas Dundas retained his parliamentary seat despite the active hostility of the government manager until 1794, when it passed to a member of his interest at a by-election, and the new Lord Dundas retained a considerable voice in the county until the election of 1812.

Sir Thomas Dundas inherited his position in Stirlingshire politics from his father, Sir Lawrence Dundas of Kerse, a wealthy merchant turned politician, who had used his riches to build up a parliamentary following after the death of the Duke of Argyll in 1761, when he placed a number of his friends and relatives in parliamentary seats, including that of Stirlingshire, where the candidate of the Argyll interest was turned out by Sir Lawrence's son. Sir Lawrence lived until 13 Dec., 1781, and until that date the politics of Thomas Dundas were essentially those of his strong-willed father who, although occasionally in Opposition, was never very far from the Administration politicians as he successfully pursued a baronetcy, and unsuccessfully, a peerage. Thomas Dundas, however, was in fact a liberal in politics, a supporter of parliamentary reform and of reform of the corrupt Scottish burghs, and in Parliament was closely connected with the Portland group, which inevitably meant that he was much more of an Opposition politician than his father had ever been. There was, however, one thing more of significance which Thomas Dundas inherited from his father besides his political interest and his wealth, for Sir Lawrence Dundas was a bitter enemy of Henry Dundas, their hostility dating from their clashes over control of the politics of the city of Edinburgh, which Sir Lawrence represented, and which Henry Dundas and the Duke of Buccleuch sought to take away from him. In consequence of this well-established rivalry, the member of parliament for Stirlingshire could hope for little or no aid for his management which might involve patronage appointments over which the Edinburgh representatives of Government had any control, but the remarkable thing about Thomas Dundas' interest in Stirlingshire is its survival in spite of this lack of a direct route to the things which freeholders were apt to crave. It was an interest, moreover, which was something more than the member of parliament, for it in fact owed its survival to the efforts of a group of gentlemen who were much more active than their nominal leader in the management of the county.

The capture of the Stirlingshire seat in 1768 was largely due to the readiness of Sir Lawrence Dundas to employ his wealth to advance his politics, and like most rich men buying their way to a position of political influence, he had created a number of nominal votes, although both he and his son were too cautious to embark upon a mass creation of such qualifications on a scale sufficient to alarm the real freeholders by the prospect of a packed roll. Dundas' real strength was his ability to get things done, for as a man who had made a fortune as a commissariat contractor had to do, he was a great 'fixer'. Sir Lawrence's connections were often of a backdoor variety, but they were nonetheless effective, and there can be no doubt that he had a very substantial following among the freeholders of the counties in which he was active. Sir Lawrence Dundas' reputation as a political 'fixer' has been put on record by Ramsay of Ochtertyre, who described him, with some exaggeration, as a politician who 'without the name of a minister' had the 'disposal of almost everything in Scotland'.[1] There can be little doubt, therefore, that Sir Thomas Dundas inherited a legacy of gratitude for favours obtained, and that this in turn helped to sustain his own, clearly Opposition, interest. Alliance with other Stirlingshire freeholders of influence strengthened the Dundas interest to the point where Thomas Dundas' tenure of the seat appeared unshakeable, for Indian patronage, obtained through the agency of the Haldanes of Airthrey and William Elphinstone among the regional allies, and from English associates active in East India politics, served to consolidate the feelings of obligation which were so vital to successful political management. Personal connections with Lord Sandwich kept open a line of naval patronage, even when the Dundas's were ostensibly in opposition to Lord North's Administration, while the family's wealth permitted them to loan money to a number of freeholders, and the initial victory over the Argyll interest in Stirlingshire in 1768 was repeated even more convincingly with the crushing defeat of Sir James Campbell of Ardkinglas in 1774, when Thomas Dundas was re-elected by the convincing margin of 44 votes to 19.[2]

The succession of Sir Thomas to the baronetcy and the leadership of the interest upon the death of his father in 1781 provided that interest with its greatest test, for it saw a very active politician replaced by a lethargic one who was, moreover, a close associate of the Prince of Wales and thus quite clearly removed from any connection with the existing Administration by the personal hostility of the king towards the prince. Stirlingshire, however, was not recovered by Administration, and Sir Thomas Dundas continued to represent the county in Opposition, and his career suggests that the power of ministers was less formidable than they might have wished the voters to believe. The period of Sir Thomas Dundas' influence in Stirlingshire indeed affords evidence not only of the ability of a political interest to survive when alienated from Government, but of its capacity to function effectively without much active guidance from its nominal leader, for Sir Thomas' position was sustained by the efforts of a group of his freeholder friends acting in unison.

The Dundas family was an ancient one, but the founder of the fortunes of this branch of the family, Sir Lawrence Dundas, was a younger son of a junior branch, who was essentially a self-made man who had built his great fortune through his success as a forage contractor to the army in Scotland, Flanders and Germany after very modest commercial beginnings in the Luckenbooths of Edinburgh. Wealth allowed the Dundas family to augment their local influence by adding to their estates in Stirlingshire and its neighbouring counties, but it was hardly possible for its representatives to make use of that favourite term of county politicians and claim 'a great natural interest', for it was essentially a new family in the power balance of the region. A further count against the family as leaders of a Scottish political interest was the fact that Sir Thomas, in particular, made his principal place of residence his estates in the North Riding of Yorkshire when Parliament was not in session. Accordingly, there were Stirlingshire gentlemen ready to view the baronet as a carpetbagger, in spite of his Stirlingshire origins among the small lairds of the county. Even in Sir Lawrence's time this opinion was current, for in 1774 he was warned that 'the handle or argument used against you is your indifference & not residence in the Country, the voters are not noticed, when they are wanted they know their value'.[3] The 'Northern Nabob' was sufficiently rich and owned wide enough estates to have made a considerable number of fictitious votes, but money alone was insufficient to maintain an interest in a county which had its superiorities split as extensively as Stirlingshire, where there was a substantial number of independent small freeholders, and indeed, any attempt to pack the roll with nominal voters might be detrimental to the interest. The proper mode of management at any time in the eighteenth or early nineteenth century demanded active and regular canvassing through the medium of a continuing round of social calls paid at the homes of the voters. Accordingly, perhaps the most surprising thing about the success of Sir Thomas Dundas as a county member of parliament was his ability to maintain his position with a minimum of social contact, and his ability to attract to his interest influential lairds resident in the district who were willing to undertake this demanding and essential task in his absence, for it was only by such means that a politician could anticipate the mood of the county. Thomas Dundas of Fingask, George Haldane of Gleneagles, Colonel James Masterton, Robert Bruce of Kennet, Sir Lawrence Dundas' brother-in-law, and William Morehead of Herbertshire, the county convener of

Stirlingshire, were all active partisans of Sir Thomas Dundas, while in a time of crisis the interest would recruit additional help among the freeholders and supplement their efforts with the services of the most competent lawyers available. Sir Thomas Dundas was in a position to pay for the talents of political lawyers, but lawyers alone would have been insufficient to maintain a political interest in the absence of the member of parliament, for lawyers, unless they were themselves, like Kennet and Gleneagles, influential barons, were a suspect breed, and many freeholders would have felt slighted had they been canvassed by an employee of the member of parliament. The employment of influential friends was not of course an ideal solution, for indeed there was no true substitute for the politician himself, regularly resident in his constituency, keeping up his own social contacts, but it was the enthusiastic support of friends which kept the Dundas interest a power in Stirlingshire for so many years.

Sir Thomas Dundas met with no opposition to his re-election in 1780, and he was again chosen without challenge in 1784, for the extent of his success in the 1774 election must have been a marked deterrent to potential rivals. By 1787, however, another interest was beginning to form, and Sir Thomas faced a new contest in the general election of 1790, but for twelve years Sir Thomas was unchallenged in Stirlingshire, and even in 1790 he retained the seat. Like his father, Sir Thomas Dundas was absent from the constituency which he represented for extended periods, and this absenteeism became more marked as he grew older. In his earlier years, Thomas Dundas was more active, and in 1775, for example, only one year after he had been elected, and therefore long before he had need of the freeholders' votes, he was paying visits and undertaking the social business of political management, though finding it less than agreeable. 'Ever since I came to Scotland,' Dundas remarked, 'I have been employ'd in visiting my ... constituents. I have either dined or stopped at the house of all our Friends.'[4] Actually it was not quite all of them, for the member of parliament excused his failure to visit two of the more remotely situated lairds by suggesting that they were 'really to far off in this dreadful weather, for it has rained incessantly these three days and the whole country is under water'.[5] Visits of courtesy, even when no election was in view, were, however, expected, and when Sir Thomas was himself leader of the interest he proved to be more and more reluctant to incur the personal discomfort of making such tours of his constituency, leaving this work to his friends in the county.

Sir Thomas further weakened his political position by another defect, for he showed himself reluctant to maintain a regular correspondence with his voters. Appearing indeed to dislike writing letters, the member of parliament tended to respond only to letters sent by close associates, but a gentleman who had shown himself friendly to Sir Thomas' interest who did not receive a prompt and full reply to correspondence was very likely to construe that neglect as a deliberate snub. Sir Thomas Dundas persistently made difficulties for himself and his interest by unnecessarily delaying replies to letters. In the case of Sir James Dunbar of Mochrum, one of the freeholders of Stirlingshire considered to be friendly to Dundas' interest, an attempt to solicit patronage produced neither action nor an acceptable answer. Sir James had a son in the service of the East India Company, and he wanted his member of parliament to use his influence to obtain a leave of absence for him, but after two years and many letters Dunbar received only one communication from Sir Thomas, and that, as a mutual friend remarked, was unsatisfactory, for it 'marked your being ill-pleased with his impatience and if I remember right you express'd that displeasure pretty warmly. You will know whether Sir James wrote to you since,' the friend suggested, 'I think he did and that he has never heard from you in return.'[6] Sir Thomas Dundas, by his own laziness in answering his correspondence, made his own task of management more difficult than it need have been, and thus deprived himself of an alternative method of keeping in touch with his county and compensating for his reluctance to reside among his constituents.

Even if Sir Thomas Dundas' connection with Opposition ensured that little government patronage would come his way save during the brief period when the Duke of Portland was in office, he was not without influence in this category of management, for it was during Sir Thomas Dundas' tenure of the county seat that a substantial number of Stirlingshire gentlemen began to find places in India for their sons. Cadetships, surgeoncies, an occasional writership, and numerous appointments as officers of East Indiamen created a desire for more and maintained that feeling of hope which was so useful to a politician who could awaken it. Sir Thomas Dundas used his influence at East India House to secure favourable voyages for Captain Ninian Lowis, commander of the East Indiaman *Woodcott*,[7] who was the son-in-law of John Munro of Auchenbowie, an influential freeholder, and by such means built up the feelings of obligation which were so useful to a political interest, and this was done frequently enough to make that interest something of a political institution by the time a challenger appeared to oppose Sir Thomas in 1787.

It was evident from 1787 that there was a strong probability that a candidate supported by Administration would come forward against Sir Thomas Dundas at the next general election, but it was from 1788 that the Opposition began to be troublesome to the sitting member. King George III became incapable of fulfilling his duties in that year and, accordingly, it became necessary for a regent to assume the functions of the head of state. The obvious and only reasonable candidate for the office of regent was, however, the Prince of Wales, whose close relationship with Opposition politics over many years made his appointment appear threatening to the Administration. However much the Prime Minister might have wished to deny the office to an enemy, he had little option but to give the regency to the heir to the throne, but he chose to pin his faith on the monarch's speedy recovery and insisted that the Prince's powers as head of state should be restricted and, in particular, his freedom to name officeholders should be limited for a time. That decision of the Administration produced a political crisis which reached from Westminster to the constituencies and, to a considerable degree, produced lasting trouble for the member of parliament for Stirlingshire who, as a member of the Prince of Wales' circle, voted with Opposition against the Administration over the regency issue. The bitter confrontation between Pitt and his allies on the one hand,

and the friends, old and new, of the Prince of Wales on the other, took the form of local trials of strength within parliamentary constituencies, prompted by the circulation among the electors of addresses designed to show support for the position of Administration. The problem faced by the incumbent representative of Stirlingshire lay in the fact that, in common with much of the Scottish electorate, the voters of Stirlingshire appeared receptive to the idea that a sovereign parliament had the power to limit the authority of a regent. It could indeed be argued that this was a logical extension of the doctrine of parliamentary sovereignty, assuming of course that it was possible to ignore the inconvenient fact, from the Administration's point of view, that the head of state whose powers were to be restricted was a necessary part of that sovereign Parliament.

Scottish opinion, according to the convener of the county of Stirling, leaned in general to the position taken by Pitt and the other ministers. 'Every where in this country Mr. Pitt's popularity has the ascendency over that of Mr. Fox,' Convener Morehead informed Sir Thomas Dundas.[8] The Administration, hard-pressed in Parliament and with the possibility of an election before it, was happy to take full advantage of this favourable climate of opinion, and encouraged its friends to call county meetings where votes of thanks to the Prime Minister might be moved, and effectively sought in this way a vote of confidence which would declare its actions constitutional and at the same time strengthen its hand in preparation for a general election. William Morehead of Herbertshire, the county convener of Stirling, as a friend of the member of parliament, appreciated how distasteful such an address would be to Sir Thomas Dundas, and postponed calling a meeting as long as he could, but, as Herbertshire reported:

> After parrying it for some time, I received a letter signed by Lord Fincastle, Sir Michael Bruce, his Son the Colonel, Mr. Ogilvie, Mr. Belsches, Mr. Ferrier, Mr. Strachan & Mr. Cadell, requesting me to call a meeting of the County of Stirling *to consider the present situation of Public Affairs and what is proper for them to do.* This was so pointed that there was no evading it. I was therefore under the necessity of calling the meeting, or I must have incurred the charge of evident partiality. I have never been more fretted at any thing of the kind. I have every reason to believe that this has been done in order to move a vote of thanks to Mr. Pitt and his friends. Knowing how disagreeable it must be for you, I have written to all your most trusty friends the state of the case, conjuring them to come up with all their strength that we may meet this unforeseen attack and if possible subdue it ...[9]

Faced with a trend of opinion generally favourable to the position adopted by William Pitt, politicians, like Sir Thomas Dundas, who had voted against Administration on the regency question, were obliged, in self-defence, to resist any move arising from among their constituents for a vote of confidence in the minister's handling of the question. Supporters of Administration in Stirlingshire who could force the issue to the point of carrying a resolution in a county meeting would create such an impression of strength that they would greatly strengthen the position of an Administration candidate at the next election, and it was already believed that such a candidate would contest the seat if there was any probability of success.

The county convener was not the only supporter to warn Sir Thomas Dundas of his danger, for his friend Henry Erskine, one of the leaders of the Scottish bar and a perceptive observer of Scottish politics, advised the member of parliament against any attempt to directly reverse the motion for an address of thanks to William Pitt. Erskine strongly urged caution, while assuring his friend that all those associated with Opposition in Scotland were attempting to check the addresses, but emphasised that, in his opinion, 'to meet the foe on the general point is perfectly vain, to fight mere opposition agt Ministry is equally so. Delay, and that on a sort of middle & equivocal ground must be our sole object . . . '[10] Erskine enlarged upon his view of the best method of meeting the challenge in a letter which he sent to one of Sir Thomas Dundas' Stirlingshire voters, in which he again urged that a direct confrontation should be avoided:

> I think it may be successfully opposed independently altogether of the great question of right on this ground, That the vote as to the powers of the two Houses obtained by the Ministers influence must ultimately prove the object of thanks or reprobation according to the use that is henceforth made of it. If it is followed up by an arrangement of the Regency consistent with justice to the heir aparent and the proper constitutional ballance between the legislative and executive branches of the Government those who disapprove the vote on the general ground may concur in praising the moderate use that has been made of it . . . On this view I would ground a motion to delay the question till the great business of the Regency shall be finally settled . . . [11]

Henry Erskine's solution to attempt to delay the motion was a sensible one, for an open confrontation between supporters of Administration and those who were committed to Opposition would be harmful to the member of parliament's interest, for it would be likely to bring out a full muster of Administration partisans, and several of them, and some of the most powerful, notably the Marquis of Graham and Sir Archibald Edmonstone, were still inactive. On the other hand, it was still vital to arrange for enough of Sir Thomas' friends to attend the meeting to ensure that Erskine's motion would be carried rather than that favoured by those freeholders who had requested the meeting. The matter was urgent enough for Sir Thomas to be asked to directly request the attendance of his friends at the forthcoming county meeting,[12] and Sir Thomas' alarm is evident in his readiness to overcome his normal dislike of correspondence for long enough to dispatch the necessary circulars. County meetings were notoriously uncertain events, for they were by no means confined to the parliamentary electors, although the freeholders whose names were included in the Stirlingshire electoral roll would of course take a prominent part. All of the Stirlingshire gentry, however, were free to attend such an assembly, and it was very difficult to predict the actions of the smaller landowners who, inevitably, were somewhat remote from the calculations of a political interest,[13] yet a defeat for the friends of Sir Thomas Dundas would imply the vulnerability of the interest, and would certainly shake its influence among the more restricted group of voting barons.

When the county meeting which William Morehead had reluctantly summoned finally met on January 9th, 1789, the efforts of the Dundas interest proved to have been sufficient to overcome the attack by the friends of Administration. The size of the gathering was clearly an unpleasant surprise for the friends of William Pitt, and one of them was in fact so taken aback that he moved for adjournment on the rather unusual grounds that the 'meeting was the fullest, but one, that he ... ever recollected to have seen'.[14] As one might expect, that suggestion provoked some laughter, and it was certainly not taken seriously by the gentlemen present, many of whom had made lengthy and difficult journeys to the town of Stirling in one of the worst months of the winter and had no intention of leaving again without finishing whatever business was intended. Adjournment for two weeks, which the instigators of the meeting now requested, was so evidently an expedient to change the composition of what purported to be a meeting intended to reflect public opinion in the county that the friends of Sir Thomas Dundas would have been extremely unwise to agree to the motion. The ministerial supporters, however, finding themselves in the minority, remained silent when they were asked if they had any other motion than one for adjournment to propose. Conversely, the friends of Sir Thomas Dundas, now sure of their strength, moved into the attack, insisting that those who had requested the meeting at such an inconvenient time should put their intended motion to the gathering. Spiers of Culcreuch, one of the freeholders, remarked that

> the conduct of the gentlemen who had requested the meeting appeared to him in an extraordinary light. He said that since they did not seem to know themselves the purpose for which the meeting had been called he would tell them. 'I know that the purpose of calling this meeting was to vote an adress of thanks to Mr. Pitt on his conduct with respect to a recent vote given by the two Houses of Parliament ... but since the gentlemen will not bring forward their intended motion, I pledge myself to this meeting to do it ... and those that think Mr. Pitt deserves such a vote of thanks will give it to him, and those who think otherwise will reject it.'[15]

Finding Spiers determined, the group of supporters of Administration, with extreme reluctance, agreed to make the motion themselves, and their hesitation was justified, for they were defeated by forty votes to sixteen.[16] Having disposed of the unwanted motion, however, the friends of Sir Thomas Dundas remembered Henry Erskine's advice and did not take the dispute further, contenting themselves with a statement that the address had been rejected 'on the ground of its being unnecessary and inexpedient',[17] even though, as William Morehead explained, the Dundas interest had sufficient numbers to have carried a vote of thanks to the member of parliament. 'It was thought better,' Morehead told Sir Thomas, 'to do nothing farther than defeat the adversaries',[18] and the defeat of the motion was an effective vindication of Sir Thomas Dundas' parliamentary conduct.

The group of Administration supporters, now known from their place of meeting as the Carron Inn Junta, although humiliated, had not been dispersed as a party in the county, and in fact it would appear that the humiliation which they had suffered was a factor in preserving their unity. Some of the minority had been offended by the actions of Sir Thomas' friends in arranging such a substantial turnout at Stirling and with the arguments used to effect that result. As one of Sir Thomas' friends remarked, 'if we had not taken care to insinuate that the vote if carried would have been a personal affront to you, we would not have had half so numerous a meeting',[19] an evaluation which is almost certainly correct, for January was never a favoured month for travel in eighteenth-century Scotland. On the other hand, even if some of the associates of the Carron Inn Junta claimed to see no attack upon Sir Thomas Dundas in their own actions, the Administration itself was fully aware of the impact of the addresses of thanks which they were actively soliciting. Lord Advocate Ilay Campbell had in fact been sent to Scotland to promote the addresses, much to the disgust of Henry Erskine, who complained that the Lord Advocate's task had been made easier by his ability to tie off with an Opposition member of parliament.[20]

The Stirlingshire freeholders chiefly involved in the attempts to secure a pro-Administration address were Colonel Andrew Bruce, a serving army officer and eldest son of Sir Michael Bruce of Stenhouse, a prominent freeholder, Robert Belsches of Greenyards, a well-known ministerialist, and Lord Fincastle, the heir of the Earl of Dunmore. The association of the principals with Sir Michael Bruce was particularly dangerous, for Sir Michael was considered to be a friend of Sir Thomas Dundas, a fact which may have induced others to join in the group's activities. Clearly the Carron Inn Junta had anticipated a poorly attended meeting which they could run as they saw fit, and they could hardly have done more to mismanage their own project for, as the convener remarked, it was scarcely conceivable that gentlemen of some consideration 'could have entered into such a scheme without some previous muster of strength or without having so much as settled the terms of their motion'.[21] It appears probable that the known ministerialists in the Carron Inn group, particularly Lord Fincastle and Robert Belsches, intended to establish a new political organisation in Stirlingshire, and they may have lacked time to concert their efforts with other friends of Administration to secure a better showing. On the other hand, there is a possibility that the men who dominated the Carron Inn group intended to enhance their own political reputations by creating their own political interest to support Administration while ignoring such potential rivals as the Marquis of Graham and Sir Archibald Edmonstone of Duntreath, whose estates made them far more significant friends of the Government, neither of whom was involved in the group's activities. Some of the less astute members of the group, notably Colonel Bruce and his father, Sir Michael, do appear to have believed that a vote in favour of Pitt's conduct would not necessarily be a vote of censure upon that of Sir Thomas Dundas, for according to one of the member of parliament's friends,

> Sir Michael & his son, particularly the latter, were a good deal nettled that the proposed vote of thanks to Mr. Pitt should have been taken up by you, or at least by your friends, as a *party matter*, that neither they nor any of the other gent[leme]n who signed the letter meant or intended any *offence* to you . . . [22]

In the course of their debates on the regency question neither Pitt nor Fox and his allies displayed much consistency, for while the latter was placed in a position of extolling the royal prerogative, the former was obliged to take up a distinctly Whiggish position. Accordingly, it is possible that some gentlemen, normally satisfied with the Opposition politics of Sir Thomas Dundas, might have been attracted to William Pitt's current position. Equally, and without undue cynicism, the Bruces' indignation could be interpreted as a natural response to a humiliating defeat and their argument that no attack on their representative was intended was no more than a means of salving injured pride.

In any event, the Carron Inn Junta did not change their plans as a result of their defeat, for they at once began to seek reinforcements as a preliminary to making a second attempt to carry their motion at a county meeting. Charles Innes, one of Sir Thomas Dundas' better-informed political correspondents, reported before the end of January 1789 that the Carron Inn group had 'been investigating & paying every attention in their power to every man they can find in the county who is possesst of a £100 Scots of valuation'.[23] Innes drew the correct conclusion, namely, that the group intended to try again for a victory in a county meeting, and warned Sir Thomas Dundas that 'whatever they may pretend to you', they 'have been wrought upon to play Mr. Pitt's game ... or they are so much ashamed & nettled at their late defeat, they are resolved of themselves to attempt another meeting from mere spite & opposition ... '[24] There was substance to Innes' suspicions for, at a meeting in Carron Inn on January 24th, it was unanimously resolved 'that the sense of the county was not fairly taken at Stirling ... the greatest part of the majority that day being composed of nominal voters and small proprietors'.[25]

The decision of the gentlemen of Carron Inn was to request the convener of the county to call a second meeting, but the implication of their resolution, that they represented the real voice of the county, is certainly unfounded. Sir Thomas' friends of January 9th included most of the nominal freeholders present, but some of them were also substantial proprietors with estates held from a subject superior, and the member of parliament's interest had in fact a small majority even of the real freeholders present. The criticism which the Carron Inn Junta chose to level at their opponents, that they manipulated the county meeting by bringing in the small proprietors, rings false when advanced by a group which was now making every effort to recruit such small proprietors for its own ranks, while it was an essential attribute of a county meeting that all proprietors were free to attend. In any question of measuring county opinion it is wise not to take statements at face value, and in spite of Lord Fincastle's printed declaration that the decision to call a second meeting of the county had been made at 'a meeting of many respectable and independent gentlemen of the county of Stirling',[26] it is notable that this great assembly consisted of only five men.[27]

Fincastle, as the spokesman of the five, who had now seen fit to reject the decision of a well-attended county meeting, wrote to Sir Thomas Dundas to insist that he did not intend a personal attack upon the member of parliament, but although Dundas replied politely and with unusual promptness, he left Fincastle in no doubt that any repetition of the address scheme would indeed be taken as an attack. 'You have really pinn'd them to the wall by your answer,'[28] remarked Innes, as he and Sir Thomas' other managers prepared to counter-attack, for if the Carron Inn Junta persisted, the Dundas party intended to beat them again, and this time to reinforce their victory with a resolution of their own.

Acquiescing in the demand for a new meeting, the Dundas party took the greatest care to canvass all who might be persuaded to attend. Charles Innes, Dundas' agent in the county, toured the entire shire accompanied by William Morehead of Herbertshire, the convener, General Campbell of Boquhan, and other gentlemen of the Dundas interest. The three gentlemen, with the aid of some of their own friends, divided the lists of freeholders, commissioners of supply and other proprietors, giving each of Sir Thomas' active friends a section to canvass, and in this manner exerted a great deal of pressure on lairds, large and small, who might otherwise have been hesitant to make another winter journey.[29] Sir Thomas Dundas had an effective political machine in Stirlingshire, and it was nowhere more in evidence than in the preparations made for the second county meeting. Gentlemen, whose support might have been in doubt if left alone, were fixed by a direct approach from a friend whom it was believed they would hesitate to disoblige, and persuaded to add their signature to a circular letter which committed them to attendance at a meeting and to support for an address to the Prince Regent.

Early in February it became clear that the Carron Inn group had again miscalculated, and that they would once more fail to muster sufficient support to carry a motion to their liking. At that point they would have withdrawn, if they had been permitted, but with urgent notices sent to the gentlemen of the county requiring their attendance at Stirling on February 14th, the friends of Sir Thomas Dundas insisted that it was too late to abandon the meeting and that it should proceed, and they could ensure that their arguments would prevail since one of their number was the county convener. On the appointed day 68 gentlemen assembled at Stirling, with the Dundas interest fully in control of proceedings,[30] and it was a simple matter to obtain general agreement for a harmless message of congratulations to the Prince Regent. The Dundas interest, however, having been put to considerable inconvenience by their opponents, determined to put their own dominance beyond dispute, and moved that 'the thanks of the meeting be presented to Sir Thomas Dundas, Baronet, the representative of the county, for his manly, steady & uniform conduct in Parliament'.[31] Having baited the trap, Sir Thomas' associates watched with delight as the Carron Inn Junta proceeded to walk into it. Foolishly, the Carron Inn group opposed the motion and met with a predictable humiliation. It would have been far wiser to have promptly offered to second the motion, perhaps with some qualification about the member of parliament's recent conduct on the regency question if this was thought worth making an issue, but it was essential to refrain from a division if the Carron Inn group wished to avoid the humiliation of a second crushing defeat which could only demonstrate their own weakness. A motion of thanks to a member of parliament who had been the choice of the county for over twenty years need not have been taken as controversial, and the wording of the motion had indeed been intended to avoid the appearance of being overtly partisan. The gentlemen of Carron Inn, however, not only opposed the motion of thanks to Sir Thomas Dundas, they insisted that their dissent should be recorded in the minutes, a record which disclosed their own ineptitude, for they could muster only seven freeholders' votes, a showing which could hardly have enhanced their own reputations in the eyes of Administration.

In spite of their recurring defeats the existence of the Carron Inn group still provided a nucleus for a ministerial party in the county, and thus posed a threat to the member of parliament, for anger at their disgrace served to unite the leaders of the group and make them available to support any candidate who should start against Sir Thomas Dundas in the interest of Administration. If the leaders of the Carron Inn Junta were unable to dislodge Sir Thomas from his parliamentary seat, there was an alternative, for in the background were the much more powerful figures of Sir Archibald Edmonstone of Duntreath, the purchaser of the forfeited estate of the former Viscount Kilsyth, which could be the means of creating many nominal votes, and the Marquis of Graham, the manager of the interest of the Montrose family. Accordingly, the friends of Sir Thomas Dundas began to prepare for a contested election as early as March, 1789,[32] and did not permit their February victory to make them over-confident. The Montrose estates, in particular, were a threat which might turn into an active danger at any time, for if the family exerted its full powers in Stirlingshire, it could make eighteen nominal qualifications with little difficulty. In addition, the head of the Montrose family was superior of lands valued at more than £3,000 Scots feued to vassals and undivided in the books of supply. Making votes on these lands was likely to be more costly, but if the commissioners of supply could be persuaded to act to divide the valuations, it was likely that a number of additional votes might be made, while further freehold qualifications could have been made by utilising lands owned by the Montrose family in property as well as superiority, though once again these qualifications would have been more costly to produce.

Perhaps the danger was less serious than it at first appeared, for had there been a concerted effort to dislodge Sir Thomas Dundas by creating fictitious votes, there is enough evidence from the freeholders' minute books of Stirlingshire to suggest that this would have been enough to rally most of the real freeholders to the member of parliament's support. Indeed, many years later, when there was no more than a suspicion that the Montrose family intended to assert its power by making nominal votes in 1821, this was sufficient to create a coalition to resist ducal power which saw Whigs and Tories unite to support a Tory freeholder, Henry Home Drummond, who in fact owed his election to the opposition Whigs.[33] Perhaps it was fear of just such a development which restrained the Marquis of Graham in 1789, for the votes were not made. A family which rightly prided itself upon its great natural interest in the county would have been unwise to act so rashly that it might be left isolated, with all the loss of face which that would entail, for it is evident that a peer who attempted to rest his power upon the nominal votes of factors, writers, and half-pay army officers would have become an object of contempt in Stirlingshire. In some counties the ability to nominate a member of parliament might have provided solace for an isolated nobleman, but in a county like Stirlingshire, there were too many small freeholders to make any victory certain. Interests used nominal voters, but equally they attempted to attract as many real freeholders as possible, and politicians took considerable pride in numbering their real as opposed to their nominal support, even if the vote of a nominal freeholder who did not scruple at taking the trust oath was just as good as that of the holder of a good freehold estate.

Any chance that the political life of Stirlingshire would return to normal was removed in March 1789, but not by the Marquis of Graham. Once again it was the gentlemen of Carron Inn who began another attack upon the member of parliament, undeterred by their previous setbacks, but on their third attempt they took care to try to ensure a poor attendance at the county meeting by giving only a few days' notice. Letters from William Morehead, the convener of the county, warning of the meeting, reached Edinburgh only two days before it was due to take place. The intention, as Charles Innes surmised, was to confine the muster as far as possible to the Carron Inn group and their friends, 'and if strong enough to bring forward an address of their own to the King', who had by that time recovered his reason, and more significantly, 'a vote approving of the conduct & measures of his confidential servants'. [34] It is in the nature of county meetings, however, that they cannot be kept secret, and although they kept Sir Thomas Dundas' friend the county convener in the dark about their intentions for some time, one of the gentlemen whom the Carron Inn Junta approached gave timely warning to Sir Thomas' agent, Charles Innes, who was therefore prepared for countermeasures.[35] Nonetheless, the Junta came closer to success at the third meeting than at the previous ones, for the meeting at Stirling on March 31st was very sparsely attended, with only 39 gentlemen present. [36] Poor attendance was perhaps to be anticipated, for this was the third such meeting in the course of the winter, and it says a good deal for the management abilities of the men who managed the Dundas interest that they were able to persuade 23 of Sir Thomas' friends to make another cold journey to Stirling.

The weather at the end of March was very severe and, as Charles Innes reported, 'for half an hour, Mr. Morehead & I thought we would have been in the minority, which would have been a most unfortunate circumstance'.[37] Innes and Morehead must have had a nervewracking half-hour as they attempted to delay the vote while they waited for their numbers to increase, and although Sir Thomas' friends ultimately prevailed, they were so alarmed by the narrowness of their victory that they refrained from pressing their advantage, and compromised with a non-controversial motion of little significance to anyone. Nevertheless, the third county meeting was a victory for Sir Thomas Dundas' interest, and like the others it was gained for him by the efforts of a group of resident gentlemen of ability associated with the member of parliament. The interest of Sir Thomas Dundas was something more than a politician and his hired lawyers, for it is evident that Sir Thomas was not the mainspring of the political interest of which he was the nominal head. Indeed, it would be difficult to quarrel with the assessment of Sir Thomas Dundas made by a political associate, who remarked that he was 'a most respectable good man but he is surely no very active politician'.[38]

The successive defeats inflicted upon the Carron Inn Junta did not make Sir Thomas' position impregnable, and by April the member of parliament was being warned that he might lose his seat at the next election. The victories of the Dundas interest in the county meetings had prevented certain defeat, but they had not ensured victory at a general election. Indeed, after studying the electoral roll, Innes advised Sir Thomas that both he and the convener were

> very apprehensive you will lose the county at the next election unless you *immediately* make great exertions and add to the number of your friends. In these circumstances we would recommend to you to come to Scotland as soon as possible that you may, *before* any other candidate appear, secure those who are doubtful or unengaged ... [39]

The survey of the freeholders which prompted Innes' warning was made in April, 1789, and it disclosed that although the roll then contained 74 names, no fewer than nineteen of them were dead or divested of the lands for which they voted, while another three would be unable to attend, leaving 52 potential voters. According to the calculations of the Dundas party, Sir Thomas could rely upon the support of 26 voters, thus leaving 26 who might oppose him, a balance which was too close for any sense of comfort should the Administration put a good candidate into the field against the incumbent. [40] Some of the difficulties which Sir Thomas faced had been caused by attacks of conscience which had affected some of his nominal voters, for his losses were not among the real freeholders, but among the fictitious ones, whose qualifications had been created by the Dundas family, a setback which flowed from some of the harsh things which judges had recently said about such votes. One of the nominals, Harry Davidson, wrote to the member of parliament, to inform him that he could

> by no means continue to hold the above qualification, without paying to you the full value of it, and when I pay you the value, I shall consider myself at perfect liberty to act upon it fully and freely, at my own pleasure and discretion, without any supposed confidence or honorary engagement whatever towards you or your family, but will act in any manner agreable to myself, and vote for or against you, as it may suit my inclinations at the time. Upon these terms I shall be ready to settle and pay the value, but if they are not agreable to you I shall immediately divest myself of my qualification ... [41]

Davidson's attitude, which was shared by a number of his nominal voter colleagues, clearly added an unexpected element of uncertainty to the political picture. If the qualifying superiority was not sold to Davidson, for example, Sir Thomas Dundas would certainly lose one of his voters, yet if he sold the qualification it might be employed against him.

The erosion of the majority normally available for Sir Thomas Dundas through desertions and deaths gave the managers of the interest reason to feel concern, for the prospect of new claimants coming onto the roll could turn the balance decisively against them. Charles Innes, in particular, was evidently greatly alarmed by the danger posed by new claims, advising Sir Thomas that

> Mr. Morehead & I see so much danger from the force that can & undoubtedly will be brought against you by some of the Carron Inn Junta, Lord Graham, the Duke of Hamilton, Sir A. Edmonstone, Sir W. Murray, Mr. Johnstone etc. that we are very apprehensive of the consequences, the more especially as Sir Archd.[Edmonstone] has no less than eleven votes ready to come on the roll, and to be used against you, while on the other hand we hardly know one in condition to come on the roll who may be friendly . . . [42]

There were in fact 23 potential claimants, who had been in possession of the lands which constituted their qualifications for the necessary time to allow them to be considered for admission to the roll, and twelve of these qualifications, not the eleven suggested by Innes, were votes made by Sir Archibald Edmonstone of Duntreath. Of the remaining claimants, one might be discounted, for he was disqualified from voting by reason of his office under the crown, while another two were in India and were thus unlikely to attend a meeting for some time. On the other hand, even the usually optimistic legal advisers of the member of parliament did not expect that he could gain the support of more than five of the new admissions, and that the remainder would be friends of Duntreath or the gentlemen of Carron Inn. If those calculations were correct, Sir Thomas Dundas stood to lose his election by a margin of ten votes:

pro [Sir Thomas Dundas]	26	Contra	26[43]
pro to be inrolled	5	Contra to be inrolled	15
	31		41

The picture which was emerging from the calculations of the Dundas interest strongly suggested that it was in the power of Sir Archibald Edmonstone to decide the next county election in favour of a ministerial candidate, assuming of course that he could arrange for his nominal voters to be admitted to the electoral roll before the dissolution of Parliament, while in the background there was a more remote danger, but which might yet become real, of the creation of additional votes by the Duke of Hamilton, upon whose estate qualifications had been made in 1774 and not subsequently employed, while the Montrose estates could contribute another flood of fictitious voters to tilt the balance even more conclusively against Dundas. The immediate threat, however, was the votes created by Sir Archibald Edmonstone who were not as yet upon the roll. Accordingly, if something could be made of the existing roll, all was not yet lost for Sir Thomas Dundas, whose own lawyers were hastily completing the sale of two qualifications to friends lacking votes in the county.[44] If the interest could retain control of the old roll on the day upon which the new claims would be considered, they could admit their own friends and find reasons to deny the claims of the enemies, at least postponing their admission to the roll, perhaps until after the election.

Sir Thomas Dundas was not the greatest asset possessed by the Dundas interest in Stirlingshire. In spite of repeated warnings of the growing threat to his position, and advice that in this crisis he should renew his contacts with the voters, Sir Thomas did not appear in Stirlingshire. By the summer of 1789 the member of parliament's absence was attracting wider attention, with his enemies beginning to say openly that they did not expect to see him in Scotland. Sir Thomas Dundas was in poor health, and there was thus some excuse for his reluctance to leave the comfort of his Yorkshire residence for the tribulations of a tour among the lairds of Stirlingshire. Unfortunately, however, for those who had to manage the interest in his absence, that Yorkshire estate was also very well situated to permit its owner to travel to the races at York and Richmond, events which were well reported in the sporting press with full details of the important personages in attendance. No one was more ready to take offence at an appearance of neglect than a Scottish freeholder, and by his readiness to place the racing calendar ahead of his constituency duties Sir Thomas Dundas was weakening the personal bonds between politician and constituents which were still a major element in the strength of an interest, and equally, if Sir Thomas' health was too poor for extensive travel, his son, Lawrence Dundas, should have been active on his behalf.[45] It might in fact be inferred that it may have been the prolonged absence of Sir Thomas rather than the bad weather which reduced the attendance of the friends of the interest at the third county meeting in Stirling. Sir Thomas' liking for the sport of kings was well known, and few gentlemen freeholders would hold a love of horse racing against him, but it was surely misguided in a politician faced with a serious challenge from Administration to refuse a request from a leading baron of the county for his attendance at a meeting in favour of reform of the royal burghs. Sir Thomas was a known supporter of burgh reform, and sincere in his support for this campaign, but he pleaded sickness as his excuse for non-attendance, and then attempted to emphasise the parlous state of his health by expressing doubt of his ability to join the Prince of Wales at York Races.[46] Sir Thomas' correspondent, not surprisingly, had a different order of priorities, and was unlikely to have been encouraged to greater efforts on behalf of a candidate for office who would not act to enhance his own political profile in his constituency.

By August 5th, 1789, it had been placed beyond any doubt that opposition was intended at the forthcoming election, for on that day Robert Belsches of Greenyards, one of the Carron Inn Junta, lodged objections to the qualifications of twenty-six of the freeholders presently on the Stirlingshire roll, all of whom, needless to say, were supporters of Sir Thomas Dundas. Belsches' action was so extreme that even the lethargic Sir Thomas was stirred to movement, and he was in fact present at the Michaelmas Head Court in Stirling on October 6th, where he was chosen preses of the meeting in a sparsely attended court.[47] On the other hand, even if the Dundas party were able to take control of the meeting at the outset, that did not mean that they could arrange all of the business to their advantage. There was no difficulty striking off the roll the names of seven freeholders who had died since the roll was last made up, but when it was time to hear the objections lodged by Robert Belsches against the freeholders in the interest of Sir Thomas Dundas, the latter had to bear in mind the deeply entrenched hostility towards nominal voters which existed in the county. It would have been politically unwise to have simply used the Dundas majority in a thinly attended meeting to repel all objections and uphold votes which were demonstrably fictitious, and in fact no effort was made to do so. Accordingly the freeholders present struck off the roll fifteen freeholders against whom Belsches had lodged objections,[48] for this time the gentlemen of Carron Inn had prepared their ground well and offered convincing documentation suggesting the nominality of these qualifications. Some of the losses were anticipated, for voters like Harry Davidson, who had no intention of taking the trust oath if it were put to him, could never have been retained. Others, however, were more unexpected, for the attack upon the vote of John Francis Erskine of Mar, and James Erskine, Lord Alva, as liferenter and fiar respectively of the estate of Mar, had not been predicted, and that vote had been regarded as a safe one for Sir Thomas Dundas.[49] The member of parliament's friends, however, successfully defended three voters against whom Belsches had instituted proceedings, and Robert Belsches did not proceed with his charges against another eight freeholders, suggesting that these had been lodged for no sound reason.

With the roll purged, it was then time to consider the new claims, nine of which were lodged for the Michaelmas meeting of 1789, and eight of them were accepted without difficulty. The remaining claimant, however, was Sir Alexander Campbell of Ardkinglas, the son of the late Sir James Campbell who had represented Stirlingshire in Parliament until 1768, and the friends of Sir Thomas Dundas had good reason, therefore, to suspect that this gentleman was intended to be the candidate who would contest the seat for Administration. Sir Alexander was an army officer serving in India and was represented at the head court by a Stirling writer, who presented a claim to a vote as an apparent heir to the superiority possessed by Sir Alexander's late father. The Dundas interest promptly rejected this inconvenient claim, citing as their reason alleged discrepancies between the dates given in the claim and those in the vouchers submitted in evidence, and ambiguity in the naming of the lands in the valuation certificate and other documents.[50] The rejection of Campbell showed the hand of an experienced political manager, for in the circumstances which prevailed in the last months of 1789 there were only two serious potential rivals who might take the field against Sir Thomas Dundas, one of whom, Sir Archibald Edmonstone, although a ministerialist, categorically denied all knowledge of a plan to oppose the incumbent, and there was no reason to doubt his word. Accordingly, the field was restricted to Ardkinglas, who with his claim to a vote had inherited the remains of his father's Stirlingshire interest, and appeared likely to have the support of the agents of government. The Carron Inn group might afford rank and file support for a government candidate, but none of them were possessed of a substantial interest of their own, as their performance in the county meetings would indicate, and such an interest was a prerequisite for a serious attack upon an established politician.

The successful exclusion of Sir Alexander Campbell's name from the freeholders roll gave Sir Thomas Dundas an important tactical advantage, for it obliged the candidate of Administration to enter a claim for admission to the voters roll at the election meeting in which he hoped to be chosen to represent the shire, and if he should fail to secure a place in the roll, he could not be elected member of parliament. The suspicion that Sir Alexander was to be the man to oppose Sir Thomas Dundas was soon confirmed, for by the spring of 1790 Henry Dundas, the government manager for Scotland, had made it clear that he intended to add Stirlingshire to his political empire, and proposed to use Sir Alexander Campbell of Ardkinglas as his intrument. William Morehead, writing to General Fletcher Campbell, another of Sir Thomas' friends, remarked that

> The Treasurer of the Navy has at length raised up a competitor to Sir T. Dundas in this county. I have intelligence that Sir Alex Campbell is on the road if not already arrived to begin his canvas, backed with the interest of administration, that of Sir Arch. Edmonstoun, and what can be collected of the late Sir James's interest . . . [51]

The friends of Sir Thomas Dundas responded to the new danger in a manner similar to that in which they had combated the efforts of the Carron Inn Junta. A group of active and influential freeholders undertook to solicit the support of their friends and acquaintances throughout the shire,[52] a practice which had been followed by this interest from its inception, for the interest which Sir Thomas headed was essentially a coalition of many smaller interests. General Fletcher Campbell, one of the active members of the group, even suggested the formation of a formal committee to direct the campaign,[53] a plan which would have had the merit of associating a larger number of freeholders with the planning of the canvass, but there was hostility among the inner circle to this idea, the feeling being that such a committee would prove unwieldy. Co-ordination was in fact left to Charles Innes, Sir Thomas Dundas' principal political agent in Scotland, but Innes in turn divided the duties of visiting and cultivating the freeholders among several of the principal barons of the interest, for this was one of those occasions when nominal voters would be an embarrassment, and indeed attention could hardly be drawn to their existence when speaking to the real freeholders. Sir Thomas himself did not fail to pay the compliment to his leading supporters of asking for their advice,[54] but as usual he did it fairly late in the campaign, and effective management was throughout in the hands of Charles Innes and the major resident freeholders associated with the interest.

In approaching the freeholders of Stirlingshire, the friends of Sir Thomas Dundas had a new argument to put forward. One effect of the decisions taken at the Michaelmas meeting of October 1789 was that the roll had been purged of practically all of the freeholders in Sir Thomas Dundas' interest who possessed doubtful qualifications. It was now possible to point out to the real freeholders that Sir Thomas stood to lose his election through the votes of nominal freeholders created by Sir Archibald Edmonstone, for that gentleman had been easily persuaded by Henry Dundas to throw his weight behind the candidate favoured by Administration. 'Every thing', in short, would 'depend on the consciences of Sir Archd Edmonstones nominal voters',[55] who, if they insisted upon their right to vote, could crush the known friends of Sir Thomas Dundas by weight of numbers. On the other hand, the threat of an election victory for Administration obtained through the votes of fictitious freeholders was an argument which could carry weight with real freeholders who under other circumstances might not be attracted to Sir Thomas Dundas' politics, and it was an argument which was advanced with some vigour by the member of parliament's allies.

Contrary to popular belief, moreover, it was not unknown for the holder of a nominal qualification to suffer from an attack of conscience at an election meeting, and according to Henry Erskine, some of the gentlemen to whom Sir Archibald Edmonstone had given votes were men of so nice a sense of honour that they would be unlikely to take the trust oath, which was hardly the best choice for the maker of tied votes to have made. In Erskine's opinion:

> Some ... will not take the oath, James Ferrier is one, Campbell of Fairfield is also one of them. He is now in London. If you press him I am confident he will stay away from the election. Col[onel] Lyon will not swear. This I am assured of by Harry Bethune to whom he said so ... [56]

A landowner who gave nominal qualifications to men with too many scruples was engaging in an expensive and time-wasting exercise, and indeed, should one man refuse the oath of trust there was a danger that the example would prove contagious, and other voters, normally more pliant, might decline to perjure themselves by swearing that they were in absolute and unfettered possession of the lands which constituted their qualifications. Erskine's advice at least gave some hope to the Dundas interest when the freeholders assembled to choose their representative on July 6th, 1790, when 53 voters attended the meeting at Stirling.[57]

The freeholders immediately divided upon the question of the choise of preses of the meeting, Sir Thomas Dundas being proposed by Robert Graham of Gartmore, while Sir Alexander Campbell's friends suggested James Bruce of Kinnaird, but although the vote was close, Sir Thomas carried this first step of the meeting by 27 votes to 26.[58] This division can be considered in another manner, for if the voting for preses had been by real as opposed to nominal voters, Sir Thomas Dundas would have had a much more convincing majority. Of the 27 who voted for Sir Thomas as preses, only five were nominal voters, whereas of the 26 who supported the interest of the candidate of Administration no fewer than eleven were nominal voters in origin, although one of that number, Dr. James Hay, who had obtained his vote from the late Sir James Campbell, considered himself sufficiently independent to have offered the vote for sale.[59]

With Sir Thomas Dundas in the chair the remainder of the election meeting proceeded in the normal way. Eleven new claims were presented to the meeting, eight of them in the interest of Sir Alexander Campbell and three friends of Sir Thomas Dundas. Of the eleven, only four were added to the roll, but all three of Sir Thomas' friends were found duly qualified to vote, while of the claimants favourable to Sir Alexander Campbell only one, William Forbes of Callender, whose estate was one of the largest in the county, was found acceptable. [60] The trust oath was freely administered, which was sufficient to rid the roll of two of Sir Alexander Campbell's friends, Colonel Lyon and Colonel Duncan, who declined to swear. However, on this occasion the freeholders did not content themselves with the oath of trust and possession for, in line with the apparent intentions of the Court of Session and the House of Lords to take a more determined stand against fictitious votes, additional and more searching questions were put to suspected voters.

One of the voters whom Henry Erskine believed would hesitate to take the trust oath did not in fact refuse to take it, although his qualification was clearly of doubtful independence. James Ferrier was qualified by his possession of a liferent of superiority and Colonel Dundas, one of the freeholders present in the interest of the member of parliament, proposed that Ferrier should take the trust oath, demanding in addition that Ferrier should tell the freeholders whether this superiority formed part of the entailed estate of the Duke of Argyll, who employed Ferrier as his legal agent. Ferrier did not have much difficulty disposing of the question of the legality of his qualification, at least to his own satisfaction, for he replied that

> altho he did not consider the question as regular, he would answer it, but would first take the liberty of explaining the nature of his freehold which he had now held for 16 years without challenge, the gift of a nobleman to whom he owes many favours. The freehold has produced to him betwixt four and five pounds sterling yearly, and he has entered vassals from whom he has received considerable compositions, particularly one of near L60 Sterling from a gentleman now present, Mr. Dunmore. That in these circumstances he feels the most thorough conviction in his own mind that this is neither a nominal or fictitious estate, altho it makes part of the Dukedom of Argyle, which is certainly held under an entail. Whereupon [as the freeholders minute book recorded], Mr. Ferrier took the said oath.[61]

The connection between James Ferrier and the estate of Argyll, evident though it was and acknowledged by the voter, was insufficient ground to justify expunging his name from the roll and the lawyer was left in peace.

At the election of 1790 fifteen freeholders were asked to take the oath of trust and possession, and six of them were more closely examined, and although only the two gentlemen who actually refused to take the oath were struck off the roll, the effect of the questions was sufficient to induce two more of Sir Alexander Campbell's friends to request that their names be removed from the roll as they were divested of the qualifications for which they had claimed a right to vote. The attack upon nominal voters was not all from one side, however, for nominality was also alleged against one of the successful claimants, William Morehead, younger of Herbertshire, the son of the convener, who claimed a vote for certain lands in the parish of Dunipace which he held in liferent and had obtained from his father. The Campbell party objected that young Herbertshire was seeking admission to the roll with a fictitious qualification created only for the purpose of giving him a vote. Morehead, however, responded by offering to take the trust oath although he declined to answer any more searching questions, and argued that a liferent given by a father to his eldest son, who would in due course inherit the fee, was less objectionable than a similar liferent given to a stranger, but it was his connection with the majority which carried young Herbertshire's name into the roll. [62]

The arguments of the contestants, and the manipulation of the meeting by the party which first secured a majority, should not, however, obscure the fact that there was a real issue in this election, apart from the desire of Sir Thomas Dundas to retain his parliamentary seat. The 1790 election was also a contest to determine if the genuine freeholders of Stirlingshire could preserve some measure of freedom of election, for there was a very real danger that such a mass of nominal voters would be introduced to the roll, whether those already made or those who might yet be made, that the only interest left in the county would be that of Henry Dundas and Administration. Had the government faction taken control of the meeting and added all of the nominal voters whom they had ready, they could have terminated all further political controversy in Stirlingshire and made the member of parliament the nominee of Henry Dundas, as had happened in other constituencies.

The freeholders minute book for this period affords evidence of this contention, for four of the claimants in the interest of Sir Alexander Campbell were qualified by liferents of superiority disponed to them by Sir Archibald Edmonstone of Duntreath, a supporter of Administration with the ability to make more votes from the superiorities of the Kilsyth estate. Two of the claimants were younger sons of the Laird of Duntreath, and failing a family quarrel they would be likely to vote as the head of their house directed. A third of Duntreath's voters, Colonel Ilay Ferrier, was a former officer of the Dutch army, who had resigned his commission in 1783, and who now hoped to secure employment in the British service at an appropriate rank, an ambition which was more likely to be successfully obtained by careful attention to the wishes of Government. The fourth of Duntreath's voters, James Cheap, was the only one with a real connection with Stirlingshire, having once been a freeholder in his own right, and Cheap had actually purchased his qualification and had paid a good price for it. Cheap had no doubt of the reality of his qualification, but he was nonetheless a friend of Government who would be unlikely to differ in his political opinions with the Laird of Duntreath, and there is some reason to believe that even that vote was given in confidence and that all four were, as Sir Thomas' party alleged, 'calculated solely to increase the political interest of Sir Archibald Edmonstone'.[63]

The freeholders rejected other claimants on technical grounds, including one of the founders of the Carron Inn Junta, Colonel Andrew Bruce, who had persisted in his hostility to Sir Thomas Dundas in spite of the reconciliation of his father, Sir Michael, with the member of parliament. Bruce had a qualification independent of his father's estate, but unfortunately for him the lands for which he claimed a vote were not described in the books of supply by the same names under which they were detailed in Colonel Bruce's charter, and his claim was accordingly rejected.[64] The majority were equally decisive in dealing with a deserter from their ranks, for James Erskine, lord Alva of the Court of Session, had arranged for a vote to be prepared for him based on portions of the estate of Mar, of which his nephew, James

Francis Erskine, was liferenter and Lord Alva was fiar. When the judge presented his claim, however, it proved to be incomplete, for his charter had 'been most improperly withheld from him for the purpose of preventing him from voting at this election by a gentleman now present in the interest of Sir Thomas Dundas'.[65] As James Francis Erskine was still an adherent of Sir Thomas Dundas and was present at the meeting, and the same charter was used by both him and his uncle, it appears likely that it was the nephew who had concealed the vital Mar charter without which there could be no question of adding Lord Alva to the roll.

The most significant of the rejected claims was that of the rival candidate, for Sir Alexander Campbell of Ardkinglas was no more successful at the election meeting than he had been at the Michaelmas court. Campbell claimed a right to vote as his father's heir in the barony of Gargunnock, but all of the estates of the late Sir James Campbell were in the hands of trustees, and it was this fact which the majority cited as grounds for rejecting the claim. Of course the major defect in Sir Alexander's title was not his inherited burden of debt and his uncertain tenure of the family estates, it was his decision to oppose Sir Thomas Dundas, for it would have demanded a much more unexceptionable title than Campbell possessed to have overcome the hostility of the Dundas party and left them without an excuse to eliminate a rival who was unfortunate enough not to be already upon the roll.[66]

The result of the election could not have surprised anyone present at the meeting, for Sir Thomas Dundas was re-elected by 28 votes to 22,[67] with four freeholders abstaining from the final vote. Had all of the claimants been added to the roll the result might have been very different, for with the addition of Sir Alexander Campbell's own vote, Sir Archibald Edmonstone's four, Colonel Andrew Bruce and Lord Alva, Sir Alexander should have carried the question by one vote. There is, however, some uncertainty about that transformation, although it appealed to the loser, for of the four gentlemen present who abstained from the final vote, three were friends of Sir Thomas Dundas and only one was an ally of Campbell. Would the abstainers have stood by and seen Sir Thomas defeated?

Sir Alexander Campbell, no doubt sustained by his knowledge of Henry Dundas' friendship, was not discouraged by his defeat and felt confident enough of ultimate success to take his protest to the House of Commons, a move which ensured that the election of 1790 continued to be fought long after the votes had been counted and result declared. The Michaelmas meeting of October 5th, 1790 was in fact a continuation of the election meeting, as the parties attempted to add to their strength in anticipation of another election. Sir Alexander Campbell's friends attempted at the Michaelmas meeting to make difficulties for Sir Thomas Dundas, in spite of the fact that they were in the minority, for they refrained from proposing one of their own friends for the position of preses of the meeting and instead named a strong-willed, and often wrong-headed, friend of Sir Thomas, and they in fact carried the election of Robert Graham of Gartmore by 18 votes to 10.[68] If they hoped that this result would produce division within the Dundas interest, however, they were mistaken, for thereafter Sir Thomas Dundas carried all before him. Three voters in Sir Alexander's interest, who had obtained their qualifications from the Duke of Argyll or from the late Laird of Ardkinglas, were struck off the roll, while an objection offered to one of Sir Thomas' friends, James Francis Erskine of Mar, was repelled. All of the successful claimants admitted to the roll were in the interest of Sir Thomas Dundas with a single exception, and that individual was disqualified from voting by reason of his office, and any possibility that this gentleman might free himself to cast a vote was removed by the fact of his serious financial difficulties which would prevent him from sacrificing his office of profit.

Before the end of 1790 Sir Thomas Dundas had therefore added three additional votes to his strength and appeared to be out of danger, but in the course of the winter the Court of Session, in a series of decisions unfavourable to the majority of the Stirlingshire freeholders, placed Sir Thomas' political future once more in jeopardy. On December 14th, 1790 the lords of session ordered the freeholders to add to their roll the name of Sir Alexander Campbell of Ardkinglas, and followed by requiring that four more of Sir Alexander's friends be admitted to the roll and three of Sir Thomas' party removed. The effect of the court decisions made the outcome of another election, should Sir Alexander's petition succeed, appear very uncertain. The decisions of the court, in the opinion of Henry Erskine, were politically motivated for, as he suggested,

> the Court of Session ... had never much decency, but in the Stirling cause they have thrown aside all shame ... as long as the House of Commons permit them to have any jurisdiction in election cases, so long must we expect to be under the guidance of every Minister, Instill this into your friend who is so warm an advocate for emancipation of Negroes, let him be so keen to free his fellow subjects in N[orth] B[ritain] ... [69]

The House of Commons, however, proved to be less subservient to the wishes of Henry Dundas than the Court of Session was believed to be, and the fact that Sir Thomas Dundas was a well-known and popular member while Sir Alexander Campbell was an unknown must have further strengthened his position, for Sir Thomas Dundas was not exposed to the hazard of another contest, which would clearly have been closely fought. Sir Thomas Dundas did not in fact have to fight another election again, for when he entered the Government with the Duke of Portland in 1794, he was awarded a peerage. The Stirlingshire seat which Lord Dundas vacated passed without opposition to Robert Graham of Gartmore, a popular freeholder associated with the interest of Lord Dundas, and at the subsequent general election the seat passed to a representative of the Elphinstone family, who were also allies of Lord Dundas and just as hostile as he had been to Henry Dundas' dominance of Scottish politics.

The successful retention of a county seat of some importance for an extended period of time by an opposition politician suggests that minister-managers were less all-powerful than popular opinion believed and they themselves liked to imply. Henry Dundas had been an arch-enemy of Sir Lawrence Dundas, the founder of the Stirlingshire interest, for they had clashed bitterly over Edinburgh politics, and Henry Dundas' enmity had followed Sir Thomas Dundas thereafter.

Yet Sir Thomas Dundas' retention of the seat was clearly not the result of his own outstanding abilities as a political manager. Great wealth and Indian patronage were assets which could be employed to advantage, but given the reluctance of Sir Thomas Dundas to undertake the burdensome duties expected of a county member of parliament, it is evident that the survival of the interest was due in large part to the participation in its management of a group of influential and active associates, drawn from the freeholders of Stirlingshire, who were willing to handle the social side of building an interest which the nominal leader neglected.

NOTES

1. John Ramsay: *Scotland and Scotsmen in the Eighteenth Century* [Edinburgh, 1888], 1, 154.

2. SRO. SC67/59/ 4/68.

3. North Riding Record Office. Zetland MS.ZNK/X/1/2, Thomas Dundas of Fingask to Sir Lawrence Dundas, 22 Dec., 1773.

4. Ibid. MS.ZNK/X/2, from Thomas Dundas of Castlecary, 5 Oct., 1775.

5. Ibid.

6. Ibid., William Morehead of Herbertshire to Thomas Dundas of Castlecary, 17 Oct., 1778.

7. Ibid., John Munro of Auchenbowie to Sir Thomas Dundas, 22 Mar., 1789.

8. Ibid., William Morehead to Sir Thomas Dundas, 2 Jan., 1789.

9. Ibid.

10. Ibid., from Henry Erskine, 3 Jan., 1789.

11. SRO. Cunninghame-Graham, GD22/1/315, Henry Erskine to Robert Graham of Gartmore, 2 Jan., 1789.

12. North Riding Record Office. Zetland ZNK/X/2, from Charles Innes, 2 Jan., 1789.

13. NLS. Saltoun MS.16738, William Morehead to General Fletcher Campbell, 6 Jan., 1789.

14. North Riding Record Office. Zetland ZNK/X/2, 'Extract of a letter from Stirling, 9th January 1789, intended to have been insert in the Mercury'.

15. Ibid.

16. Ibid., 'Minutes of the Stirling Meeting, 9th Jan., 1789'.

17. Ibid.

18. Ibid., from William Morehead, 10 Jan., 1789.

19. Ibid., from Charles Innes, 24 Jan., 1789.

20. Ibid., from Henry Erskine, 3 Jan., 1789.

21. Ibid., from William Morehead, 10 Jan., 1789.

22. Ibid., from Charles Innes, 24 Jan., 1789.

23. Ibid.

24. Ibid.

25. SRO. Cunninghame-Graham, GD22/1/315, Lord Fincastle to Robert Graham of Gartmore, 14 Jan., 1789.

26. Ibid.

27. North Riding Record Office. Zetland ZNK/X/2, Charles Innes to Sir Thomas Dundas, 3 Feb., 1789.

28. Ibid., from Charles Innes, 28 Jan., 1789.

29. Ibid., from Charles Innes, 3 Feb., 1789.

30. Ibid., 'Minutes of the Stirlingshire Meeting, 14 Feb., 1789'.

31. Ibid.

32. Ibid., from Charles Innes, 31 Mar., 1789.

33. Ronald M. Sunter, Stirlingshire Politics, 1707–1832, Edinburgh Ph.D., 1971, 381–385.

34. North Riding Record Office. Zetland ZNK/X/2, from Charles Innes, 31 Mar., 1789.

35. Ibid.

36. Ibid.

37. Ibid.

38. Donald Ginter, *Whig Organization in the General Election of 1790* [Berkeley, 1967], 51–2, Laurence Hill to William Adam, 6 Apr., 1789.

39. North Riding Record Office. Zetland ZNK/X/2, from Charles Innes, 6 Apr., 1789.

40. Ibid., 'Roll of Freeholders, Stirlingshire, 17th April, 1789'.

41. Ibid., from Harry Davidson, 3 Mar., 1789.

42. Ibid., from Charles Innes, 6 Apr., 1789.

43. Ibid., 'List of Freeholders who are ready to be inrolled and to vote at next Election'.

44. Ibid., from Charles Innes, 4 Jul., 1789.

45. Ibid., from Charles Innes, 29 Jul., 1789.

46. SRO. Cunninghame-Grahame, GD22/ 1/315, Sir Thomas Dundas to Robert Graham of Gartmore, 17 Aug., 1789.

47. SRO. SC67/59/4/281, Stirling Freeholders Minute Book.

48. North Riding Record Office. Zetland ZNK/X/2, 'Gentlemen whose names stand on the roll at present, but cannot vote and must be struck off'.

49. SRO. SC67/59/4/284.

50. SRO. SC67/59/4/306.

51. NLS. Saltoun MS.16739, William Morehead to General Campbell, 6 Mar., 1789.

52. Ibid., Charles Innes to General Campbell, undated.

53. Ibid., from Charles Campbell, also undated.

54. Ibid., Sir Thomas Dundas to General Campbell, 22 Jun., 1790.

55. North Riding Record Office. Zetland ZNK/X/2, from Henry Erskine, 23 Mar., 1790.

56. Ibid.

57. SRO. SC67/59/4/316–7, Stirling Freeholders Minute Book.

58. Ibid., SC67/59/4/318.

59. Sir Charles Elphinstone Adam, *The Political State of Scotland in 1788* [Edinburgh, 1887], 328.

60. SRO. SC67/59/4/339, Stirlingshire Freeholders Minute Book.

61. Ibid., SC67/59/4/323.

62. Ibid., SC67/59/4/337–8.

63. Ibid., SC67/59/345–7.

64. Ibid., SC67/59/4/339.

65. Ibid., SC67/59/4/344.

66. Ibid., SC67/59/4/357–362.

67. Ibid. SC67/59/4/363–4.

68. Ibid., SC67/59/5/1–2.

69. North Riding Record Office. Zetland ZNK/X/2, from Henry Erskine, 16 Feb., 1791.

7

The Destruction of a Political Interest: Berwickshire and Lord Marchmont, 1779–80

Berwickshire in 1779–80 affords an example of the self-destruction of a political interest which had, prior to that period, named the Member of Parliament for at least a century.[1] This was a county with one very powerful interest, that of the Earl of Marchmont, who successfully influenced many of the smaller lairds, of whom there were an unusually large number.[2] The great Marchmont interest destroyed itself by making a wrong choice of candidate, for as Henry Dundas once pointed out, the choice of candidate was vital. The individual chosen was not a matter of indifference to the freeholders,[3] even when they were otherwise willing to take a lead from a great landowner. The events which unfolded in Berwickshire, moreover, provide a good illustration of the danger of seeking the support of enemies to secure an immediate political advantage. The successful candidate in this contest secured his place by a compromise with a rival group, but the success so obtained proved to be Pyrrhic victory, for a seat in parliament, obtained at very high personal cost, could not be retained in face of the reviving hostility of temporary allies, who undoubtedly got the best of the bargain.

The dominant interest, headed by the elderly Hugh Hume, third earl of Marchmont, had met with some relatively ineffective opposition some years earlier from the rival branch of his family, the Homes, earls of Home,[4] and although the much greater wealth and territorial base of the Marchmonts prevented Home's enmity from becoming a serious threat to Marchmont's control of the county, the very extent of the latter's dominance was liable to cause resentment, and Marchmont was fortunate in having as the representative of his interest chosen by the freeholders, James Pringle, a gentleman popular with most of the gentry of Berwickshire. Pringle represented the county from 1761 to 1779, and had he continued in Parliament Marchmont would in all probability have continued to name the member of Parliament until the end of his life, for a popular candidate and the gratitude and goodwill built up by many years of successful distribution of patronage made the Earl of Marchmont's interest formidable.

Pringle, however, decided that he would not again be a candidate at the next general election, and notified his friend Lord Marchmont of his intention, which of course, for the first time for many years, raised the question of an alternative candidate to represent the Marchmont interest.[5]

Lord Marchmont had been active in politics as early as 1734, when he first sat in the House of Commons as the representative of Berwick-upon-Tweed, and had been a representative Scottish peer without intermission from 1750. The earl held government office, as Keeper of the Great Seal of Scotland,[6] and had been accustomed over a long period to exercise power and see his will as paramount in the county of Berwick. Lord Marchmont's desire to impose his will upon others led the earl into a disastrous error of judgement, which not only divided the county, but split his own family and broke the strength of the Marchmont interest in Berwickshire. Faced with the impending retirement of Pringle, whose 'chief pride and satisfaction in being in Parliament' was that he 'had the happiness to enjoy the confidence and favour of the County',[7] Lord Marchmont determined to replace him with a gentleman of unusual unpopularity, Sir John Paterson of Eccles.

Paterson, in sharp contrast to his well-liked predecessor, was described in a document produced during the ensuing political turmoil as

> a man whose sentiments are mean and whose conduct is contemptible, who is only known in his neighbourhood by pitifull squables with his tenants and dependents, who has become famous in the County Courts for unjust and trifling law suits with servants, tradesmen and shopkeepers, and infamous in the Supreme Courts for knavish attempts of a greater magnitude ... [8]

The litigious Sir John, however, had one substantial asset in his favour in Lord Marchmont's eyes: he was his son-in-law.[9] Sir John's object in seeking to enter parliament was mercenary — he hoped to secure a crown office for himself — and Pringle's impending departure created the necessary opportunity. Accordingly, probably at Paterson's prompting, Lord Marchmont persuaded Pringle to resign the seat in advance of the general election by securing for the outgoing M.P. the right to retain his office of Master of Works.[10] That resignation, moreover, was arranged without any prior notice reaching the gentlemen of Berwickshire, who were thus deprived of an opportunity to organise any realistic opposition to the candidate put forward by Lord Marchmont, and Sir John Paterson was duly elected to represent the county for the balance of the parliament at a by-election on 15th April 1779. The election of Paterson 'by Lord Marchmont's influence before the electors in generall had time to form any plan for opposing him'[11] was the cause of considerable disquiet in the county, not merely among those who would normally have been enemies of the Marchmont interest, but even among those who should have been regarded as its sure friends. Perhaps if Lord Marchmont's own influence in government circles had been greater, the error would not have been too serious, for if Paterson had been quickly provided with a suitable place and as rapidly replaced as the candidate of the Marchmont interest by someone more popular with the freeholders, there would have been no lasting damage. Unfortunately, however, Marchmont was unable to secure such a place for his son-in-law, who would therefore, in all probability, wish to continue for another parliament.

Among those unhappy with Lord Marchmont's nomination of Sir John Paterson, with no pretence of consultation with the gentlemen of the shire, must be included some of the other members of the earl's own family, in particular his grandson, Hugh Scott, younger of Harden, whose mother was Lord Marchmont's youngest daughter, and even Marchmont's only son, Alexander Hume, Lord Polwarth, whose possession of a peerage of Great Britain,[12] combined with the advanced age of the earl [who had been born in 1708], made his opinions more significant than would normally have been the case with a dependent son. Lord Polwarth did not openly oppose his father, but he was clearly behind his nephew, when Hugh Scott decided to come forward as a candidate at the general election.

Hugh Scott advised his grandfather that 'many who voted at last will not willingly vote the same way at the next', and suggested that he would himself make a better standard-bearer for the Marchmont interest in view of Sir John Paterson's unpopularity. [13] The Scotts of Harden were themselves important landowners in the region: Walter Scott of Harden, Hugh's father, was the chief of the Scott family,[14] and after Lord Polwarth, who was childless, Hugh Scott was Marchmont's heir. A young man, who had not yet had an opportunity to make enemies, with personal influence and closely connected to the Earl of Marchmont, would appear to be an unexceptionable candidate and indeed, as Hugh told his friend and uncle, Lord Polwarth, he was not given an immediate refusal by his grandfather: 'Lord M[archmont] ... as far as I can observe ... seems far from determined to push the present scheme with vigour, if he was convinced it was not popular'.[15] On the other hand, if Scott did not meet with a hostile reception, he received no encouragement either, which appears to have been anticipated by Polwarth, who seems to have had similar experiences with his father. Polwarth remarked to his nephew shortly after the by-election and Hugh's approach to his grandfather that

> A superior has it always in his power to avoid entering on subjects he dislikes, & there are people who are perfect masters of the art of saying the most when they mean the least, rendering their meaning unintelligible, & laying in for the power of saying hereafter that they had given you advice wch you neglected, & consequently blaming you, act as you please ... [16]

If Hugh Scott took his lukewarm reception by Lord Marchmont to indicate that he would not incur his grandfather's anger by coming forward as a candidate, he was to be rapidly disillusioned.

Hugh Scott did not intend to oppose the Marchmont interest, rather he hoped to be the means of saving that interest from the consequences of an error of judgement and to hold it together for his friend Polwarth, whose succession was unlikely to be long delayed in view of his father's age. Indeed, Polwarth was much more insistent upon Hugh Scott coming forward as a candidate than the latter was to act decisively and possibly come into conflict with his intimidating grandfather, contemplating at first no more than a canvass by the two competitors, to determine whether Paterson, the sitting member, or himself would be most acceptable to the gentlemen of Berwickshire, with both candidates equally representative of the Marchmont interest. This, however, was to reckon without the determination of Lord Marchmont to give the county a candidate of *his* choice, for the approach contemplated by Hugh Scott clearly put the choice of candidate in the hands of the freeholders in reality as well as in constitutional theory, and that had never been the situation in Berwickshire in Lord Marchmont's lifetime. When he persisted in his intention to canvass the county, Hugh was told bluntly that he should not divide the interest lest he open the way for another party to take control of the election and return an enemy of the Marchmonts, while this denial was reinforced by letters to the freeholders from Sir John Paterson informing them that he had not engaged in any compromise and would himself be a candidate at the next general election.[17] With the door to Marchmont's support closed so abruptly, Hugh Scott appears to have been contemplating acquiescence in his grandfather's wishes, for he was a young man who might reasonably hope to succeed on another occasion, perhaps after Paterson had been satisfied or after his grandfather's death, but his uncle advised a different course. Lord Polwarth wrote:

> You were told 'Those who promise to be your friends are not to be trusted, they mean to divide the interest, & by that means ruin it' Now if you act, it will be said, 'you were told what would be the consequence, & that you are ruining the interest, with a great deal about young fools, & old wiseacres, bad advice, obstinacy, want of duty, & so farther.' You are also told, 'If you are the choice of the majority of the friends, it will give pleasure to see you etc.' Will he put you in a way of knowing that choice without asking. If you do ask, *vide supra*, if you do not, 'why it is your own fault, you might have done it, I told you you I had no objection, would you have the gentlemen throw themselves at your head?' ... I see no motive worth a moments thought to stop you ... To divide the interest sounds ill, but in reality is it not much better that the County should be divided between two relations of my family ... than have the enemy unite the foes, & get many stragglers from us? ... a head of opposition once fairly form'd will take a great deal of killing ... [18]

The decision to act on Lord Polwarth's advice and persist in his opposition to Sir John Paterson proved to be a costly adventure for Hugh Scott, but it is clear from Lord Polwarth's correspondence that more than personal ambition drove him to it, for his uncle continued to exert pressure to keep him from retracting. When Hugh Scott returned from London to the county in May 1779 to let it be known that he was willing to become a candidate, it is clear that he was still influenced by Lord Marchmont's arguments, and indeed his argument to Polwarth against openly declaring as a candidate so long before a general election proved to be prophetic:

> if our enemies unite & we seperate we stand a bad chance. If therefore I had become an actual candidate without a very considerable knowledge of the state of the county I might have been forced by my adherents to stand it out to the last & by the Bart. being equally stubborn have let the interest slip through our fingers into the hands of some formidable opponent ... I am sure the principal object we have in view is the preservation of your family interest ... [19]

Scott clearly hoped to evade a serious confrontation with Lord Marchmont, and foresaw the difficulties which indeed did arise when both Paterson and Scott persisted in opposition to each other, thus making an opening for enemies of the Marchmont family interest. Polwarth, however, did not share his nephew's doubts and told him plainly to stop vacillating and declare himself a candidate:

want of decision so falsely call'd prudence, spoils more business than any ten other causes ... The foundation you built upon was Sir John's unpopularity, do you find that altered? You never expected support from my father, & your conversations with him make you the best judge of what is his opinion ... I know no medium betwixt going or standing still, betwixt being openly a candidate or giving it up; if you mean to oppose Sir John, oppose him; if not, give it up ... [20]

Polwarth's concern was primarily the threat to the family interest caused by his father's attempt to impose an unpopular candidate upon the county for a second time, and indeed there was some reason to fear that, with both Marchmont and Polwarth commonly resident in England, the traditional family influence might diminish through lack of consultation with the voters of Berwickshire. Marchmont himself had a legacy of gratitude for past favours upon which he might draw, but Marchmont was an old man and Polwarth feared that his father's interest might not pass to him if it was strained to breaking point through its association with Sir John Paterson.

Lord Polwarth, Hugh Scott, and the latter's father, Walter Scott of Harden, the organisers of opposition to Sir John Paterson, did not immediately contemplate opposition to the Marchmont interest, for they saw themselves as part of that interest. On the contrary they hoped to unite that interest in support of a popular candidate by securing by means of a preliminary canvass, conducted long before an election was in view, a clear indication of the sentiments of the voters. In face of such an indication of opinion, Lord Marchmont, it was hoped, would remain neutral and Sir John Paterson would withdraw in order to permit the usual easy victory for the Marchmont family interest at the general election. In this view, Polwarth, while refraining from active canvassing for his nephew, did everything else to favour his candidacy, going so far as to write a letter of good wishes which might be shown to every voter in order to demonstrate that Hugh Scott was not, in the opinion of the heir to the title, acting contrary to the interest of the Marchmont family.[21]

The division within the Marchmont interest created opportunities for other interests which could not normally have hoped to successfully challenge Lord Marchmont and his friends. Hugh Scott was at first apprehensive that the Duke of Gordon, hitherto a friend of Lord Marchmont's, might introduce his own candidate,[22] and if that threat did not materialise, there was clearly danger from an influential long-time enemy of the Marchmont family, Patrick Home of Wedderburn. Moreover, the divided Marchmont interest encouraged other candidates, unconnected with any large interest, to contemplate entering the contest, thus fragmenting the roll still further.

When Hugh Scott declared himself a candidate early in June 1779, he advised a voter that Lord Marchmont 'was determined to support Sir J[ohn] P[aterson] at the G[eneral] E[lection] having I imagine given him a promise of his assistance without knowledge of the real state of the C[ount]y, taking his information from that quarter only ... '[23] But if the earl's support was not expected by his grandson, neither did he anticipate the degree of rancour with which Lord Marchmont would campaign for the re-election of Sir John Paterson. After a preliminary survey of voters in a portion of Berwickshire, Scott was ready to suggest that if Marchmont would maintain a neutral attitude in a contest which was restricted as yet to the peer's son-in-law and grandson, he was confident of success.[24] Lord Marchmont, however, was far from neutral, and the more his grandson persisted, the more infuriated the elderly peer became, and the fact that his own son was involved in opposition to his will, a fact quickly drawn to his attention by Sir John Paterson, did not soothe his temper.

Lord Marchmont inspired in many of the freeholders feelings of apprehension on the one hand and gratitude for past favours on the other. Many freeholders approached by Scott and his friends were willing to wish him well, and clearly many were also very unhappy with Sir John Paterson as their representative, but at the same time some of them were unwilling to give a commitment to vote for Scott, when such a promise would mark them in opposition to Lord Marchmont. Sir John Stuart of Allanbank, for example, who not only believed Paterson to be an unsuitable representative but also entertained thoughts of his own son as a candidate, was ready to admit to Hugh Scott that the reason for not taking a stand against Paterson was his 'fear of having his place taken from him ... if he irritated the Bar[one]t too much'.[25] Accordingly, although Stuart was friendly, that friendship was not to be counted on as a vote, for he had written to Lord Marchmont promising to follow him in whatever he desired. There were many freeholders like Sir John Stuart in this county which had been dominated by Lord Marchmont for so many years. Lord Polwarth rightly urged Hugh Scott to redouble his efforts and to 'trust no single voter who does not absolutely secure you his vote, for no stone will be left unturn'd to biass all waverers against you, & every general good wisher will shrink under the rod like Sr John Stuart'.[26] But even those afraid to offend Lord Marchmont by open opposition might possibly be persuaded to stay away from the election rather than vote for Sir John Paterson. That at least was the solution to the problem contemplated by Sir John Stuart's son, who informed Hugh Scott of his concern to learn while in Italy that Paterson had been elected to replace James Pringle:

> because ... *it is not* nor *will be* the real sense of the County that he should represent us. If Lord Marchmont thinks so he is grossly mistaken & my respect and regard for his L[or]d[shi]p lead me to think on finding his mistake he will be sorry he has engaged his interest. Tho' I cannot at present engage to anyone ... I cannot in honour give *him* my vote in any event ... [27]

More dangerous to Hugh Scott's chance of election was the considerable body of freeholders who retained genuine feelings of gratitude for past acts of friendship by Lord Marchmont, who could count on the legacy of a lifetime at the centre of political life and lengthy association with government. As Hugh Scott ruefully remarked:

> many people told me they are under such obligations to Ld M[archmont] as not to look upon themselves in this particular independent, but that they hope Ld M[archmont] will not desire them to go against me. And at their desire I write this

post to my Grandfather to beg he would not use his influence with them ... I know this will not have the smallest effect. Still it becomes me to use every means & leave nothing undone which there is a possibility of my afterwards regreting that I did not do ... [28]

Far from refraining from interference, Marchmont became more violent in his hostility to his grandson, going so far as to demand that voters holding qualifications created on the Marchmont estate vote for Sir John Paterson, whatever their personal inclinations.[29] Fictitious votes were of course given to their holders to enable them to support the political interest of their author, but in the circumstances of a contest as yet confined to members of the Marchmont family, it was considered unusually ungentlemanly to deprive voters of their choice of the family member to represent the interest. George Brown of Ellieston, and William Riddel, two voters in this situation, were presented with an ultimatum to vote as directed or surrender their qualifications, and indeed both men later secured liferent qualifications elsewhere, Ellieston from Scott of Harden and Riddel from Mrs. Edgar of Newton,[30] indicating that they did indeed succumb to pressure to the point of surrendering their votes. Extreme measures like this did of course alienate the genuine freeholders still further, and had Hugh Scott been in his own mind an enemy of the Marchmont interest he might have made more of this alienation. Unfortunately, as he was acting with the heir to that interest, Hugh Scott found himself ever more embarrassed by the earl's intransigence, for as he remarked to Polwarth,

If I were a declared & determined enemy to your family I should point out the measures proposed & rejoice at them because they must disgust & give offence. But still retaining a great degree of esteem & affection for the author of these measures it gives me uneasiness to see him acting in such a manner as to incur universal disapprobation of his conduct ... [31]

Equally, Lord Polwarth felt constrained by his relationship to their opponents from acting as his own wishes suggested, for he felt unable to ask freeholders directly for their votes and felt unable to do anything which would 'bear the most distant appearance of want & duty to' Lord Marchmont.[32] On the other hand Hugh Scott canvassed with a letter in his possession written by Polwarth whose careful wording was intended to 'be intelligible to those who chuse to understand, & yet gives no hold to such as mean to pervert ... '[33]

The close friendship between Lord Polwarth and Scott, and their reluctance to make a clear statement of their opposition to Lord Marchmont introduced an element of uncertainty into their own position. Where that could lead became clear when a baseless but plausible rumour began to circulate in the county suggesting that Hugh Scott was a dishonest associate of the detested Sir John Paterson. The report suggested that Hugh Scott 'stood merely to keep off another candidate & that when there was no longer any danger of that' Scott was to withdraw, leaving the field clear for Paterson.[34] The rumour appears to have originated with the rival Home of Wedderburn faction, for in a document emanating from that group it was suggested that

As Sir John had been introduced into his seat by artifice and surprise, many of the electors from the near connexion of the two Candidates were suspicious that Lord Marchmont and his friends meant to preserve him by the same means . . . [35]

The discreditable rumour was understandable but completely unfounded, for although Polwarth and Hugh Scott could choose their friends, relatives like Sir John were imposed upon them, and the hostility within the Marchmont family was only too real.

The possibility that the friction within the Marchmont interest would subside became ever more unlikely, largely because of the strength of the rumour of Scott's complicity with Sir John Paterson, for in order to refute the arguments used by his enemies Scott felt compelled to undertake that he would persist to the last with whatever support he might gain. That resolution was a far cry from Scott's original plan for a tentative canvass to determine that he was the stronger candidate, while allowing withdrawal should Sir John prove to have too much support. Lord Polwarth remarked, at the opening of the canvass,

if my father is determined to support Sir John Paterson heartily, you then have a fair opening to get out at. You may say, you was deceiv'd, you thought the ground would have born[e] you, & therefore rather than divide the interest & do mischief, you will give up.[36]

Clearly, however, the stated resolution to persist in opposition to Sir John up to a vote was shutting the door on any withdrawal by Scott, and the Marchmont interest could only be reunited if Sir John Paterson declined to stand again, which was unlikely unless he was first provided with a place, a prospect in itself improbable.[37]

The approach made to Lord Advocate Henry Dundas by Hugh Scott and his father widened the breach still further, and for that reason they had delayed making such an application for assistance because they knew Lord Marchmont disliked Henry Dundas and, as Hugh told his uncle, Polwarth, 'while the other side kept within bounds we were cautious of giving offence'.[38] However, when Marchmont's open hostility made such an approach essential lest the weight of Government be cast into the balance on the other side, the Scotts' learned to their surprise that Marchmont himself had attempted to forestall them by making an agreement with the Lord Advocate.[39] Dundas, however, found an alliance with another group which, whether it knew it or not, was breaking up the Marchmont interest, much more congenial, in that it opened a way to Henry Dundas' future domination of the county in which he already had many friends. There is a somewhat naive assumption on the part of Hugh Scott that Henry Dundas was his disinterested friend. No doubt, as Hugh pointed out, the Lord Advocate 'from the variety of his connexions' had it 'much in his power to break any third party'. But whether Henry Dundas would 'exert himself to the utmost to do it,' as Hugh expected, depended entirely upon whether or not it was to Henry Dundas' advantage to do so.[40] The Lord Advocate, however, was an influential and determined enemy of Sir John Paterson, and for that reason the Scotts counted themselves fortunate to have his assistance.

During the canvass of the county by the two candidates, the grave of the Marchmont interest was dug industriously by the indiscreet and unthinking actions and statements of Sir John Paterson. Admittedly, Paterson could have done nothing without the concurrence of Lord Marchmont, but it appears that the earl, perhaps carried away by the strength of his own anger at what he considered the disloyalty of his son and grandson, fell more and more under the malign influence of Sir John, whose advice proved to be very damaging to the family interest. In particular, Paterson's threat that Lord Marchmont would split his estate into votes and 'by that means bring about 40 new votes into the field'[41] which would secure Sir John's re-election against all opposition, was unlikely to be well received by the freeholders whose wishes were thus to be set aside. In any county in Scotland where a considerable body of real freeholders existed such a statement would have aroused fury, and Berwickshire was no different. In short, as an opposition 'Memorandum about the Berwickshire Election' suggests, many of the principal landowners 'thought the County dishonoured by having such a Representative, and themselves insulted by having him avowedly forced upon them by Lord Marchmont's nominal and fictitious votes'.[42] As it turned out, there were not forty votes to be made on the Marchmont estate, but even the number completed, twenty-two, was a formidable group, and most of them were men who would vote as Sir John Paterson should direct. 'Your whole estate is divided in 400£ valuations, & many given to Northumberland farmers . . . ,' Lord Polwarth was advised. 'I know many Gentlemen who refused them. I must own I felt some degree of indignation at superiorities upon Ld M[archmont]'s estate being offered at the Cross of Edin[burgh] to any body that would take them.' [43]

Even with the new nominal voters, five of whom were successfully added to the freeholders roll at Michaelmas 1779, Paterson and Marchmont appeared to be losing their battle, for Scott's chance of success was enhanced by the inactivity of Patrick Home of Wedderburn, the leader of the anti-Marchmont party in the county, who, if he had not declared for Scott, had given qualifications upon his estate to the Lord Advocate and his nephew, both of whom were engaged to support Scott.[44] The mass creation of nominal voters through the splitting of the Marchmont estate, moreover, was of great assistance to Polwarth and Scott, for 'the appearance it has of tyranny sets all the lesser lairds against' Paterson.[45] In addition there were already votes being secured for Hugh Scott through Dundas' assistance such as John Buchan of Letham who offered his support 'if the Lord Advocate was for him'.[46] On the other hand there were also freeholders whom Scott had 'every reason to think inclined to our side' who refused him because, as in the case of Alexander Robertson of Prenderguest, Lord Marchmont wrote to him and he felt 'bound in gratitude for a favor received a few years ago to comply' with Marchmont's solicitation in favour of Paterson. [47]

Sir John Paterson did not hesitate to threaten all whom he felt he could influence in that way, even Lord Polwarth himself, whose attention was drawn to the inconvenience he might experience should his annuity from the Marchmont estates be stopped. It was not an idle threat, for in the spring of 1780 Polwarth complained to Walter Scott of Harden that he was in urgent need of £1,000, for

> they have most ingeniously found out, that they shall probably plague me by not paying me my Annuity, & therefore rather than miss an opportunity of being in the wrong, & of shewing to what littleness they are capable of descending, they are defrauding me of what is justly my due, by my marriage articles ... [48]

Lord Marchmont's actions were already appearing to have a negative impact upon the Marchmont interest as early as October 1779, for from what Polwarth could determine in London, 'the matter seems completely understood & in its proper light, as Power, Force & Artifice against Popularity, Affection & Sincerity'.[49] Polwarth, moreover, could not help reflecting that should his father die before the election the situation would alter completely, 'because all the forced votes will undoubtedly ebb to me, & many made ones will not be such notorious blackguards as to vote my own votes against me, even supposing their friend fool enough to desire it'.[50] Lord Marchmont, however, proved to be more durable than his son believed likely, and indeed survived his son by several years.

The divisions within the Marchmont family were deepened in November 1779, when Lord Marchmont dismissed his law agent, Thomas Cockburn, W.S., for communicating with Polwarth. According to the latter, Cockburn had committed 'no less heinous a crime than writing me a most innocent letter'.[51] Innocent or not, Cockburn was in a most unenviable situation between his employer and his employer's heir, and he had already incurred the anger of Sir John Paterson when he refused to canvass the freeholders on his behalf.[52] Unfortunately for Cockburn, it was Paterson's accounts which were believed by the Earl of Marchmont, and the stories circulated via Paterson in the county, which undoubtedly fuelled the earl's anger, suggested that the lawyer had represented Lord Marchmont 'as an old feeble, insignificant man', and Polwarth as the man to whom the gentlemen of the Marchmont interest looked.[53] There was enough truth in that suggestion to make it plausible, and nothing was more likely to infuriate so arrogant a nobleman as Marchmont, as Paterson must have known. From Polwarth's letter to Cockburn regretting his dismissal, it is evident that the contents of Cockburn's communications could not have been notably indiscreet, for Polwarth's description of 'a fair & friendly communication' [54] does not suggest the betrayal of an employer. On the other hand, it is known that Cockburn also communicated with Polwarth through Hugh Scott, suggesting that Polwarth should think carefully and take advice before signing any documents which might be forwarded to him for signature, though in this case too, it might be argued that in so doing the lawyer was acting in the best interest of the Marchmont family, though not perhaps as the current head of that family might have wished.[55] At all events, Polwarth and everyone else involved did not doubt that the prime mover in this event as in all the other steps in the contest for control of Berwickshire politics was Sir John Paterson. Polwarth wrote:

I can only lament an old man of the most superior abilities allowing himself to be so guided. My feelings as to the guider may be more severe, but to quarrel openly with him [as long as it can with honor be avoided] would be like flying in my father's face ... A time will come when all this shall be repaid with interest, & then Sir John may feel how dangerous the anger of a patient man ... [56]

Unfortunately for the best interests of the Marchmont family their quarrel went on too long, for on November 29th, 1779 the enemies of that family made their first move towards opposition, meeting in Duns 'to consider of some plan to prevent Lord Marchmont from forcing a Member of Parliament upon them by dividing his whole estate into nominal and fictitious votes'.[57] The meeting was called by George Home of Branxton, an Edinburgh lawyer who was the principal manager of the interest of Patrick Home of Wedderburn, and the holder of one of the latter's nominal votes. Among those present or invited to this gathering were Robert Hay of Drummelzier, William Hall of Whitehall, Alexander Renton of Lammerton, Sir John Stuart of Allanbank, Archibald Douglas of Douglas and other substantial landowners and men of influence, in whose ranks Home of Wedderburn must be included, though the latter for some reason appeared reluctant to become a candidate himself.[58] Douglas was in fact the first to be invited to allow his name to stand,[59] and when he hesitated, both Renton and Hall came forward on what they described as the 'Independent Interest'.[60]

According to George Home's calculations, in November 1779 the election was quite open. There were 94 freeholders on the Berwickshire roll, but of that number, perhaps eight or ten were certain to be absent, some in India or America, and others being too infirm to travel to an election, thus reducing the total possible attendance to about 84. Sir John Paterson was estimated to have 22 sure votes, though this might be supplemented by the 17 additional nominal voters who still had to be enrolled, perhaps at the general election, and certainly at the Michaelmas Head Court of 1780. Home was unwilling to allow Hugh Scott to have more than 18 confirmed and certain votes, while he believed there were 24 who were strongly opposed to both the Marchmont candidates [who were still rumoured to be working in collusion]. The supporters of the candidates declared and the known enemies of the Marchmont family totalled 64 freeholders on the roll. The remaining 20 were doubtful, so clearly the election might go to any candidate, and the prospect of overturning the Marchmont interest was feasible.[61] George Home did not believe that Hugh Scott would give up easily, for his father, Scott of Harden, had stated 'in the most positive terms that he is determined his son shall stand the Election if he should have only ten votes; and that no consideration will ever make him unite his interest with Sir John Paterson's '.[62] The great fear of this enemy of Lord Marchmont, however, was that the latter would at the last order Sir John Paterson to give up rather than see the family interest overthrown, and that indeed would have been the sensible course, but a determination to defeat Hugh Scott had so gripped Lord Marchmont that he appears never to have considered a compromise with his grandson which might have kept the interest together. On the contrary, Sir John Paterson, though perhaps without Marchmont's knowledge, in the last resort was ready to make an arrangement with the enemies of the Marchmont family had they been willing to accept it.

Doubts about Hugh Scott's will to oppose his grandfather persisted even after he had begun to assure voters that he would stand the contest whatever support he might receive. Late in November 1779, for example, George Home wrote, though he did not send, a paragraph which indicated his thoughts on the question:

> My opinion of Mr. Scott . . . does not permit me to believe he will keep his resolution should Lord Marchmont insist upon his altering it. Hugh Scott has no very distant prospect to Lord Marchmont's succession and the stake is great.[63]

Gradually, however, this readiness to think the worst of Scott because of his relationship to Marchmont was overcome, and even determined enemies of Marchmont's domination of Berwickshire, such as James Dickson of Antonshill, began to accept Scott's honesty and to believe that 'he was neither dependent on nor connected with the great Peer in this political contest, on the contrary stood in direct opposition to him'.[64] On the other hand, as Scott obtained more and more promises of support by insisting 'that he was never to join in any respect with Sir J[ohn] P[aterson]',[65] he greatly restricted his own freedom of action to the point where only the death of Lord Marchmont and the succession of Polwarth to that title might have kept the Marchmont family interest from destruction.

The addition of two more candidates was an added complication, but William Hall of Whitehall soon gave up upon finding during a canvass that support was uncertain.[66] As he pointed out to George Home of Branxton, the freeholders' friendship was little to the point: 'they shake and squeeze me by the hand; they drink and wish me all success; they offer me meat and lodging; their females smile upon me; but alas not a word will they speak, speaking to the purpose . . . '[67] The other self-styled Independent, Alexander Renton of Lammerton, proved more dangerous to Scott, even though there seemed little prospect of his winning a majority of the freeholders to his cause, for Renton was the instrument used by Henry Dundas to take the initiative away from Scott and his friend Polwarth. Scott was not particularly alarmed when he found Renton was his rival, for although the latter was a member of the interest of Home of Wedderburn and his ally, Hay of Drummelzier, Scott could take comfort from the fact that neither of these influential figures was a candidate. Renton, it was felt by the Scott party, was only a 'person by whom their strength & consequence is to be tried & shown',[68] and that had they thought themselves likely to succeed, one of the leaders of the anti-Marchmont interest would have been the man. The strength of the third, or Independent party, was mainly in the eastern section of the county, and there Scott found little support. Equally, however, he could take comfort in the fact that Marchmont and Paterson could do little there either, and clearly, since the third party was strongly hostile to Lord Marchmont's domination of the county and his attempt to enforce his will by creating many nominal votes, it was hardly to be expected that Renton, Wedderburn and their friends could join with Paterson.[69] Accordingly, when the election came, it was to be anticipated that the third party would join Scott in order to keep out Sir John Paterson. The reluctance of one of the principal members of the third party, Hay of Drummelzier, to see his estate broken up to make votes,[70] determined that in the race to add votes to the roll which Marchmont and Paterson had begun, the third party could not win without the alliance of Scott who had already promised every voter he had met that he would not abandon the contest until the election had taken place.

The contest between the two stronger candidates, Scott and Paterson, however, had become so bitter that rational analysis became ever more difficult for the principals. It was at that point that the Lord Advocate and his associate, the Duke of Buccleuch, seized their opportunity to take effective control of Berwickshire politics. Dundas, a voter in Berwickshire qualified by a nominal vote on the Wedderburn estate, had been an active supporter of Hugh Scott, who considered him a staunch ally, and the Advocate had indeed fixed a number of votes for Scott. However, in spite of every effort, none of the candidates could secure a clear majority of the roll, and Sir John Paterson began to cast about desperately for allies. Sir John approached Sir John Stuart of Allanbank and his son, who controlled a total of five votes,[71] with a suggestion that present support would be repaid by assistance in securing the younger Stuart's election when Sir John had been provided with a place and retired from Parliament.[72] When the Stuarts rejected his approaches, Sir John turned to the known enemies of the Marchmont interest, the Homes of Wedderburn and the third party who were engaged to support Renton of Lammerton.[73] Sir John told them that he much preferred Renton to Hugh Scott, and attempted to secure some compromise with them to divide the Parliament, but at all events to defeat Scott. It was an unlikely plan, since the whole object of the third party had been to keep Sir John Paterson from securing re-election, but it was this approach which gave Henry Dundas his opportunity, for he took it to Hugh Scott, for whom he was acting almost as a manager, and strongly urged the necessity of Scott making terms with the third party, lest they make a different arrangement with Paterson,

The plan proposed to Scott called for him to abandon his candidacy for the Berwickshire seat and join with his friends in supporting a candidate to be named by the Duke of Buccleuch. Such a candidate, with the support of Buccleuch, the Lord Advocate, Scott's friends, the third party, and, as Polwarth put it, 'all worshippers of the rising sun',[74] would ensure Sir John Paterson's defeat. In return for his compliance, Scott was at first promised possession of a burgh seat for three years, to be followed by his election for Berwickshire when the incumbent should step down under the terms of the suggested arrangement, leaving Scott in possession of the county seat for the remainder of Parliament.[75]

In listening to such a proposal from the wily Lord Advocate, Hugh Scott forgot what had been the object of his own candidacy, namely to preserve the Marchmont interest for his uncle Lord Polwarth from the destructive effect of Lord Marchmont's support of Sir John Paterson. The arrangement to which Scott was listening would replace the Marchmont interest with that of Buccleuch and the Lord Advocate, and Polwarth at least sensed the danger in that development even if his nephew did not. In the first place, even if Scott entered Parliament under the patronage of the Duke of Buccleuch, who would also return his man for the county, the benefits were surely a lot more apparent for Buccleuch than they were for Lord Polwarth. As he pointed out to his nephew, 'it will be said that the Duke has beat my father & got possession of Berwickshire. An idea w[hi]ch will not augment my weight'. [76] Moreover, there was a danger in any such arrangement which disposed of the freeholders without consultation, for as Polwarth warned, 'Are you sure the Gentlemen of the County will bear being turned over so compendiously? You may remember how much was said last year ... about cramming down throats etc. Will the Gentlemen bear the idea of your leaving them now & telling them you shall want them in three years? '[77] The bargain as proposed to Scott also called for an immediate sacrifice for a prospect of future help, yet if the bargain caused resentment among the freeholders, might not this be used as an excuse for the Buccleuch incumbent remaining as Member until the end of the Parliament? 'Then who insures your Berwickshire election at that?' Lord Polwarth emphasised, telling his nephew in the plainest terms that unless he was elected for Berwickshire at this election, the Lord Advocate and Buccleuch would control the county, and 'you either never will be a member at all, or at least, if you are, it will be on the Duke of Buccleuch's interest '.[78]

Lord Polwarth's initial reaction was correct. The project was a trap, and unfortunately for Scott and Polwarth they were induced to enter it. The terms of the proffered agreement were modified, apparently in Scott's favour, but the resulting bargain essentially put Hugh Scott into a position of dependence on others, and those others were not friends of the Marchmont family. The bargain struck between the third party and Scott was arranged by George Home, on behalf of Renton and the third party, and Henry Dundas, acting supposedly in the interest of Scott.[79] The arrangement divided the Parliament, allowing Hugh Scott to sit for the county of Berwick for at least four years. At the end of that term, a group of influential gentlemen of the Wedderburn interest might, at their option, call upon Scott to resign his seat and support the election of Renton or another of their friends for the remainder of the Parliament, while Scott in turn would be provided with the Linlithgow Burgh's seat currently occupied by Sir James Cockburn. The last sweetener offered to Scott was singularly implausible, for considering the expense of contesting a burgh district, why would an incumbent give up the seat in favour of another and lose his investment? In the event, however, Scott accepted the arrangement, frightened by the threat that unless he did so, the third party would reach an agreement with Paterson, and the result of the election was placed beyond doubt.

Even the shrewder Lord Polwarth, who saw more deeply into political questions than his nephew, was not unimpressed by the revised arrangement:

> The present plan, of your now coming in, aided & supported by the third Party, only on the condition of giving up your seat at the requisition of four gentlemen with the power of then demanding Sir James Cockburn's seat, appears to me so much in your favour ... that there can be no doubt ... of the propriety of you agreeing to it. In my opinion the requisition never will be made, because it is death to Sr James Cockburn ... [80]

Indeed, even if Hugh Scott was required to resign his seat, that would not, in Lord Polwarth's opinion, be a particularly serious setback, for Polwarth was not to be a party to the agreement. Accordingly, Polwarth, should he have succeeded his father by that time and reunited the Marchmont interest, could run a candidate against the man put up by the third party at the by-election, and replace him with Hugh Scott at the following general election. Apparently Polwarth had got over his initial misgivings about the effect of allowing the Duke of Buccleuch and the Lord Advocate to get a strong foothold in the county and had forgotten their connection with Home of Wedderburn. Polwarth too was dazzled by the plan held out to them by Henry Dundas, that of 'turning out our competitor, & seeming to unite the county'.[81]

The Berwickshire election result was determined long before 21st September 1780, when the freeholders met to choose their representative. Of those present, 50 voted for Hugh Scott, younger of Harden, and 35 for Sir John Paterson,[82] but the agreement through which Scott had obtained this majority was common knowledge, and Paterson promptly appealed to the House of Commons, arguing that his defeat was the result of a corrupt bargain, a view which the Parliamentary Commissioners shared, thought not to the extent of seating Sir John, whose own party had been built upon extensive interference with the freedom of election by a Peer. The battle within Parliament was expensive and prolonged and it ended in the unseating of Scott and the calling of a new election, held on 12th April, 1781.[83] The appeal to Parliament was Sir John Paterson's last throw, for he had clearly hoped to be seated by order of the House of Commons. The county was unmistakably hostile to Paterson, and accordingly he declined to oppose Hugh Scott, who was returned without opposition at the new election, though still unreconciled to his grandfather.[84]

During the Parliamentary hearings relating to the election of 1780, one of the facts brought to light by the evidence of George Home of Branxton, the manager of the Wedderburn interest, was that Scott had not needed to make any compromise with the third party, for they had been committed to support him in any event.[85] As Scott later remarked, he had been 'needlessly drawn into a compromise which afterwards gave my friends & myself much vexation & trouble & ended in a reduction of my Election'.[86] In those circumstances it would appear unlikely that Scott would have immediately made another such bargain with the third party when it had been shown to be unnecessary as well as illegal. Indeed, according to Scott, the Lord Advocate had actually burned the written contract after a dinner held in the Duke of Buccleuch's London residence the day after the election was held to be void, with the words 'Now you are satisfied'.[87] At the 1781 election meeting, Walter Scott of Harden, Hugh's father, had intended to make a public statement that the bargain was at an end, but was dissuaded by Henry Dundas on the grounds that 'such a declaration was unnecessary as this was perfectly understood to be the case by all Parties'.[88]

There the matter rested until 1783, when it became abundantly clear that the understanding of the parties was far from perfect, for the Wedderburn party demanded Hugh Scott's resignation, this time without mention of a substitute burgh seat, an element of the agreement which had presumably vanished in the smoke of the burned contract. Something else had changed by 1783. Hugh Scott was deprived of the aid of his uncle, for Lord Polwarth had died in 1781,[89] survived by his still embittered father, whose hostility prevented Scott from succeeding to the Marchmont estates upon his own death.[90] Thus Scott, the disinherited heir to the Marchmont estate, was clearly just as independent as any candidate could be, yet the Wedderburn party was resolved to remove him.

Hugh Scott found himself in an impossible position. To be sure, there was now no written contract binding the third party to himself and demanding his resignation when the Wedderburn faction should demand it. On the other hand it was common knowledge that such an arrangement had been made in 1780. Scott and his friends held that the contract had been voided by the nullification of the election to which it related, but as the spokesman of the Wedderburn party, George Home, pointed out, 'After the first Election was reduced do you know of any old compromise being departed from?'[91] The argument advanced by the third party was that Scott was unable to free himself from the compromise in the absence of a public statement at the time, which as we have seen was prevented by Henry Dundas. The Duke of Buccleuch appears to have taken no part in this attack upon the Member of Parliament,[92] but Patrick Home of Wedderburn declared publicly at a county meeting in Duns that Scott was bound in honour to resign his seat, and this opinion was reiterated by George Home,[93] one of the two men who had drawn up the original agreement. The other man involved in the drawing up of the compromise, Henry Dundas, adamantly refused to take any part in resolving the dispute, a decision which effectively destroyed Scott's position.[94] He was faced with a hard choice of alternatives. On the one hand, he could retain the seat which had cost him so dearly, and be denounced by his enemies as a man without honour. Alternatively, he could resign his seat and give it to the Wedderburn interest, whether or not they were represented by Renton of Lammerton or Home of Wedderburn himself, and once they had possession there was obviously little chance of dislodging them when Lord Marchmont's enmity was unabated. Yet was there any real difference between resigning at once or continuing to retain the seat with many of the gentlemen convinced by gossip that the Member was a man of dishonour? Clearly Scott's re-election would be unlikely in any event. In short, a bargain of convenience placed Scott in the hands of his enemies, and there was no way of escape. His friend, David Hume of Ninewells, who acted as an intermediary with the Wedderburn party, advised Scott in the strongest terms to resign, because

> the dispute has become too notorious to be hushed up and forgotten ... An appeal to the Public, by printing your correspondence, would now only serve, at best, to inform people that you and Mr. Home utterly differ ... If, on the other hand, you remain content with retaining your seat, having given no explanation whatever to the County at large, I am much affraid that you shall sustain a damage a thousand times more important than your seat can compensate, were it a longer and more certain tenure than it is. This you may be assured of, that in case of your so doing, the tongues of the whole third party ... will be active in propagating an account of the matter, the

most possible to your discredit and disparagement. And the world, I am sorry to say, would be too ready to give ear to them ... [95]

Ninewells' advice was to resign, making a public declaration of the motives which led Scott to do so, and explaining that he did so because he did not choose to have his 'honour in the mouths of people'.[96] A resignation enforced by a compromise would of course lead to the House of Commons voiding the election of Renton or an alternative enemy, and Scott could honourably return to the battle in a new election which Parliament would order. It was good advice, and Scott would have been well advised to take it, for that alone afforded a prospect of recovery from this deadly attack made upon what every eighteenth-century gentleman valued more than anything else, his honour. Scott, however, hesitated too long, trying desperately to persuade Henry Dundas, who had been the author of the original and, as the Lord Advocate must have been well aware, unnecessary compromise, but Dundas saw his interest in taking no part in this dispute, for the Wedderburn party were among his own friends and their victory essentially gave Henry Dundas a stronger footing in the south-east. The general election came too soon for Hugh Scott, finding him still in possession of his seat and his position as a man of honour seriously eroded. Accordingly there was no purpose to be served in running once again on 27th April, 1784. Patrick Home of Wedderburn was chosen without opposition to represent the county of Berwick. Walter Scott of Harden remained the leader of a considerable interest in the county, but Hugh Scott was, understandably, so sickened by his brief experience of political action that he never again attempted to enter Parliament. Whatever Scott had done in the last period of his tenure of the Berwickshire seat, he would have been misrepresented. Retaining the seat doomed any chance of securing re-election, yet to have accepted Ninewells' advice was also dangerous, for what might the Wedderburn faction have made of Scott's hesitation in resigning? To resign was to admit that a bargain existed, yet the hesitation appeared to demonstrate that he had attempted to evade a bargain which involved his honour. No wonder Scott remarked in a letter to Gilbert Elliot later in life that

> before you were born I was for years rendered so perfectly miserable by a contested election and all its consequences, such as breaches of family connections, and private friendships, that I hear of a contest in which I may be called upon to take part with horror ... [97]

Undoubtedly Scott's political activity cost him a great inheritance, for his grandfather, Lord Marchmont, never forgave him. Membership in the House of Commons brought no benefits to Scott as an individual in the brief term for which he sat, merely additional expense, and an agreement with false friends was the means of nullifying Scott's personal influence in the county of Berwick. Lord Marchmont, by his readiness to accept bad advice from his unpopular son-in-law, Sir John Paterson, so broke his family interest when his remaining relatives refused to acquiesce that the Marchmont interest was never the same again.

Dictation by a peer was the one thing that no county with a substantial body of freeholders would tolerate, and that fact had been established long before 1779–80 as a constant in Scottish county politics. Management required more finesse than Paterson and Marchmont possessed, and the crudity of their approaches to the freeholders effectively undermined Lord Marchmont's influence in the county.

The argument put forward by the Wedderburn party was impossible to answer, for even had Hugh Scott made a public appeal to the gentlemen of Berwickshire, the fact of doing so would have been made to rebound upon his own head, for the enemy would have argued that not content with attempting to break a solemn engagement, he was now attempting to defraud their party of its just reward under the compromise by creating the possibility of a nullification of the election, by making the bargain public. In short, Scott was completely boxed in, and in this one is tempted to see the devious hand of Henry Dundas, who undoubtedly benefited by Scott's political extinction. Even if one concedes all of the Wedderburn argument that Scott was not at liberty to withdraw from an agreement once made, no matter that the election to which it related had been voided, the fact remains that the compromise had been quite unnecessary in the first instance, for Scott was going to win anyway with the third party's aid. The curious thing about the episode was the sudden appearance of a new party, built around two friends of the Lord Advocate, Patrick Home of Wedderburn and his nephew, George Home. Although there was no clear evidence of collusion between Dundas and the Wedderburns, their intentions must have been well known to the Advocate, who indeed voted upon a fictitious qualification given him by Wedderburn. In all probability, and even allowing for the partisanship of a friend, Thomas Cockburn was not far from the truth when he complained that

> out of the friendship and assistance of Lord Advocate, and of his Lordship's most intimate friends in politics & otherways, Mr. Home of Wedderburn & Mr. G. Home, there issued a venemous composition. Ld. Advocate and Mr. G. Home secretly contrived to raise up what they called a third Party. Wedderburn & G. Home the ostensible authors, & G. Home the conductor. Out of this composition, spectres and apprehensions were imagined and held out. Mr. Scott's progress was marr'd and at length the foul compromise was the fruit. Mr. Scott was wounded in the house of his friends.[98]

NOTES

1. SRO. Scott of Harden, GD157/2945/ 1/13, Parliamentary Committee on the Berwickshire election, evidence of George Home.

2. Ibid. GD157/2886/1/1–2 and GD157/2886/2, Freeholders Roll, 1778, with comments.

3. SRO. Melville Castle, GD51/1/198/26/7, from Henry Dundas, 6 Feb., 1802, 'in ane independent Scotch county every thing depends on the choice of a Candidate'.

4. Sir Lewis Namier and John Brooke [eds.], *The History of Parliament: The House of*

Commons, 1754–1790[London, 1964], i, 473.

5. SRO. Scott of Harden, GD157/2887/1/1–2, James Pringle to Walter Scott of Harden, 5 Mar., 1779.

6. Sir James Balfour Paul, *The Scots Peerage* [Edinburgh, 1909], vi, 20–22.

7. SRO. Scott of Harden, GD157/2887/1/1–2, James Pringle to Walter Scott, 5 Mar., 1779.

8. SRO. Home of Wedderburn, GD267/14/14, 'Memorandum about the Berwickshire Election'.

9. Balfour Paul, *Scots Peerage*, vi, 20–22.

10. SRO. Scott of Harden, GD157/2887/1/1–2, James Pringle to Walter Scott, 5 Mar., 1779.

11. SRO. Home of Wedderburn, GD267/14/14.

12. Balfour Paul, *Scots Peerage*, vi, 20–22.

13. SRO. Scott of Harden, GD157/2911/1, Hugh Scott, younger of Harden, to Lord Polwarth, 30 Apr., 1779.

14. Namier and Brooke, *The House of Commons, 1754–90*, iii, 412–3.

15. SRO. Scott of Harden, GD157/2911/1, Hugh Scott to Lord Polwarth, 30 Apr., 1779.

16. Ibid. GD157/2914/1, Lord Polwarth to Hugh Scott, 29 Apr., 1779.

17. Ibid. GD157/2882/2, Sir John Paterson of Eccles to the Freeholders of Berwickshire, 15 May, 1779.

18. Ibid. GD157/2914/2, Lord Polwarth to Hugh Scott, 9 May, 1779.

19. Ibid. GD157/2911/2, Hugh Scott to Lord Polwarth, 25 May, 1779.

20. Ibid. GD157/2914/3, Lord Polwarth to Hugh Scott, 1 Jun., 1779.

21. Ibid. GD157/2914/5, Lord Polwarth to Hugh Scott, 28 Jun., 1779.

22. Ibid. GD/157/2911/2, Hugh Scott to Lord Polwarth, 25 May, 1779.

23. Ibid. GD157/2915/7, Hugh Scott to John Stuart, younger of Allanbank, 18 Jun.,1779.

24. Ibid. GD157/2911/2, Hugh Scott to Lord Polwarth, 25 May, 1779.

25. Ibid.

26. Ibid. GD157/2914/4, Lord Polwarth to Hugh Scott, 16 Jun., 1779.

27. Ibid. GD157/2914/2, John Stuart, younger of Allanbank, to Hugh Scott, 30 Jul., 1779.

28. Ibid. GD157/2911/1–2, Hugh Scott to Lord Polwarth, 29 Jun., 1779.

29. Ibid. GD157/2911/6, Hugh Scott to Lord Polwarth, 11 Jul., 1779.

30. Sir Charles Elphinstone Adam, *The Political State of Scotland in 1788* [Edinburgh, 1887] 58–74.

31. SRO. Scott of Harden, GD157/2911/1–2, Hugh Scott to Lord Polwarth, 29 Jun., 1779.

32. Ibid. GD157/2914/6, Lord Polwarth to Hugh Scott, 29 Jun., 1779.

33. Ibid. GD157/2914/5, Lord Polwarth to Hugh Scott, 28 Jun., 1779.

34. Ibid. GD157/2911/1–2, Hugh Scott to Lord Polwarth, 29 Jun., 1779.

35. SRO. Home of Wedderburn, GD267/14/14, 'Memorandum about the Berwickshire Election'.

36. SRO. Scott of Harden, GD157/2914/3, Lord Polwarth to Hugh Scott, 1 Jun., 1779.

37. Ibid.

38. Ibid. GD157/2911/7, Hugh Scott to Lord Polwarth, 2 Aug., 1779.

39. Ibid.

40. Ibid.

41. SRO. Home of Wedderburn, GD267/14/14, 'Memorandum about the Berwickshire Election'.

42. Ibid.

43. SRO. Scott of Harden, GD157/2911/8, Hugh Scott to Lord Polwarth, 13 Sep., 1779.

44. Ibid.

45. Ibid.

46. Ibid. GD157/2914/21/1, John Buchan of Lethem to Henry Dundas, 4 Oct., 1779.

47. Ibid. GD/157/2911/8, Hugh Scott to Lord Polwarth, 13 Sept., 1779 and GD157/2886/2, Freeholders Roll.

48. Ibid. GD157/2929/1, Lord Polwarth to Walter Scott of Harden, 5 Mar., 1780.

49. Ibid. GD157/2914/9, Lord Polwarth to Hugh Scott, 12 Oct., 1779.

50. Ibid.

51. Ibid. GD157/2914/10, Lord Polwarth to Hugh Scott, 18 Nov., 1779.

52. Ibid. GD157/2943/18, Thomas Cockburn to the Earl of Marchmont, undated [Nov., 1779].

53. Ibid. GD157/2911/10/ 1–2, Hugh Scott to Lord Polwarth, 9 Dec., 1779.

54. Ibid. GD157/2943/17, Lord Polwarth to Thomas Cockburn, 18 Nov., 1779.

55. Ibid. GD/157/2911/9, Hugh Scott to Lord Polwarth, 8 Nov., 1779.

56. Ibid. GD157/2943/17, Lord Polwarth to Thomas Cockburn, 18 Nov., 1779.

57. SRO. Home of Wedderburn, GD267/14/14, George Home of Branxton to Archibald Douglas of Douglas, 20 Nov., 1779.

58. SRO. Scott of Harden, GD157/2945/1/12–13, Parliamentary Committee on the Berwickshire Election, evidence of George Home.

59. SRO. Home of Wedderburn, GD267/14/14, George Home to Archibald Douglas, 20 Nov., 1779.

60. SRO. Scott of Harden, GD157/2911/10/1–2, Hugh Scott to Lord Polwarth, 9 Dec., 1779.

61. SRO. Home of Wedderburn, GD267/14/14, George Home to Archibald Douglas, 20 Nov., 1779.

62. Ibid.

63. Ibid. A paragraph deleted from the draft of George Home's letter to Archibald Douglas, 20 Nov., 1779.

64. SRO. Scott of Harden, GD157/ 2950/6, James Dickson of Antonshill to George Home, 19 Nov., 1779.

65. Ibid.

66. Ibid., William Hall to Hugh Scott, 25 Jan., 1780.

67. SRO. Home of Wedderburn, GD267/14/14, William Hall to George Home, 7 Dec., 1779.

68. SRO. Scott of Harden, GD157/2911/11, Hugh Scott to Lord Polwarth, 1 Feb., 1780.

69. Ibid. GD157/2911/10/1–2, Hugh Scott to Lord Polwarth, 9 Dec., 1779.

70. Ibid. GD157/2940/3, Hugh Scott to Walter Scott of Harden, 14 Mar., 1780.

71. Ibid. GD157/2945/1/19–20, Parliamentary Committee on the Berwickshire Election, evidence of Sir John Stuart.

72. Ibid.

73. Ibid. GD157/2945/1/14, evidence of George Home.

74. Ibid. GD157/2914/14/1–2, Lord Polwarth to Hugh Scott, 5 Aug., 1780.

75. Ibid.

76. Ibid.

77. Ibid.

78. Ibid.

79. Ibid GD157/2945/1/14, Parliamentary Committee on the Berwickshire Election, evidence of George Home.

80. Ibid. GD157/2914/15, Lord Polwarth to Hugh Scott, 18 Aug., 1780.

81. Ibid.

82. Ibid. GD157/2945/1/1, Parliamentary Committee on the Berwickshire Election.

83. *Scots Magazine* report, Vol.43, 146–7, March 1781.

84. Namier and Brooke, *The House of Commons, 1754–90*, 474.

85. SRO. Scott of Harden, GD/157/2945/1/13, Parliamentary Committee on the Berwickshire Election.

86. Ibid. GD157/2917/7, intended letter of Hugh Scott to Patrick Home of Wedderburn, undated, Oct., 1783.

87. Ibid. GD157/2954/10, Hugh Scott to George Home, 5 Sept., 1783.

88. Ibid. GD157/2954/7, Hugh Scott to Henry Dundas, 5 Nov., 1783.

89. Balfour Paul, *The Scots Peerage*, vi, 20–22.

90. *Ibid.*

91. SRO. Scott of of Harden, GD157/2950/4/2, George Home to Hugh Scott, 18 Nov., 1783.

92. Ibid. GD157/2953/2, Hugh Scott to George Brown of Ellieston, 27 Oct., 1783.

93. Ibid. GD157/2954/14, Hugh Scott to Henry Dundas, 15 Oct., 1783.

94. Ibid. GD157/2954/5, Henry Dundas to Hugh Scott, 6 Nov., 1783.

95. Ibid. GD157/2917/5/1–4, David Hume of Ninewells to Hugh Scott, 27 Nov., 1783.

96. Ibid.

97. Ibid. GD157/2883, Hugh Scott of Harden to the Hon. Gilbert Elliot, Oct., 1812.

98. Ibid. GD157/2951/4, Thomas Cockburn to Walter Scott of Harden, 15 Dec., 1783.

8

The Limits of Patronage: the Defeat of David Scott in the County of Angus, 1795–6

The defeat of the Marchmont interest in Berwickshire was in large part self-destruction by a family quarrel, but a contributory factor was the active opposition to the earl shown by Henry Dundas, a more potent source of patronage than Marchmont, whose office of Keeper of the Great Seal of Scotland only put him on the fringes of government and certainly did not imply a right to command significant Scottish patronage. Henry Dundas was one of the most powerful political managers to operate in Scotland, yet even he was not unbeatable, and a member of parliament whose usefulness to the Minister was evident could be rejected by the freeholders of his county in spite of possessing not only the most active assistance which Henry Dundas could provide but also unusually extensive patronage of his own. The fate of David Scott, the member of parliament for Angus, and the difficulties which he encountered with his constituents in 1795–6, indicate the complexity of the task of managing a county electorate even when the incumbent was generously provided with the power to reward friends, for Scott in this period was Deputy-Chairman of the East India Company.

Perhaps it was David Scott's involvement with East India Company politics which was his undoing. Scott lost his support in Angus in spite of having helped many of the freeholders by providing employment in India for their kinsmen, and although the member of parliament was ready to complain of ingratitude on the part of those whom he had aided, he appears to have been largely the author of his own misfortune by losing touch with the opinions of his constituents. Freeholders were rarely bought by patronage. Patronage gave leverage to aid in their management by permitting a politician to capitalise upon the natural feelings of gratitude which were aroused by timely assistance. On the other hand, any voter in a county expected to be recognised as a man of some importance in his community, and that meant that a wise member of parliament went out of his way to consult the gentlemen of his county on every suitable occasion. David Scott's defect in the eyes of many of his constituents was not that he acted contrary to the wishes of the county in Parliament, or that he made improper use of his office; they complained that he was failing to involve the gentlemen freeholders in determining questions in which they felt that they had a right to a voice. Rightly or wrongly, Scott was seen by a substantial number of the gentlemen of Angus as taking advice only from a small clique of gentlemen with whom the Member of Parliament associated, while ignoring the remainder and thus disparaging them. One of the critics, Colonel Alexander Duncan of Lundie, assured Scott that he had

> never intended to insinuate that you had used your influence in the County improperly, on the contrary I am of opinion that your conduct with regard to the

Public Good of the County was perfectly correct, and uniformly directed for its interest ... but alas sometimes affections of less importance and seemingly trifling, influence the human heart.[1]

The essence of effective management in a Scottish county was taking care that such 'seemingly trifling affections' did not break the interest. The pride of the gentlemen freeholders could never safely be wounded by an appearance of taking them for granted, and David Scott was guilty of just such an offence.

Scott *was* a busy man, for his concern with Indian affairs was extremely time-consuming. He was, as Henry Dundas pointed out to a freeholder, Dundas's 'right hand man in the administration of India',[2] and the nature of Scott's official position in the East India Company prevented him from spending much of his time in the county of Angus where he was a substantial freeholder. Accordingly, David Scott got into the way of dealing with matters of local concern through some of the leading gentlemen with whom he regularly corresponded, including Sir David Carnegie of Southesk and Lord Douglas, both of whom had considerable interest and property in the county, a practice which lay at the root of his subsequent troubles. In the first place, by his actions Scott enhanced the influence, already powerful, of his intermediary, Sir David Carnegie, while at the same time he gave offence to many of the freeholders when something was presented to a county meeting as a *fait accompli*.

David Scott of Dunninald was not a Sir John Paterson, detested by his fellow lairds, for even an opposition survey of the county prepared in 1788, when Scott was the ministerial candidate, emphasised his popularity in the county, while one of his political opponents testified that he had the greatest respect for Scott's character.[4] Influence, popularity and respect, however important, were not enough, however, for David Scott lost the county of Angus and was forced to retire to the venal burgh district of Dundee, where his wealth and patronage successfully kept him in Parliament.

In reality, Scott was much less secure than he looked, in part because of his practice of using Sir David Carnegie to manage the county for him. Clearly, when Carnegie then chose to come forward as a candidate in opposition to the incumbent, Scott was at a disadvantage, many of the freeholders having promised their votes to Carnegie before Scott learned that opposition was intended,[5] and some of them at least did so under the impression that Carnegie, Scott's political agent in a former election and subsequently manager of his interest, acted with Scott's approbation.[6] Yet more threatening to Scott's chance of re-election was the fact that Sir David Carnegie acted in alliance with the gentleman who led the largest single political interest in the county, William Maule of Panmure, the brother of the Earl of Dalhousie, who had inherited the extensive estate of the Earl of Panmure, for the Panmure interest had customarily enjoyed the leading political role in the county through a combination of personal connections and employment of nominal voters. Together, Carnegie and Maule formed a dangerously strong opposition to the incumbent even when the latter had the strongest possible assistance from Government.

As soon as it had become apparent that David Scott's seat was seriously threatened, Henry Dundas, then at the height of his influence in government, intervened on his friend's behalf, but at the same time he made it quite clear that he still hoped to regain influence over Sir David Carnegie, for Scott was virtually ordered to avoid making the political quarrel a personal one:

> I totally disapprove of your writing any letter to Sir David Carnegie or doing or saying anything that can be construed into an opinion that your contest has in the smallest degree put you out of humour. I never once in the course of a long political life knew any man in the world get substantial benefit in any politics ... by mixing personalities with them, but I have known twenty examples to the contrary. I therefore do not give you ... an *advice* but impose it upon you as a prohibition ... [7]

Sir David's influence in the county principally resided in his personal connections, for although the Southesk interest was substantial, his estate did not permit the massive creation of additional qualifications. Panmure, on the other hand, already had many nominal qualifications manufactured by the late earl, and for that reason appeared to be the greater threat. Henry Dundas, however, believed that William Maule could be, if not eliminated as a danger, rendered powerless to remove the valuable Mr. Scott from Parliament.

William Maule, as the second son of the late Earl of Dalhousie, had inherited the Panmure estate, while his elder brother obtained the Dalhousie lands. Lady Dalhousie, however, was still alive, and William Maule's right to command the holders of nominal qualifications on the Panmure estate was unclear, if his mother could be persuaded to endorse David Scott at Henry Dundas's bidding. Dundas's task was made easier by the fact that Indian patronage had been obtained for members of the Dalhousie family and an argument of ingratitude could be employed, as Henry Dundas so well knew how to do, to counter any sign of wavering loyalty. As Lady Dalhousie was reminded:

> Yr Ladyship will recollect the very great anxiety to procure a Writership for yr Son. I applied to & got it from Mr. Scott. You must naturally suppose that I cannot fail to be a good deal hurt, if without any reason on earth, his brother on the first occasion takes a decided part against a person who at my request had become the benefactor of his brother. In short it unhinges all those ties & obligations in life, by which one is enabled to support & aid one's friends.[8]

A few days later, Dundas rubbed the lesson home by advising Lady Dalhousie that David Scott could not have had the slightest suspicion of Dundas's having asked such a favour 'for Mr. Maule's brother if I had entertained the remotest idea that Mr. M. meant to act hostilely to him in the County he represented '.[9] The attack on Maule's mother was pressed so effectively that she was induced to make her personal friendship for Dundas and Scott publicly known, and by implication to repudiate the current holder of the Panmure estate, an act which did indeed have its effect upon some of the liferent voters attached to the Panmure family.[10] With less powerful freeholders Dundas was equally determined, writing to Admiral Duncan, the brother of Colonel Duncan of Lundie, that if Lundie 'had been a

Freeholder in Mid Lothian & taken a part against the Advocate, it would not have hurt me more than his taking a part against Mr. Scott '.[11] The Government, Dundas made plain, was strongly interested in securing the re-election of a member of parliament whose attendance in the House of Commons was vital to the administration, for according to Dundas:

> If you were to ask either Mr. Pitt or me whether there is any connexion of ours wither in or out of Parliament, whose aid is of more use in the conduct of much essential publick business, *there is not one*. Under these circumstances I have only to regret that I have not the more means to aid him.[12]

From Dundas's manner of expressing his determination to aid Scott it is apparent that this was not merely one seat among many in Henry Dundas's Scottish empire but something truly significant to Government, and it thus appears still more surprising that on this occasion the government manager suffered a defeat.

In the county of Angus a popular, well-connected and patronage-rich Member was unable to retain his seat even with the most earnest exertions on his behalf by Government. A man like David Scott should have been able to build for himself an impregnable position in the shire based solidly on foundations of gratitude for services rendered and hopes for services to come. When the opposition appeared, Scott himself was too ready to suggest that the freeholders of Angus were uniquely greedy and ungrateful, but was that a fair evaluation of the character of the gentlemen of Angus? Scott, in fact, created the opposition which unseated him through his perhaps necessary preoccupation with Indian affairs, for it was that which opened a distance between the representative and the freeholders, which is made clear by the response of some of them when asked to give their reasons for hostility. The cause of their disenchantment with Scott may at a distance appear trivial, but it was always easy to antagonise the barons through an appearance of neglect of their views, and in Scott's case that neglect was actual, for he acted only through a coterie of associates, ignoring the mass of the voters. Colonel Alexander Duncan 'embraced the first opportunity of joining the independent Freeholders to support Sir David Carnegie', for 'it was but too evident that a certain set of gentlemen were the only persons consulted in any thing related to the County'.[13] Such conduct in any county with a substantial number of independent freeholders would have caused trouble, and in Scott's case there could be no question of ignoring the independent gentlemen and relying upon nominal voters when the estate with the largest supply of such nominals, that of Panmure, was in the hands of an enemy.

The touchstone of the opposition to Scott was the formation of a new fencible regiment to be associated with the county, one of many such temporary units raised for home defence during the wars with France. Angus already had smaller company-size formations for internal defence, and the idea of a regiment for that purpose was one which originated in London, as David Scott admitted.[14] The dispute was over the provision of officers to the new regiment, and here Scott's lack of contact with the freeholders, whose aid was essential for the successful launching of such a regiment, hampered both his own career and the organisation of the unit. Colonel Duncan appeared to be expressing a widely held opinion when he complained to the Member of Parliament that

> It was but too evident that a certain set of gentlemen were the only persons consulted in any thing relating to the County, witness the appointment of the officers to the Regiment which was endeavored to be crammed down our throats without the consent or approbation of more than one or two gentlemen, with whom I am determined never to associate . . . [15]

The fencible regiment had become associated with a particular segment of the Angus gentry, namely, those associated closely with the Lord Lieutenant, Lord Douglas, and it is evident that no serious attempt was made to secure the prior agreement of the county before proceeding. When Duncan and other prominent freeholders were informed of the plan, they were at the same time told that Douglas of Brigton and other friends of Lord Douglas had been named captains.[16] Moreover, Scott himself, in November 1794, wrote to the convener of the county 'expressly recommending Captain Hunter as an *excellent officer* to be Lieutenant-Colonel', an opinion which was not shared by Colonel Duncan.[17] The difficulty in short, as Duncan reported that a freeholder at the county meeting had complained, was that the unit had become 'more a family than a County Regiment'.[18]

The close association of the regiment with the Douglas family and its friends effectively alienated many of the freeholders, including apparently Maule of Panmure, in spite of the fact that he had been given an opportunity to raise the regiment and had declined.[19] David Scott in fact appeared to be bewildered by the unexpected hostility to a Douglas-raised regiment, for, as he complained to Colonel Duncan, not only had Panmure refused to organise the regiment, but Duncan himself and Colonel Fotheringhame, the convener of Angus, were considered to be unwilling to undertake additional duties. Indeed, Colonel Duncan had complained that the demands of his office of Deputy-Lieutenant were 'too severe' for his health.[20] What Scott failed to anticipate, however, was the unnecessary alienation of many freeholders occasioned by the absence of any attempt at consultation. They had simply been informed 'that Colonel Douglas of the West Lowland Fencibles has engaged to raise a Regiment of Fencibles to serve in Great Britain or Ireland, and that it is his wish as well as that of the Lord Lieutenant, that the Regiment should be considered as more particularly attached to this County'.[21] The gentlemen of the county had approved of the idea of a regiment and agreed to name it the Angus Fencibles, but the nomination of the officers to such a regiment was felt by a number of them to be something which should be considered at a county meeting. The practice followed when a great landowner raised a regiment, that of distributing commissions to friends and relatives, often in return for sharing in the expenses of finding recruits, was considered not to be applicable in this situation where the gentlemen of Angus might be called upon to meet some of the costs of raising what purported to be a county regiment. Indeed, the Angus gentry specifically reserved judgement on whether any such support would in the circumstances be given, promising only that upon completion of the companies raised for local defence they would consider the question of financial support for Colonel Douglas's regiment.[22]

The Member of Parliament and Lord Douglas had involved Sir David Carnegie in their discussions when a fencible regiment was first projected, and indeed Carnegie was one of the leading figures in the small group of gentlemen through whom Scott dealt at arm's length with Angus questions, but Carnegie insisted that the launching of the regiment was done in a manner contrary to his advice, particularly on the question of the lieutenant-colonelcy, claiming

> that it was my opinion [Captain Hunter] should obtain the consent & approbation of the Captains of the Angus Volunteers & of the principal gentlemen of the County before he took any one step in the business ... when I came down, I found the Regiment going on, but that neither the officers above mentioned nor the gentlemen had given their approbation.[23]

The raising of troops, regular, volunteer and fencible, created labour shortages in Angus as elsewhere, and a new regiment, fully associated with the county, would clearly make matters worse. Accordingly, although the consent of the freeholders might have been expected in view of the external threat and the fear of insurrection, resentment at taking their support for granted produced a formidable backlash. Indeed, in view of Carnegie's advice that the principal gentlemen of the county should be consulted, those who were *not* consulted had some reason to feel affronted. The opposition clearly was not personal, as it had been in the case of Sir John Paterson in Berwickshire, for Scott himself told Robert Dundas, the Lord Advocate, that 'far the greater number told me that "they were angry with others" who were considered to be my first political friends & that by voting for Sir David they hoped to hurt them'.[24] Scott assured the Lord Advocate that during his canvass he had learned that the freeholders would have accepted all of the new levies 'had my friends not carried matters with such a high hand'.[25]

Even after David Scott abandoned his business in London in order to hurry to Scotland and commence a canvass of the county, he still appeared to be confused by the freeholders' rejection. Indeed, Scott's bewilderment is understandable, for all the unpopular actions of which the freeholders complained, from a choice of a collector of the cess to the dispute over the Angus Fencibles, had been concerted by a group of freeholders which included his opponent, Sir David Carnegie. Scott's conclusion, however, that the freeholders had been imposed upon by Carnegie, was unwarranted, for the fault lay with Scott himself, who should never have encouraged the emergence of any intermediary between himself and his constituents. On his own admission, David Scott had created an arbitrary division in questions of interest to the county and had confined his attention to only one portion, for, as he told Colonel Duncan:

> I deemed myself particularly obliged to Sir David Carnegie for allowing himself to be the channel of communication between the County & me, and for acting as a principal in all County matters. In regard to the County itself, I never lost sight of its great interest, such as Coal Duty, Bridges, Turnpikes, Supplies of Men for

Government etc. There I recommended as coming immediately under my attention as Member for the County — but as to the interior management of Forfar, of Road Meetings, Appointment of Collector of Cess, or in short any local regulation or arrangement, I never interfered, from an idea that it would be officious and improper when so many gentlemen on the spot [were] better informed than me in such affairs . . . [26]

Scott, with the best of intentions, brought trouble upon himself by his attitude. Certainly there were many questions relating to the county which should have been decided by the gentlemen themselves, but that was precisely what had not been happening and what had induced their revolt. Decisions were made in accordance with the wishes of a small group of Angus landowners close to the Member of Parliament without consulting the remainder of the county gentry. Scott's opponent, Sir David Carnegie of Southesk, until then one of Scott's inner circle himself, was well placed to suggest that good advice was being ignored and that all county questions were settled by Lord Douglas and his associates as they pleased. Indeed even some of Scott's explanation to the Deputy-Lieutenant, Colonel Duncan, could be held to support such an argument.

When David Scott began his canvass in August 1795, the battle was already lost. He began with the hope of dispelling the belief that a group of gentlemen close to him had made improper use of his influence,[27] but unfortunately it was too late for such explanations, even if they had carried conviction. A majority of the freeholders were already secured by Sir David Carnegie, and the opposition now included not only political enemies exasperated by the management of the county, but also men whose support Scott had counted certain, who had been induced to promise their votes to Carnegie in the belief that Sir David, who had been known to be Scott's 'political Agent for the County',[28] was coming forward by agreement with the incumbent who must have determined to retire from Parliament. This misapprehension, if such it was, was the result once again of Scott's distance from his constituents. A failure to maintain personal contacts made an unannounced decision to retire from the Commons, in order to concentrate on Indian affairs, quite plausible. There is no evidence that Carnegie ever suggested such a thing, whatever rumour might be current, but it was a poor political manager who would see, as Scott did, a majority of the voters in his county secured by an opponent before he 'in fact had known of any opposition'.[29] Political agents were normally Edinburgh lawyers familiar with all the intracacies of electoral law, and Scott's excessive reliance on a major landowner with a great interest of his own in the constituency was undoubtedly inviting trouble should the agent quarrel with his principal. A writer who was an employee, rather than a laird who was a temporary ally, was the only safe channel of information, and even then the Member was expected to maintain far closer contact with the individual freeholders than Scott had been willing to attempt.

It may have been some consolation to Scott that he found during his tour of the county that his personal popularity was unimpaired, for, as he told Robert Dundas:

Every person, *I except none* declared themselves highly satisfied with my public conduct, & only had to regret that such parts of it in regard to the Fencibles & Volunteers Corps as have been thought exceptionable were acts of Sir David & his friends & Not mine ... [30]

But that did not materially improve his position, for as he admitted to the Lord Advocate, Sir David would have a majority of five votes at the Michaelmas Head Court, and although like so many politicians Scott looked on the bright side and insisted that if he could only gain five votes from his rival it would count double,[31] the hope of doing so was surely unrealistic when even those who had good reason to have felt grateful for Scott's patronage had deserted him. But Scott's denunciation of such deserters betrays a mistaken view of the power of patronage and what it should confer. Scott believed that a freeholder aided in some way was, or should be, a bought dependent, remarking that:

> Some & I am sorry to say not a few, from having bad heads & far worse hearts left us in a manner too infamous to describe. Perhaps they sunk under the weight of obligation, & though they would best exonerate by breaking thro' every tie of gratitude. Mr. Dundas experienced this in still more extreme degree than me ... [32]

Freeholders could rarely be bought in the manner London-based politicians appeared to believe. Patronage did induce a feeling of gratitude, and that could be the basis of great political power, but this did not eliminate the need for continuing and careful management and the maintenance of close contact with the individual freeholders. Nothing caused greater resentment than the impression that a voter was taken for granted, and even worse that his vote had been bought by assistance given in the past. Patronage was seen in the counties as an act of friendship, and the best politicians never lost sight of that fact or failed to preserve the appearance of close personal friendship with the recipients of patronage. David Scott, in short, had become too much of a London politician through his preoccupation with East Indian affairs, and it led to misunderstanding of his fellow-barons in Angus.

With the majority of the freeholders engaged to his rival, one solution which occurred to Scott was to resign his seat immediately, by applying for the Chiltern Hundreds, in order to permit Carnegie to replace him for the remainder of the Parliament.[33] The reasoning here was that many freeholders who had promised support to Carnegie did so only for one election, leaving them free to vote as they chose at a subsequent contest. Unfortunately for Scott, Sir David Carnegie had foreseen this possibility and had sought the freeholders' support at the next *general* election, and promises of such support could not be considered redeemed by a vote at a by-election.[34] Moreover, there was some reason to doubt Scott's interpretation of some of the responses of freeholders who had committed themselves to Carnegie, for the assumption that they would at a second election return to Scott was certainly not based on firm evidence. Hunter of Blackness, for example, told Scott

> That he would vote at the Michaelmas Head Court for me to be Preses, & with us in preventing any persons being kept off the Roll that were our friends, & had a right to

come on. That on the first ellection he must vote for Sr David, *but be it soon or late* he would vote on the second for me against Sir David & every person whatever except Mr. Maule himself.[35]

What if the rival candidate at the general election turned out to be William Maule of Panmure, now a determined ally of Sir David Carnegie? Given Maule of Panmure's interest in the county and his family's history of political activity, that was a prospect which showed every possibility of being realised.

In any contested election there were individuals whose support might be won, if not immediately, at least on a subsequent occasion, and David Scott was tempted by the idea of resignation in order to make the general election a second contest. Scott was convinced that his disadvantage resulting from Carnegie's prior application could be overcome and that some of the freeholders were vulnerable to attack. James Chaplain of Colliston, for example, had, according to Scott, 'sold his vote for four hundred Pounds or as good which he got in an Ensigncy. If a similar principle operates & he has sense to distinguish he will come round assuredly'.[36] Several other individuals were considered to be susceptible to pressure from their relatives in India, and communications from there might be expected before a general election, for Scott had naturally sought the good offices of those whom he had aided.[37] Moreover, the efforts of Henry Dundas with Lady Dalhousie had borne fruit, and several of the freeholders who normally voted with the Panmure interest, and were indeed engaged to Carnegie, might be detached at a subsequent election. Patrick Chalmers of Auldbar, an independent freeholder, told Scott that he had promised support to Sir David Carnegie 'from a principle of gratitude to Maule, as supposing it for the Panmure family, but he now found Maul[e] acted . . . against the interests of the whole family'.[38] Accordingly, Scott began to canvass energetically for the freeholders' votes at a second election, since it was clear that Sir David was going to secure the first one, reinforcing the Scott interest meanwhile with a few new nominal votes, though clearly that approach could not be taken too far without alienating the county even more seriously. Unfortunately for Scott, he could not spend the necessary time to cultivate his constituents, for Indian business recalled him to London in September, where the Chairman's gout necessitated the presence of the Deputy-Chairman of the company.[39] Scott fully intended to return to Forfar in time for the Michaelmas Head Court, and indeed feared that an attempt might be made at that meeting to diminish his position still further by voting him out of the chair and thereafter 'to keep voters off the Roll . . . who have a right to be brought on & to admit good & bad on the other side'.[40] The head Court, however, had to be held without the Member of Parliament's attendance, for Scott found it impossible to leave London because of the absence of Henry Dundas,[41] the Minister responsible for Indian affairs, which once again permitted Scott's enemies a clear field in Angus. Needless to say, they made the best use of their opportunity to stir up further discontent with the representative.

Of the five leading interests in Angus, two, William Maule of Panmure and Sir David Carnegie of Southesk, were Scott's enemies, and another, Lord Douglas, was an ally. Canvassing added the majority of the Ogilvies, 'the ancient Clan of the County',[42] to Scott's supporters, but the Earl of Strathmore, whose family interest was second only to that of Panmure in Angus, declined to commit himself. In spite of that the situation was not irredeemably lost, and Scott's powers of patronage might win a few mercenary friends, for the Member was determined to spare nothing in this direction: 'An Ensign to be made a Lieut[enant] is nothing —Bengal, Madras or Bombay Cadet [ships] could be had'.[43] The combination of a willingness to try to please and a misunderstanding of the opinion of the county, however, led Scott into further difficulty and played into the hands of his rivals.

In a letter to John Graeme, a writer to the signet who acted for Scott in the Angus political work, the Member of Parliament made a statement whose meaning is less than clear:

> The stamps you must speak to the Gentn. addressed in the inclosed, what expectations he may hold out, & you may pledge yourselves for it. I can't treat on such a subject.[44]

The gentleman referred to above was, in all probability, Robert Graham of Fintry, a freeholder who was among the most active of Scott's friends and closely associated with him in the canvass of the county. That remark communicated to Fintry appears to have led the latter to claim in conversation with George Dempster of Dunnichen, another important freeholder, that the administrator of the Stamp Office in Angus, John Rankine of Mains of Dudhope, one of Scott's opponents, was to be deprived of his office which was to go to William Allison of Fallows in return for his vote.[45]

A letter from Scott to the Lord Advocate appears to confirm that such an intention was in Scott's mind, for he remarked that

> Mr. Allison told me he certainly would not vote against me but he could not promise to vote for, but referred me to your Lordship. I have reason to believe he wants an office in the Stamps about L300 p. annum only, which has been held by another for several years & which would be far better disposed of than to him ... Allison would not speak out to me but I could see the above. I think his is a life rent vote but he must be kept in humour.[46]

William Allison was in fact qualified on a liferent obtained from the late Earl of Panmure,[47] but as with a number of other voters so qualified, the division in the Panmure family offered Allison an opportunity to act independently of William Maule of Panmure, and to insist that his vote was an independent one. The exact nature of the conversation between Graham of Fintry and Dempster is of course impossible to determine, but Dempster was given the impression that David Scott had suggested that Dempster had been shown a plan to replace Rankine with Allison, a claim which he hotly denied. The story, moreover, was given wide currency, to Scott's detriment, for as he told Dempster:

> Some have written ... that there could be no doubt of my intentions for that Mr. Dempster had declared I had communicated it to him. I have written them "No

consideration would make me accept of a Man's Vote who could venture to insinuate my having an intention different from what I expressed. I therefore entirely exonerated all them from their promise, who could be mean enough to conceive such an idea of me." I can't say what number of Votes I may have lost by this Paper War relative Mr. Rankin ... but ... it is impossible for me to compute the damage wch has been done me ... The County of Angus could be no object on earth for me, for putting up with insult, & some of those correspondents abt Rankin seem not to know what insult is ... [48]

In fact, after being bombarded with letters from the many friends of Rankine, David Scott was attempting to secure Rankine's vote rather than replace him. An associate of Scott in the Indian shipping interest employed one of the sons of Rankine of Dudhope as a clerk, and this gentleman strongly urged Rankine to think of his other sons and to promise support to Scott at a second election even if he was committed to Carnegie at the first one. As Scott reported to one of his friends in Dundee, Rankine had been told that

One Son in the *Ld Thurlow* Indiaman Midshipman ... could have got through my influence advanced in the service as fast as his years would qualify him & another that wished to be a Cadet he could have got me to appoint had I not found that they were the Sons of Dudhope ... [49]

Scott advised David Anderson, one of his Angus friends, to make a point of 'getting as if accidentally into conversation with Dudhope on the subject and point out how absurd it is to sacrifice the interests of his family to compliment'.[50] Dudhope, however, refused to bite in spite of the obvious damage which his attitude may have occasioned to the careers of his family. But the damage had already been done to the Scott interest, in Angus in all events, for when the Provost of Dundee again suggested removing Mr. Rankine from his office in the Stamps in September 1796, David Scott made it quite plain that he had had enough of Rankine and his office, telling the Provost:

If you knew the volumes & volumes of letters which I had received in favour of Mr. Rankin at Forfar & the ill will which was industriously raised against me for a supposed intention of mine to do as you now propose, I dare say you would be satisfied that it would be improper in me at present to disturb the tranquillity of your neighbourhood ... [51]

David Scott certainly had no love for Rankine, being of opinion that he had 'merited dismission over & over again',[52] but the suggestion that this might be contemplated in order to secure a vote had done the Member of Parliament immense harm in the county. Scott blamed his friend Graham of Fintry for the blow, claiming that Fintry's 'communication to G[eorge] D[empster] brought upon me a most voluminous correspondence & no doubt ill will',[53] but even if Fintry acted rashly there can be little doubt that Scott had indeed contemplated the action which he so strenuously denied, and equally it is clear that even the most confidential associates of Scott in his campaign for re-election were not kept fully informed of the Member's thinking.

From London the situation in Angus did not look as bad as it did in Scotland, and even in late January 1796 David Scott could still write optimistically to his Scottish friends suggesting that his evaluation of the freeholders' roll would give him a majority of six at a second election, though this was based on a number of assumptions to the effect that all undeclared voters and liferenters would divide equally and that some of the more elderly supporters of Sir David Carnegie would fail to make the journey to Forfar to cast their votes. Scott, however, was equally clear that he would prefer not to run at all than be defeated, believing that 'it matters not whether by a majority of 2 or 10'.[54] In those circumstances, with the possibility of victory resting upon such unproven assumptions, the certainty which Scott sought was not to be found in the county of Angus, but success at a second election was in his mind when he resigned his seat in order to re-enter Parliament as the Member for the Dundee district of burghs.[55] That hope turned out to be impossible to satisfy, for Sir David Carnegie was replaced at the general election by William Maule of Panmure, and David Scott remained as the Member for the burghs. Indeed, for a Member of Parliament in Scott's situation, busy, wealthy and well supplied with the powers of patronage that burgh councillors valued in their representatives, the burghs seat was a better choice than a county, though perhaps an even better alternative might have been the Cornish borough which Scott was once offered and refused during his struggle to retain control of Angus.[56]

In one view, David Scott's term as the representative of his native county was ended by a fencible regiment, the collectorship of supply and a minor excise office, but in reality all these are symptoms of Scott's great fault, his failure in management. County management was never just the distribution of places and pensions, for there was no Scottish politician better placed to satisfy the freeholders than David Scott. Good management required something more than patronage. It demanded close attention to what in far-off London might seem trivial matters of detail, but which in Forfar appeared matters of great moment. Above all the touchiness of the Scottish freeholders could never be safely ignored. They were very ready to take offence at any sign of a slight, and what greater disparagement could they receive than to be ignored in questions on which they felt they had a right to be consulted? Scott enjoyed a valuable personal popularity, but it was the popularity of a stranger, and there is little evidence that David Scott ever contemplated spending several months a year cultivating the freeholders in endless rounds of dinners, and drinking sessions. Perhaps he might have escaped censure for his failure to maintain close social ties with the gentlemen because of the extenuating circumstances of his high office in London, but to devolve the duty of cultivating the voters upon Sir David Carnegie was surely imprudent when the latter had just as good a claim to represent the shire.

David Scott never fully appreciated what had created the opposition to his retention of the Angus seat, seeing only the worst form of ingratitude in William Maule, for example, and complaining that although I had heap'd attentions on him, & bestowed such essential favours on his family, I yet marvelled not at his conduct, because I conceived that wine & its concomitant weakness are equal to blind all the virtues he might have been possessed of . . . [57]

Scott never seemed to consider that William Maule of Panmure might have felt justified in his opposition, by the fact of his own exclusion from any share in the management of Angus, in view of his family interest in the shire. A writership to Maule's younger brother was unlikely to create a tie of absolute dependence, and Scott, whatever attentions he heaped upon the Laird of Panmure, did not involve him in political management, relying rather upon Lord Douglas and Sir David Carnegie. Patronage and the support of powerful Ministers was not enough to compensate for bad management. Of the two, management skill was much more significant than patronage, particularly in the counties. Burgh magistrates saw a golden future before them when they offered their support to David Scott, and even a man of his resources had difficulty keeping up with the demands of the councils of Perth, Cupar, St. Andrews and Dundee, but the kind of management which worked for Scott in his burghs was quite insufficient in the county.

NOTES

1. SRO. Melville Castle, GD51/1/198/2/12, Colonel Alexander Duncan of Lundie to David Scott, 13 Aug., 1795.
2. Ibid. GD51/1/198/2/6, Henry Dundas to Robert Graham of Fintry, undated [July, 1795].
3. Sir Charles Elphinstone Adam, *The Political State of Scotland in 1788* [[Edinburgh, 1887], Freeholders roll of Forfarshire, 158.
4. SRO. Melville Castle, GD51/1/198/2/10, Colonel Alexander Duncan to David Scott, 23 Jul., 1795.
5. India Office Records Home Misc. 728/186–191, David Scott to Robert Dundas, Lord Advocate of Scotland, 7 Sep., 1795.
6. Ibid.
7. C.H. Philips [ed.], *The Correspondence of David Scott, Director and Chairman of the East India Company, 1787–1805* [London, 1951], i, 38, Henry Dundas to David Scott, 1 Aug., 1795.
8. SRO. Melville Castle, GD51/1/198/2/7, Henry Dundas to Lady Dalhousie, 16 Jul., 1795.
9. Ibid. GD51/1/198/2/9, Henry Dundas to Lady Dalhousie, 21 Jul., 1795.
10. India Office Home Misc. 728/186–191, David Scott to the Lord Advocate, 7 Sep., 1795.
11. SRO. Melville Castle, GD51/1/198/2/8, Henry Dundas to Admiral Duncan, 21 Jul., 1795.
12. Ibid.
13. Ibid. GD51/1/198/2/10, Colonel Alexander Duncan to David Scott, 23 Jul., 1795.
14. Ibid. GD51/1/198/2/11, David Scott to Colonel Alexander Duncan, 9 Aug., 1795.
15. Ibid. GD51/1/198/2/10, Colonel Alexander Duncan to David Scott, 23 Jul., 1795.
16. Ibid. GD51/1/198/2/12, Colonel Duncan to David Scott, 13 Aug., 1795.
17. Ibid.
18. Ibid.
19. Ibid. GD51/1/198/2/11, David Scott to Colonel Duncan, 9 Aug.,.1795.

20. Ibid.
21. Ibid. GD51/1/198/2/12, Colonel Duncan to David Scott, 13 Aug., 1795.
22. Ibid.
23. Ibid. GD51/1/198/2/13, Sir David Carnegie of Southesk to Colonel Duncan, 4 Sep., 1795.
24. India Office Home Misc. 728/186–191, David Scott to the Lord Advocate, 7 Sep., 1795.
25. Ibid.
26. SRO. Melville Castle, GD51/1/198/2/11, David Scott to Colonel Duncan, 9 Aug., 1795.
27. Ibid.
28. India Office Home Misc. 728/186–191, David Scott to the Lord Advocate, 7 Sep., 1795.
29. Ibid.
30. Ibid.
31. Ibid.
32. Ibid.
33. SRO. Melville Castle, GD51/1/198/2/5, Lord Douglas to Henry Dundas, 30 Aug., 1795.
34. India Office Home Misc. 728/195–203, David Scott to John Graeme, W.S., 11 Sep., 1795.
35. Ibid. MS.728/186–191, David Scott to the Lord Advocate, 7 Sep., 1795.
36. Ibid. MS.728/195–203, David Scott to John Graeme, W.S., 11 Sep., 1795.
37. Ibid.
38. Ibid.
39. Ibid. MS.728/211–216, David Scott to James Guthrie of Craigie, 12 Sep., 1795.
40. Ibid. MS.728/205–207, David Scott to James Chaplain of Colliston, 11 Sep., 1795.
41. Ibid. MS.728/240–1, David Scott to Major Erskine, 28 Oct., 1795.
42. Ibid. MS.728/132–3, Sir J. Smyth Burges to James Ogilvie of Ruthven, undated, [Nov., 1795].
43. Ibid. MS.728/195–203, David Scott to John Graeme, W.S., 11 Sep., 1795.
44. Ibid.
45. Ibid. MS.728/120–130, David Scott to George Dempster of Dunnichen, 27 Nov., 1795.
46. Ibid. MS.728/186–191, David Scott to the Lord Advocate, 7 Sep., 1795.
47. Adam, *Political State of Scotland in 1788*, Forfarshire Freeholders Roll.
48. India Office Home Misc. 728/128–130, David Scott to George Dempster, 27 Nov., 1795.
49. Ibid. MS.728/131 and 728/133–4, David Scott to David Anderson, 27 Nov., 1795.
50. Ibid.
51. Ibid. MS.728/513, David Scott to Provost Thoms, 15 Sep., 1795.
52. Ibid. MS.728/144–5, David Scott to Lord Douglas, 20 Dec., 1795.
53. Ibid.
54. Ibid. MS.728/181–5, David Scott to John Graeme, W.S. and other Angus friends, 21 Jan., 1796.
55. Ibid. MS.728/ 304, David Scott to Robert Graham of Fintry, 27 Feb., 1796.
56. Ibid. MS.728/211–216, David Scott to James Guthrie of Craigie, 12 Sep., 1795.
57. Ibid.

9

Ministerial Power in a Small County: the Peeblesshire Election of 1732

The influence of powerful Ministers, aided as it was by a steady flow of patronage, was very real. On the other hand, it should not be assumed that possession of such powers confirmed a Minister's control of a contested county election. Any politician who took a hand in a county election could find himself hard pressed, and not merely in the larger counties where the supply of patronage could never hope to match the needs of a majority of the freeholders. Even counties with small electorates of around twenty voters could provide hard political battles in which the candidate favoured by Administration was by no means sure of victory. The by-election held in the county of Peebles in 1732 provides an example of the uncertainty of control by the Administration, for although the Government candidate ultimately prevailed, the contest turned at one point upon a single vote on the date of election. The number of freeholders in the county of Peebles was never large, and it is clear from the closeness of this contest that the 'managers' were unable to secure a safe majority of even a small electorate by bribery. Patronage was a factor in securing the return of the Administration candidate, but it was certainly not enough to put the question beyond dispute, and it was decided only on the day of election itself.

The Peebles election of 1732 was occasioned by the death of John Douglas, the brother of the Earl of March, who had represented the county since 1722. The March interest was normally dominant in Peebles, but John Douglas's death completed the eclipse of this interest begun in 1731 by the death of the earl, for the current holder of the title was a minor. Freeholders who had formerly taken their lead from Lord March and his brother thus found themselves freed from former obligations to that family, and they showed little willingness to accept advice from the late earl's widow, even though she did take a hand in the question of the succession to the parliamentary seat.

When John Douglas had last been elected, in 1727, he had been opposed by Sir James Nasmyth of Posso, a Peeblesshire baronet, who had indeed accused Douglas and his brother of having rigged that election meeting.[1] Now, with the Douglasses removed by death, Sir James tried again, and in March 1732 came forward as a candidate with the powerful support of the Duke of Argyll and the Earl of Ilay, who were strongly opposed to another gentleman who had offered his services to the freeholders of Peeblesshire, Sir Alexander Murray of Stanhope.

Influence in political questions was extremely diffuse, for it was not merely a matter of Argyll and Ilay, or their political deputy, Lord Milton, writing directly to freeholders to seek their vote and interest for Nasmyth. That was done where there seemed any prospect of success in cases where an obligation had been incurred by a freeholder and friendship was to be expected. Equally, however, the rallying of a political interest for a contested election was a matter of adding together many lesser interests, with the Administration seeking the aid of other gentlemen who might have influence upon the freeholders of Peebles. Milton and Ilay, for example, employed their own connections with Lord Elibank, Lord Minto, the Master of Ross, and Thomas Cochrane of Wester Stanley, a commissioner of excise, all of whom were believed to have the ability to influence voters in this county to support the candidate adopted by the Administration. The chain of influence could be further attenuated. Lord Milton, for example, approached the Master of Ross, who in turn sought the intervention of Sir James Lockhart with the Peebles freeholders.[2] The influence of relatives was eagerly sought, for a freeholder might not care to disoblige a kinsman. The Administration approached the Peebles freeholder, Geddes of Kirkurd, through his brother, who readily promised that he would 'undertake for Kirkurd notwithstanding his great friendship with Sir Alexander Murray of Stanhope', and that laird was in fact successfully attached to the Government party.[3]

An approach to a gentleman of influence required care, however, for the possibility of misunderstanding and disobligement was always present. Sir Gilbert Elliot of Minto, a lord of session, had long been closely associated with the Argyll family in politics, and it was therefore natural that he should be approached for his assistance with some of the freeholders with whom he was connected. Indeed, when Lord Minto was directly approached by Sir James Nasmyth, he had declined making a declaration, a refusal which was attributed to the fact that 'he had not heard how Earle Isla was disposed'.[4] Unfortunately the message which reached Lord Minto did not make it at all clear how Ilay and Argyll wished him to act, for the letter sent by Argyll simply asked Minto 'to use his interest to keep out Stanhope in all events'.[5] Upon receipt of that request Lord Minto acted to try to keep out Sir Alexander Murray of Stanhope, but not by throwing his support behind Sir James Nasmyth. Minto persuaded one of his own friends, Sir Alexander Murray of Blackbarony, the chief of the Peebles Murrays, to declare himself a candidate.

Blackbarony had strong interest in the county, and could count on the friendship of a number of lairds, particularly those of his own name, including Lord Elibank, who described Blackbarony as his 'very good friend and Chief'.[6] The obvious advantage created by Blackbarony's standing, however, namely the division of the Murrays between the two Sir Alexanders, was negated by the remaining candidate, for Sir James Nasmyth made it plain that if Blackbarony stood, then he would join forces with Stanhope to keep him out,[7] and as the freeholders began to divide into three parties a dangerous situation began to emerge for the Administration. If Nasmyth made good his threat to join Stanhope, the latter would in all probability be elected by a substantial majority, but the greater danger was in fact the possibility of a junction between the two Murray baronets, with the Murray family dominant in Peeblesshire independent of Administration.

A three-cornered contest fought to the last was scarcely more encouraging for

Government, for Thomas Cochrane took a pessimistic view of Sir James Nasmyth's chances, admitting that Sir Alexander Murray of Blackbarony's standing had 'disordered some of our Electors that was for Sir Alex. Murray of Stanhope, if he stand it will give Stanhope some truble, but be what I can lairne Sir James Nesmyth hes not a chance for it'.[8]

Sir Alexander Murray of Stanhope was able to attract substantial support, for he had a persuasive manner in conversing with the freeholders in their homes. On the other hand, with one of them at least, Stanhope talked too freely, for he had almost secured a promise of support from the brother of Geddes of Kirkurd, when he disclosed that

> he had left London in haste, without waiting for Earle Isla's recommendation, hoping to carry the election by his own interest without the aid of any great man. This made Mr. Geddes stand off, who told Sir Alexander that he Geddes was under many obligations [to Lord Ilay] and that he could not imbark with Sir Alexr. till he knew Lord Ilay's wishes.[9]

With some other gentlemen, however, independence of Lord Ilay was a positive advantage, and Lord Traquair, Robert Murray of Murrayshall, Hay of Drummelzier, and other Jacobite gentlemen gave Stanhope their support, though the fact that few Jacobites would take the oaths to Government which would qualify them to vote made their support less useful. Jacobite gentry did, however, have their own connections and powers to influence voters, so their support was not as ineffectual as it might at first glance appear, while the assistance of the Duke of Roxburghe and Lord Lintoun was also valuable in establishing Sir Alexander Murray of Stanhope as a strong candidate. [10]

In addition to Blackbarony, Stanhope, and Sir James Nasmyth, the freeholders with the greatest personal interest in the county were William Carmichael, the brother of the Earl of Hyndford, Alexander Murray of Cringletie, a relative of Blackbarony's who had formerly represented the county in Parliament, and Williamson of Chaplehill, the sheriff-clerk of Peebles. All of them were believed to be susceptible to pressure from Administration or from those connected with it, but before they could be fixed it was first essential to improve Sir James Nasmyth's situation by removing any danger of a union of the two Murray baronets against him. Accordingly Ilay and his deputy Milton, employing Lord Elibank as their intermediary, arranged a compromise which resulted in the withdrawal of Blackbarony in return for his appointment as sheriff. Blackbarony had stood, according to Elibank, only on condition that he was 'assured of the Earle of Ilay's interest and support',[11] and that support had already been given to Nasmyth, but Blackbarony's affairs were in disorder and he was in desperate need of some remunerative office, while he was in fact also negotiating the sale of a portion of his estate to Lord Ilay himself.[12] In short, it was a comparatively easy task to detach Blackbarony from his own political ambitions and to swing his support behind Nasmyth by an offer of patronage. According to James Armour, the lawyer appointed by Lord Milton to manage the Peebles election, Blackbarony controlled several votes, alleging that he commanded 'two or three' freeholders 'who possibly might have declar'd for Stanhope ... and its thought will carry them whither he pleases'.[13] Blackbarony's unequivocal declaration of allegiance to Argyll and Ilay on March 30th,[14] and Lord Elibank's assurance that the Laird of Blackbarony had written to all his friends and relations to follow his example and support Sir James Nasmyth, were therefore of considerable help to Administration, Elibank in fact claiming that 'six good votes' would be switched to Nasmyth by this arrangement.[15]

The removal of Blackbarony as a candidate, which at the same time placed a friend in the important position of sheriff, clearly was an example of management by bribery, one of Milton's correspondents remarking that the laird had 'swallowed the bait of the Sheriffship most greedily',[16] but this is an example of a single office gaining a number of votes, for the same writer pointed out that Blackbarony 'has writte to all his friends that their voting for Sir James Nasmith, will be as oblidging to him, as if they voted for himself'.[17] A carefully planted patronage bribe could sometimes yield results of real significance, but it is equally clear that there was no question of attempting to bribe a significant number of the voters, and indeed what could have been found to use for such a purpose? The death of the late sheriff-principal, John Douglas, had left a vacancy in the county of Peebles which would in any event have to be filled, and Lord Milton and Lord Ilay used the office to good effect. It had not in fact been difficult for Lord Elibank and his two associates, the Master of Ross and Sir Gilbert Elliot, to persuade Blackbarony to see his interest in accepting a sheriffship now, rather than some possible office in the future, assuming he was successful in an uncertain political contest. At the same time it was also quite certain that if by persisting and thus dividing the county Blackbarony allowed Stanhope to secure election, any chance of Government favour would be gone for ever.

Blackbarony in turn intended to use the office of sheriff to help his own friends, insisting on his right to name a sheriff-depute, for which he favoured appointing his kinsman, Alexander Murray of Cringletie, an important freeholder who as yet was undeclared.[18] The Laird of Blackbarony, however, quickly found that his bargain with the wily politicians in Edinburgh was not quite what it seemed. Blackbarony had supposed that he would be stepping into the place of the late John Douglas, as sheriff-principal of the shire, but that office had long been the possession of the family of the Earl of March, and Blackbarony was forced to content himself with the office of sheriff-depute, though he did obtain the right to name his deputy, the sheriff-substitute.[19] The appointment of the other standing officer of the sheriff court, the clerk, was specifically denied to Blackbarony, and retained by the Government for future use, and, in fact, Blackbarony's descent, as the Master of Ross put it, 'from being a great prince'[20] to a minor member of Administration, was a very poor bargain.

Having safely eliminated one of the more powerful potential enemies, the Administration turned to the remaining influential freeholders who were as yet undeclared. Lord Minto, at Ilay's request, persuaded Lord Hyndford's brother, William Carmichael, if not to support Nasmyth, at least to stay away,[21] while Williamson of Chaplehill, because of his long association with the March family as sheriff clerk during the sheriffship of the late earl and his brother, was considered likely to be directed by the Countess of March, particularly as he had already not only promised to vote as she directed but to make his brother follow his example.[22] The remaining freeholder with a strong personal interest in the county, Alexander Murray of Cringletie, was not only a member of Blackbarony's family, but was considered susceptible to Lady March's influence, for he hoped to obtain the post of chamberlain to the infant Earl of March. It appears that Cringletie had quarrelled with Blackbarony in the past, but it was confidently believed that he would 'lay hold on this opportunity of making up' the quarrel between them.[23] The agents of Administration accordingly had every confidence that Sir James Nasmyth 'will have a greate majority '.[24]

Over-confidence was one of the commonest errors of political agents and their employers, and it was particularly prevalent in this election, for most of the bold predictions and exertions of influence had little real impact upon Sir James Nasmyth's campaign. The only significant assistance which the schemes of Administration obtained for their candidate was through Sir Alexander Murray of Blackbarony, whose gratitude for the sheriffship induced him not only to write to his friends to solicit their support for Nasmyth, but even persuaded him to arrange for one of his friends, Stuart of Escog, to accompany Sir James Nasmyth during his tour of the county, thus making the Murray chief's position clear.[25]

Murray of Stanhope, however, was not without strength in the county, for even before the election was called he could already count on the support of a number of freeholders, and before the date of election he added to his friends William Carmichael, Murray of Cringletie and Williamson of Chaplehill, in spite of the efforts of the Administration. Moreover, from the Administration's viewpoint, there was a further danger stemming from their own success in arranging for Blackbarony's withdrawal, for it might tempt another gentleman to try his fortunes. Luckily for Milton and Ilay, only the eccentric Laird of Prestongrange showed any inclination to enter the contest while it was in progress, for a third candidate invariably made the results unpredictable and hazardous for a political interest. Prestongrange, however, was badly placed for canvassing, for he was in a debtors' prison, although it was for a time reported that the laird had hopes that his wife would 'advance as much money as to liberate him out of prison'.[26] Lady Prestongrange apparently had other ideas, for at any event Prestongrange did not appear either as candidate or voter.

The bait intended to snare Alexander Murray of Cringletie proved insufficient. The office of chamberlain of the March estate, which Cringletie desired, was in the gift of members of the Douglas family, and for that reason the Administration had felt confident that a letter from the Earl of Morton to reinforce Lady March's request would be quite sufficient to fix Cringletie for Sir James Nasmyth. They were wrong, and it was soon reported that 'notwithstanding all that Earle Mortoune has hitherto wrote to him', Cringletie had 'declared openly for Stanhope'.[27] Murray of Cringletie had not only declined to make up his quarrel with Blackbarony and refused Lord Morton's request, he 'made it a merit with his party, that Earle Mortoun's letters should not move him, showed them openly to encourage the other freeholders to disregard the solicitations of all persons whatsoever'.[28]

Williamson of Chaplehill and his brother, Williamson of Cardrono, were considered to be attached to Lady March and also subject to influence from Sir Gilbert Elliot of Minto. Once again nothing came of these connections, for their votes were not secured for the Administration candidate. Lady March was a zealous supporter of Sir James Nasmyth,[29] but her wishes were ignored by Chaplehill, the dominant member of his family, for Cardrono was said to be 'absolutely determined by his brother'.[30] Lord Minto might have done something with the Williamsons, but he refused to stir and indeed seemed 'less zealouse in this matter than he would have been if his project had been gon into, of setting upp Black Barrony'.[31] Minto's lukewarm support of Nasmyth had another unfortunate consequence for Government, for he had asked William Carmichael, Lord Hyndford's brother, to stay away from Peebles on election day, but Carmichael, left alone thereafter by Minto, was persuaded to become an active supporter of Sir Alexander Murray of Stanhope and to become one of the leading members of his party.

Sir Gilbert Elliot of Minto's lack of enthusiasm was almost certainly caused by disappointment at the demolition of his scheme to secure the seat for his friend Blackbarony, but he took refuge in an argument that he had promised not to interfere with the Williamsons. Thus, a lord of session who had been associated with the Argyll family throughout his political career did not exert his powers to try to influence two voters considered important by the Administration managers, one of whom was of opinion that 'all would be sure, yea even tho' they were only prevail'd upon to stay away'.[32] The Williamsons were not only present, however, the Laird of Chaplehill was again a key figure in the Stanhope party.

The failure of Ilay and Milton to build a clear majority for their chosen candidate may perhaps have been due to the strength of their opponent as a canvasser, for one of Milton's agents described Sir Alexander Murray of Stanhope as 'a person of great activity and address',[33] and in a contest as close as this one was shaping up to be, decisive bribery need not be on one side only. It was in fact to be apprehended that if the contest could not be settled beyond dispute well before election day, Stanhope might find an opportunity to tip the balance in his direction, for 'if the thing should come within a measuring cast, Sr James is close fisted and Stanhope is capable of going a ridiculous lenth with his money'.[34]

In spite of all efforts by Government and its supporters, as the date of election drew near there was absolutely no certainty that Sir James Nasmyth would be successful. On April 27th, when James Armour, the customs official and lawyer charged with direct management of the election for Administration, came to Peebles, he found the freeholders already assembled in the shire town, divided into two parties quartered at different inns. In his view the result of the election on the following day was extremely uncertain in spite of his own efforts and those of Lord Elibank, who for three weeks had been devoting himself almost exclusively to this contest. Reviewing the roll, James Armour found that the freeholders would divide ten against ten.[35]

The election meeting on 28th April was a lengthy one, running from noon that day to five the next morning before it was finally settled in Sir James Nasmyth's favour. This election was won and lost on the question of control of the proceedings in the election meeting itself, and here Sir Alexander Murray of Stanhope's friends thought themselves secure, for they included in their party a previous member of parliament, Murray of Cringletie, and Williamson of Chaplehill, the sheriff-clerk. When an election meeting was held there was a statutory procedure for its conduct, one feature of which was the initial assumption of the chair by the last elected member of parliament, who would then ask the freeholders to choose the preses, or presiding officer, for the remainder of the meeting. The 1681 regulatory act, moreover, appointed 'that failing the first or second Commissioner of the county last nam'd members of parliament, that the Shirif Clerk or Stewart Clerk should proceed to collect the votes upon the question, who should be preses'.[36] With both a former member of parliament and the sheriff clerk in their ranks there was reason for the Stanhope party to feel confident, and Sir Alexander Murray of Stanhope came into the election meeting at the head of his friends joking 'upon carrying his point against such powerfull opponents as the Duke of Argyll and the Earle of Ilay'.[37] James Armour, the Administration's agent, however, had not been idle, and he justified the Minister's confidence by producing a scheme in the course of the night of the 27th/28th which turned the tables on the opposition. Stanhope, in fact, appears to have enjoyed the support of most of the gentlemen of Peeblesshire, for even the Administration's observers remarked that he 'had a great many gentlemen to bring him into town',[38] but there were many otherwise qualified voters whose Jacobite politics kept them from participating and most of them were adherents of Stanhope. Most of the gentlemen of that persuasion 'came no further than the Tolbooth doore ',[39] but that still left Stanhope with ten votes and apparently control of the critical first stages of the election meeting. Indeed, Stanhope should have had a clear majority had he himself been qualified, but he 'had not been upon the rolls for 20 years before',[40] having apparently withdrawn from political life after his defeat by John Douglas when he had been as ill-prepared as on this occasion. It was certainly unwise to attempt to secure enrolment at the same meeting at which election as member of parliament was sought.

James Armour's night of hard thought had produced a plan which he sprang upon the freeholders when they assembled. Armour and the sheriff, Sir Alexander Murray of Blackbarony, had been busy in the forenoon, while the freeholders were making leisurely preparations for their noon meeting and no doubt recovering from the heavy eating and heavier drinking of the night before. Armour had noticed that the commission of Williamson of Chaplehill issued by the late sheriff, Lord March, was unusual in that it was not a life appointment, but only during pleasure, and concluded that it was a mandate 'which perished with the death of the mandator'[41] being confirmed in that opinion by the fact that Chaplehill had been given a new commission in the same terms by the last sheriff, John Douglas. Thus Chaplehill, their 'mortal enemy', could no longer function as sheriff clerk because his commission was extinct. Having to their mind found good reason to remove Williamson of Chaplehill from office, Armour and Blackbarony decided to name a new clerk, choosing one of the freeholders, Veitch of Bogend to fill the position, in spite of the fact that Blackbarony's commission as sheriff-depute specifically debarred him from naming such an officer. There was no end to the ingenuity of the legal mind in a political contest, however, and Armour pushed the doubtful Blackbarony to appoint Veitch by insisting that as the writ from the Crown ordering the sheriff to call an election meeting was in his hands, it 'must needs imply that every thing must be done to accomplish that end, and that therfor to appoint a Clerk pro re nata to that speciall effect must be in the sheriff's power'. [42]

Armour, however, had a good point to make when he suggested that the sheriff himself could not function as such unless he was qualified by taking the oaths of allegiance and assurance before the election meeting, and to do that it was necessary to have a sheriff clerk before whom the oaths might be sworn. Accordingly, a special meeting of the sheriff court was assembled before the meeting of the freeholders, at which William Veitch, armed with his commission from Blackbarony to act as clerk, qualified the sheriff, and Blackbarony in turn qualified Veitch and the sheriff-substitute, Hay of Haystoun, and all 'were in their places when the freeholders came in, where Stanhope and his friends were in a sort of consternation'. [43]

Armour's ingenuity gave Sir James Nasmyth's friends possession of the essential writ of election, which otherwise would have had to be surrendered to the Stanhope party upon the demand of Williamson of Chaplehill, and with the writ went control of the vital first stages of the election meeting. Armour had been equally ingenious in finding a method of eliminating the unwanted services of the former member of parliament, Alexander Murray of Cringletie. Armour and Sir Alexander Murray of Blackbarony held that Cringletie could not assume the chair on the ground that John Douglas had held the parliamentary seat in two successive parliaments after Cringletie had retired from the legislature, and failing him the chair must be taken by the sheriff clerk, now of course Veitch of Bogend, one of Nasmyth's friends.

Taken by surprise by this unexpected development, Stanhope and his friends could think of nothing more than making a written protest that Cringletie should be allowed to preside and that Williamson of Chaplehill's commission was good until it was recalled, but that did not improve their position, for Veitch kept his seat and the writ, and proceeded to take the votes on the question of who should be preses. As expected, the twenty freeholders present divided equally, with ten freeholders voting for the sheriff-substitute, Hay of Haystoun, and the ten of Stanhope's party for William Carmichael.

William Veitch of Bogend, the sheriff clerk, then tilted the balance decisively in favour of Sir James Nasmyth by observing

> that the scale must be casten some way or other, and that he thought Blackbarony's vote, the Sherrif, and his own, the Clerk's being both freeholders tho not yet added to the roll, but both present with their titles in their hands, ought to determine it, for that no other way appear'd, upon which they voted Haystoun preses . . . [44]

Naturally, the procedure adopted by Blackbarony and Veitch did not have much appeal for Sir Alexander Murray of Stanhope, who 'fell into a rage, and cryed that this was the Earle of Ilay's power', going on to vilify the sheriff 'as one appointed for a turn whose time would be verry shorte ".[45] Haystoun, however, immediately assumed the chair and they proceeded to elect a clerk to the meeting, an office for which it was undesirable to retain Veitch who was a freeholder and would thus have been deprived of his vote. In his place the Nasmyth party chose Henry Balcanquall, whom James Armour described as one of his servants, and this time the vote was very clearly in favour of the Nasmyth party, for Veitch of Glen, who had voted with Stanhope on the question of the preses, now adhered to the Nasmyth party for the remainder of the contest. Rarely was an election a safe predictable thing, for voter behaviour was often quite erratic: a promise to act in a particular way could be fulfilled by as narrow an interpretation of the promise as a voter might please. In the case of the Laird of Glen it would appear that a rash promise to support William Carmichael for preses had been kept, but thereafter he followed his own inclinations. Accordingly with both the sheriff and the sheriff clerk abstaining, the position of clerk was settled in favour of Balcanquall by eleven votes against nine.[46]

As always in a contested election, there were a number of new claimants seeking enrolment, and it was here that control of the machinery of the meeting was vital, for it would determine the order in which such claims were considered, and a majority could ensure that their own friends were placed upon the roll and their enemies excluded. In some counties, such as Stirling, the freeholders quite early in the eighteenth century attempted to make the order of consideration of claims more certain and possibly more impartial by having them registered by the sheriff clerk on the date of submission with the relevant documents, and thereafter heard them in that order at the freeholders' meeting, but that was not the custom of the county of Peebles where the preses of the election meeting had considerable latitude to determine the order of consideration of claims. James Armour was standing beside Sir James Nasmyth in the meeting room and he at once put into his hand a list of claimants in their interest, five in all, Blackbarony, Veitch of Bogend, the Laird of Borland, the Laird of Horsburgh younger, and Stewart of Tombey. At Nasmyth's prompting Hay of Haystoun, the preses, at once secured the enrolment of Blackbarony and Veitch before the opposition had realised what was happening, and by the time they did, it was too late.

Sir Alexander Murray of Stanhope, realising too late that his party was becoming a hopeless minority, protested that 'the meeting should next proceed to consider the titles of some whom he desired might be added to the roll, before they should proceed further in the list first offered'.[47] With a show of evenhanded impartiality, Hay of Haystoun submitted with a good grace, agreeing that any two claimants whom Stanhope wished to name should be considered next. When they were proposed, both Baillie of Colends and Murray of Cardon were rejected by the majority, before they threw a derisive gesture in Stanhope's direction by admitting him to the roll. The preses then returned to the former list and the majority admitted another three of Sir James's friends and rejected another of Stanhope's,

Dickson of Whitstead, to leave the roll divided sixteen to ten in Nasmyth's favour.

The meeting had become more and more heated as the contest continued, and William Carmichael, it was reported, 'turn'd more fowle mouth'd, saying, that he was against Sr James Naismith on purpose to oppose those that had taken him by the hand, and say'd that he meant my Lord Ilay',[48] and was indeed reported to have attempted to influence other freeholders against the Minister in order to secure the liberty of the shire. Sir Alexander Murray of Stanhope also became exasperated as he saw his election slipping away from him, and ordered a clerk named Alexander Shaw to make minutes of the meeting independently of those prepared by the appointed clerk. James Armour would have taken a short way with this rival clerk, having advised the sheriff and Haystoun to make a motion to turn everyone who was not a freeholder out of doors. Neither, however, had the courage to take that advice and Stanhope's clerk continued to minute proceedings, which reached a different conclusion from the official version.

Late in the meeting, the Nasmyth majority, their enthusiasm waxing with the increasing certainty of their victory, rubbed the face of the most obnoxious of their enemies in the dirt by striking William Carmichael off the roll. The removal of Carmichael was engineered on very poor legal grounds, for he had been enrolled since the last election in 1727 without challenge, and it was his original title to enrolment which was now seized upon as grounds for expelling him. Sir James Nasmyth alleged that Carmichael was not in fact the King's vassal:

> his titles were a charter from the Crown to the Earle of Hyndford his brother unexecuted in its precept, for that brother was never infeft, that he and his brother had granted an assignation of the charter and precept to Mr. William whereupon he stood infeft, as assigney, that tho' this was sufficient to convey the estate, yet a vassal could not be imposed upon the King without his own consent, that Earl Hyndford was nominee in the charter, that the King had never acknowledged Mr. William and therfor he was not the King's vassal. [49]

This was an extremely doubtful argument in law, and it was certainly not the place of a freeholders' meeting to expel from their roll a freeholder presently enrolled whose circumstances remained unaltered, but the Nasmyth majority enthusiastically voted Carmichael off the roll, 'which so surprised and confounded him that he was observed to sit all night thereafter silent, changing colours and biteing his nails, that I dare say they shall not need a pairing this moneth to come'.[50] James Armour certainly did not attempt to justify the grounds for Carmichael's expulsion, contenting himself by remarking that 'whatever was in this objection, Mr. William had become so obnoxious to the greatest part of the meeting that he was thrown out'.[51]

In political questions, however, it was dangerous to have too much fun at the expense of a minority, for that unnecessary gesture cost the Nasmyth party one of their own votes: a freeholder who had to this point sustained their cause, Horsburgh, showed his displeasure by transferring his vote to the Stanhope party in the final question. Elections were never won until the final question had been asked, and in this county where so many lairds were Jacobites at heart, if not always openly, there was uncertainty until the oaths of allegiance and assurance had been taken to qualify the voters for the election of a member of parliament. In the event, the loss of Horsburgh was not serious, for although Sir James Nasmyth lost the services of Burnet of Barns, who declined the oath of allegiance, his opponent also lost a supporter, Robert Murray of Murrayshall.

On Murray of Stanhope's calculation, he should have had thirteen voters rather than the nine of the official record, but even so it still placed him in a minority, and the election was concluded with the return of Sir James Nasmyth of Posso chosen fourteen against nine, to represent the shire of Peebles. Armour, whose manipulation of the meeting had contributed so materially to that result, was quickly rewarded by a place in the salt establishment,[52] while Nasmyth took his place among the supporters of Administration in the House of Commons. Sir Alexander Murray of Stanhope made another attempt to wrest the seat away from Nasmyth at the general election of 1734, when the contest was again pushed to an equality of votes, which on that occasion was beyond the sheriff's ability to resolve, for he made a double return. Nasmyth, however, retained the seat until 1741 when the seat was regained, without opposition by Alexander Murray of Cringletie.

It is clear from the events in the county of Peebles that even a manager of the stature of Lord Ilay, aided as he was by a very able deputy Andrew Fletcher, lord Milton, based in Edinburgh close to the scene of action, was unable to be certain of the return of a candidate whom he favoured. The kind of overconfidence which created the legend of the Minister's absolute mastery of Scottish politics was often very far from accurate in its description of political power. In the case of this election, for example, James Armour was advising Lord Milton at the end of March that he had really nothing to do, since all was determined by the wishes of Ilay and Argyll:

> My Lord the Duke's and Lord Isla's friends did so chearfully exert themselves in what they thought would be agreeable to those great men, that I was left little else to do, but to be punctual in conveening their friends together, and carrying their messages . . . [53]

As Armour described the political situation in the county, there was really no contest at all, for 'supposing Lord Minto carry's for Sir James the votes of Cardrono, Chaplehill and Haystoun reckon'd at present undetermin'd [we] will have about 18 or 19 votes of the 25 voters'.[54] That kind of reporting reaching Ministers in London suggests a possible explanation of the legendary reputation of ministerial power, which is no more accurate because it happened to be believed by the politicians themselves. Even with one of the three undetermined votes mentioned by Armour, in the event Sir James Nasmyth went into the election meeting with only ten votes. The power of politicians, great or small, was the ability to call in obligations, for the feeling of obligation could indeed make a freeholder feel a need to vote as his friend desired, just as Geddes refused to declare his voting intention until he heard Ilay's wishes, citing his many obligations to the Minister. Influence without the tie of a sense of obligation was much more tenuous, and personal friendships could, if they came into conflict with that feeling of obligation, matter little, as Geddes of Kirkurd showed when voting against his personal friend, Sir Alexander Murray of Stanhope. Equally the tie of obligation could force a freeholder to support a candidate for whom he felt no affection. In the case of Kirkurd, for example, his vote for Sir James Nasmyth was 'purely out of respect' for Lord Milton, 'for he was far from having the least attachment to Sir James, that he was greatly ruffled and freted by a law suit which as he imagined Sir James did groundlessly keep up against him for a long time, till such time as the Court of Session gave it against Sir James'.[55] When one bears in mind that this was an election in which the loss of one vote would have determined the outcome in favour of Sir Alexander Murray of Stanhope, it is clear that the assumption of total superiority made in the early weeks of the contest, and duly reported to Ilay in London, was far from accurate. Geddes, Veitch of Glen, or even one of the Jacobite lairds, had he been willing to compromise with his conscience for the occasion, could have tipped the balance against the ministerial candidate, whose apparently convincing majority looks somewhat less convincing upon close examination.

The account given of the actual events in Peebles on the day of election has been taken from the private letters sent to Milton by his agents in the town, Vaughan and Armour, and it would thus appear to give a fairly accurate picture of what occurred, although it should be added that it does not coincide with the version given by Sir Alexander Murray of Stanhope in his petition to the House of Commons.[56] Stanhope concurs with Armour in his complaint that William Veitch, the sheriff clerk, and Sir Alexander Murray of Blackbarony voted for the preses of the meeting in spite of the fact that they were not as yet enrolled. Stanhope also alleged, however, that he had asked for the oaths of allegiance and assurance to be taken, and that his friends did so qualify, but the sheriff and his friends had declined. In this case an advantage may have been seen in taking the oaths at a particular time in the proceedings, for they were not put until *after* the rolls were made up and Nasmyth made use of the voice of Burnet of Barns in those questions. Apart from this the petition takes the standard form of arguing that unqualified opponents were inserted in the roll, while qualified friends were kept out, and of course Stanhope naturally adverted to the unjustifiable exclusion of William Carmichael, who had voted at a previous election upon the same qualifications. The surviving evidence, however, would suggest that the return of Sir James Nasmyth could be justified; but as an exercise of Lord Ilay's power, of which Stanhope complained, it was a rather weak performance. In the contest there was something less than generosity in the distribution of patronage. If James Armour was well pleased with his reward, the same could not be said for Blackbarony and his sheriff-substitute, Haystoun, the latter having been very unwilling to accept this subordinate office.[57] James Armour, who had been consulted by Milton and asked to suggest a suitable candidate for sheriff, had believed, like Blackbarony, that the office was to be that of sheriff-principal, which had been held by the late John Douglas in the King's gift, but the valuable office was retained by the Administration, and the Laird of Blackbarony was fobbed off with the position of depute, while Haystoun was thus downgraded from depute to substitute, the latter being a notoriously poorly paid post. Management of the election through the distribution of rewards or hopes of reward was never attempted here, even though the number of voters was small enough to have made that means of influencing the electorate possible, and in fact there is no substantive evidence that wholesale bribery was ever employed, even in a by-election like this one, where the competition for available patronage was obviously less fierce than it would have been during a general election. The patronage which was employed, was employed with a very sparing hand to effect a particular object, and the intention was to do considerably more than win one vote.

NOTES

1. Journal of House of Commons 21/46, 203.
2. NLS. Saltoun, MS.16551, the Master of Ross to Lord Milton, 30 Mar., 1732.
3. Ibid. MS.16548, James Armour to Milton, 23 Mar., 1732.
4. Ibid.
5. Ibid. MS.16551, G. Vaughan to Milton, 8 Apr., 1732.
6. Ibid. MS.16550, from Lord Elibank, 28 Mar., 1732.
7. Ibid. MS.16551, from G. Vaughan, 8 Apr., 1732.
8. Ibid. MS.16549, from Thomas Cochrane, 28 Mar., 1732.
9. Ibid. MS.16548, from James Armour, 23 Mar., 1732.
10. Ibid. MS.16550, from Lord Elibank, 18 Apr., 1732.
11. Ibid., from Lord Elibank, 28 Mar., 1732.
12. Ibid., from Lord Elibank, 7 Mar., 1732.
13. Ibid. MS.16548, from James Armour, 28 Mar., 1732.
14. Ibid. MS.16550, from Sir Alexander Murray of Blackbarony, 30 Mar., 1732.
15. Ibid. MS.16550, from Lord Elibank, 30 Mar., 1732.
16. Ibid. MS.16548, from James Bogle, 4 Apr., 1732.
17. Ibid.
18. Ibid., from James Armour, 30 Mar., 1732.
19. Ibid., from James Armour, 11 Apr., 1732.
20. Ibid. MS.16551, from the Master of Ross, 30 Mar., 1732.
21. Ibid. MS.16548, from James Armour, 29 Apr., 1732.
22. Ibid., from James Bogle, 4 Apr., 1732.
23. Ibid.
24. Ibid.
25. Ibid., from James Armour, 30 Mar., 1732.
26. Ibid., from James Bogle, 4 Apr., 1732.
27. Ibid., from James Armour, 13 Apr., 1732.
28. Ibid., from James Armour, 18 May, 1732.
29. Ibid., from James Bogle, 4 Apr., 1732.
30. Ibid.
31. Ibid. MS.16551, from G. Vaughan, 14 Apr., 1732.
32. Ibid. MS.16548, from James Armour, 13 Apr., 1732.
33. Ibid., from James Armour, 15 Apr., 1732.
34. Ibid. MS.16551, from G. Vaughan, 8 Apr., 1732.
35. Ibid. MS.16548, from James Armour, 3 May, 1732.
36. Ibid.
37. Ibid. MS.16551, from G. Vaughan, 29 Apr., 1732.
38. Ibid.

39. Ibid.
40. Ibid. MS.16548, from James Armour, 3 May, 1732.
41. Ibid.
42. Ibid.
43. Ibid.
44. Ibid.
45. Ibid. MS.16551, from G. Vaughan, 29 Apr., 1732.
46. Ibid. MS.16548, from James Armour, 3 May, 1732.
47. Ibid.
48. Ibid. MS.16551, from G. Vaughan, 29 Apr., 1732.
49. Ibid. MS. 16548, from James Armour, 3 May, 1732.
50. Ibid. MS.16548, from James Armour, 29 Apr., 1732.
51. Ibid., from James Armour, 3 May, 1732.
52. Ibid., from James Armour, 18 May, 1732.
53. Ibid., from James Armour, 30 Mar., 1732.
54. Ibid.
55. Ibid., from James Armour, 29 Apr., 1732.
56. JHC 21/924 and 22/12.
57. NLS. Saltoun, MS.16548, from James Armour, 11 Apr., 1732.

Part III
Maintaining a Burgh Interest

10
Maintaining Interest in a District of Burghs

The electorate which chose the representatives of the royal burghs of Scotland was much more clearly defined than that of the counties, for it was restricted to members of the burgh councils. In each of the towns involved in parliamentary elections, the magistrates and councillors were themselves elected each year by the votes of the previous council, a pattern which is general, though with a number of local variations relating to the manner of electing trades representatives; the number of voters, accordingly, was not only small but essentially oligarchic. Disputes regarding the elegibility of voters, therefore, were normally related to the municipal politics of one of the towns, where some divergence from the accepted constitution of the burgh was alleged to have occurred, or where the corrupt practices of a candidate had been so blatant as to invite an appeal to courts or parliament.

The burgh councils were well aware of their own significance in parliamentary elections, and many of them proved to be adept at extracting the maximum possible profit from those who sought to represent them, something which could sometimes be facilitated by further reducing the number of palms which might require greasing through profitable, if illegal, bargains with other councils in their district to co-operate for their mutual advantage. In the district which included the royal burghs of Jedburgh, Haddington, Lauder, Dunbar and North Berwick, for example, the votes of two of the burghs, Jedburgh and Haddington, were of little importance while the three other towns remained in alliance to return the member of parliament. The Dalrymple family, who were dominant in North Berwick, and the Maitlands, who controlled the burghs of Lauder and Dunbar, effectively shared the parliamentary seat, although the two-town strength of the Maitlands demanded that Lord Lauderdale's candidate should sit for two parliaments before giving way to a Dalrymple.

Although an aristocratic family might have great influence in a burgh, as the Maitlands had in Dunbar and Lauder, this did not imply that they had the only voice in a town's affairs. Power in a royal burgh was normally in the hands of a group which controlled the decisions of the town council, and although a patron might well be associated with this managing inner circle, it was really a collective leadership. The existence of such an inner circle has been established by the indiscretions of some of them in putting their agreements into a written document, which in turn became an exhibit in judicial proceedings. Such agreements would stipulate that those members of council who belonged to the managing group would act together in all time coming, and that the group would abide by the wishes of the majority of their own number when they dealt with such questions as the admission of new councillors or the choice of a suitable representative in parliament. Those who were detected in this offence, which was of course a conspiracy to restrict even further than had already been done by the burgh constitution the freedom of the town to choose its political leaders, were probably the most shortsighted and distrustful of the burgh oligarchies, who felt themselves compelled to provide written evidence of their crime. In fact, however, the remarkable continuity of membership which appears in so many burgh councils strongly suggests that such arrangements were common, and that extended membership of a managing group provided the leading members with the experience and confidence to act for themselves in parliamentary politics.

The manner of holding a council meeting to choose a burgh delegate, who would travel to the returning burgh of the district and there give his vote for a member of parliament, was one aspect of a town's affairs which was closely regulated by statute. The authority to hold a council meeting for the purpose of choosing a delegate was given in the form of a precept, issued by the sheriff of the county in which the burgh was situated, to whom the parliamentary writ had been delivered. The sheriff, in turn, was obliged to issue his precept to the chief magistrate of the burgh within four days of receiving the writ, under a penalty of £100, the standard fine imposed for a variety of political offences by the Act 16 George 11. cap.16 [1743].

Upon receipt of the sheriff's precept, the chief magistrate resident in the town was again compelled to act within a certain time, in this case two days, to summon a special council meeting by giving personal notice to every councillor, or by leaving a notice at his home within the burgh. The purpose of that meeting of council was not in fact to choose the delegate, but to fix a date upon which such an election might take place, and an election meeting could not indeed be held until a further two days from the date of the organisational meeting had elapsed.

When it came to the election, however, procedure was unfortunately less well controlled, for although the common clerk of the burgh was required to take an oath against bribery, laid down by the Act 16 George 11, and it was normal for all of the councillors to take the oaths intended to exclude Jacobites from participation in parliamentary elections, there was one curious oversight in the regulatory statute. Any elector present might require that every voter should swear under oath that he had not accepted a bribe, but if no magistrate or councillor asked for this to be done, the oath could not be employed. Obviously, if bribery had been widespread, the easiest method of avoiding the offence of perjury was to refrain from putting the oath to the council. When all preliminaries had been accomplished or avoided, the council would then proceed to elect its commissioner, or delegate, by the votes of a majority of the council members present, and the individual named to this post might or might not be himself a councillor, for it was not even necessary that he should be a resident of the town. The office of commissioner was in fact often assumed by the actual candidate for election to parliament whom the burgh favoured, for that was a sure means of making certain of one vote on the day of election and guarding against any untimely second thoughts by town or delegate.

The actual election of the member of parliament followed a similar procedure, when the four or five burgh commissioners met together in the town house of the returning burgh, together with the candidates and their principal supporters. During the election the commissioner of the returning burgh was of particular importance, for in the event of an equality he was permitted a casting vote, which not infrequently was decisively and vigorously employed with scant regard to legality. The duty of returning the member of parliament was one which rotated around the towns of the district, according to an order of precedence determined by the old Scottish Parliament, and the year when a town was in this situation was one of the highlights of the career of a burgh magistrate, for the town assumed an importance which its size and population might not otherwise warrant. In a warmly contested election, a handful of men in a single burgh, the inner circle of that town, could for all practical purposes name a member of parliament by the manner in which their delegate chose to exercise his casting vote. In the election meeting the competence of the assembled delegates was restricted to the duty of verifying the commissions which they produced from their towns, each duly authenticated by the affixing of the common seal of the burgh in question, and thereafter the clerk of the returning burgh took the votes of the delegates. That at least was the legal position of burgh delegates, but in fact the involvement of so many burgh politicians with county politics sometimes led the commissioners to confuse their functions with those of freeholders in their head courts which, unlike the towns, were empowered to judge the validity of a claim to a vote.

The politician who hoped to secure the parliamentary representation of a burgh district was obliged to follow methods quite different from those which would be appropriate to a county interest. Like the county interest, however, a burgh interest demanded constant attention, for the heart of the politician's problem was the need to manage several towns at the same time. With only Edinburgh enjoying the luxury of its own representative and the remaining sixty-five towns being grouped in fourteen districts of four or five burghs, the difficulties facing politicians would have horrified their English contemporaries. A group of four towns, scattered perhaps over as many counties, presented major problems of control, for even if a gentleman carried influence in one community, he might have little to say in the remainder located far from his own estates. The scattered properties of some of the leading peers made a few of them influential burgh managers, but there was in fact no district of burghs which could be considered safely dominated by a single family, and it is in this sense that Scotland might claim to have had no rotten burghs, for there were no town seats which were susceptible to the easy forms of political control available to a number of English landowners, whose local power allowed them to nominate members of parliament.

In another sense, however, the Scottish royal burghs were rotten enough, for the systematic corruption of the electors was one of the leading aspects of burgh management, strongly marking it off from county politics; while if bribery would not suffice, politicians would readily contemplate a resort to violence to effect a change in the composition of the electorate. The politics of the counties, like those of the burghs, involved jobs and rewards for the friends of a politician, but the methods were more restrained, and there was much more concern to maintain the appearance of independence. Burgh voters had their own ideas of independence, and indeed they did have their own unique kind of independence, but they rarely suffered from inhibitions about the desirability of making the best possible bargain for themselves in return for their political support. Where a freeholder might have been induced to promise his vote in a county election many months, or even years, before an election took place, and would often consider himself bound in honour to vote according to that promise, a councillor was much more likely to reach his decision during an election contest, after summing up the potential usefulness of the candidates to himself and his community. Most Scottish burghs were influenced by neighbouring landowners, and such magnates could perhaps be seen as the patrons of the community near which they lived, but even if the great man was listened to with respect, there was normally an overriding consideration. Few burghs would willingly throw away the benefits which their vote might bring them simply to oblige a neighbour, and the vote was only to be obtained by making it worth the council's while to agree to a particular course of action. It was, in particular, felt to be essential that the town's vote should not be wasted by being given without hope of success, and it would be pointless for a landowner to attempt to make a council persist in a plan which could result in the town being outvoted by four votes to one, for such a result would simply undermine the authority of the managing group within the town and the patron alike.

The system of grouping towns to return a single member of parliament had the effect of making political control precarious, for it was quite possible for each burgh in a district to look to a different patron, or even for each town to have competing patrons associated with factions within the municipal councils. Landowner influence was a factor in burgh politics, and a great family, by a suitable mixture of personal influence, traditional claims to loyalty, access to patronage, willingness to spend money in a community, and even, as a last resort, readiness to intimidate, could obtain a commanding position in a town. Dominance, however, was closely linked to the magnate's proximity, for an absentee, unless very well supported by resident kinsmen, could not expect the same degree of deference which might be accorded a resident landowner. In 1753, for example, the provost of Peebles suggested that Lord March's power in that community had been eliminated by his absence, remarking that if the earl 'resided among them an interest in that place would naturally arise to him, but in the way he is at present, his interest is altogether inconsiderable'.[1] A landowner might, however, reside close to a town, exert great influence over its council and feel sure of the burgh's vote, but that would not give him a safe parliamentary seat, for the remaining towns might or might not be under similar influence from their own neighbours but would undoubtedly have their own views. Success in a burgh election demanded compromise, and even when such bargains were engineered they were rarely durable. Burgh politics had a built-in instability in spite of the continuity of membership in so many of the councils, for there were too many variables, and it was this fact which made the ordinary burgh councillors significant in parliamentary politics. Examination of any district of burghs can confirm what William Ferguson wrote of the northern burghs, that 'the small men who sat on the town-council, though overshadowed by the parliamentary politicians and for the most part manipulated by them, emphatically were not cyphers'.[2]

Landowners might interfere in the management of the neighbouring burgh, but there was usually a limit to the deference shown to a patron by a council, for councillors did not like to back a loser. They might defer to the great man of the district, but they were equally insistent that the town's vote should not be lost, and would use that argument to excuse their making the best bargain they could for their own advantage. Effective management united local influence with a willingness to spend money to extend that influence to other towns, and particularly the town which, by rotation, would be returning burgh at the next general election. Burgh politics also demanded some connection with Government, for there was no better way to impress the burgesses than by providing demonstrations of the politician's power to reward friends with patronage appointments. A burgh interest required a secure base for future operations in one town, and demanded that careful attention be paid to the composition of the town council because of the frequency of elections. Annual elections, even by self-electing councils, did permit the possibility of unreliable elements creeping in unnoticed at a Michaelmas election, and the politician had to devote considerable care to ensuring that his friends retained their majority. But there were other dangers, much harder to avert, for in a small community resident councillors could become hostile to one another for reasons which had nothing to do with parliamentary politics, but if the quarrel led to a revolution in the composition of the town council, it could make the town's vote elusive when next it was in demand.

Retaining the degree of control which would permit a politician to count on the support of a burgh delegate at a parliamentary election required some nice calculations. The politician was expected to reward his friends, and the object sought was often a patronage office, but the inability to supply such offices for more than a fraction of the town council could create jealousy. The disappointed could begin to feel neglected, and in that state they were apt to listen to the agents of another candidate who might promise changes. The problem intensified, if anything, with the passage of time, for when parliament in its wisdom decided that many officeholders should no longer vote in parliamentary elections, the balance of power in some councils was held by men who might well feel neglected by the incumbent member of parliament. The situation which could arise in a burgh council is indicated by David Ballingall, a general of the Royal Marines, who was an important figure in the politics of the burgh of Inverkeithing in 1820. General Ballingall remarked that 'on our side David Wishart belongs to the custom-house boat, Daniel Adamson to the Customs, John Dove to the Lazarette, Mr. Bonthron, master of the Quarantine Cutter'.[3] In a council with two parties within it, four of the majority were officials barred from voting in parliamentary elections, although, as Ballingall pointed out, 'they can vote for Magistrates and new Councillors at Michaelmas'.[4] Patronage could create discontent as easily as it could extend influence, and effective management required that hopes be maintained even among those who could not be satisfied, lest frustrated ambitions developed into an attempt to unseat the existing magistrates.

Politicians often found entertainment a necessary stopgap with which to hold the friendship of potential deserters who could not be supplied with anything more substantial in the way of reward. Lord Rothes, a leading burgh patron of the early eighteenth century, remarked on one occasion that it was 'necessary to give folk their gutts full of drink, since I'm affraid it will be all that severalls will gett who are gaping for places'.[5] On the other hand, food and drink in themselves were insufficient to win or retain influence in a town, and sufficient councillors had to actually obtain places, or other evidence of the politician's desire to oblige, to whet the hopes of the remainder. Food and drink would be consumed, and would indeed be expected, but the disposal of a burgh's vote demanded some more lasting proof of a politician's usefulness to the community and its councillors.

In building interest in a burgh district, an obvious starting point was with the gentry families involved in the affairs of the towns, for they had to be conciliated wherever possible, a task which would be easier for a Minister or other Government manager than a member of parliament, and it would be done much along the lines suggested by the Laird of Brodie in 1727, when advising how to arrange favourable returns from the northern constituencies for the interest of the Earl of Ilay and the Duke of Argyll. The burgh of Nairn was controlled by Rose of Kilravock and his son, both of whom had been friendly to the Ilay interest but were now 'sour'd at not being taken notice of'.[6] Brodie advised that Government place their cousin, Robert Rose, in the customs service and that, at the same time, an obliging letter from Ilay or his brother should be sent to them. Expressions of personal regard from men high in Government service, reinforced by some evidence of the value of their friendship, remained the appropriate method of manipulating the landed families who had infiltrated the burgh magistracies, and whose treatment was essentially similar to that shown to freeholders, for they were of course the same individuals. The overt bribery and the debauching entertainment approach was directed at the lesser men in council, but these men, nonetheless, had their own political significance, and were rarely the dupes of those who thought to use them.

Direct influence by major landowners was not unusual, particularly in the case of the smaller burghs. Landowners themselves might occupy some of the council seats in towns which they used for political purposes, a practice which could lead to the somewhat embarrassing degree of success achieved by the Marquis of Annandale in 1721, when he found himself simultaneously provost of Annan and of Lochmaben, two of the burghs of the Dumfries district. A peer at the head of two burgh councils was not likely to be well received by the House of Commons in the event of a disputed election, and Lord Annandale accordingly decided to surrender the provostship of Annan until the following Michaelmas. The change, it might be added, was more cosmetic than real, for the vacant provost's chair was filled by Lord William Johnston, the earl's brother.[7] In 1822 the landowner-provost was still to be found in the burgh of Dornoch, where the Marquis of

M

Stafford held the office of chief magistrate,[8] and the pattern could be repeated in burgh after burgh. Forres, for example, was effectively dominated by the chief of the Grants from 1760 to almost the end of the century,[9] while in central Scotland Culross was strongly influenced by the Cochrane family. Even in towns which had no single patron to whose wishes the council would defer, rival landowners were frequently associated with the parties within the council, as were the Cunninghams and the Hendersons at Inverkeithing, and the Erskine and Argyll interests at Stirling.[10] Occasionally a burgh council might become restive if proprietors of rural estates became too intrusive, as in 1781, when a minority group within the council of Arbroath protested against the naming of Sir David Carnegie as one of the councillors of the town on the ground that he was 'neither trader nor residenter', [11] but such protests are rare, and even in this case the minority was associated with another landed gentleman of the area.

However much a landowner-politician might talk of 'his burghs', the influence of outsiders could not be pushed too far with any degree of political safety, for it could antagonise a portion of the community. Good management demanded, as far as possible, quiet towns, where no dispute was allowed to arise to bring the validity of the town's vote into question. Accordingly, to ensure such peace, it was essential for a politician to pay heed to the prejudices of the communities against non-resident councillors, for if a few non-residents were acceptable, too many of them, and particularly where they occupied the magistrates' offices, could cause problems. A politician with an eye to retaining his own influence in a town was wise to allow for this antipathy to strangers, lest it stir up trouble at an annual election of a new council or even at a parliamentary election. The people of the burgh of Forres, for example, found the neighbouring landowner Sir James Grant of Grant quite acceptable as their provost, but there were always two resident bailies in the town, and the Laird of Grant's chief ally in Forres, Bailie Duncan Grant, continually urged his chief to exercise care when making up the list of potential new councillors. In 1779, after discussing with his colleague, Bailie Forsyth, the suitability of a number of candidates for election to council, Duncan Grant told Sir James that Forsyth 'wish'd to know who were to be our council in town, press'd strongly ... recommending to you respectable people, for our own credit who were in the magistracy, & having a majority of council in town'.[12] When the Grants controlled Forres, the town council included many landowners who were indeed non-residents, but the need for peace in the town ensured that a majority of council were in fact indwellers in Forres.

If a burgh council did fall into the hands of strangers, the result could be very damaging for the political interest which wrongly believed that this was a route to safe control of the community, for the burgesses were by no means so indifferent and uninvolved in politics as their lack of voting power might suggest. Popular dislike could cause sufficient difficulties to call into question the burgh's vote in a parliamentary election, the very thing which any politician hoped to avert, and at the very least it made for an unquiet town.

In the mid-eighteenth century the burgh of St. Andrews became dangerously restive under the management of magistrates who had no more interest in the community than the disposal of its vote in parliamentary elections. A group of non-residents commanded a majority in council and showed marked indifference to the community's interest, filling offices as they saw fit and perpetuating themselves in office for many years. In the words of a petition which reached Lord Milton in 1747, describing the situation which had prevailed in 1744:

> There were then in Council Provost Douglas living at Dalkieth 21 years Provost without intermission, Laurence Gib eldest Baillie, residing as Tide Surveyor at Ferry-port-on-Craig, 15 years a Baillie, Provost Lindesay at Isle of Man, Mr. Lewis Douglas living at Ed[inburgh], Rot. Douglas, Tidesman at Pittenweem, & others & severall Seafaring Men, seldom at home.[13]

The resentment of the townspeople towards a council composed of so many absentees had induced the incumbents to quieten them by passing an act of council in 1741 restricting the term of office to three years, which was sufficient to keep the opposition silent for another three years, until the Michaelmas election of 1744, when the majority turned out of council their three chief critics and rescinded the act restricting the term of office. This flouting of public opinion induced the burgesses to contribute sufficient money to take an appeal to the Convention of Royal Burghs which in due course issued a decreet arbitral restoring the burgh consititution and declaring that residence was a requirement for membership of council. The trouble came to a head in 1745 when a number of the absentee councillors were unable or unwilling to travel to St. Andrews and a majority was found to enforce the Convention's decree.[14] Judicial proceedings before the Court of Session then followed, and in effect the town was disputed between the non-residents and the residents for some time. No politician with any sense of the needs of management would allow discontent to reach such levels as to invite appeals to convention or courts, for a disputed council meant a disputed vote, which could overturn an election. The burgh reformers of St. Andrews, needless to say, made their own political attitude clear at once: they, like the group whom they had displaced, were friends of Administration, and their rebellion was due entirely to their concern at seeing 'the patrimony neglected, the streets etc. going to ruin, under the administration of men who had no interest nor connection in the place'.[15] Intelligent political managers took care to prevent that kind of rebellion of the burgesses by ensuring that resident magistrates were available in the community and that a substantial number of councillors would in fact be men with a real connection with the place; in consequence some councillors were drawn from the ordinary burgesses of the towns.

The merchants and tradesmen who sat in council were not cyphers, and some of them could take a significant part in parliamentary politics, aided as they were by the continuity of membership which was found in these self-electing councils. Long service as a councillor and magistrate could give a man a shrewd understanding of the lairds and politicians who attempted to manipulate him, and individuals of this type were not without the ability to, in turn, manipulate the politicians. Long service was common. In 1821, for example, the provost of

Glasgow, Laurence Craigie, had been a councillor for twenty-three years. Craigie was not unique, for Bailie John Hamilton could boast thirty-one years of council membership, while John Ballantyne, the deacon of the hammermen, had been forty-four years in council.[16] When a politician approached such men for their support, they were not to be put aside with promises, for the politician who failed to make good what he had offered was likely to find himself faced with the same men at the next election. Councillors expected a return for the town's vote, ranging from favours for the town itself to employment opportunities for their friends and, not least, to gifts for such deserving individuals as themselves.

Burgh magistrates and councillors were rarely reluctant to demand favours, and indeed, on occasion, they would show a distressing lack of a sense of what was politically possible. With a clear eye to the main chance a magistrate might demand more and yet more from an increasingly exasperated politician who, at the same time, could scarcely afford to break with him. One member of Administration complained in 1747 that he was being continually pestered by Cunningham of Balbougie, the provost of Inverkeithing, who had

> taken it in his head to write me once a week wt a hundred & fifty demands in each letter, & which is more has got a Brother, who I never saw either, who writes me from Flanders packets as big as clock bags wt letters inclosed to other folks in ym wch I have five or six shillings to pay, desiring advancement in the army.[17]

Modesty was rarely one of the virtues of burgh magistrates, and Provost Cunningham and his brother were merely carrying to extremes what was the normal attitude of those with a town's vote at their disposal. They were not to be induced to part with that vote without an adequate return, to the distress of many a politician like Lord Rothes, who complained of the council of St. Andrews in 1715 that there was 'no doing with any of these people without promising to serve them. Lord knows how I'll get them all pleas'd'.[18] When George Dempster required the support of the same town in 1762, the attitude of the councillors had not changed, for Dempster told one of his friends that the election in St. Andrews would 'turn on a single vote' unless he was able to 'provide a councillor's son in a Kirk'.[19]

Bribery could take a collective form, for the group could seek something as a council instead of, or in addition to, individual matters. It was collective bribery of the council of Selkirk which ultimately determined the outcome of the election in the Linlithgow district of burghs in 1747. In that election the councillors of the Linlithgow district struck a rich vein of gold, for this was one of the early political ventures of Lawrence Dundas of Kerse, one of the wealthiest of the mid-eighteenth-century politicians, and a gentleman who, throughout a long parliamentary career, spared neither 'his money [n]or his pains'.[20] Linlithgow was the returning burgh for a four-town district in 1747, a group which comprised, in addition to that town, Selkirk, Lanark and Peebles, a spread which ensured that no single landowner could dominate all of them. It was not, of course, necessary for a candidate to secure a unanimous return, and in this instance the support of Linlithgow and one other burgh would be sufficient, for Linlithgow's casting vote as returning burgh would ensure that in the event of an equality the result would go according to the wishes of the council of Linlithgow.

There was no shortage of candidates for the honour of representing the four burghs. At the first suggestion of an election a son of the Laird of Dundas, an important neighbour of Linlithgow, appeared a likely prospect, while James Carmichael, a brother of the Earl of Hyndford, who had interest in Lanark and Peebles, was ready to enter the contest and quickly strengthened his position by securing the powerful friendship of Henry Pelham and the Duke of Argyll, whose support was a virtual guarantee of Carmichael's ability to provide patronage to deserving allies.[21] Two other candidates were also in the field, for the Earl of March, whose estates were adjacent to the burgh of Peebles, initially favoured a gentleman named Veitch, while a fourth aspirant was to be found in Captain Harry Fletcher, an army officer, son of Lord Justice Clerk Fletcher of Milton, whose family hoped that a seat in parliament would prove the 'most effectual way to get him out of his banishment in Gibralter'.[22] Almost immediately, however, the field of candidates altered, for the family of Dundas of Dundas decided to withdraw from the contest, appreciating perhaps that it was likely to be an expensive venture, and no doubt reconciled to the retreat by their knowledge that one of their kinsmen, better provided with funds, was ready to enter the battle. The newcomer was Lawrence Dundas of Kerse, a Stirlingshire laird who was building a fortune as a financier and commissariat contractor, and who appreciated the value of parliamentary influence to a businessman involved in Government contracts. Lawrence Dundas persisted in his attempt on the Linlithgow district in spite of the hostility shown to his candidacy by the Duke of Argyll and his allies in Administration, but Dundas's rejection by the Ministers did not endanger his own lucrative business as a Government contractor, for he had wisely established good relations with the Duke of Cumberland, whom even Ministers hesitated to offend.[23]

The returning burgh, Linlithgow, should have been the chief objective of the candidates, for its vote was likely to be essential to success in a closely fought contest, and here the Dundas family already had influence because the town was situated near their estates in West Lothian and Stirlingshire. On the other hand, Linlithgow was in no way dominated by the Dundas family, for there were many other neighbouring proprietors with friends in the burgh, notably the Duke of Hamilton, who had asked for a patronage appointment for Provost Bucknay from the Marquis of Tweeddale, when the latter was Secretary of State, in 1742.[24] Local influence, however, could be stretched to breaking point, and a landowner who exerted too much pressure on a town which was close to his estates could alienate more voters than he gained, and it would appear that this was one of the considerations which induced the Laird of Dundas to abandon his scheme of obtaining the seat for his own son, thus leaving the ground clear for Lawrence Dundas of Kerse. Town councils disliked such pressure, particularly when there was certain to be a keenly fought contest in the district in which their town would enjoy a casting vote in case of need. In those circumstances a premature declaration by the town would deprive the council of an opportunity to strike a better bargain for themselves with another candidate; and to follow blindly the direction indicated by a neighbouring landowner would clearly imply that the burgh was the property of the great man which he was free to dispose of at will, presumably for his own benefit rather than for that of council and community. The people of Linlithgow, accordingly, appear to have resisted the pressure from Dundas, for by the middle of June the council was reported to be badly split, with seven of its members committed to the Dundas family and the remainder not only opposed to this course, but quite displeased at what they viewed as a rash commitment by the seven Dundas partisans.[25] At this time the council of Linlithgow had twenty-seven members, and most of them took a much more cautious line when solicited for their support and were evidently determined to resist all pressure until they had an opportunity to view the field of candidates and decide where their own interests lay. The majority of the Linlithgow council, it was reported, had been 'so much disobliged' by the speeches of Dundas partisans 'that 16 of them have joynd hands avowedly to oppose the great ones'.[26] An informed observer of the political scene in Linlithgow remarked, no doubt correctly, that this hesitation and the alliance of the sixteen councillors was 'intended to raise the mercat'.[27] In a hotly contested election it was not likely to be advantageous to give for nothing what might command a better price, and an immediate declaration by Linlithgow would simply ensure that the potential largesse would be distributed elsewhere.

The burgh council of Linlithgow contained a number of particularly venal citizens, and several of the group who had shown such early eagerness to endorse the Dundas party's claim to the town's vote must be included in that category. According to a series of character sketches prepared for the Fletcher party in order to arrive at a plan for winning them over, some of the Dundas party were less than safe votes. There was, for example, an innkeeper sitting in council who could be characterised as a

> greedy fool, perpetually wavering, but sensible enough to be silent, till he knows, or thinks he knows, which side or party to bring to his house that will spend most money. He is certainly attach'd in his heart to B[uckna]y, from which L[awrence] D[undas]'s frequent entertainments at his house has in some measure withdrawn him. But tho' he has in compliance to L[awrence] D[undas] & his party shaken hands with them & declared for them, he is not staunch, setled, or to be depended on ... He hath got no bribe nor indeed the promise of any, & was originally made to declare or rather to disemble, on purpose to draw L[awrence] D[undas] & his Compy. to his house to spend money ... [28]

The political agent of Captain Fletcher was convinced that the innkeeper could easily be persuaded to reconsider his support of Lawrence Dundas, and it appears that the lady of the house was the more dominant personality and that the attack would have to be made by this route, for Mrs. Carlaw was

> venal to the last degree ... The case as to money spent in her house must be represented truely, viz. that it will soon cease of course, & with it all future hopes for many years. That her husband's conduct to the provost is extremely

exceptionable ... That therefor it's hop'd a woman of her sense will in the present occasion act like herselfe & consider the solid intrest of her family & secure her husband's conduct against all possible objections from both partys by prevailing on him to go out of the way quietly ... [29]

There was little that was certain in burgh elections, and if Lawrence Dundas had secured the early promises of some of the councillors, he was not misguided enough to regard them as firm friends, for all voters remained subject to pressure from other parties until the election was over. The cardinal error in burgh politics was overconfidence, and if Lawrence Dundas was free from this fault, the same could not be said for one of his rivals, James Carmichael, the brother of the Earl of Hyndford, who had been endorsed by the great men of Administration.

To have the active support of Administration was no doubt a great advantage for it clearly made it easy to provide demonstrations of the candidate's power to obtain patronage places in the towns which he was contesting. Carmichael, however, became overconfident and began to take support for granted, convinced that the friendship of the Duke of Argyll and Henry Pelham put his election beyond dispute. From the first, Carmichael had the vote of Lanark, where most of his own influence lay, and was confident of securing the support of Selkirk by his own efforts, while he believed that his connection with Administration would get him Lord March's interest in Peebles.[30] Accordingly, Carmichael neglected to do what was really necessary for success in this election at the right time, for he failed to compete actively for the support of Linlithgow, the returning burgh. Linlithgow was left to Dundas and Fletcher for much of the contest, and it was already clear that something more than the influence of the neighbouring peers and lairds would determine the vote of that burgh, for as one observer remarked, 'its probable who first offers mony to the 17 at Lithgoe will break them'.[31] James Carmichael, by his failure to appreciate that Linlithgow would not necessarily support the candidate endorsed by Administration, allowed the town to pass by default into the hands of a rival.

As the competition continued, however, Carmichael was encouraged by the narrowing of the field, for one of his rivals, Captain Harry Fletcher, withdrew in face of the Duke of Argyll's obvious displeasure, and Andrew Fletcher, younger of Saltoun, who had been acting for his Gibralter-based brother at Linlithgow, returned to that town to canvass for James Carmichael. This development was the outcome of a compromise arranged by the Duke of Argyll's friends in Scotland, which left Carmichael to demonstrate what he could do in the towns in a clear contest with Lawrence Dundas, for Veitch, Lord March's candidate, also agreed to withdraw.[32] The arrangement was an unfortunate one for Administration, for they fixed upon a candidate who was unable to meet the challenge. It was a political compromise of a kind frequently encountered in eighteenth-century Scottish politics. In return for a clear field, Carmichael and his brother Lord Hyndford agreed to repay the expenses already incurred by the Fletcher family at Linlithgow and to unite their own interest with that of Lord March in the county election of Peebles, but the arrangement did not provide the Government with a strong candidate in the Linlithgow burghs, a contest in which the Duke of Argyll was vitally interested, for he was determined to deny the seat to his enemy Lawrence Dundas. In all probability the energetic Fletcher family would have had a far better chance of defeating Dundas, even with an absentee candidate, than did the lethargic and notably parsimonious Carmichael. The Fletcher party had been actively campaigning in the most significant burgh from the opening of the contest, but upon being given a clear field in Linlithgow, Carmichael did nothing to build up his own interest there. Conversely, the disappointed Fletcher family were assumed to be willing and able to swing the votes of their Linlithgow friends to another candidate. The Fletcher interest in Linlithgow had been created by the lavish expenditure of money [for they provided entertainments to counterbalance those which were staged by Dundas] and by holding out to the undecided councillors prospects of economic revival through the establishment of new manufacturing facilities in the burgh, a scheme which a friend of the Fletcher interest believed 'would be of great service & would make all arguments from the other side vanish'.[33] But with Fletcher no longer a candidate, these arguments of potential economic benefit would come more easily from a man who expected to sit in the legislature rather than from a third party, and it is evident also that the Fletchers no longer had any reason to pour additional money into Linlithgow after the enforced withdrawal of Captain Harry Fletcher.

Linlithgow was the primary objective of Lawrence Dundas, a candidate well provided with money and willing to disburse it to further his political ambitions. Dundas was shrewd enough to know that he would be resisted in every possible way by the Argyll interest and its candidate, and he took precautions to guard against the prospect of bribery charges at Linlithgow, while at the same time effectively gratifying the venal councillors and burgesses by employing an ingenious and relatively undetectable form of bribery which was given in the guise of compensation for forage taken from the townspeople by troops passing through the burgh, a scheme which was open only to Dundas in his capacity as commissary for bread and forage in Scotland.[34] The office of commissary was useful in another way, for it allowed Lawrence Dundas to remove from Linlithgow one of the councillors whom he was unable to win over: Robert Gardiner was a subordinate officer in Dundas's department, and in that capacity could be ordered to travel to Fort William to report on the state of the provisions in that distant garrison.[35] Dundas made full use of his connections with the military authorities, and he could also hold out to the eager councillors the prospect of a recommendation for the construction of barracks in the town, a form of development which was always popular in small burghs eager for the business which would be brought by a resident garrison.[36] Given the position and connections of Lawrence Dundas and the absence of the other candidate, it is hardly to be wondered that the Dundas interest steadily grew in Linlithgow and was strongly supported by the ordinary residents of the town, for it was not at all clear that he was out of favour with the current Administration.

Lawrence Dundas had, indeed, attempted to make his own compromise with the men in power, attempting to persuade them that he would be a suitable member of parliament devoted to the interests of the crown, but there was never any real prospect of securing the endorsement of Administration when the Duke of Argyll had influence, convinced as he was that Dundas was 'a mortal enemy & ... spring & author of all or most of the mischief against all our friends when he attended the Army'.[37] Accordingly there was no further room for compromise, and the contest would be pushed by both Dundas and Carmichael, although in reality most of the pushing came from Dundas, for James Carmichael was already convinced that he had secured the parliamentary seat. Carmichael believed he was sure of the support of three towns out of four, and that he could accordingly ignore Linlithgow and its casting vote. Lanark was indeed sure for Carmichael, he believed that Lord March's influence in Peebles would give him that burgh's vote, and he had struck a bargain with the power-broker of Selkirk, William Wauch, the town clerk, for a third vote. In politics, however, very little is ever sure until the votes are counted, and Selkirk's support was much less certain than Carmichael believed; indeed his own experiences with Clerk Wauch should have counselled caution. The agreement between James Carmichael and William Wauch required the candidate to pay, for the use of the town council of Selkirk, the sum of £160, which certainly looked like a very inexpensive way of obtaining a parliamentary seat. Carmichael, however, failed to pay Wauch the sum stipulated in the bargain, perhaps because he was over-cautious in parting with his money or because, through inexperience, he took too much for granted, but when he met Wauch again the candidate found that the price had risen. At the second meeting Wauch told Carmichael that now '£400 was the word, and unless he would instantly agree to pay or secure that sum, that their town would declare for Laurie, who had offer'd ... £600 ... '[38] Upon receipt of this unwelcome news James Carmichael quickly 'struck hands for £400 ' and was reported to have 'given security for it and looks upon Sel[kirk] as dead sure, and says he is absolutely sure of Lanerk '.[39]

While James Carmichael was bribing the town clerk of Selkirk, Linlithgow was writing to Lawrence Dundas to advise him that, if he could secure the vote of another town, they too would support him and thus secure his election; and it is interesting to note how quickly the ranks of the council of Linlithgow began to close when it became probable that the election would be carried by their casting vote. On the fairly safe assumption that the generous Mr. Dundas would spare no effort to secure the vote of either Selkirk or Peebles, the council of Linlithgow, having weighed up the alternative, a candidate who had ignored their burgh, not surprisingly decided that their Stirlingshire neighbour was likely to prove a greater asset as their representative. In making their offer of support to Lawrence Dundas, the council, it was reported by friends of Administration, all 'went into this measure, except Kennoway, Paterson & two or three more of the 17' who had hitherto declined to commit themselves to a candidate.[40]

Dundas and his friends could not have been greatly surprised by the change of heart at Linlithgow, for they had been making determined efforts to encourage such a development, and their attention had by no means been restricted to the members of council. Linlithgow, like all of the Scottish burghs, was governed by a self-electing town council whose members alone had a voice in choosing a member of parliament. On the other hand, the restricted franchise should not be taken to imply that the ordinary townspeople had no share in the outcome of a contested election, nor was Lawrence Dundas a politician who failed to appreciate their usefulness in exerting pressure upon the council of the burgh. Lawrence Dundas's methods were discussed more fully in relation to a later election, but there is no reason to question their application to this one, for many of the neighbouring gentry and tenant farmers were brought into town, reinforced by people from the town of Falkirk. Dundas was always 'attended with great numbers . . . whom they canton in councillors houses',[41] and their attendance was further encouraged by daily entertainment which was extended to the general population. By 'throwing money to the populace', Lawrence Dundas made himself popular in the town, while his vociferous supporters crowded the streets 'drinking and huzzaing'.[42] The mob had a role in a contested election which should not be underestimated, and it is evident from a report on the Selkirk election of 1754, when Lawrence Dundas had his own methods turned against him, that the mob did in fact exert a significant degree of pressure upon the more timid councillors.

In 1754, when Andrew Pringle came to Selkirk, he found Lawrence Dundas 'prevalent in the Council and in the Mob . . . however, next day, by . . . proper measures the Mob was made unanimously ours, which produced good effects, and now . . . we have 16 to 16 and the casting vote on our side'.[43] In 1747, however, Linlithgow was filled with enthusiastic supporters of Dundas, and the councillors must have been encouraged to make their offer by the knowledge that this action would enhance their own popularity. Merchants and tradesmen were subject to pressures which did not necessarily involve their corruption. Neighbouring proprietors and their tenants brought business to the town which could be withheld, while no man of business, even if securely placed in a self-electing burgh council, could really be indifferent to a personal unpopularity which could cost him a lot more than a few broken windows. When such risks were undertaken for a politician, the reward had to be sufficient to outweigh the hazards of becoming the object of the mob's wrath, and in the Linlithgow of 1747, with one candidate conspicuously ignoring the members of council, and the other both generous and popular, there was little reason to hesitate any longer.

It is known that some of the Linlithgow councillors were not in fact offered bribes by Lawrence Dundas, yet they gave him their support. The evaluation of Dundas's friends in council prepared by the Fletcher party, for example, discusses in a disparaging way William Inglis, a journeyman tanner, who, in spite of being brought into council by some of Dundas's opponents, had become one of Dundas's partisans. The man was 'exceeding poor & naturally honest, tho' of very frail understanding . . . and hath little or no ambition above a belly full, a hearty botle, & a trifle in his pocket'.[44] The Fletcher agent, however, stated explicitly that Inglis had given his support to Dundas without receiving anything in return, and he was equally certain that Inglis could not be persuaded by any offer to change his vote. It was councillors of Inglis's type who would be most likely to follow the popular will in such a contest, and if one would hesitate to claim that they could ever have amounted to a majority of council, there were at least some who would bow to the popular will, and this in turn could change the balance of power within a council.

With a conditional promise from Linlithgow, Lawrence Dundas had every reason to intensify his efforts to gain another burgh, at whatever cost, and the only likely prospect was Selkirk. 'Laurie is now at Selkirk,' a correspondent informed Lord Milton, 'I wish he mayn't send Wauch back to town to make a third bargain'.[45] James Carmichael, the candidate of Administration, was far too careless to be a successful burgh politician, for he had already lost Linlithgow in spite of inheriting the Fletcher interest there and possessing the substantial advantage of Government aid. Carmichael had indeed so ignored that town that Lawrence Dundas was successfully posing as the candidate close to Government, and, as one of Carmichael's critics remarked, whereas Dundas had 'gone to Lythgow with a great posse, spared nothing & promised the Government was to build barracks etc.,'[46] Carmichael, the Government candidate, had done nothing material to build an interest in the town before the council had committed itself publicly to the popular Lawrence Dundas. Now the election was to be snatched from Carmichael by the vote of the burgh of Selkirk, a vote which he chose to consider safely bought, declining to make further efforts in the town and thus permitting Lawrence Dundas to exert his powers of persuasion unchallenged.[47]

The election was determined by the vote of the burgh of Selkirk, and that vote could only be obtained for money, as James Carmichael had already learned from his dealings with the town clerk, William Wauch. The councillors of Selkirk were in fact desperate for ready money, for they had been encountering difficulties in their management of that impoverished burgh, and had recently lost an action in the Court of Session brought at the instance of the Selkirk weavers. The decreet issued by the Court on July 17th, 1744 ordered the burgh council to make a payment of £139 to the plaintiffs, and the decreet, most inconveniently for the councillors, insisted that the public revenues 'were to be noways burdened'.[48] Accordingly, the magistrates and councillors of Selkirk had been awaiting the coming of an election with some eagerness, for in their need they had been obliged to issue bonds of £160 Sterling to meet the demands of the decreet and other legal expenses, and the bonds, together with the unpaid interest, were still outstanding. That was not the end of the troubles of the council of Selkirk for, perhaps encouraged by the weavers' success, some of the inhabitants of the burgh had commenced another action in the Court of Session 'for alledged misapplication of the town's revenue'.[49] In the event of a second defeat in the Court of Session, who could predict what sums might be demanded from the councillors? In such circumstances, the candidate whom Selkirk would endorse could only be the one who showed the greatest willingness to loosen his purse strings and aid his friends.

James Carmichael compounded his first error in failing to conclude a bargain when Wauch offered it to him, for when he found himself forced to offer £400 for the burgh's use, he would have been better advised to place it immediately in the hands of the burgh magistrates. A promise from Carmichael for future payment proved to be insufficient to prevent the burgh of Selkirk from concluding a new bargain with Lawrence Dundas, and Dundas paid only £300, but it was to be paid immediately after the election of a delegate. According to a statement made by Bailie Andrew Scott, who was evidently an undeclared supporter of Carmichael [for he signed the statement on July 30th, 1747], Scott, in company with another magistrate, Bailie Thomas Laurie, met with the manager of the Dundas interest in Selkirk at Laurie's house. Lawrence Dundas's agent, Dr. John Rutherfoord of Faldonside, authorised the payment of £300 Sterling for the use of the burgh council the day before the delegate was chosen and, in return, the two bailies promised to use their interest in order to elect one of Lawrence Dundas's friends, Robert Dundas, younger of Arniston, advocate, as the burgh's delegate to go to Linlithgow and there cast the town's vote for a member of parliament. The two bailies then communicated their agreement to the burgh treasurer, John Fairbairn, 'and in general the bargain was known and understood by the whole Councill, who did agree to accept of it'. [50]

On the day of election of a delegate, the two bailies again met with the Laird of Faldonside to ask for their money, but the latter, supported by an Edinburgh lawyer, adamantly refused until he saw Robert Dundas duly chosen and supplied with the town's commission, being of opinion, as Scott remarked, 'that it was not so proper for Mr. Lawrence Dundas's interest to pay money till after the delegate was elected, and that there might be a snake in the grass ... immediately after the election it should be paid'.[51] Bearing in mind Clerk Wauch's negotiations with Carmichael and the fact that the burgh's commission would have to bear a seal affixed by the same gentleman, the caution shown by Faldonside appeared justified, for there were many precedents for councillors accepting bribes from both parties. On the other hand there can be no question that money changing hands at the election itself was a particularly blatant example of corruption, and the facts were scarcely concealed, for, as soon as council had chosen Robert Dundas to be their delegate, the two magistrates hurried off to the home of the dean of guild, where Rutherfoord of Faldonside and his legal adviser awaited them with one hundred guineas in ready money and a bill for £195, payable in ten days, which was in fact paid by Rutherfoord on July 27th.

The Selkirk magistrates appeared already to have repented of their bargain and to have felt that they had been over-modest in their demands, for they asked Rutherfoord to engage on behalf of Lawrence Dundas to 'relieve the magistrates and town council of Selkirk of a proces depending against them in Session at the instance of several burgesses for alledged misapplication of the town's revenue'.[52] In this, however, the bailies were unsuccessful, for even a gentleman of Lawrence Dundas's wealth was unwilling to safeguard a burgh council against the consquences of a misapplication of revenues, for that kind of undertaking could well prove to be throwing money into a bottomless pit, and would have virtually guaranteed that the remaining burgh property of Selkirk would have been plundered. Lawrence Dundas, when consulted by his Selkirk agent and now sure of a parliamentary seat, was willing to give an additional £50 'towards relieving the council of that proces',[53] and, moreover, the Dundas party were ready to relieve the council of the charges of an advocate, for Robert Dundas agreed to serve them in the matter of the process without charge, but there was to be no question of a blanket guarantee of payment of any award made against the council.

The money paid to the council of Selkirk — and Bailie Scott was quite insistent on the point — was utilised to pay the outstanding bonds, while any residue was to be employed for repair to the burgh church, although such statements are impossible to confirm or refute. Clearly, however, the election of the Selkirk delegate had turned on the question of cash. Carmichael's party began the bargaining with their negotiations with the town clerk, and as Lord Milton remarked, Clerk Wauch's interest 'would have effectually secured the Election' for Carmichael, 'had not our own artillery been turned against us, and had we not been overpowered by the root of all evil'.[54]

Carmichael was too slow in reaction and far too reluctant to spend money when money alone would serve him. James Carmichael was advised by a friend at Selkirk that 'Mr. D[unda]s was bribeing high',[55] and there can be little doubt that the corruption of the Selkirk councillors went well beyond the collective gift stressed by Bailie Scott, but Carmichael did nothing. Instead of launching an immediate counter-attack, Carmichael and his friends 'rely'd on their bargain ',[56] a decision which left the council free to listen to the arguments of the Dundas party and then to vote as self-interest dictated.

While Selkirk and the parliamentary election were slipping away from him, James Carmichael was engaged at Linlithgow, to which he had belatedly turned his attention. Carmichael and his family had agreed to 'bestow £600' upon the councillors of Linlithgow,[57] and that sum employed at the right time might well have been sufficiently attractive, particularly if reinforced by promises of future patronage. But by the time Carmichael paid any attention to Linlithgow the town was already lost, and among the burgesses at large pro-Dundas feeling was so strong that it was necessary to negotiate secretly with a few councillors who were thought to be willing to reconsider their position should the arguments be sufficiently persuasive. Since Carmichael had shown no talent for such delicate negotiations, he was advised to delegate the duty to William Alston, a writer experienced in election matters, and on the evening of July 19th the two set off from Edinburgh for the burgh of Linlithgow. On approaching the town the carriage was stopped, and Carmichael dismounted half a mile from the town limits while Alston, who was not known in the place, went on alone to the house of Bailie Kennoway. The magistrate would send for his two closest associates and discuss with Alston 'wither the artillery may be plaid off to porpos & if it can, they will conveen the troops and concert their schemes, before the enemy know that ther's any designe upon them'.[58] On the other hand, should Alston find that bribery would not carry the councillors to Carmichael, the lawyer had an additional task. 'If the fort is impregnable & proof agt our artillery', Alston would learn from Kennoway and his friends 'how the other side imploy'd theirs and take the proper protests. This is all that could be done on so short a warning'.[59]

A campaign in which the Government candidate found himself hiding on the edge of the burgh limits, while a stranger attempted to learn something of the state of the council, had evidently been grossly mismanaged, and as Lord Milton complained, when some money expended in the town might have done some good,

Carmichael 'did nothing to purpose, but believed they would be for him because they drunk his drink and eat his meat'.[60] Councillors were not to be so cheaply won, for they all had their own views and interests with which the candidate would be wise to make himself familiar, and even an offer of money at the last moment, when feelings were high in the streets of the burgh, was unattractive. Councillors might be unscrupulous in pursuit of their own advantage, but many of them would hesitate to bring upon themselves the wrath of the mob by breaking their promise to the popular candidate. It was not merely Carmichael who deluded himself, however, for even the experienced Lord Milton, usually well informed of all that transpired in Scottish elections, suggested to the Duke of Argyll that Carmichael was still sure of election, for he had Lanark in his hands, Peebles through the agency of Lord March, and the promise of Selkirk as conveyed by William Wauch. In this view Linlithgow would see reason and 'come back to g[overnment]'.[61] This too was wishful thinking, and not merely because of the venality of the Selkirk magistrates, for Lawrence Dundas, with his talk of barrack construction, was not suggesting that he was in opposition to Government, leaving many of the councillors less than certain whether Carmichael or Dundas had the ear of Administration. The contest demonstrated that the influence of landed families, however useful this might be to a candidate, was ancillary to such matters as patronage, offers to be useful to the community, and simply the provision of the cash for which councillors stood in urgent need. In all of these categories Lawrence Dundas was effective, successfully persuading the councillors to see their own interests as identical to his own.

The election was now a formality, for although James Carmichael had the support of the delegates of Lanark and Peebles, Dundas, with Selkirk and Linlithgow, was in complete control thanks to the casting vote of the returning burgh, and on July 22nd, 1747 Lawrence Dundas was named the member of parliament. Lawrence Dundas's tenure of the seat was brief, however, for on March 7th, 1748 a committee of the House of Commons awarded the seat to James Carmichael, principally on the ground that the council of Selkirk had failed to take an oath against bribery before proceeding to their election of a delegate.[62] In fact, this decision appears to have been a measure of the Duke of Argyll's dislike of Lawrence Dundas, for Carmichael had failed to take appropriate steps to prepare the ground for such an appeal, and none of the Selkirk voters present at the meeting had asked that the oath be put.[63] An appeal on the ground of bribery, however, would have been unwise, for the losing candidate was equally guilty of the offence, and accordingly Dundas was unseated essentially on questionable procedural grounds used to disqualify the delegate of Selkirk, and it was done in spite of the fact that the delegate in question, Robert Dundas, younger of Arniston, took the matter so much to heart that he was led to threaten retaliation against Ministers of the Crown.[64]

The election for the Linlithgow burghs can be regarded as typical, for a candidate offering his services to a burgh council would rarely suggest that he was in opposition to the Government, a statement which would have effectively undermined whatever interest the candidate had built up. Money, the willingness of the candidate to spend it freely, and his readiness to make undertakings and promises to the community were decisive, for councillors expected more than entertainment.

Bribery certainly had its place in the calculations of burgh patrons and politicians. Without rewards for friendship, no interest, however powerful its landed base and apparent influence, could maintain its position over the long term. Captain Patrick Rigg, the leading figure in the council of Cupar, remarked in 1795 that 'every man of good sense must know, that any person wishing to keep a borough must at times do good and pleasant things to his friends'.[65] A steady flow of patronage at all times was advisable, but in a hotly contested election this flow of 'good and pleasant things' had to be augmented by something more than the normal patronage. On occasion the transactions were of such a form that they can be regarded in no other light than as the purchase of a vote, or attempts to do so.

In 1767, George Dempster, the Member for Dundee burghs, was being run very hard by a Perthshire gentleman, Robert Mackintosh of Auchintully, who was well provided with funds since he had been set up by Dempster's enemy in East Indian politics, Lord Clive.[66] Dempster, in the heat of the contest, was led to commit some indiscretions at Cupar which led to his arrest and subsequent criminal proceedings.

The evidence against Dempster is admittedly somewhat tainted, for his enemy in Cupar, Bailie Robert Geddie, following a Michaelmas election at which the Bailie had been turned out of council together with his friends, had issued a proclamation 'offering a reward of £100 Sterling, to the discoverer of any act of corruption, over and above the sum offered, received, or refused, with the indemnity provided by act of parliament'.[67] An offer like that, as the *Scots Magazine* pointed out, was standing temptation to perjury, but from Dempster's private correspondence it is clear that bribery formed a normal part of his political management in these burghs. Accordingly, if we ignore the blanket accusation levelled against most of Dempster's friends in the council of Cupar, that they only gave him such support by reason of gifts, promises or securities, and instead concentrate our attention on the more specific examples of corrupt practices, for which a witness was forthcoming, we are probably on fairly firm ground. According to the criminal letters against Dempster, the member of parliament had met with one of the council, James Morres, the deacon of the waulkers, at the home of the convener of trades, who was a Dempster partisan, where Dempster tried to persuade Deacon Morres to support his interest in council and 'did repeatedly offer to, and press the said James Morres to take money, and to give his promise'.[68] Dempster was alleged to have 'at last ... put three different parcels into one of the waistcoat-pockets of the said Deacon James Morres, each of which contained twenty notes for one pound Sterling each, of what is commonly called the Dundee bank', an establishment of which Dempster was the principal proprietor. James Thomson, another of Dempster's targets, was deacon of the fleshers, and in his case Dempster, after suggesting 'that a trading man was always wanting money, promised, that if he the said James Thomson would say the word, he would believe it, and would give him anything he would ask or demand',[69] though apparently

Deacon Thomson did not take up this tempting offer. John Smith, a Cupar tanner who expected to be brought into council at the ensuing Michaelmas election, was invited to support the interest of Dempster and Provost Baxter, and Dempster, 'in order to enforce his solicitations, took out of his pocket four parcels of banknotes, containing ... eighty pounds Sterling ... saying ... that it would relieve him, and pay his debts'.[70] Clearly, merchant councillors commanded a higher bribe than council deacons, rating twenty pounds more in the scale of corruption. James Campbell, an innkeeper, and one of the associates of Bailie Geddie and, like the bailie, turned off council at Michaelmas, was advised that 'if he would go in with, or stand by, the said Provost John Baxter's leet', Dempster 'would immediately give him fifty pounds Sterling'. Another councillor turned off at the burgh election, David Preston, changekeeper in Cupar, was visited prior to that meeting by Dempster, who, 'after asking ... whether he owed any money, and the said David Preston answering, That he was a silly body that neither owed not had owing to him the said George Dempster corrupted, or attempted to corrupt him ... by an offer of fifty pounds Sterling'.[71]

Partly by such methods, George Dempster gained what he quaintly described as 'a most amazing victory in Cupar ... I have beat corruption on its own ground ... I found things desperate there, in three days we set 'em to rights ... '[72] The manner of Dempster's success, however, landed him in a series of expensive lawsuits and finally forced him into the expedient of withdrawing from the parliamentary election at the last moment in favour of a friend. The friend, who also secured his election for a county, chose to sit for the latter, allowing Dempster to return to the attack successfully in the burghs and secure his return in the by-election.[73] Dempster's activities at Cupar attracted unusual attention, but that was all that was extraordinary about the contest. Bribery was a frequently employed tool in any contested burgh election, and even when a councillor refused a bribe, cynical contemporaries were apt to wonder what he had got from the other side to retain his loyalty. In 1818, for example, *The Scotsman*, when reporting the refusal by a council deacon of Stirling of the rather startling offer of £2,000 'rather than vote contrary to his conscience', far from conceding that the councillor might have scruples, speculated:

> How argumentative and persuasive must the morality of the mentor have been, who managed to keep that son of St. Crispin firm in the faith to Ministers, and how many weighty and substantial reasons must he have produced before he succeeded.[74]

Firm evidence of the size of individual gifts is of course difficult to secure, for it was not likely to be carefully recorded in a book which might fall into the wrong hands, but by repute, at least, the gifts received by councillors were substantial. Charles Rampini, the sheriff-substitute of Moray and Nairn, writing in 1898, described the events of the hotly contested parliamentary election of 1820 in the Elgin district as it was remembered in the burghs. It was alleged, for example, that Lord Fife had given a gift of a psalm book to James Cattanach, the deacon of the wrights of Elgin, in itself a modest enough gift. The psalm book, however, was believed to have aided the deacon in more than his devotions, for it was said to have contained three £100 notes between its pages. No doubt hard evidence is lacking for this popular belief, but, on the other hand, hundred pound notes must have been scarce commodities in the Elgin of 1820, and their changing must have been widely remarked. Even more conclusively there was evidence of extensive bribery of councillors by the Grant family, Lord Fife's opponents in that election, in which real property changed hands. According to Sheriff Rampini, the Grants conveyed to Deacon Steinson 'a well-biggit close', which the sheriff remarked as having recently been sold by the last heir of that family. The sheriff indeed suggested that the only council deacon to have failed to add to his wealth during the election was Alexander McIver, the deacon of the shoemakers, who was said to have 'refused £2,000, and the liferent of a farm, for himself and his son'.[75] In short, although it is hard to state precise and accurate values for bribes given to councillors, there appears to be little doubt that many of those sitting in burgh councils were able and willing to satisfy their own greed when a parliamentary election was contested with vigour, and they were most certainly not the mere pawns of greater men, there to do their will, and it was that degree of self-interested independence which was the occasion of much of the political violence which disfigured burgh elections.

Political violence was not uncommon in Scottish burgh elections, and if the instigator might on occasion be a burgh patron angered by opposition to the point of desiring vengeance, the normal motive was to attempt to swing the balance of power within a council back to the friends of the politician by securing the absence of a few enemies. Violence could of course vary greatly in scale. At one extreme it might include the near-legal arrest of a councillor for debt, in order to prevent his attendance at an important meeting, which was usually easily effected, for men engaged in trade were invariably burdened with debt, but violence could be much more openly illegal coercion of the council members, in which fear was intended to intimidate and restrain opponents from attending the election.

In the case of the arrest of a debtor, the politician would obtain possession of the instruments establishing the debt from a third party. Thus prepared, he would obtain a warrant for the commitment of the debtor and with the aid of a court officer make the arrest. Timing was of the essence, for the man to be taken had to be arrested at the last possible moment, preferably as he was making his way to the town house to take part in the election meeting, for that alone would ensure that the councillor would be absent. Timely warning would permit the freeing of the debtor by payment of the obligation. Such arrests were usually brief affairs, and the messenger happily let his prisoner go free at the conclusion of the election meeting, thus demonstrating that this was electoral sharp practice rather than a genuine attempt to collect an unpaid debt. If this tactic was almost normal in burgh politics, it was certainly not unknown even in the politics of the counties, and county politicians were sometimes put to considerable difficulty to find sufficient cash to pay the debts of their voters should this be necessary to secure their presence. In 1734, for example, Sir James Grant of Grant sent a desperate appeal for cash to Robert Grant of Tammore, the factor of Lord Elchies' estate, pointing out that his opponents 'have gott all the captions they can to be execut against our Friends'.[76] Sir James had only £600 on hand to pay such demands, clearly having been taken by surprise by his opponents. The Grants had an additional £600 on its way from an Edinburgh bank, but that could not reach the north before the election meeting, and accordingly the friends of the Grant party were asked to put into the debt-paying fund all ready cash available, though with the promise of early repayment. In burgh politics, where the arrest for debt was a more common tactic, no politician of experience would fail to have a substantial sum of money available to free his friends if needed, for it was often required. On the other hand, some of the methods used to ensure the absence of hostile voters went far beyond mere arrest for debt, and were manifestly illegal.

In 1740, for example, Captain Munro of Culcairn, supported by eighty armed men, carried off ten of the councillors of the burgh of Dingwall, and although the excuse was once again their alleged debts, this had all the appearance of a raid on the town by the Munros and obviously prevented any free election.[77] Pushed to such extremes, arrest of councillors invited the attention of the judicial authorities, as did the kidnapping of councillors who declined to absent themselves when requested to do so.

The arrangement of a convenient absence from a vital election was another approach taken by politicians who wished to engineer a change in the balance of power within a council. A councillor would be approached after he had promised his support to a particular candidate, and if he could not be detached, he might be asked to depart quietly from the town and return when the election had passed. One of the Linlithgow councillors in 1747 named Wardrop, who was attached to the interest of Lawrence Dundas, was to be approached by Dundas's enemies and offered 20 guineas on his arrival in Glasgow and a further 30 guineas when he reached Port Patrick, as an inducement to abscond. There was an element of persuasion employed beyond the mere fact of bribery however, for Wardrop:

> As he is a V[i]l[ai]n . . . must be assured in express terms, his being brib'd by both parties is well known. That his vote will be infallibly cast, he punish'd, ruin'd etc. To prevent all which, there is no security for him but in a decent retreat. These hints may be solidly improven by adding, that work in his weaving way may be instantly given & continued to him . . . [78]

The unannounced departure of a councillor, bribed and threatened though Wardrop might have been, could be argued to be a voluntary excursion to Port Patrick, but councillors could find themselves making even longer journeys of an involuntary nature. The Dumfriesshire royal burgh of Lochmaben was notorious throughout Scotland for the political outrages which were committed there, and in one case which attracted attention in 1790 it was disclosed that a councillor named Walls had been kidnapped and taken as far as London before he could regain his freedom. Walls was allegedly arrested for debt, but in reality his offence was to persist in opposing Sir James Johnstone and refusing to accept a bribe of £200 to 'take a walk . . . on the day of election'.[79] Taken prisoner by armed men in his own fields, Walls was removed from the town before he could cast his vote, but on this occasion it was not merely the election that was called into question. The High Court of Justiciary, no doubt incensed by the frequency of such abuses at Lochmaben, made an example of the kidnappers, although, needless to say, Sir James Johnstone, their master, was not punished. The immediate offenders, however, after suffering whipping through the streets of Edinburgh, were sentenced to banishment, but it is remarkable that even where the offence was so flagrant, one of the judges was able to suggest that 'he was inclined to mitigate the punishment . . . as it was one of those crimes which the common people did not think would be attended with such fatal consequences'.[80] The opinion of the Lord of Justiciary is in itself an indication of the extent of the practice of arranging artificial arrests for debt, which were in fact forcible detentions to subvert elections.

The holding of voters, who had been persuaded to engage their support for a parliamentary candidate, to ensure that they did not change their minds before the day of election, was essentially another form of kidnapping, and their detention, even if comfortable, was nonetheless confinement. In 1791, for example, when a heated contest for the representation of the Dunfermline burghs was in progress involving three candidates, one of them, Captain Campbell, appeared to have secured the support of a majority of the council of Dunfermline. That majority was reduced by the efforts of Colonel Erskine of Alloa, a friend of Captain Cochrane, one of Campbell's opponents. The Colonel invited ten of the councillors of Dunfermline, including two of the deacons who had already given their promises to Campbell, to visit him at Alloa House for dinner. Once they were safely inside its walls, the councillors were not permitted to return to Dunfermline and were 'kept closs confined by a strong Gaurd surrounding the house and under constant intoxication until the day of Election, when they were brought back to Dunfermline in carriages under a Gaurd with the Colonel at their head and put into the Council house without being allowed to speak to any person whatever'.[81] The well-watered councillors, including Campbell's erstwhile friends, duly showed their gratitude for their extended dinner by electing Colonel Erskine to be their delegate by 12 votes to 10. Detention of this kind was, however, much riskier than arrest for debt. In the case of a real debt, providing there was a careful regard for the forms of legality, a member of council could be prevented from casting a crucial vote unless the debt was immediately paid. But detention of a number of councillors would be a strong ground for appeal to the House of Commons or to the courts, particularly if one of the detained men could be persuaded to claim that he had been detained against his will, which would not be too difficult to do by holding out to a greedy man visions of what might have been done for him had he been available for discussions prior to the election.

Detention of voters was a common ground of appeal. Typical of the reaction of a losing candidate defeated by such an expedient was the petition of Colonel Grant in 1780 complaining of the return of Major-General Staats Long Morris, the candidate of the Gordon family in the Elgin district of burghs. A number of the councillors of Inverurie, one of the towns of this district, were claimed by Grant to have been held prisoners in the castle of Keithhall, the seat of the Earl of Kintore, and thereafter to have been conveyed to the election under an armed guard of the earl's followers, while the Duke of Gordon was also alleged to have used similarly strong measures to influence the voters in other burghs.[82] From a private letter, however, it would appear that after Colonel Grant had obtained a promise of support from the council of Inverurie, two of his voters had been won over by Lord Kintore. They had, as Grant put it, 'deserted', and had not been kidnapped. Nevertheless, Grant contended that their detention at Keithhall in order to prevent them changing their minds for a second time gave him grounds for an appeal designed to overturn the election of a delegate from that town.[83]

Where noblemen and lairds were active in a burgh's politics, they could display much shortness of temper towards those who cared to oppose their wishes. In the Elgin election of 1715, for example, while the usual accusations of bribery and undue pressure were raised, the choice of a delegate for that burgh supporting the interest of Colonel John Campbell of Mamore appears to have been secured by a particularly persuasive argument employed by one of the councillors. According to the petition against the return of Campbell, 'Robert Dunbar of Grangehill declared to them that if they offered to protest against his being elected delegat . . . his sword was to the fore and that he would be delegat who would or who would not', upon which the Laird of Grangehill was duly chosen by the votes of ten councillors against a bold minority of six.[84]

Improper pressures upon councillors in contested parliamentary elections were by no means restricted to the North or to such relatively remote communities as Lochmaben, for towns within easy reach of the capital were subjected to the most serious illegalities by politicians in no way inhibited by the proximity of the superior courts of justice. In the burgh of Inverkeithing, a contest arose for the office of provost, a dispute which was of course closely linked to parliamentary politics. The candidates for the office of chief magistrate were John Cunningham and Sir Robert Henderson of Fordell, with the latter as the aggressor attempting to overthrow Cunningham's power in the burgh. Sir Robert Henderson began by seeking support from the trades deacons and, failing to detach them from Cunningham's interest, he insisted that such deacons could have no voice in the election of a council. The right of deacons to participate in burgh elections in Inverkeithing was admittedly of recent origin, for it dated from an Act of the Convention of Royal Burghs of 25th June 1742, but the Laird of Fordell took a stand on that very point, insisting that only an Act of Parliament was competent to alter the burgh sett, and that the convention had exceeded its powers. In accordance with this belief, real or feigned, Fordell obtained a warrant from two justices of the peace forbidding the deacons of trades of Inverkeithing sitting in the old council from participating in the election of the next year's magistrates and councillors. Fordell himself, supported by his ally, Bailie Hugh Grandiston, and reinforced by a constable, barred the entrance to the council chamber of Inverkeithing and refused to permit the deacons to enter. The constable, summoned by Bailie Grandiston, was in an unenviable position, for Provost Cunningham ordered him to allow the deacons to pass, while the bailie was as determined in his orders to refuse them entrance. As a result of these measures, however, Bailie Grandiston secured a majority in council, and this group duly chose Sir Robert Henderson of Fordell to be their new provost in Cunningham's place.[85] According to the losing party, however, Fordell had an additional source of influence which suggested the manner in which his majority was obtained, for as a great coal owner, Sir Robert had brought into the burgh 'a great mob of coaliers, tenants and other people'[86] with whose support he was enabled to intimidate many of Cunningham's friends, an allegation which is in all probability correct, for there was no class of society which aroused more fear in neighbouring communities than the Scottish serf coaliers. The irregularities at Inverkeithing were so extensive that the Lords of Session were induced to reverse the result of the council election and remove Sir Robert Henderson and two of his allies from office, basing their decision upon the well-documented forcible exclusion of the council deacons from the council chamber. Sir Robert Henderson's attempt on the provostship was not the only such illegal act in the burgh of Inverkeithing, however, for in 1760 a contest between Captain Robert Haldane of Airthrey and Admiral Francis Holburne became even more heated, and the admiral, in danger of defeat, resorted to a most potent form of persuasion:

> For a week previous to the election, the town was filled with all the Press Gangs in the Firth. There were above sixty sailors, armed with swords and pistols, in town. They paraded through the streets at all hours of the day and night, and intimidated the inhabitants by threats of being pressed. Besides these sailors, there were three Lieutenants of Men-of-War, who commanded the Press-Gangs, and a great number of midshipmen; and a Press Cutter lay in the bay, close to the town for several days before the election; and all of them disappeared immediately after the election was over.[87]

Attempted intimidation and removal of political opponents was practised well into the nineteenth century. In 1820, for example, there was a notoriously disorderly election in the Elgin district, in the course of which one of the magistrates of Elgin came close to being permanently removed from political activity:

> Bailie Francis Taylor, acting Chief Magistrate, was captured at his garden-gate by a party of the Duffs, carried ... to the seaside, where an open boat was procured to transport him to Sutherland, but a storm and head wind having got up, they were seventeen hours on the passage, and, after nearly losing their lives, they with the utmost difficulty got into the harbour of Brora ... [88]

After this experience, Bailie Taylor was understandably reluctant to make another sea passage, and his return by land was sufficiently delayed to change the balance of power in the vital election at Elgin. This setback so incensed Lady Ann Grant, an opponent of the Earl of Fife and the Duff faction, that she summoned 700 Grants and other tenants from Strathspey to march on the town, a threat which was countered by Lord Fife calling an estimated 1,500 of his tenants and friends to Elgin. Clearly, in the second decade of the century, there was every prospect of a lively clan battle, which seems to have been averted only by the alarmed Sheriff of Moray and the clergymen of Elgin who persuaded Lady Grant to order her people back to Strathspey on their undertaking to maintain order at the ensuing election in a fair manner.[89]

Holders of government office resident within a royal burgh frequently had considerable influence on its politics, and many were indeed members of council. Accordingly, to the people of one of the burghs, a clear test of the influence and potential usefulness of a politician was his ability to retain his friends in their places and equally to secure the removal of hostile officials. A candidate who failed to provide such a demonstration when necessary was apt to find enemies insinuating that he was unacceptable to Government and that the town should look elsewhere for its representative. In 1753, when Captain Robert Cunningham was candidate in the Duke of Argyll's interest for the Dunfermline district of burghs, he found that all of the Government employees in the burgh of Inverkeithing were his enemies, with the result that some of the councillors began to believe that the Captain did not have the support of the influential duke. It was not an unexpected development, for as the Captain remarked, 'these are strong arguments to convince weak bodies, that know nothing of what is going on beyond the walls of their town'.[90] Captain Cunningham's solution was to urge that an example be made of one of the officials, James Bell, the Stampmaster, for 'you cannot find a more undeserving object'. But the place would have to be transferred quickly to a Cunningham supporter, for 'if something of this sort is not done, *power* will be undervalued, and the Duke of Argyll's protection will soon be thought not worth the asking in a disputed election '.[91] Equally, a distribution of new appointments among friends, or potential friends, indicated in the most effective manner to the people of a burgh where power lay, and these places were frequently sought by the politicians. In 1807, for example, Robert Dundas was urged to secure a Treasury warrant to be an exciseman for John Horn, deacon of the tailors of Dunfermline, because this was essential for the maintenance of a Government interest in that town.[92]

The magistrates and councillors of the burghs were not the passive objects of external manipulation. In every town the composition of the council had a membership which varied in its social rank, and more importantly perhaps in intelligence. Every burgh had its leaders who, in the manner of John Galt's Provost Pawkie, were able to establish themselves unshakeably in a position of local power. A magistrate might be a loyal servant of a patron, he might be a rogue distrusted with good reason by all politicians, or he might be a man who acted genuinely in the interest of his community as well as for his own advantage, but dominant personalities with the intelligence to manage their colleagues continued in council year after year. Leaders of a council could secure such influence even when a council was under the direct patronage of a great landowner resident in the district who was obviously respected. A good example is t o be found in the burgh of Montrose, which saw Lord Panmure as its patron, a nobleman who was shown great respect by the townspeople. On the other hand this did not mean that Lord Panmure's wishes would determine the composition of the burgh council, where at one Michaelmas election the choice of the new magistrates and councillors was manipulated in a masterly fashion by one of the bailies in direct opposition to the wishes of the patron.

Bailie James Bisset reorganised the council of Montrose to suit his own wishes and did so in spite of his apparent 'zeal for Lord Panmure's interest' prior to the election.[93] Lord Panmure had relied upon the chief magistrate, Provost George Ross, to arrange for the election to the new provostship of Thomas Douglas, one of Panmure's friends then in the council, and to defeat the efforts of the leader of the rival group in council, David Doig, to obtain the chief magistrate's place. In pursuit of this plan, Panmure had requested Bailie Bisset to call upon him at Panmure House, where Bisset led the Earl to believe that he was zealous for his interest. Upon his return to Montrose, Bailie Bisset went to Provost Ross and persuaded him to delay the council meeting for a day, and then, as the indignant Ross recounted, spent the night with Doig persuading the remaining councillors that Provost Ross 'had joined in a Jacobite scheme to rent & destroy the Whig Councell'. The following day, when the council of Montrose assembled to elect its successor, 'the zealotts were all furious'with Ross '& without the least shewe of reasone told' the provost that his plot was discovered and they 'would take care of [Ross] ackordingly'.[94] Bisset, the man who had arranged for this misunderstanding, was, according to Ross, 'paciefying them & giveing them fair words', with a view to mislead Provost Ross, who was, as he admitted ruefully, in 'noe dread but I wase to have his own vote & intrest'.[95] Provost Ross, thoroughly misled by Bisset's words, advised his own friends to follow Bisset's lead in the voting which would follow as the new councillors were chosen.

In accordance with the customs of Montrose, the old councillors then adjourned for supper, but when they reconvened to choose their new magistrates, Ross got a nasty surprise. Provost Ross immediately proposed Lord Panmure's friend, Thomas Douglas, for the office of provost, and David Doig was also put into the leet for that position, but with this accomplished Bisset threw off the mask of friendship for Ross and deference to Lord Panmure's wishes. Addressing the council, Bailie James Bisset, as Ross put it in his report to Panmure,

> saiyd a great deall of nonsense in favours of keeping your Lordship's intrest, but that there was no compairison betwixt & spliting the Councill; therefor he voted for Provost Doig. I swear I never wase so trickt in my lifetime . . . [96]

Bailie Bisset, needless to say, gave Lord Panmure a somewhat different version of the events of the burgh election. According to Bisset, when he returned to the burgh from Panmure House, he found the councillors, with the exception of Provost Ross, 'agreed on Prov. Doig to be put into the Chair, but on this condition that your Lordship's friendship should be strictly regarded. So that it was simply impossible to overturn that determination'.[97] Ross, however, went into the council meeting with five votes in a council of which only fourteen members could be present. Bailie Bisset had control of three of the remaining votes,[98] so it is evident that it was the latter who acted as kingmaker, overturning the existing administration and replacing it with that of Provost Doig. The only consolation for the noble patron in all this was the new chief magistrate's promise to his friends that he would support a candidate favoured by Lord Panmure, an undertaking whose value could in no way be predicted. What was clear was that a council had been formed without regard to the expressed wishes of Lord Panmure, who was left to make what he could of the result, and Bisset was now a power in council who could not be safely ignored.

Councillors so strongly entrenched in power were not to be treated lightly by patron or politician, and they, like the freeholders, had their own views distinct from those which interested the great men. Like freeholders, they had sons in need of employment, if in business they sought commercial favours and contracts, they expected as a perquisite of office to be entertained after a Michaelmas or election meeting, even when there was little opposition, and on occasion they sought and received gifts. As in the counties, patronage and politics went hand in hand. On the other hand, one must also suspect that on occasion councillors may have been quite willing to accept a suggestion that they should arrange to be absent from a violently contested election, for it could bring them the enmity of those who could harm them, whichever way they voted. Perhaps few politicians were as vindictive as Lord Fortrose, who remarked on one occasion of an opponent that 'my intention is to ruin totally his Family, that his children may remember who it was that their Father disobliged',[99] but the Lanark voters 'threatened by gentlemen ... with loss of custom and personal enmity' in 1818 were not alone in receiving that kind of warning.[100] Voting in an open election was not a decision to take lightly, even in the self-electing and venal system of the eighteenth century, and patronage received from one party had to be set against the enmity of another. Perhaps an urgent business trip to Edinburgh, London or wherever was the wisest course? One tends to see a councillor selling his vote to the highest bidder, but in fact that might not be at all easy to do, for if some politicians were prepared to bribe an opponent into temporary friendship, there were others, such as Lord Advocate Hope, who set themselves firmly against that practice, preferring instead to reward steady friends to the exclusion of others; for as he put it:

> I am ... a great enemy to half-measures, & to that mistaken policy of buying an enemy, instead of rewarding a friend, & therefore would rather bestow his place [as postmaster] on a firm friend, than buy him off by the fear of losing it, especially as the fellow would probably secretly undermine us after all ... [101]

In burgh politics there was much more of what can only be called ill-concealed bribery than would be seen in county politics, but the idea that dispensing patronage and cash bribes was all there was to burgh management is mistaken, and those politicians most familiar with the day-to-day workings of burgh management were rarely deluded into believing that their control was absolute. Lord Rothes, who had a hand in the politics of most of the Fife towns, complained 'that all these sort of people are so fickle that one is never sure of 'em till all is over. But we must make the best we can of 'em ... '[102] Which was all that any patron could do with the burgh councillors.

Even the most influential politicians could be forced to make an undignified retreat by burgh councils when faced with imminent defeat. In 1761, for example, when the city of Edinburgh was strongly influenced by the Duke of Argyll, the latter failed to persuade the burgh council to accept his candidate for member of parliament. The man favoured by Argyll, Alexander Forrester, was unpopular with the community, and there were soon good grounds for fearing that the council might reject Forrester in favour of John Fordyce, a gentleman unacceptable to the Duke of Argyll. Burgh councillors were normally unresponsive to public pressure as a result of their self-electing constitution, but if the public became concerned about an issue, they had their ways of making the councillors take notice. In a letter written to Argyll, Lord Milton observed that

> what hurt us most was the instructions of the whole corporations to their Deacons prohibiting them to vote for Mr. Forrester, and the customers of merchants as well as tradesmen threatning to leave their shops if they voted for Mr. Forrester ... '[103]

Faced by the threat of the council giving way to popular pressure if Argyll persisted, the duke had no alternative but to drop Forrestor and ask his friends to vote for a more acceptable candidate.

Where a leader in council possessed a Government office, this undoubtedly created a channel of continuing influence, for even when gratitude might diminish, removal was still a threat. Indeed, in the case of the not inconsiderable number of councillors who held appointments which made them non-residents of their communities for lengthy periods, it was not even necessary to go so far as to secure their dismissal. In 1790, for example, Erskine of Cambo pressed Henry Dundas to secure the recall to duty of 'Robert Louthian, one of the present Magistrates of Kilrenny, and late Master of his Majesty's Ship Amphion ... on such a station as to prevent him being present at the next Michaelmas Election ... at Kilrenny ... '[104] The opposite course, that of obtaining leave for army and naval officers to attend an important council meeting, was also within the power of politicians with Government connections. Moreover, those officeholders actually resident in a burgh, such as officers of customs and excise, could be, and often were, employed to influence merchant councillors to follow a desired course by a selective enforcement of the laws against smuggling. One councillor might find his goods seized, while another, equally culpable, but a member of another political interest, was left in peace.[105] The message was quite clearly indicated by such actions, and to persist in opposition might prove ruinously expensive. In all the sea-coast burghs in the eighteenth century there was an extraordinary interest in the placement of officers of the customs service, a greater interest than the salaries of the posts would appear to warrant, and a politician unable to secure some of these places for his friends was on shaky ground.

Maintaining an interest in a burgh was a permanent activity, for a council required constant management and a flow of patronage sufficient to maintain the hopes of those who had not yet been recipients of such favours, for as Lord Rothes remarked, 'selfish views goe a great lenth wt most people'.[106] A patron was expected to demonstrate his generosity and concern for the community by providing for his friends, and also by making liberal donations to the poor and for public works, from repairs to kirk and town-house, to harbour construction. In September 1767, Sir Lawrence Dundas helped consolidate his interest in the city of Edinburgh with 'a very liberal donation to the merchants and trades of Edinburgh; £300 to the poor of the merchant company, £200 to the merchants maiden-hospital, and £500 to the trades maiden-hospital'.[107] £1,000 in one gesture did create a suitable impression, but that impression would not have been lasting had not Sir Lawrence reinforced his usefulness to the community on numerous other occasions. Politicians and influential landowners of the neighbourhood invariably headed the subscription list for any community project, and this was no more than was expected of them. To do less was to encourage the growth of an opposition of the discontented and greedy around some more generous or wealthier gentleman, and that in turn was to invite even higher costs in a contested election. Burgh management, above all, required money. Those politicians unwise enough to engage in burgh management with less than was required could ruin themselves by persisting in political activity. It was certainly easier to meet the necessary charges if the politician was acceptable to Government, but even those so situated were ill-advised to persist in a burgh contest without a sizeable private fortune. Of all the ways of entering the Parliament of Great Britain, a severe contest in a Scottish burgh district was the least attractive, and some who took this route lived to regret it.

Burgh members who had spent heavily in order to obtain and retain their seats were not disposed to add to their burden by coming into conflict with the Government if they could avoid it, and in this regard the Whig politician T.F. Kennedy caught the attitude of the burgh member who had obtained a seat through heavy expenditure of his own money and wished to retain it, in his description of Robert Downie of Appin. Downie, the member of parliament for the Dunfermline district, was clearly in favour of a bill which the opposition had introduced in the House of Commons, for as Kennedy related:

> I happened to pass along one of the back benches on which R. Downie was sitting. He stopped me and said, "Maister Kennedy, that's an excellent bill o'yours — that Jury Bill." I replied, "I am happy to hear you say so, Mr. Downie — I had not hoped to have your support — but I think it will come on tonight, and I hope you will stay in the House that I may have your vote." "Na, na, Maister Kennedy, that's a very different thing — it's an excellent bill, and I wish you may succeed, but if I was to vote wi' you and gang against the *government*, hoo could I gang to the Treasury next day, beggin' for eight and twenty thoosand *damned scoondrels*," [the people of the burghs he represented] "that would never do, Maister Kennedy — but persevaire, Maister Kennedy, and *never mind me*."[108]

There were many like Robert Downie among the representatives of Scottish burghs, but it was not inevitable that a burgh member should be in the Government interest, for on occasion, in spite of the best efforts of Government managers, an opposition candidate could capture a seat, although for much of the eighteenth century it was an open questions whether he would be able to retain it if he did not quickly enter the ranks of Administration. However distasteful a burgh member of parliament might find his constituents, he had to accustom himself to taking account of the greed, vanity and ambitions of the councillors of his towns, or he would not long retain the seat. Such a politician, moreover, was required to demonstrate not only his adherence to an administration which dispensed the things which councillors desired, but that his own services were of sufficient value to ensure a steady flow of patronage came through his hands; for if any doubt arose on this head, the burgh leaders would begin to seek an alternative representative.

Burgh councillors, in general, never lost sight of their own personal advantage, and for many of them their power to choose a member of parliament constituted their principal asset. Perhaps there would be few who would be as shameless as the councillor-son of one of the bailies of Inverkeithing who, in the election of 1818, not only accepted bribes but admitted it before a parliamentary committee investigating the complaint of a defeated candidate that his rival, John Campbell, had obtained the seat by corrupt means. According to the account printed by *The Scotsman,*

> This candid witness, with the utmost coolness, swore, that he himself received from an agent of Mr. Campbell's different sums, amounting in the whole to upwards of £500, in consideration of promising his own and his father's votes for the Delegate in the interest of Mr. Campbell, and that after pocketing the money they both voted on the other side . . . [109]

The unreformed burgh councils of Scotland had rogues in plenty, but the essential fact remains that, even if they were guilty of criminal behaviour in bartering their votes, they were clearly not the dependents of the men who hoped to use their services. It was the continuous element of uncertainty pervading burgh politics which made the task of the cultivator of burgh interest both expensive and wearing. In short, there were many easier ways to enter the Parliament of Great Britain than as the representative of a Scottish burghs constituency.

NOTES

1. NLS. Saltoun MS.17532/181, 'Memoriall, Selkirk & Peebles, Mar. 1753 '

2. William Ferguson, 'Electoral Law and Procedure in Eighteenth and Early Nineteenth Century Scotland', University of Glasgow Ph.D., 1957, 336.

3. SRO. Melville Castle, GD51/1/198/26/45, General David Ballingall to Melville, 2 Apr., 1820.

4. Ibid.

5. SRO. Montrose, GD220/5/458, Lord Rothes to Montrose, undated, c. Jan. 1715.

6. NLS. Saltoun MS.16535/48, Alexander Brodie of Brodie to Milton, 7 Jul. [1727].

7. Annie Steel, *Records of Annan, 1678–1833* [Annan, 1933], 66–68.

8. *Parliamentary Papers* 1823, XV, *papers relating to the Royal Burghs of Scotland,* provides the composition of councils in 1822.

9. Robert Douglas, *Annals of the Royal Burgh of Forres* [Elgin, 1934], 99–104, and SRO Seafield papers, correspondence of Bailie Duncan Grant, describe the period of Grant dominance.

10. Ronald Sunter, 'Stirlingshire Politics, 1707–1832', University of Edinburgh Ph.D., 1971, 430–509.

11. George Gay, *The History of Arbroath* [Arbroath, 1876], 359.

12. SRO. Seafield, GD248/57/1, Bailie Duncan Grant to Sir James Grant, 17 Sep., 1779.

13. NLS. Saltoun MS.17532/116, 'Case of St. Andrews'.

14. Ibid. MS.17532/ 117–8, 'Memorandum concerning the town of St. Andrews.'

15. Ibid. 'Case of St. Andrews'.

16. *Glasgow Courier*, 30 Aug., 1821.

17. NLS. Saltoun MS.16650, John Maule to Milton, 26 May, 1747.

18. SRO. Montrose, GD220/5/458, from Lord Rothes, 12 Jan., 1715.

19. SRO. Dalhousie, GD45/14/431, George Dempster to Lord Panmure, 20 Jun., 1762.

20. NLS. Saltoun MS.16681, Provost John Bucknay to Milton, 26 Sep., 1753.

21. Ibid. MS.16642, from James Carmichael, 19 Jun., 1747.

22. Ibid. MS.16643, Lord Milton to Ronald Crawfurd, 13 Jul., 1747.

23. Ibid. MS.16645, Andrew Fletcher, younger, to Milton, 5 Nov., 1747.

24. NLS. Yester MS.7045, the Duke of Hamilton to Lord Tweeddale, 26 Feb., 1742.

25. NLS. Saltoun MS.17532/106, 'State of the Town Council of Linlithgow', 19 Jun., 1747.

26. Ibid. MS.16647, from Hamilton of Innerwick, 21 Jun., 1747.

27. Ibid. MS.16649, from Alexander McMillan, 14 Jul., 1747.

28. Ibid. MS.17532/220–222, 'plan for making the following persons ... '

29. Ibid.

30. Ibid. MS.16643, from George Cheap, 29 Jun., 1747.

31. Ibid.

32. Ibid. MS.16643, Milton to Ronald Crawfurd, 13 Jul., 1747.

33. Ibid. MS.16646, from Robert Gardiner, 8 Jul., 1747.

34. Ibid.

35. Ibid. MS.16646, from Robert Gardiner, 9 Jul., 1747.

36. Ibid. MS.16641, Milton to the Duke of Argyll, 17 Jul., 1747.

37. Ibid. MS.16641, from the Duke of Argyll, 12 Jul. [1747].

38. Ibid. MS.16649, from Alexander McMillan, 14 Jul., 1747.

39. Ibid.

40. Ibid.

41. Ibid. MS.16681, from John Bucknay, 11 Oct., 1753.

42. Ibid.

43. *HMC*21, Supp. Report on the MSS. of the Duke of Hamilton, 177, Andrew Pringle to the Duke of Hamilton, 11 Apr., 1754.

44. NLS. Saltoun MS.17532/220–222, 'plan for making the following persons ... '

45. Ibid. MS.16649, from Alexander McMillan, 14 Jul., 1747.

46. Ibid. MS.16641, Milton to the Duke of Argyll, 17 Jul., 1747.

47. Ibid. MS.16649, from Alexander McMillan, 18 Jul., 1747.

48. Ibid. MS.16653, 'Statement by Bailie Andrew Scott, 30 Jul. 1747.'

49. Ibid.

50. Ibid.

51. Ibid.

52. Ibid.

53. Ibid.

54. C.S. Terry [ed.], *The Albemarle Papers* [Aberdeen, 1902], ii, 453–4, Milton to the Duke of Newcastle, 29 Aug., 1747.

55. NLS. Saltoun MS.16649, from Alexander McMillan, 18 Jul., 1747.

56. Ibid.

57. Ibid. from Alexander McMillan, 19 Jul., 1747.

58. Ibid.

59. Ibid.

60. Ibid. MS.16641, Milton to Argyll, 17 Jul., 1747.

61. Ibid.

62. Romney Sedgwick [ed.], *The History of Parliament: The House of Commons, 1715–54*, i, 402.

63. NLS. Saltoun MS.16643, from Ronald Crawfurd, 21 Jul., 1747.

64. Ibid. MS.16643, 'Memorandum Mr. James Carmichael, Augt. 1747. '

65. SRO. Melville Castle, GD51/1/198/10/41, Patrick Rigg to Robert Graham of Fintry, 13 Jun., 1795.

66. *Scots Magazine*, Aug. 1768, 407–9.

67. *Ibid.*

68. *Ibid.*

69. *Ibid.*

70. *Ibid.*

71. *Ibid.*

72. SRO. Messrs. Tod Murray and Jamieson, W.S., GD237/106/9/6, George Dempster to John Henry Cochrane of Rochsoles, 11 Oct., 1767.

73. *Journal of the House of Commons*. vol. 32, 55, 267–8.

74. *The Scotsman*, 6 Jun., 1818.

75. Charles Rampini *A History of Moray and Nairn* [Edinburgh, 1898], 274–5.

76. H.D. Macwilliam [ed.], *The Letters of Lord Elchies*[Aberdeen, 1927], 212–3, Sir James Grant to Robert Grant of Tammore, 11 May, 1734.

77. Ferguson, 'Electoral Law and Procedure', 315–6.

78. NLS. Saltoun MS.17532/220, 'plan for making the following parsons ... '

79. *Scots Magazine*, Jan. 1791, 44–47.

80. *Ibid.*

81. SRO. Melville Castle, GD51/1/198/10/29, James Campbell to Henry Dundas, 1 May, 1791.

82. *Scots Magazine*, Dec. 1780, 639.

83. SRO. Seafield, GD248/58/1, General James Grant to Sir James Grant of Grant, 17 Sep., 1780.

84. William Cramond, *Records of Elgin* [Aberdeen, 1903], i, 389.

85. William Stephen, *History of Inverkeithing and Rosyth* [Aberdeen, 1921], 221–4.

86. *Ibid.*

87. *Ibid.*, 225.

88. E. Dunbar, *Social Life in Former Days*, second series [Edinburgh, 1866], 168.

89. *Ibid.*

90. NLS. Saltoun MS.16682, Capt. Robert Cunninghame to Milton, 28 Sep., 1753.

91. Ibid.

92. NLS. Melville MS.1053, James Horne to Robert Dundas, 20 Aug., 1807.

93. SRO. Dalhousie, GD45/14/431, Provost George Ross to Lord Panmure, 22 Sep., 1753.

94. Ibid.

95. Ibid.

96. Ibid.

97. Ibid., James Bisset, 25 Sep., 1753.

98. Ibid., from George Ross, 18 Sep., 1753.

99. W. Ferguson, 'Electoral Law and Procedure', 328.

100. *The Scotsman*, 6 Jun., 1818.

101. SRO. Balnagowan Castle, GD129/24/83/19, Charles Hope to Sir Charles Ross, 1 Sep. [1802].

102. SRO. Montrose, GD220/5/ 458, Lord Rothes to Montrose, 12 Jan., 1715.

103. NLS. Saltoun MS.16718, Lord Milton to the Duke of Argyll, 4 Apr., 1761.

104. SRO. Melville Castle GD51/1/198/10/14, document marked 'Received 9th of August 1790 from Cambo'.

105. W. Ferguson 'Electoral Law and Procedure', 312–3.

106. SRO. Montrose, GD/220/5/440, from Lord Rothes, 26 Dec., 1714.

107. *Scots Magazine*, Oct. 1767, 556.

108. Henry Cockburn, *Letters on the Affairs of Scotland* [London, 1874], footnote, 196–7.

109. *The Scotsman*, March 6, 1819.

11

Personal Ambition and Burgh Politics: the Failure of the Duke of Montrose in the Glasgow District of Burghs, 1714–16

Politician-patrons could manipulate and calculate in order to secure the return of a friend who would support their interest in Parliament, but all those calculations could be brought to nought by the self-interest of a burgh councillor. The politics of the Glasgow district of burghs in the period 1714–1716 illustrate the loss of a seat through that kind of conflict, and the limitations placed upon a patron's freedom to impose a candidate upon councillors who had their own views.

The Glasgow district, in addition to that city, included three smaller burghs, Rutherglen, Dumbarton and Renfrew, already overshadowed by the regional dominance of Glasgow, the growing wealth of whose merchants gave them connections with all of the remaining councils. Glasgow was accustomed to being represented in Parliament by one of its council, and had since the Union obtained that result through its collective influence in the other communities, united with the interest of a powerful patron, James Graham, fourth Marquis and first Duke of Montrose. Superficially, Glasgow should have been extremely deferential to the Duke of Montrose. The Duke, with extensive estates in the vicinity of Dumbarton and holding the regality, or barony, of Glasgow as a feudal jurisdiction, and thus controlling part of the city and its suburbs, was a formidable figure.[1] Moreover, since family ties were still strong, Montrose could count on the friendship of a number of merchants of the Graham name who took their lead in politics from their chief. Montrose had a good deal of say with Sir James Smollett, the leading figure in the burgh of Dumbarton, and with the Duchess of Hamilton, one of the patrons of Rutherglen, though in the case of that town Campbell of Shawfield and the city council of Glasgow itself also had influence. The remaining town, Renfrew, was dominated in this period by Campbell of Blythswood who, like Shawfield, was also connected with Glasgow and its merchant community.

The Duke of Montrose was not the only politician who aspired to control the Glasgow district and its representative, for the Duke of Argyll was also in a position to influence his clansmen, the Campbell merchants and lairds of the region. Family influence of this nature was by no means confined to the Glasgow district, which was admittedly close to the lands of the two dukes in question, for even in the east-coast burgh of St. Andrews, a Bailie Campbell was expected to abandon a previous engagement and fall in with the wishes of his chief in the election of 1715.[2]

Merchants in a growing trading city like Glasgow, whether connected by family ties with a great magnate or not, had a good reason to seek a political patron in the early eighteenth century. What they required in a patron was access to

Government. Court connections were vital, and the council of Glasgow was fully conscious of the degree to which the trade of the city could be helped or hindered by the actions of Administration. The lord whose friendship they sought was expected to be a channel of communication between the burgh and the Court, and it was for that reason that Provost Roger of Glasgow wrote to Montrose that 'for advice and council I know none I can depend upon so safe as yr Gr[ace]'.[3] Montrose, who held the office of Secretary of State from September 1714 to August 1715, and was in addition chancellor of the University of Glasgow, seemed an obvious choice for patron of Glasgow, even without his own ability to hurt or aid those citizens living within the regality. With his Court connections Montrose was clearly in a position to perform useful services for the merchants of the city, and in the election of 1715 Montrose and the city were in agreement that they should seek the re-election of the competent sitting Member, Thomas Smith.

The candidates in the election of 1715 were in fact both Glasgow merchants, Thomas Smith, the representative of the city since 1710, and Daniel Campbell of Shawfield, a merchant closely connected with the Duke of Argyll, and thus quite unacceptable to the Duke of Montrose. In the last months of 1714, however, the normal rivalry of the two great men of Dunbartonshire was temporarily in abeyance, at least on the surface, for both dukes were strong supporters of the Hanoverian Succession, and King George I was not firmly seated upon the throne as yet. The Jacobite threat, which came to a head in a serious rebellion shortly after the election of 1715, led the dukes to sink their differences and agree to Thomas Smith's re-election for the Glasgow district. Argyll agreed to write to his friends in the district to inform them of his decision,[4] and apparently did so. However, this was to reckon without the ambitions of Daniel Campbell of Shawfield who, in spite of this news from his chief, came forward as a candidate in opposition to Smith; indeed Shawfield quickly gained a useful point by placing one of his friends in the provost's chair at Rutherglen.[5]

Had it not been for the unusual circumstances of the Jacobite danger, a declaration by Shawfield would have been followed immediately by a battle for dominance between the interests of the two dukes, but in the prevailing situation Montrose, in particular, was extremely anxious that no suggestion of a quarrel between himself and the Duke of Argyll should be aired, for the Jacobites were only too eager to hint at disputes between the two Whig nobles for their own ends.[6] The initiative does appear to have been taken by Daniel Campbell on his own account. That at least was the opinion of Mungo Graeme of Gorthie, the Perthshire gentleman who was Montrose's principal agent in Scotland, and a shrewd observer of the contemporary political scene. As Gorthie interpreted these events, Argyll had indeed written to Shawfield and his other friends seeking their support for Smith, but Shawfield, determined to supplant Smith, had

> taken the cunning way, to write to the d[uke] that he would serve him as he desired, but thought it reasonable that Th. Smith & every body else should know that he had it from him, and yt he should be under his speciall direction, and if he can tell the d[uke] that he is not to expect this, and that [Smith] haveing been first recommended

by yr Gr[ace], unless he makes this previous capitulation, it would be a throwing away of d[uke] A[rgyll's] interest to make up yours, if his Gr[ace] should persist in his first resolution of having him to support Th. Smith ... [7]

Gorthie's suggestion may be surmise, but it was probably fairly close to the mark, for Shawfield was eager to secure the seat, and his approach to Smith, also detailed by Gorthie, suggests both that he knew his opponent's likely response and that he was setting the scene for an attempt to persuade Argyll to withdraw his support from Smith by persuading him that he was throwing away his interest in favour of the Duke of Montrose. Smith was told by Shawfield that 'if he would do right things [meaning, if he would be ye d[uke] of Ar[gyll]'s man] he would may be let it drop to him'. Thomas Smith, apparently a man of some independence, replied that 'he would not say so much to any man',[8] an answer which appeared to suit Shawfield's purposes. The latter, moreover, insisted in the towns that he had received no commands from his chief to support Smith, and went so far as to allege that it would become evident within a few days that Argyll's support was given to himself.[9]

It does not appear that Argyll reversed his earlier decision or gave active support to Shawfield, and Smith himself did not believe that the Campbell chief was hostile, whatever Shawfield might suggest. But sufficient confusion was created in the public mind to create some doubt about the attitude of the Argyll family, which was at best lukewarm to Smith's re-election, because of the latter's connection with the Montrose interest, for Campbell of Blythswood received a letter from Lord Ilay, the brother of the Duke of Argyll, advising him to act as he saw fit in this election.[10]

On the other hand, even if Argyll was not an active supporter, Thomas Smith's re-election appeared likely. There was no substantial opposition to him in his own city of Glasgow, and Montrose arranged for him to have the support of the delegate of Dumbarton through Sir James Smollett. [11] At the same time, the Duchess of Hamilton was an active supporter of Smith in Rutherglen. 'She has sent her servants severall times their with allowance to spend what money they pleased, and has been so very sollicitous in the matter as to cause one or two of them to be brought to her self, where she took them engadged.'[12] With the duchess's help, Smith was able to add Rutherglen to his two other towns, Glasgow and Dumbarton, limiting Shawfield to Campbell-controlled Renfrew, though Rutherglen's support was conditional, Smith believing that council would only 'stand firm if they are not bought with money'.[13] In the event Smith's re-election in February 1715 was secured, although this was by no means the end of it. Shawfield remained a contender for the seat should another opportunity arise, while the uneasy agreement of the two dukes did not outlast the year 1715.

Smith and the Montrose party were politicians too experienced to rest on their laurels after their electoral success. Burgh management was an ongoing process, or a strong position soon deteriorated to nothing. Glasgow council was remodelled at Michaelmas 1715, with 'some of Shawfield's particular friends thrown out not by accident but by design',[14] while Montrose's gift of the office of bailie-depute of the regality of Glasgow to the Member of Parliament was said to have 'pleased wonderfully the people here'.[15] But Shawfield still had a party, as did the Duke of Argyll, whose influence was augmented by his defeat of the Jacobite danger, a fact which could not help but enhance his reputation in that Whig town. Provost Aird, the leader of the Argyll party in Glasgow council, though not in command of a majority of council, was still taking 'more than ordinary pains to recommend' the Duke of Argyll to the town, and 'to interpret every step made by his Grace as done with a particular view to the advantage of the town of Glasgow'.[16] The enhancement of the Argyll interest in the city was furthered by a visit from the Earl of Ilay, followed shortly thereafter by the Duke himself, whom

> his favorites have been taking ... time to perswade us ... is to come incognito, and that he'll be angry if the least notice be taken of him, and to conceal his entry, Shawfield has written circular letters acquainting the neighbouring Lords and gentlemen that his Grace is to be with us the morrow, that no body may hear of it, six piece of cannon are to be fir'd three time when he comes to the ports while the musick bells play all the time, and that no body may see the entry the train bands are to line the streets ... [17]

Unfortunately for the Montrose interest in the district of Glasgow the competent Member of Parliament, Thomas Smith, had only a brief tenure of his seat, falling ill in London during the winter of 1715–16. On January 12th the Duke of Montrose was warning his friends to be on their guard and to prepare for a by-election, for 'there are small or rather no hopes of poor Mr. Smyth's recovery',[18] and indeed Thomas Smith died on the morning of the 19th.[19] The problem which emerged almost as soon as the vacancy was created was the lack of a suitable candidate acceptable to the Montrose party. Daniel Campbell, this time openly the Duke of Argyll's man, was obviously going to be a formidable opponent, but the choice of candidate to oppose him was effectively restricted to a member of Glasgow council, since Glasgow was unwilling to accept another. As Gorthie put it, 'a stranger we can't think of',[20] which limited Montrose to the leaders of the council of the city, none of whom were, in the duke's opinion, in any way so well qualified for the post as the late Thomas Smith.

As soon as Smith's death was known in the city, Provost Bowman of Glasgow communicated with his counterpart at Rutherglen, the recently elected Provost Spence, and received from the latter an undertaking that his burgh would go in with Glasgow.[21] If this agreement held, that was sufficient to carry the election, since Rutherglen was the returning burgh, whose casting vote in a four-burgh district was sufficient to return the Member with the assistance of one other delegate, so the Montrose party began the campaign in a very strong position only to see that position crumble to complete defeat, wrecked on the ambitions of a Glasgow councillor.

The basic difficulty was put to the Duke of Montrose at the outset by one of his partisans, Principal Stirling of Glasgow University, who alleged that 'ther's a great penury of men tollerably fitt'.[22] The two leading men in Glasgow council were Provost Bowman, and the late Provost, John Aird, a man close to the Duke of

Argyll; the candidate to oppose Daniel Campbell would have to be one or other of these men. 'The last will yield to the first if he'l stand, but if he does not it will be next to impossible to get it put by him,'[23] Montrose was informed. Whatever the patron might wish, a member of Glasgow council was alone acceptable to that town, and in the current composition of that council that left only two possibilities. Montrose had no doubt about which one he preferred, finding that the only thing he could say for John Aird was that 'they don't call him D[aniel] C[ampbell] ... bar that I know no other difference'.[24] Aird was regarded by the Montrose interest as untrustworthy, for as Mungo Graeme of Gorthie pointed out, he was

> vain, and a certain prey to such as will be at pains to whedle him with hopes, and I doubt much, but that familiarity [with the Duke of Argyll], which is begun, if it be improven by a winter's politicks at London may at last bring D[aniel] C[ampbell] and him upon one foot, and so good bye to our good toun ... [25]

Unfortunately for the Montrose interest, if Aird was an unacceptable candidate, the alternative, Provost Bowman, was only marginally better. He was 'honest and sincere, but weak to a wonder', [26] and in council the chief magistrate was generally dominated by the more dynamic John Aird. Provost Bowman, moreover, was extremely reluctant to allow his name to be advanced as a candidate to succeed Smith, whereas all accounts agree that Aird was ambitious to sit in parliament. Bowman had some assets for the Montrose interest, however, for he was the incumbent chief magistrate and, in addition, was a Rutherglen man, which gave him some additional influence in that burgh. The Duke of Montrose was in no doubt about his suitability, although the available choice was admittedly somewhat limited, writing Gorthie that 'the Provost must be brushed up and Jo[hn] Aird disapointed if possible'.[27] Gorthie, on the other hand, rightly had some qualms about pushing an unwilling man to stand for election, and while he was in full agreement with his chief about the desirability of Bowman standing in preference to Aird, doubted the practicality of the scheme, and tended to take refuge in the thought that 'any of the two will dissapoynt Shawfield'. [28]

When the Duke of Montrose showed no enthusiasm for John Aird as a means of defeating the Campbell interest, his friends again suggested that Aird might be the lesser of two evils, for although

> Yr Gr[ace] has a right enough notion of Aird ... if ye'l take it in this case, that he stands in opposition to D[aniel] C[ampbell] and shall carry it, the case is not so bad as at first it would seem. For ... it baulks D[aniel] C[ampbell] and states him in opposition to d[uke] A[rgyll] ... '[29]

The greater danger, as Gorthie came to appreciate, was that Daniel Campbell might succeed by default. Provost Bowman's unusual modesty in hesitating to agree to become a candidate was preventing an effective campaign from being commenced, for even if John Aird might not 'have the impudence to oppose Bowman openly',[30] if Bowman would do nothing for himself, Aird saw no reason to do it for him. The inactivity of the Montrose/Glasgow interest was giving

Daniel Campbell a free hand. Rutherglen, the vital returning burgh, suddenly began to look vulnerable, for even if Provost Bowman believed that the town would support Glasgow in the election, his own inactivity was shaking Provost Spence and his colleagues. Even Bowman had qualified his statement that Rutherglen was secure with the proviso, 'except Shawfield bribe highly',[31] and the latter had now hit on a very persuasive argument with the councillors of Rutherglen. Daniel Campbell was patron of the parish of Rutherglen, 'and thereby has some right to the teinds'.[32] Campbell, accordingly, offered to give the teinds, or tithes, to the council of the burgh, though obviously only if certain conditions were met, and the town began to reconsider its hasty decision to go with Glasgow in the forthcoming election.

Although the Montrose party hastily sought the opinion of counsel on the validity of Shawfield's claim, the fact that it was listened to in Rutherglen demonstrated that Shawfield had taken the offensive with some prospect of success. Equally, the Campbells did not neglect Glasgow itself, for in January 1716 Daniel Campbell called upon Provost Bowman and presented him with a letter from the Duke of Argyll in his own favour, at the same time modestly suggesting that he had not sought the seat, but was merely submitting to pressure from 'one that had done all he could for the good town's safety & advantage',[33] while inferring that Glasgow council should do the like. The strength of that kind of appeal lay in the fact that the merchants of Glasgow did indeed feel grateful to Argyll for standing between them and a Jacobite assault. Bowman quickly called the council leaders together and, while they refused to accept the Duke's recommendation on the grounds that 'the town of Glasgow [what ever other burghs had done] had strictly observ'd an act of the Royal Burroughs enjoyning them to elect one of yr own Council',[34] it was plain from what was said during the meeting that there were many councillors unwilling to disoblige the Duke of Argyll. Indeed, several councillors succeeded in having a clause inserted in the reply to the letter to the effect that 'whomsoever they choose he would be in his Grace's Interest'.[35] Argyll also approached the Duchess of Hamilton for her support, and although the Duchess 'was not fond of Shawfield', it was to be feared that the fact that Lord Selkirk, the Duchess's son, was now a partisan of Argyll, would prevent her from taking her former active part in this election.[36] In short the Montrose interest was starting to show weakness, and that fatal inactivity was taking its toll.

Admittedly there was no candidate available who was so well qualified for the position as the late Thomas Smith, and as Montrose plaintively remarked, 'it is to be wisht there were not such a penury of persons fit for that charge',[37] but the principal lack in the Montrose interest was an efficient campaign manager in Glasgow able to actively combat Daniel Campbell. The man who had undertaken this task for Thomas Smith, John Graham of Dougalston, was absent for the 1716 by-election, and Mungo Graeme of Gorthie, who tried to fill the gap, was unaccustomed to burgh management. Gorthie, indeed, showed a growing irritation with the councillors of Glasgow as the campaign continued to languish, complaining that

its a base province I own to be manageing with people who generally are both fools
and false. Theirs ane adress requisite in such a management that I'm quite a stranger
to, and by no means have I inclination to learn it, or rather I think I'm not capable, so
upon the wholl I say we want a politician to be a commander in chief, who knows how
to set the proper engines to work . . . [38]

The absence of an effective co-ordinator was becoming critical, for even if the vote
of Glasgow was secure, Rutherglen was threatened, Renfrew was Shawfield's, and
Sir James Smollett, the great man of Dumbarton, was taking his cue from the
developments elsewhere and was showing reluctance to give a firm commitment.
His answer to a request for support to the Montrose interest was that he would 'do
yr Gr[ace] all the service he can, but does not declare positively'.[39] It was an
unhappy sign, and although Gorthie was convinced that Smollett 'won't care to
disobleidge directly', he feared that he 'may find ways enough of makeing it
miscarry, and he not to blame, if he has a mind to wheedle'.[40]

Provost Bowman was, after great pressure, persuaded to agree to come forward
as a candidate, but it was then too late to retrieve a losing campaign. John Aird to
the last moment had remained convinced in his own mind that he would be the
candidate rather than the chief magistrate, or if Rutherglen should be lost, that he
might be chosen Glasgow's delegate rather than have the city affronted by the
defeat of its Provost, and the suspicious Gorthie believed that Aird might have in
view securing an opportunity

> of obleidgeing d[uke] A[rgyll] by giveing his vote to D[aniel] C[campbell] without
> disobleidgeing the town at the same time, because it will be plain that D[aniel]
> C[ampbell] carrys it without him. In those views he's not only inactive himself, but
> keeps all his friends so . . . [41]

Whether or not Aird was a friend of Daniel Campbell of Shawfield — and few
observers seemed to think he was — he was certainly an ambitious man proud of
his acquaintance with the Duke of Argyll, and convinced that he would himself
make an excellent member of parliament. This opinion of his abilities was not
shared by others, Montrose indeed questioning what would be thought of an
interest that pitched 'upon him as ye fittest person which no man on earth but
himself can think'; [42] and there is no reason to doubt that Argyll's views for once
coincided with those of his political rival.

On the other hand, even if Aird was unattractive to the politicians as a candidate,
the fact remains that the ex-provost was a power in Glasgow, and his strength in
council completely undermined the Montrose interest in this election. Rutherglen's vote was lost 'merely thro' the inactivity of our people' [43] of Glasgow, as
Gorthie pointed out. The council of Rutherglen, left alone by the Glasgow people,
reached their own understanding with Daniel Campbell for their present
advantage, and the cause of this crucial defeat, which of course cost the Montrose
party the election, was not in doubt. As Gorthie pointed out:

> Our Election . . . is gone quite wrong. Ruglen had gott proposals from our toun and
> had promised not to conclude any thing with D[aniel] C[ampbell] till once they

should acquaint our provost. But they have broke their word, and concluded their treaty with D[aniel] C[ampbell] so that when our provost sent over to Ruglen yesterday morning to know what resolution they had come to ... He had ane answer ... that upon reasonable accounts they had promised their vote to D[aniel] C[ampbell]. I take it that Aird has been rogue in all this matter. Bowman is weak and wheedled by the other. All that his freinds can do cant keep him from letting Aird into his secrets, and he is able to diswade him from the measures that his freinds give him. In a word knaves and fools are ill to guide ... [44]

Daniel Campbell of Shawfield, in marked contrast to the incompetent Bowman, conducted a shrewd and effective campaign for his own election:

D[aniel] C[ampbell] by his emissarys is insinuateing to several people what risque the town will run by disobleidgeing d[uke] A[rgyll], and this inactivity of the Magistrates makes those insinuations beleived, for they rekon that its the prospect of this inconveniency which makes the Magistrates shy to act with that vigor they did before ... [45]

In the circumstance of this unaccountable inactivity of the civic leaders of Glasgow, what other conclusion could the bailies of Rutherglen reach than that so sedulously pointed out by the partisans of Shawfield, namely that they feared the Duke of Argyll? Why not take Shawfield's offer, benefit themselves and their community and avert such a fate? In short, as one of Montrose's friends remarked, 'there is no opposing popular humor sett on fire by bribes & lyes '.[46]

A more effective candidate could have made much more of the contest than poor Bowman did, for the Duke of Montrose had sufficient Court influence to gain posts for his friends, and such gifts as that of King's Chaplain, given to Principal Stirling,[47] could have been turned to advantage to demonstrate that favours were not to be sought only through the Duke of Argyll. Indeed there is some reason to believe that Shawfield himself must have been close to admitting defeat during the campaign, for some of the arguments used by his partisans have a note of desperation about them:

There is one argument used for Shawfield which is extraordinary, viz. that if he carry not the election his Lady will miscarry who is now with quick child, and that may be of unspeakable loss ... [48]

The growing belief, even in Glasgow, that the friendship of the Duke of Argyll was the route to Court favour was never effectively dispelled. No doubt the Duke of Montrose was correct when he told Gorthie that Glasgow 'won't mend their c[redi]t by sending up D[aniel] C[ampbell]',[49] but his friends failed to impose that belief on the voters.

An incompetent candidate, moreover, with an ambitious false friend in the council of the city, was a burden no patron could overcome without an effective manager capable of forcing the candidate to act in his own best interest, and when the council of Glasgow at last met to choose its delegate to the election at Rutherglen,

provost Aird took fairly off the mask and propos'd that the provost should be
instructed to vote for Shawfield ... but the Clerk whispering the provost that such
an instruction being against the nature of the writs would make the deed null, they
proceeded no further in that matter but went in to choice of yr Elector ... [50]

The delegate so chosen was Provost Bowman, for whom a majority, which
surprisingly included Aird, voted, but unfortunately Provost Bowman left the
meeting convinced that he was obliged to vote as the majority of the council
wished, and he was left in no doubt that the general opinion was that Glasgow
should accept what was now inevitable and endorse the winning candidate, Daniel
Campbell, who, with two towns and the casting vote of Rutherglen, could no
longer be stopped. As one of Montrose's friends complained:

How the provost will vote I cannot tell, tho I an affraid it will be for Shawfield. He is
absolutely under Aird's Government, and a very silly man. The Pr[incipal] & I have
been useing our endeavours to perswade him to vote for himself, but in short we have
no body but fools or knaves to deal with ... [51]

Even after that devastating setback for the Montrose interest in Glasgow,
Mungo Graeme did not abandon all hope, for there was still the prospect of a
petition against Shawfield's return, assuming that Bowman could be persuaded to
reject Aird's advice and vote for himself. On the other hand this action which
Gorthie was pressing so strongly was only possible if Provost Bowman received
the support of the delegate of Dumbarton. Accordingly, Gorthie wrote to Sir
James Smollett to say 'that if Glasgow was assured of Dumbarton's vote, their
might be a way gott to have a fair hitt for it'.[52] Sir James, however, declined to give
a direct answer, urging that the matter be dropped since Rutherglen was lost. Sir
James, in short, had, as Gorthie remarked, decided 'to trim with the rest'. [53]

An interest which, superficially, looked impregnable, having considerable
influence in both Glasgow and Dumbarton through extensive properties and
feudal jurisdictions, family connections and patronage, was routed by a rival
interest, and one cannot escape Mungo Graeme's conclusion that it was primarily
the work of one man, whose personal ambition was behind the fatal inactivity
which gave Daniel Campbell his opportunity:

I told yr Gr[ace] in the beginning that this inactive spirit which I then observed was
the worst omen that could be, and that P[rovost] A[ir]d was the occasion of it. Its
certain he has been the only occasion of looseing this, and I believe, because he saw he
was not to be the man.[54]

Of course there was something more to the defeat than Aird's ambition, important
thought this was. The lack of an effective manager for the Montrose interest, able
to do what Bowman clearly was incapable of doing for himself, was damaging, for
that was what allowed Daniel Campbell to wage such an effective campaign by
creating an impression that the friendship of the Duke of Argyll was
indispensable, and reinforcing that by successful bribery. Certainly Aird was
disposed to believe that Glasgow must have Argyll's friendship, and the

importance of that in a council where, 'when once Aird proposes a matter theres no opposing it, and Bowman signs letters and concurrs with him even in things he is against',[55] cannot be overemphasised.

One of John Aird's first actions after Daniel Campbell of Shawfield's election was to hurry to Edinburgh to wait upon the Duke of Argyll and seek his help for Glasgow in the matter of repayment of the town's charges during the late rebellion. Clearly the impression had been created in Aird's mind, and in his friends', that this was the only route to Government favour. An influential patron, with access to Government patronage, could be defeated in an important political contest by his inability to manage a strong personality in a burgh council, and had the mortification of seeing his principal rival replacing him as patron of this important district. With an enemy in possession of the parliamentary seat, it was difficult to recover the lost influence through distribution of patronage without being open to misrepresentation and appearing to strengthen the Campbell interest, who naturally claimed that such appointments were obtained through them. Meanwhile, needless to say, Shawfield did not relax his efforts in the burghs, and by Michaelmas 1716 it was being reported that 'thers not one man who was suspected of favoring the D[uke] of Montrose . . . left in the toun council of Glasgow'.[56] Burgh councillors were not the passive objects of the patron's manipulation. They had to be managed with great care, and on this occasion sufficient care was not expended. Mungo Graeme of Gorthie, who had no love for burgh councillors, was undoubtedly accurate in his view of them and their self-interested views:

> They are wiser then to be directed, they think they can't be wrong when they put themselves under the protection of those they think has the power . . . the secret is they have [their] own views . . . There are some that are not so, but every where those are generally the fewest . . . [57]

Gorthie's comment was by no means restricted to councillors of Glasgow, but was true of Scotland as a whole in this period. Councillors could be managed, but their management required both skill and attention, for they were rarely unquestioning followers of a great man.

The difference between the two elections from the viewpoint of management could hardly have been clearer. The former Member, Thomas Smith, who in December 1714 'longs mightily to hear of the writes comeing out, for this affair is a terrible burden upon them all and a constant fatigue . . . '[58] was as different from the lethargic and reluctant Bowman as night from day. The Duke of Montrose, however, though rightly doubting both John Aird's trustworthiness and abilities, might have been better advised to accept some of the advice which Gorthie gave him, for had Aird received the support of the Montrose interest, Bowman could hardly have taken offence in view of his own reluctance to serve, and Aird promised to be a more active candidate than the incumbent Provost. As Gorthie put it, 'rather then D[aniel] C[ampbell] have it, I rather ten times Aird had it'.[59] If defeating the Campbells was the chief priority for the Montrose interest, as it should have been, then Aird, however dishonest and foolish, was a candidate with more potential than the man whom Aird dominated. But even allowing for these errors of judgement by the Duke of Montrose, the fact remains that the principal reason for the success of Daniel Campbell of Shawfield in the 1716 election was the personal ambition of a single councillor in one of the towns of the district.

NOTES

1. Feudal jurisdictions which included the suburbs of a town gave the possessor considerable influence in the burgh. See also the regality of Dunfermline possessed by the Marquis of Tweeddale, in Chapter 12.

2. SRO. Montrose, GD220/5/440, the Earl of Rothes to the Duke of Montrose, 7 Dec., 1714.

3. BL ADD MS.9102, Provost Robert Roger to Montrose, undated, c. Jun. 1708.

4. SRO. Montrose, GD220/5/811, Mungo Graeme of Gorthie to Montrose, 15 Oct., 1714.

5. Ibid.

6. Ibid.

7. Ibid.

8. Ibid.

9. Ibid., from Mungo Graeme of Gorthie, 18 Oct. and 22 Oct., 1714.

10. Ibid. GS220/5/812, from Mungo Graeme of Gorthie, 20 Dec., 1714.

11. Ibid. GD220/5/813, from Mungo Graeme of Gorthie, 21 and 24 Jan., 1715.

12. Ibid., from Mungo Graeme of Gorthie, 21 Jan., 1715.

13. Ibid. GD220/5/364, Thomas Smith, dean of guild of Glasgow, to Montrose, 30 Nov., 1714.

14. Ibid. GD220/5/529, Prof. Charles Morthland to Montrose, 30 Nov., 1715.

15. Ibid. GD220/5/813, from Mungo Graeme of Gorthie, 24 Jan., 1715.

16. Ibid. GD220/5/529, from Charles Morthland, 30 Nov., 1715.

17. Ibid., from Charles Morthland, 26 Dec., 1715.

18. Ibid. GD220/5/818, the Duke of Montrose to Gorthie, 12 Jan., 1716.

19. Ibid., Montrose to Gorthie, 21 Jan., 1716.

20. Ibid., from Mungo Graeme of Gorthie, 23 Jan., 1716.

21. Ibid.

22. Ibid. GD220/5/620, Principal John Stirling to Montrose, 20 Jan., 1716.

23. Ibid. GD220/5/818, from Mungo Graeme of Gorthie, 23 Jan., 1716.

24. Ibid., the Duke of Montrose to Gorthie, 26 Jan., 1716.

25. Ibid., from Mungo Graeme of Gorthie, 23 Jan., 1716.

26. Ibid. GD220/5/819, from Mungo Graeme of Gorthie, 17 Feb., 1716.

27. Ibid. GD220/5/818, from the Duke of Montrose, 26 Jan., 1716.

28. Ibid., from Mungo Graeme of Gorthie, 30 Jan., 1716.

29. Ibid. GD220/5/819, from Mungo Graeme of Gorthie, 2 Feb., 1716.

30. Ibid. GD220/5/628, from Charles Morthland, 3 Feb., 1716.

31. Ibid.

32. Ibid. GD220/5/819, from Mungo Graeme of Gorthie, 2 Feb., 1716.

33. Ibid. GD220/5/628, from Charles Morthland, 24 Jan., 1716.

34. Ibid.

35. Ibid.

36. Ibid.

37. Ibid. GD220/5/818, the Duke of Montrose to Gorthie, 31 Jan., 1716.

38. Ibid. GD220/5/819, Mungo Graeme of Gorthie to Montrose, 3 Feb., 1716.

39. Ibid.

40. Ibid.

41. Ibid., from Mungo Graeme of Gorthie, 2 Feb., 1716.

42. Ibid. GD220/5/818, the Duke of Montrose to Gorthie, 31 Jan., 1716.

43. Ibid. GD220/5/819, from Mungo Graeme of Gorthie, 22 Feb., 1716.

44. Ibid., from Mungo Graeme of Gorthie, 15 Feb., 1716.

45. Ibid., from Mungo Graeme of Gorthie, 2 Feb., 1716.

46. Ibid. GD220/5/628, Charles Morthland to Montrose, 17 Feb., 1716.

47. Ibid. GD220/5/819, the Duke of Montrose to Gorthie, 16 Feb., 1716.

48. Ibid. GD220/5/628, from Charles Morthland, 3 Feb., 1716.

49. Ibid. GD220/5/819, the Duke of Montrose to Gorthie, 11 Feb., 1716.

50. Ibid. GD220/5/628, from Charles Morthland, 17 Feb., 1716.

51. Ibid.

52. Ibid. GD220/5/819, from Mungo Graeme of Gorthie, 22 Feb., 1716.

53. Ibid.

54. Ibid.

55. Ibid. GD220/5/628, from Charles Morthland, 2 Mar., 1716.

56. Duncan Warrand [ed.], *More Culloden Papers* [Inverness, 1923–9], ii, 147, the Laird of Grant to Duncan Forbes, 17 Oct., 1716.

57. SRO. Montrose, GD220/5/819, Mungo Graeme of Gorthie to Montrose, 17 Feb., 1716.

58. Ibid. GD220/5/812, from Mungo Graeme of Gorthie, 20 Dec., 1714.

59. Ibid. GD220/5/819, from Mungo Graeme of Gorthie, 2 Feb., 1716.

12

Popular Issues and Burgh Politics: the Election of 1734 in the Inverkeithing District of Burghs

---

The general impression which might be formed of burgh politics is of a struggle of personalities for control of burgh councils, with an absence of real issues and a lack of concern for anything beyond the personal interests of the participants. Venal self-interest was indeed one of the characteristics of many of the burgh councillors, but there were issues which could push bribery and corruption into the background. Indeed, just as did the freeholders of some of the counties on occasion, burgh councils would sometimes feel so strongly about issues that instructions would be given to their member of parliament to ensure that he would know the wishes of his constituents on questions which were expected to be discussed in the next session of parliament. Burgh members, like their counterparts from the shires, were expected to meet with the men who had elected them, to discuss legislation which might be of interest to the towns [while not neglecting to keep the councillors well supplied with food and liquor on such occasions]. Interest in affairs outside the community was strong enough to make the regular supply of a selection of newspapers one of the duties expected of a member of parliament in a burgh district, while on occasion a local issue could arouse such popular feeling that it came to overshadow every other consideration in an election contest. The Dunfermline burghs election of 1734 was one such contest, for the issues were sufficiently popular to oblige a majority of the burgh councils, perhaps against their own wishes, to support a candidate in opposition to the Government. In fact, a false return nullified the act of self-sacrifice by giving the seat to the losing candidate, a man more acceptable to the Earl of Ilay, but three out of five towns had been willing to oppose that powerful Minister and continued in their attitude beyond the 1741 general election before self-interest again resumed its normal place in their calculations.

The election of 1734 was the culmination of a determined effort, both in Scotland and in England, to defeat the Administration of Sir Robert Walpole and his Scottish ally, the Earl of Ilay. The Government had suffered a loss of popularity and prestige as a result of a hazardous attempt to enact excise provisions which had proved to be unacceptable to the country at large, and a powerful group of Scots lords, allied to Walpole's English enemies, began to prepare for the next general election. One of the constituencies which the opposition, or 'patriots' as they styled themselves, had hopes of securing was the Dunfermline district of burghs, a group of five towns spread across four counties in the Forth valley, Dunfermline, Inverkeithing, Queensferry, Culross and Stirling.

One of the leaders of the opposition, the Marquis of Tweeddale, enjoyed considerable influence in two of the burghs, Dunfermline and Queensferry, in virtue of his hereditary office of bailie of the regality of Dunfermline, whose lands surrounded the burgh of Dunfermline and thus brought many of its inhabitants within reach of its feudal court. Queensferry also, to a lesser extent, was influenced by the holder of the regality court of Dunfermline. Another of the opposition party, Thomas Erskine, commonly called Lord Erskine, the son of the attainted Earl of Mar, was the sitting member at the dissolution, and had a considerable interest in the towns and among the neighbouring gentry. The burgh of Inverkeithing was much less influenced by the 'patriots', for its town council was controlled by Henry Cunningham of Boquhan, the member of parliament for Stirlingshire, and a loyal follower of Sir Robert Walpole, who had maintained his burgh interest, perhaps as a form of political insurance. The fourth town of the group, Culross, was mainly influenced by the neighbouring Cochrane family, but it was notoriously venal and was likely to go to the highest bidder, while the fifth community, Stirling, was considered by informed observers to be controlled by friends of Administration, with Cunningham's influence paramount. The Patriot party, aided by Tweeddale's influence in Queensferry and Dunfermline, appeared to have some hope of the seat when the group began to plan their electoral strategy for the anticipated general election, but in fact there was nothing about this contest which went according to expectation, for in Dunfermline, which Lord Tweeddale considered his town, he was challenged by one of his own servants, one of the bailies-depute whom he had appointed to hold his feudal court. The gentleman in question, Captain Peter Halkett, a son of the Laird of Pitfirrane, together with his father, enjoyed considerable personal influence in the burgh council of Dunfermline where the family had long been powerful, and when it came to open conflict between Halkett and the 'patriots', the councillors of the town were to be forced to decide who was the more to be feared, a bailie-depute resident in the community, or his superior, the absentee peer.

The member of parliament at the dissolution, Lord Erskine, had secured his seat at the previous general election in 1727 with the assistance of Lord Ilay and Henry Cunningham, bartering Erskine influence in Stirlingshire for Cunningham's help in the towns, but by 1733 Erskine was in opposition, while Henry Cunningham was completely loyal to Sir Robert Walpole and would soon reap his reward in the form of the governorship of Jamaica, which left no room for compromise. In their plan for the general election the Patriots fixed upon Lord Erskine as a suitable candidate for the county of Stirling, where the Mar family still enjoyed a legacy of influence among freeholders with long memories, which would therefore create a vacancy for a Patriot candidate in the towns, and the man chosen was Lord Erskine's uncle, James Erskine of Grange, a lord of session, and brother of the late Earl of Mar.

Lord Grange had long been considered a steady adherent of the Earl of Ilay, but disappointment at his inability to overcome Sir Robert Walpole's prejudice against the Erskines for their Jacobite past appears to have led Grange to make this break. Lord Lovat, a friend of both Grange and Ilay, deplored the judge's decision, but added, 'I cannot vindicate my Ld Grange, but I wish they had not provoked him to make this odd step '.[1] Grange was a valuable acquisition for the opposition, for he was a man of energy and ability[2] while the judge's known friendship with the more extreme elements in the Church of Scotland was an additional benefit in this constituency, which was at the heart of the quarrel between the evangelical and moderate groups in the church. The current leader of the evangelicals, Ebenezer Erskine, was one of the ministers of Stirling, while his brother and ally, Ralph Erskine, served a church in Dunfermline, and the two ministers could be influenced the more easily by Grange in that they were related, albeit remotely, for the two Erskine ministers were descended from the third Lord Erskine who had died at Flodden.

In the middle of the eighteenth century, when almost the whole population of a parish attended their parish church, the assistance of a popular minister gave a substantial political advantage to the parliamentary candidate able to enlist his services, and in this district that assistance was ready to hand for the Patriots. The reverend Ebenezer Erskine blamed all of his difficulties with the church courts upon the interference of Lord Ilay, and his personal opposition to the government manager was firmly established by the time of the election. Erskine's attitude was well known in his community, where on one occasion he had horrified one of Ilay's followers by his preaching, in which he was reported to have

> inveighed scandalously against presentations, and against the Peer personally, and sayd that if his Lordship's ancestors could be witnesses of his actions at present they would be shocked at it, and this Mr. Erskine is one of the madd men that refuses to take the oaths to the Government ... [3]

When Lord Grange decided to join the Patriots, he saw at once the possibilities which this conflict between Ilay and the influential minister of Stirling might create, for after Ebenezer Erskine and his associates had come into conflict for several years with the majority in the General Assembly of the Church of Scotland, the Assembly Commission at last concluded that the minister of Stirling should be suspended from his functions, an order which the reverend Ebenezer ignored and which no minister had yet been hardy enough to attempt to execute in Stirling, where the population were strongly attached to their ministers. In Lord Grange's opinion, this created a real opportunity for the Patriots to overturn the influence of Lord Ilay in the burgh council of Stirling by enlisting popular support which would be mobilised by the clergy. Grange suggested that 'when I[la]y is losing all confidence among them, it is a proper time for others to gain it; and that popularity among a great body of people may be of use even to a great man, especiallie about the time of Elections'.[4] Grange's own connection with the two minister brothers was not, however, simply induced by thoughts of immediate political advantage, for Lord Grange was genuinely interested in matters of theology, and his ability to hold his own in conversations on such questions gave him a reputation for piety which made the judge the confidant of several clergymen, in spite of his scandalous private life.[5]

The Marquis of Tweeddale quickly agreed to Grange's suggestion that the Patriots should make use of the evangelical party in their elections, for Lord Ilay was so unpopular with the Seceders that hardly more than an indication of sympathy was required from the opposition to win their wholehearted support. Certainly it was quite unnecessary to endorse the position taken by Ebenezer Erskine and his associates. There was no need, as Grange remarked,

> to declare fot these people's sentiments, but only to speak agst the violent measure that they seem to be threatened with ... and wish that things may go softly, and that the particular views of those in Church and State who are so hot & fierce may not embroil the Nation and draw on the powerful to persecute, & honest well meaning people & faithfull subjects to K[ing] George to suffer by Fines, Prisons & Dragoons ... [6]

It was opposition to lay patronage which had precipitated the Original Secession in 1733, and the Government was not in fact likely to endorse the sort of persecution which Grange suggested, but this reminder of the persecution of the Covenanters in the Restoration era was the sort of tool which Grange would employ with the intransigent ministers, who were only too apt to see themselves as the spiritual heirs of the persecuted of the previous century.

It was widely believed in the towns of the Dunfermline district that Lord Ilay was chiefly responsible for the decision by the Assembly Commission to suspend the troublesome minister of Stirling, and that opinion, properly used, was clearly likely to assist the Patriot cause in the election of a member of parliament. In a normal election it was advantageous for a politician to be known as a friend of Government with official patronage at his disposal, but in the exceptional circumstances of 1733–34 that was not the case. Friends of Government among the burgh councillors did their best to conceal their true sentiments because of the force of public opinion, aroused by the issue provoked by the minister of Stirling and the General Assembly's response to that challenge. A preliminary canvass of Stirling, undertaken by Lord Erskine before he withdrew in favour of his uncle, suggested that the Erskines had reason to suspect the professed friendship of the chief magistrate, provost Littlejohn. The provost, it was reported, was 'Mr. Cunningham's man, & consequently Lord Ilay's. But all that Town, & the Provost allso, pretend to be firm to Lord Erskine ... '[7] The reason for this marked reluctance to be known as a friend of Lord Ilay's was made clear by one of the government agents in Stirling, who reported that 'our touns people are all mad with the affair of their Minister Mr. Erskine who continues to preach as he use to doe'. The minister, the agent went on, 'is one who has a great deal to say with most of the Magistrates & all of them hears him preach'.[8]

Lord Erskine's visits to the burghs were made five months before the date of the general election in his capacity as sitting member, and at first glance there did not seem to be any reason why Lord Erskine could not have contested both his old constituency and the county of Stirling, for it was not uncommon to secure election for two seats and subsequently relinquish one of them to a friend in a by-election, as this was a useful means of guarding against defeat. However, the political situation in 1733 made this expedient inadvisable. The difficulty was the attitude adopted by the goverment candidate Henry Cunningham of Boquhan, for

Cunningham deliberately played down his own connection with Lord Ilay, and attempted to persuade the towns to give the reversion of their votes to himself in the event of Lord Erskine's declining to represent the district. Should Erskine succeed, therefore, in both county and burghs and elect to sit for the county, Cunningham hoped to make the subsequent by-election in the towns a formality. Conversely, should Lord Erskine elect to sit for the towns, the freeholders of the county would be deeply offended by the slight, and much of the Erskine interest in the county would disappear leaving the Cunningham-Ilay interest as the beneficiary. Since the Patriots hoped to secure both seats, the only solution was to bring forward two candidates, and in the case of the towns James Erskine of Grange was adopted.

James Erskine of Grange made his own expedition through the burghs during the Christmas vacation of the Court of Session in 1733-4, but as late as November government agents had not given up hope of regaining this deserter from the Ilay faction. One of Ilay's agents, indeed, in a burst of wishful thinking, suggested that Grange was cooling towards the Patriots and was about to make his peace with Government, but if Ilay was ever ready to believe this he was quickly disillusioned, for his informant was forced to admit that the agent had been mistaken and that his only reason for the story was that Grange

> came streight from his couch to Lucky Thomas [tavern] & got so drunk that when he came in not speaking so warm in it the omisn. was only owing to his being drunk & not able to speak at all, for he is keener than ever ... & declars pretty openly that so long as Sir Robert Walpole keeps in he can hope for nothing ... [9]

The hope of overturning the Walpole Administration was the only real motive for Grange's action in seeking a parliamentary seat, for he was in serious financial difficulties. As recently as 1732 Grange had approached Lord Ilay through the Solicitor General for Scotland to seek permission to dispose of his seat in the Court of Session for the best price he could get in order to clear his debts, after which he hoped for some alternative employment.[10] But on that, as on all previous occasions, Grange found that loyal service to Lord Ilay did not outweigh his family's connection with Jacobitism in the calculations of Sir Robert Walpole.

A preliminary canvass carried out by Lord Erskine during the summer of 1733 enabled the Patriots to form a realistic estimate of their political strength in the towns and, from the outset, it was apparent that Henry Cunningham would be difficult to dislodge from the burghs of Inverkeithing and Stirling. The Patriot party, however, had hopes of the remaining three towns of the district, Culross, Queensferry and Dunfermline, in all of which the Seceders were influential, while in two of the burghs Lord Tweeddale believed that his own influence would be decisive. In the summer of 1733 the Patriots believed they could count on the votes of Queensferry and Dunfermline, allowing them to concentrate most of their efforts to secure a third town, of which Culross looked the most vulnerable. In a five-burgh district, like this one, with each town council choosing a single delegate, three out of five was quite sufficient, but in burgh politics there was never any room for complacency, and the fortunes of the two parties fluctuated widely as the campaign progressed.

During his Christmas tour of the towns Lord Grange was gratified by his speedy conquest of the town of Stirling, where there was only one topic of interest, namely the suspension of the burgh minister, Ebenezer Erskine. Henry Cunningham of Boquhan had turned out to be more vulnerable than had appeared to be the case during the first canvass, in spite of his own efforts in Stirling, which he had also visited during the Christmas season. Cunningham, finding himself at a disadvantage in the great issue of the day in the town, tried to make the best of a bad case by attempting to turn Ebenezer Erskine's difficulties to the advantage of Government. According to Lord Grange, Cunningham had 'put in the heads of some of the Council of Stirline, that if they had declar'd for me it would hurt Mr. Ebenezer Erskine by exasperating E[arl] of Ilay at him',[11] There was a certain plausibility in this line of attack, for it would obviously have some appeal to councillors who did not wish to break with Government but who at the same time had no desire to appear as opponents of the formidable Ebenezer Erskine, who would have no hesitation in denouncing their conduct from the pulpit. Fortunately for Grange, his presence in the town enabled him to turn this potentially dangerous attack before any real harm could be done, and he accomplished this by the simple expedient of suggesting that those who believed Ebenezer Erskine might be harmed by a declaration by the town council of support for a Patriot candidate should ask the minister for his opinion. As Grange anticipated, that opinion was given in Ebenezer Erskine's usual forthright style, for he 'openly declar'd, that could not hurt him at all, for he had allready felt L[or]d Ilay's violence, and doubted not but he would do all the mischief he could to all the faithfull Ministers & fast friends of the Church of Scotland'.[12] Thus encouraged, the reluctant councillors gave way and declared their intention of supporting James Erskine of Grange at the next general election.

While this mutual concern for the inflexible minister of Stirling was at the heart of the management of the council of that town, it should not be supposed that more traditional methods of burgh electioneering were neglected, and Henry Cunningham did in fact secure the support of one of the councillors, the deacon of the butchers, who had previously offered his support to Grange, with an offer of sixteen fat wethers for his shop. But the deacon was the only councillor ready to stand against the tide of public opinion, and it was a very doubtful success, for, as Grange related, the good deacon promptly went to the Erskine party to see if they would top the bid: ' The Rascall had openly demanded from my factor 8 Guineas, on wch condition he would be for me'.[13] Treachery and lack of scruple were common enough in burgh politics, but in the current state of public opinion the deacon did himself more harm than good by his greed, for not only did Grange's factor decline to bribe the man, Cunningham learned of the attempted treachery and kept his sheep, while 'now none in the town will drink a chopin of ale with the fellow, nor keep company with him', [14] which was unlikely to have helped his business.

Success at Stirling was an unexpected bonus for the Patriot party, but simultaneously matters took a turn for the worse in one of the towns which they had believed would be theirs, and indeed it was upon this town that the strength of the Patriot challenge was based. Dunfermline had been considered, in the context of traditional politics, to be a fairly safe vote, for the judicial authority of the Marquis of Tweeddale, as bailie of the regality, gave him a considerable voice in the burgh's affairs. Contrary to common belief the old heritable jurisdictions did not dwindle into insignificance in a uniform way between the end of the seventeenth century and their abolition after the Jacobite Rising of 1745–6. Some of these courts may have atrophied, but others, and notably that of Dunfermline, retained an active life in this period. The regality of Dunfermline included an extensive portion of West Fife in the vicinity of Dunfermline, while the court's jurisdiction over the operation of the ferry service across the river Forth gave the Marquis of Tweeddale some influence in the burgh of Queensferry, from which the ferries sailed. The regality court in this period met between thirty and forty times each year,[15] and shortly after this election pressure of business demanded an increase in the court's sittings to two days each week throughout the year.[16]

Lord Tweeddale naturally did not spend his life dispensing justice to the people of West Fife, and a court as busy as this required the services of several judges. Accordingly, the Marquis appointed three or four local gentlemen to act as bailies-depute, holding their offices during his pleasure, and in appearance therefore the court was fully controlled by the holder of the heritable office who could take the office of judge from one man and give it to another. While these officers acted as Lord Tweeddale's servants, as they were in name, Tweeddale dominated Dunfermline, whose suburbs lay in the regality, and there could be few councillors of the burgh who would care to refuse his requests. It was this situation which made the Patriots so confident that they could count on the support of Dunfermline, where powerful influence was likely to reinforce public opinion, for the church question was just as strong here as it was in Stirling, and Ralph Erskine, Ebenezer's brother, and his colleague, the ministers of Dunfermline, were equally hostile to Lord Ilay. Henry Cunningham did his best to attack the councillors of the town by arguing that James Erskine of Grange was a Jacobite at heart, but it was an unconvincing performance. As Grange remarked:

> he raill'd at me & said he had gather'd up the letters I wrote to the voters of Stirline Shire wch he was to print at London, that to some I wrote L[or]d Erskine was a Whig bred at Geneva, to others that he was a Torry like his Father, & according to my own heart, and more such damn'd stuff, wch tho I had been rogue enough to write so doubly, I would not have done in so poor a strain ... who would be so great a beast as to write so grossly to a wholle shire, & to neighbours who could not but meet & compare their letters? But there is not a lie so gross that may do me hurt, wch these men do not with impudence put against me ... [17]

It did not take long for Cunningham to find that he was unlikely to be able to accomplish very much in Dunfermline, where he appears to have been welcomed only by those councillors who kept inns. Grange reported gleefully:

He had an entertainment at Chalmers, to which Veitch refused to go because he kept a public house himself, and therefore ... [Cunningham of Boquhan] order'd another at his house, and for want of company most of it and the punch was given to the beggers at the door. The two Bailies and Convener refused to go near him, and he was but ill attended by the rest, who after they let him make two great bowls of punch all declared that they would only drink wine, & the punch was given to the beggers who I suppose are now his best friends in that town ... [18]

An attempt by Cunningham to regain his influence with the leaders of council in a private meeting was no more successful than the entertainments, for the member of parliament was told bluntly that they were unhappy with his conduct, for 'he had been for the Excyse Bill',[19] and his defence of his action did not satisfy his critics. Cunningham's reception at Culross was no better,[20] and he was forced back upon the centre of his power, Inverkeithing, where he was himself the provost.

Henry Cunningham of Boquhan's identification with unpopular causes may have eliminated him as a serious threat to a Patriot victory in the district, but there was a new danger which threatened to destroy much of Grange's early success. One of the councillors of Dunfermline, Captain Peter Halkett, began to make it clear that he intended to offer his services to the towns, building upon a strong family interest in one of them. Halkett's father, Sir Peter Halkett of Pitfirrane, was himself a magistrate of Dunfermline, and the family had long been influential in the burgh, while the Captain was one of the most active of Lord Tweeddale's bailies-depute in the regality, an office which made many Dunfermline people reluctant to cross him. Halkett did not at first seek votes for himself in an open manner, but asked instead that councillors should reserve judgement until all of the candidates were known, refraining from an immediate declaration for James Erskine of Grange. The declared supporter of Administration, Henry Cunningham, quickly acquiesced in this approach, asking that voters delay their decisions until the conclusion of the final session of the old parliament when the situation might become clearer. In the circumstances it was a clever approach, for many of the councillors were currently under strong public pressure to oppose government measures, and that pressure might slacken with the passage of time. Councillors, moreover, rarely liked to put any distance between themselves and the things which Government could provide. Delay might prevent them from making a decision which might hurt them for the duration of a parliament. Halkett concealed his own intentions to some extent, for when his friends asked councillors to delay their declaration it was possible for them to argue that Halkett was merely keeping up his family interest and enhancing his own importance in the politics of the towns, which would not preclude his throwing his support behind a Patriot candidate at a later date.

Halkett's decision to attempt to secure the seat for himself appears to have been prompted by thoughts of what Government could do for him, combined with family pride and resentment at the continuance of the Erskine family's dominance of the constituency. James Erskine described Halkett as a slave to Lord Ilay,[21] but the fact remains that Government alone could serve the Halkett family in their desire for legislation to facilitate the family's coal operations,[22] while Halkett's own career as an army officer was likely to improve if he was of political value to the Administration. There were some things which only good relations with Government could facilitate in the eighteenth century but, whatever the motive, it was clear as early as January 1734 that Captain Peter Halkett was not to be counted among Grange's friends in the council of Dunfermline. It had also been learned, moreover, that Captain Halkett had been in contact with the Earl of Ilay's deputy in Scotland, Lord Milton, a fact which had been disclosed by the latter's uncharacteristic indiscretion in talking of the new arrangement with 'foolish & too hasty boasting '.[23] Warned by his enemy, Grange attempted to counter Halkett's influence in Dunfermline by making another visit to the town, this time accompanied by Lord Tweeddale, when 'all did so strongly declare their adherence to Ld. Marquis and aversion to Sr Robt. Wallpole, E. Ilay, Ld. Millnton & all who should join them'[24] that the Patriot cause again looked secure.

Dunfermline, like Stirling, was much taken with the affair of Ebenezer Erskine, since one of the ministers of Dunfermline, Ralph Erskine, was a brother of the stubborn minister of Stirling. Accordingly, in both burghs, the clergy were valuable propagandists for the Patriot cause, and in Dunfermline Ralph Erskine and his colleague Wardlaw

> dealt a good dale among their people & gave very broad hints in the Pulpit, of their duty to be publick spirited, & not to partake of other men's guilt, wch they must do if they did not employ their interrest heartily to bring in such as they had reason ... to believe sincere friends to their king & Country & to our civil & sacred Rights, Libertys & Priviledges, & if they did not oppose all who, under any pretence or temptation whatsoever they should see going in with our Oppressors ... [25]

Ministers when delivering such messages from the pulpit could make it very plain which individual they had in mind, even without naming names, and after being treated to such a discourse one Sunday, Captain Halkett was so incensed that he approached Ralph Erskine to complain that the words appeared to be directed at him. Ralph Erskine could not deny it, but if Halkett thought he could intimidate the minister he was mistaken, for, as Grange related happily:

> Erskine put it to him roundly, whether he was in any concert with E[arl] Ilay? he could not deny it, & for his vindication alleadged the promise he had given. Erskine replyed, that such a promise was dishonourable & sinfull, & that the Captn could not ... expect the concurrence of any honest man ... [26]

This not being the outcome he had contemplated, Halkett, who did not know when to leave well alone, persisted, suggesting that there was scriptural precedent for keeping his promise to the Earl, but he picked a most unfortunate illustration:

> The captn in defence of standing to his promise, urged the example of Herod who, tho' reluctantly, kept his word to Herodius & beheaded John Baptist. Erskine answer'd, Fy upon the Tyrant, why did he not gar scourge the whore & swish her out of his Court, & honestly break the sinfull filthy promise he had made like a Villain. Wardlaw us'd no less freedom with him. He is in a prodigious rage at both ... [27]

The quarrel between Captain Halkett and the two ministers effectively reduced Halkett's influence in the burgh and, according to information reaching Grange, 'some who had great favour for him before and would hardly believe it possible he could act thus ... will scarcely see him or speak with him ... [28]

Unfortunately for the management of the Patriot cause, they did not follow up this success by removing Captain Halkett from his office of bailie-depute, for Lord Tweeddale, feeling that Halkett was no longer a threat, hesitated to humiliate the man by taking the place from him. Tweeddale showed unusual reluctance to accept the advice which Grange pressed upon him and returned to London leaving Halkett as his deputy in the regality of Dunfermline; it would appear that Tweeddale was ready to take Halkett's allegations at face value, accepting the story that Halkett was only trying to maintain a natural political interest in the towns without intending to press his candidacy to a conclusion. In short, the Marquis suggested that 'the turning him out of the deputation in my absence might do more harm than good',[29] but this policy of letting matters drift until Lord Tweeddale should return from London had potentially harmful consequences. How were the citizens of Dunfermline, including the councillors of the burgh, to view this situation? They feared Halkett's power, and without a positive assurance that the Marquis of Tweeddale had broken with his bailie they did not care to disoblige Halkett. As Grange remarked, 'they fear that your L[or]d[shi]p & he will at length make up matters and so he'll continue in power as a Bailie-depute & still be countenanced by you, & he will never forgive their standing by your L[or]d[shi]p's Interrest, & would wreck his vengeance on them'.[30] Grange was giving Tweeddale sound advice in suggesting that Halkett had been too long a bailie-depute, but Tweeddale persisted in retaining a disloyal deputy until he could attend to the matter personally when he returned to the area.

The failure of Henry Cunningham of Boquhan to overcome the hostility of the clergy and councillors in several of the towns alarmed some of his old friends, who began to suspect that this might be the moment to abandon a sinking ship while there was still time. The alarm they felt was occasioned by the suspicion that the opposition forces might prove too strong for the Walpole Administration and that there might be a change of Government, with a consequent diversion of the flow of patronage from those who remained too long with the defeated Ministers. Notable among those determined to remain a friend of Government, whatever the Government, was John Cant, the town clerk of Inverkeithing, an official normally tied closely to the interest of Cunningham, the provost of that burgh. Cant, moreover, was going to be one of the major figures in the ensuing general election, for Inverkeithing would be the returning burgh and the town clerk would act as returning officer. Cant had accompanied Henry Cunningham during his round of canvassing in January 1734 and had not been impressed by their reception. He rapidly opened communications with the opposition candidate, James Erskine Grange, and the latter made a point of arranging a meeting with this potentially valuable, if quite untrustworthy, ally, whom he found drowning his sorrows in an Edinburgh tavern. This made communication a little difficult for, according to Grange:

Mr. Cant is so eternally & monstrously drunk here, that I have not got him fully spoke to. But he pretends to be for us & says that [Henry Cunningham of] B[oquha]n's head is turn'd . . . and that now he sees him like to be out of all the other Towns & left by every body . . . Inverkeithing's Vote must not be lost . . . [31]

Clerk Cant's fear that a change of Government might find Inverkeithing excluded from the flow of patronage if the town persisted in its loyalty to a losing cause was not his only worry. Cant's old associates, Henry Cunningham and Lord Milton, were pressing him as returning officer to give the election to the candidate of Administration however the town delegates voted, and although the town clerk was quite unscrupulous enough to do as he was asked, he was naturally apprehensive of the outcome should his friends lose control of parliament. The returning officer was in this mood of apprehension when Grange found him, and Cant insisted 'that he will not risque for any man the money he has allready gain'd, nor incur the pains of that damn'd dreadfull Act [as he calls it] the Bribery & Corruption Bill'.[32]

Grange knew better than to place much trust in John Cant, but the clerk's ready betrayal of Henry Cunningham's secrets was useful, allowing the Patriots to form an estimate of the extent to which bribery would be employed, for Clerk Cant informed them that Cunningham had brought to Scotland bills on the Royal Bank for a thousand pounds, and that almost five hundred guineas had already been disbursed before Cunningham returned to London. No doubt, as Grange remarked, 'the creature is monstrously false',[33] but John Cant's information was of value in planning the remainder of the Patriots' campaign. The Government clearly would spare no expense to defeat Grange, and there was more than a trace of envy in his criticism of his rival's methods: 'That fool as he goes about makes not use of eating & drinking with people so much for an opportunity of speaking to them & warming their Hearts, as to make a sputter and show of expence, wch he fancy's makes him admir'd as a brave generous gentleman'. [34]

Lacking the resources to bribe as extensively as Henry Cunningham, Grange made public opinion his main strength, keeping up pressure on the burgh councillors by the popularity of his cause with the people of the towns, and although the latter were without votes, that did not mean that they were powerless. If they became aroused, it was nor merely the business of councillors which might suffer a setback, but even their persons might suffer harm if they flouted the popular will. In order to obtain that popular interest, the efforts of the clergy were supplemented by the distribution of printed Patriot propaganda. The flow of information was essential in the opinion of some of the Patriot leaders for, as Grange suggested, 'things may happen this session of Parlt. very proper to give our countrymen just sentiments & a right spirit before the election '.[35] The proper method to awaken the right spirit was to arrange the distribution of 'pamphlets & papers to be sent to us from London ',[36] although it is likely that only single pamphlets would in fact be sent, to be reprinted locally, and there was even an attempt to establish a weekly newspaper in Scotland to support the opposition cause, but that project at once ran into financial difficulties. A further development of the Patriot propaganda campaign was the printing and distribution of a highly relevant Act of Parliament, just before the elections. 'We have in the press the Act agst Bribery & Corruption that it may be distributed,' wrote Grange, 'for as the Courtiers proceed, it is necessary that the Act be known to all.'[37] Grange showed a keen interest in this attempt to sway opinion, and he continued to distribute a regular parliamentary newsletter for several years after the 1734 election.

Propaganda, unfortunately, can recoil upon its users, and although the Patriot efforts were instrumental in raising the level of interest in what was happening in the last session of parliament before the general election, what did happen did not prove advantageous. As the bailies and councillors, whose natural inclinations were nearly always to support the men in power, watched events at Westminster with new interest, they began to find good reasons for hesitation. Had Grange's friends continued to make the running in parliament, there is every reason to suppose that he would have had very little further trouble, and perhaps even Inverkeithing might have declared for him, but that did not happen. Sir Robert Walpole recovered from the setback caused by the Excise Bill, and from the Patriot correspondence it is evident that Scottish opposition began to flag as soon as government recovery was evident. Grange at least was fully aware of the damage which this loss of momentum in parliament would do to their electoral chances and, in a letter to Lord Tweeddale, Grange stated his fears bluntly:

> If on the Triennial Parlt. the Vote of Credit etc. there be not a hearty opposition, the Country will not believe that the Patriots are in earnest or good for any thing, and our numbers & friends in this Country will drop off as snow melts before a hot sun. Tho you come to be defeat, yet if there be an honest bold & hearty batle, our troops will continue in heart; otherwise most of them will desert ... God forbid that this session go over without some publick noted popular appearance by the Patriots. We shall otherwise lose the election.[38]

Unfortunately for Grange's hopes, the Triennial Bill was thrown out by a vote of 247 to 184 in the House of Commons, after a rather ineffective debate by the opposition,[39] and the Court party made the most of that victory to strengthen their position in Scotland. One of the more serious consequences of the Government's recovery was the near certainty that Lord Ilay and Lord Milton would again crack the whip over the heads of the returning officers. 'The Court will drive the returning officers to do as they direct them,' Grange pointed out, '& the great appearance of their success will easily perswade these officers to obey blindly.'[40]

With a parliamentary victory to encourage them, the Court party redoubled their efforts in the towns of the Dunfermline district. In Stirling a resident Court manager was set to work in the person of Captain Charles Campbell, who was supplied with a portion of the funds in Henry Cunningham's hands. Here the old charge of Jacobitism was raised again against the enemies of Administration, another expedient which might provide a loophole for councillors who had deserted Henry Cunningham to return to the government fold with decency. Grange and his friends had little difficulty disposing of this allegation but, as

Grange shrewdly observed, 'it is not the strength of the objection wch in such case is noticeable, but that men want to have an objection & when driven from this will take up another. The truth is, all this proceeds from the unexpected ... superiority of the Court in Parlt. and that the Patriots have attempted little'.[41]

The Administration's campaign, co-ordinated by Lord Milton and Henry Cunningham, was designed to assist their friends in municipal office to defy public opinion by confusing the issues. Almost certainly Henry Cunningham of Boquhan had long since abandoned any intention he may have had of sitting again in parliament, for he had his eye firmly fixed upon a colonial governorship. But so long as Cunningham continued to canvass actively, Captain Peter Halkett, the true Court candidate, could pose as an independent. Even when the results of the January canvass had made it plain that Cunningham could not hope to succeed and a new candidate of Administration would be necessary, the Court managers deliberately concealed their intentions once again by setting up an alternative candidate, Captain Charles Campbell, their agent at Stirling. Captain Campbell, in spite of being closely related to both Milton and Ilay,[42] was induced to spend his own money in both the Dunfermline and Glasgow burgh districts in 1734, only to be dropped by the Court in both constituencies. The candidacy of Campbell was very useful to the Administration, however, for in the Dunfermline district the candidacy of an avowed Courtier gave some plausibility to Captain Halkett's continued pose of independence, which seemed to convince those councillors who wanted to believe it was true.

Captain Halkett concentrated his attention on his own town of Dunfermline, where he used every means he could think of to persuade the council to choose him to be delegate to represent the burgh at the election meeting at Inverkeithing. Grange was horrified to find that the Dunfermline council was not only inclined to enter into Halkett's proposal, but might even permit the Captain to give the burgh's vote in his own favour should this be enough to secure the election. The council intended that Halkett should otherwise vote for Grange, but the latter's comment on the likelihood of his obeying instructions from the council appears justified in view of Halkett's known communication with Lord Milton: 'Tying down is a jest unless the Delegate be a man of reall honour, [wch after what I have seen of the Captn I can not help thinking is not quite his character] for his vote will stand good, tho given contrary to what he was ty'd down to'.[43] Grange, rightly, considered Halkett an enemy, but the difficulty in Dunfermline was occasioned by the fact that in spite of his quarrel with the ministers of the burgh, Halkett had never openly admitted that he was an ally of Lord Ilay. In the circumstances there were many in Dunfermline who considered that their formidable bailie-depute, still apparently with the favour of Lord Tweeddale, had as good a claim to represent their town as James Erskine of Grange. The parliamentary recovery by the Government further strengthened Halkett's position, for even after a visit to the burgh by Lord Ilay himself made it difficult to conceal a connection between Halkett and the Court manager, some members of council 'would fain perswade themselves that he cheats that Peer'.[44] Rather than demonstrating a remarkable degree of obtuseness, the councillors' attitude is probably to be attributed to a

desire to avoid a breach with either the Government in office or the influential
clergy of the town. Halkett himself promoted the illusion by keeping up the facade
of independence and denouncing the known supporter of the Walpole
administration, Henry Cunningham, but, as Grange observed, 'it will be found
that Boquhan is not to stand against me, but the Captn. himself'.[45]

The Government's success in the last session of parliament in overcoming the
opposition suggested to Inverkeithing and its town clerk that they might have been
over-hasty in contemplating a change of allegiance and, as soon as the news from
London suggested that Sir Robert Walpole was not in immediate danger, they
returned to their old allegiance. Thus, as the campaign entered its final phase, the
political situation in the district changed once more. James Erskine of Grange
could still be sure of the votes of two towns, Stirling and Queensferry, in spite of
the best efforts of Captain Campbell at the former town where he admitted that
risking his life 'by drinking ... day and night for three weeks' had been to little
purpose.[46] On the other hand, Captain Peter Halkett had replaced Cunningham as
the chief rival, for the latter had 'nothing at all to say in Dunfermline or Cullross.
The Captn. has, & on Boquhan's giving up is promised Inverkeithing'.[47] If Halkett
could persuade the council of Dunfermline to give him the vital commission as
delegate in preference to Grange, he had a good chance of securing the election,
and he spared no effort to gain his point.

Two votes might be enough to secure Halkett's return, for John Cant, anxious to
regain the favour of the men in power after his temporary lapse, would not hesitate
to favour the candidate of Administration. Grange at least had no doubts about the
likely conduct of the returning officer, complaining that

> whoever the Court setts up will be return'd by Cant. If the rascall did in the least
> hesitate about what is the advantageous side for him, perhaps he may venture to
> disobey the Court's commands, & for once be a little honest, but as things go he will
> run farther & faster against us than they could allmost desire him; and they will
> promise to stand betwixt him and all hazard. He knows that if I prosecute him, the
> Session will not condemn him [of wch he boasts allready] and that E[arl] Ilay will be
> the great judge in the appeal ... [48]

The probability of a false return, even if he secured a majority of the delegates,
compelled Grange to take precautions, and by arranging to be elected for the small
county of Clackmannan, which had been unrepresented in the previous
parliament, he tried to ensure that he would obtain a parliamentary seat in any
event. Should Grange succeed in securing the Dunfermline burghs seat, another
Patriot could easily replace him in Clackmannanshire which, at this period, was
dominated by the Erskines. As yet, however, the Patriots had only two of the five
votes in their hands, Stirling and Queensferry, to which they would have to add
Dunfermline to complete their majority. Conversely, the loss of either of the towns
already in their hands would end the contest, a possibility which had not escaped
the notice of Captain Halkett and the government managers.

In March 1734 Halkett paid a visit to Stirling, where he continued to act the part
of the independent gentleman, but he found it too strongly for Grange to make a

serious impression upon the councillors. Their leader told Halkett that he was sure Grange was for the Country, but 'fear'd he was for the court, in wch case he needed not expect that Town'.[49] Halkett, however, was not so easily put off, and 'next day his brother Mr. Wedderburn & other of his friends were very busy among the Councillors'.[50] Halkett had reason to persist, for he must have been aware of a Court scheme, of quite Machiavellian character, intended to effect a major alteration in the town council of Stirling.

The dispute between the majority in the General Assembly of the Church of Scotland and the radical group led by Ebenezer Erskine had culminated in a decision by the Assembly Commission to suspend Erskine and his friends if they declined to make an apology for their conduct. Ebenezer Erskine, however, was the last man to withdraw from a position which he had taken, and he appeared more inclined to believe that it was the General Assembly which should apologise to him for their tolerance of lay patronage. That was the situation in the spring of 1734 when Church affairs started to interact even more closely with burgh politics. The formidable minister of Stirling had refused to surrender to pressure, and the Commission accordingly ordered a minister to proceed to Stirling and intimate Erskine's suspension from his own pulpit, and 'to require the Magistrates to protect him in so doing, & to take instruments if he was refused or met with violence.'[51] Nothing was more certain that that any minister charged with such a task would meet with a hostile reception in Stirling, but what is less certain is whether the decision to make the attempt was entirely fortuitous, and there is some reason to suspect that Lord Ilay, or more probably Lord Milton, had a hand in it. There is no doubt that they stood to benefit from the action, for should the magistrates decline to co-operate or fail to protect the minister charged with the unpopular duty, it would, as Grange observed, 'make them lyable, & so our friends will be prosecuted ... & give a handle to Lord Ilay to disturb the election'. [52]

The minister chosen for this uncongenial task was James Richardson, the minister of Aberfoyle, but this gentleman had been presented to his current charge by one of the Patriot lords, the Duke of Montrose. Accordingly, it appeared to Grange that Richardson might be susceptible to pressure from friends of his patron, particularly when their advice might save him from injury. The duke was then in England, but Mungo Graeme of Gorthie, the manager of his Scottish affairs, was urged to prevent Richardson from travelling to Stirling, for the situation in the burgh had become critical:

> paines are taken to perswade them, that in their present situation because of their Minister, there is no safety for them [the Magistrates] without Ld Ilay's freindship, and that to offend him farther is to be undone ... and the secret friends of ... the Court, who formerly behov'd to say otherwise because the current of the town was with us, do now begin to speak that for the sake of Ebenezer & their own safety they should yield to Ld Ilay ... [53]

Grange pointed out that there was no necessity for Richardson to risk his health by braving the unhappy burgesses of Stirling, for his lawyer's eye had spotted a loophole in the Assembly Commission's instructions to the minister of Aberfoyle.

Richardson was to read the sentence of suspension in Stirling 'on or before the 4th Sunday of Aprile. Who knows but he may be sick, or what accident may happen on that Sunday so as to justify or excuse his not going to Stirling?'[54] After the named date the Commission's order would of course lapse, and Richardson would have avoided what promised to be a singularly unpleasant experience. On the other hand, Grange did not intend to trust Richardson's own self-interest to induce him to develop a diplomatic illness, and steps were taken to make certain that he could not in any event reach Stirling. Guards were to be posted on every road leading to the town when they learned of the day on which Richardson contemplated making the journey:

> so as such as wish to meet & protect him on the way can not be disappointed ... there may be some that he is not acquainted with, who are resolved to meet him & hinder any to offer violence or affront to him, but will hinder him to proceed and make him return, but in great civility & without doing him any sort of harm.[55]

However it was arranged, Grange carried his point, for Richardson did not appear in Stirling to create a riot which might justify the prosecution of the magistrates, and his absence probably decided the election of the Stirling delegate in Grange's favour, for the council had become nearly equally divided over the issue.[56] By a combination of bribery and assurances that to support Lord Ilay was to act in the best interests of Ebenezer Erskine, the Court party in Stirling came back from almost nothing to eight out of twenty councillors able to attend the election. In Stirling, moreover, the practice in the event of a tie was to give the casting vote to the dean of guild, a member of the Court party, rather than Grange's friend the provost, which meant that had the Court been able to intimidate two magistrates with fear of a prosecution they would have chosen the delegate, and that in turn would have determined the election for the district. But with the fear of riot dispersed, Grange's friends recovered and increased their majority in council to five before the date of election of a delegate,[57] a reversal brought about once more by Grange's talent for mustering public opinion to put pressure upon the burgh oligarchy.

Just when the Court was employing the affair of Ebenezer Erskine against him, James Erskine of Grange turned the attack by reversing their arguments. With the main threat of riot dispersed, Grange put indirect pressure upon the councillors by persuading the people of Stirling that they might hope for a restoration of their popular minister, not through the agency of Lord Ilay, but through the General Assembly of the Church. Grange pressed his ally Lord Tweeddale not to miss this opportunity, for if they could persuade the Assembly to

> remove the offence of the strict people [who are all firm & earnest against the Court and abhorre E[arl] I[la]y & Sr Robert Wallpole] about the Act 1732, and in consequence get the 4 outed Ministers brought in again, it will be a vast slur on Ilay & greatly recommend the Patriots to the country ... This will in particular oblidge ... the town of Dunfermline & allso Stirline, Queensferry & Cullross, and likewise a great many in Inverkeithing ... [58]

The General Assembly of 1734 did go some way towards meeting the objections of Ebenezer Erskine and his party, but compromise was abhorrent to Erskine, and the concessions were insufficient to prevent Erskine and his group from breaking finally with the Church, but in the political field Patriot success was complete, as is evident in the statements made by government agents in the burghs. The agent at Stirling, for example, complained that 'the town are all madd with the hopes that the Assembly will restore their Minister', and were threatening violence against known government supporters.[59] Thus, by playing skilfully on the population's sympathy for Ebenezer Erskine, Grange recovered his footing in the burgh council and could count on that delegate as secured.

The decision to press in the General Assembly for compromise also paid political dividends in Dunfermline, where Grange's popularity was so great that the council ultimately rejected Captain Halkett as their delegate in favour of Grange, although not without a bitter confrontation in the council chamber.[60] With little difficulty in Queensferry for the Patriots, Grange therefore came to the election meeting in Inverkeithing with three delegate votes, while Inverkeithing, in the Court interest, had been joined by the delegate of Culross, where bribery had been extensively employed. It might be thought that with three votes out of a possible five Grange was already secure, but elections were rarely concluded as easily as that in the Scottish burghs.

Government control of the returning burgh was a great advantage, and the election meeting was manipulated by the experienced Henry Cunningham of Boquhan, the provost of Inverkeithing, who had arranged for his own election as burgh delegate. On the day of election, May 18th, 1734, Henry Cunningham had already been governor of Jamaica for several weeks, but he remained in Scotland to work for a Court victory in the Dunfermline district where the Administration was showing more than usual determination in its efforts to prevent James Erskine from obtaining a seat, having attempted to exclude him in advance by legislation prohibiting Scottish judges from sitting in the House of Commons.

The preliminary steps went without incident, as John Cant took the necessary steps to qualify himself to act as returning officer, and Henry Cunningham produced his commission as delegate for Inverkeithing. Cunningham's commission was approved by the remaining delegates without debate, as was that presented by Provost Wingate, the representative of Stirling, but it was this seemingly innocuous procedure which determined the outcome of the election, for it enabled Provost Cunningham to claim the right to control the remainder of the meeting.

When the third delegate presented his commission, unanimity came to an abrupt end, for James Erskine of Grange, the delegate of Dunfermline, received a very different reception from that accorded to Wingate and Cunningham. The provost of Inverkeithing produced a string of objections to Grange's commission and vote, ranging from 'gross bribery and corruption, threatenings, acts of violence and by unlawful combinations', to 'undue influence of certain Noble Peers of this realm particularly by one possessed of a jurisdiction interfiring with the jurisdiction of the burgh of Dunfermline'.[61] Objections to Grange personally were added for good measure and, in particular, it was alleged that a recent Act of Parliament[62] which disqualified judges of the Court of Session from sitting in the House of Commons barred Grange from taking part in an election meeting. All this wordy outburst was of course really quite irrelevant to the business in hand. In the first place, a burgh election meeting was not competent to consider such questions as the means by which a commission was obtained, let alone whether the burgh of Dunfermline could be considered independent of the regality court of Dunfermline and Lord Tweeddale, for they were empowered only to determine the authenticity of the documents produced and whether they had been sealed with the common seal of the town in question. All Cunningham's objections, moreover, shared one defect: they were simple assertions by the provost of Inverkeithing, who did not, and could not, produce any shadow of proof. However it was evident from Grange's known financial difficulties that whatever other Patriot gentlemen may have attempted, his capacity for bribery was limited. It is known that the joint expenses of both Grange and his nephew, Lord Erskine, the candidate for the county of Stirling, in the period August 1733 to February 1734, amounted to a total of only £195, almost all of it spent on entertainment of electors,[63] a practice which scarcely constituted bribery in the eighteenth-century sense.

The allegation of influence by 'certain Noble Peers' had an element of truth in it, but once again no evidence was advanced to sustain the charge, and in view of Captain Halkett's activities it was clearly a case of the kettle calling the pot black. The objection to Grange personally was no better, for although he was considered dangerous enough to induce the Administration to secure an act of parliament to exclude him from parliament, the act could only do so while Grange was a lord of session, and Grange had responded to the statute by resigning his place on the bench, which he was surely free to do, for as he put it, 'there is no law in Scotland tying any of the Judges to the Bench as the laws of Scotland tyes a coal-heugher to work at his coall pitt till dismiss'd by his employer'.[64] In any case the act had said nothing about voting, and if a judge might vote as a freeholder in a county election, why could he not cast a vote as a delegate of a burgh council?

Cunningham raised a further objection which, on the face of it, was more relevant, for there was a defect in the sheriff's precept which had authorised the burgh council of Dunfermline to choose a delegate. For some reason the precept of the sheriff of Fife had been wrongly dated, for it stated it had been signed by the sheriff on May 13th when it was already in the hands of the burgh magistrates on the 12th. There does not appear to have been any political motive behind this error, and it was probably connected with the need to produce a large number of such precepts in this county with so many royal burghs, but Cunningham insisted that it voided the Dunfermline election, even though the delegate had been chosen subsequent to the precept date. On the other hand, if Dunfermline was to be disfranchised by the sheriff's error, the same treatment should have been given to Inverkeithing, the remaining Fife town in the district, for the error was also made in their precept. Unfortunately for Grange, however, no objection had been made to Cunningham's commission and the Inverkeithing vote was now unchallengeable.

After long and increasingly heated debate the meeting passed to consideration of the commission of Bailie John Rolland, the delegate of Culross, when Grange in turn raised irrelevant objections in no way connected with the validity of Rolland's commission. What does emerge from the argument, however, is a strong probability that this town's vote was obtained by Administration through corrupt means. Grange asserted that a majority of the Culross council

> did last winter write a letter ... craving from the person to whom the said letter ... was directed money to be given them or their community in view of this present election, and that they are accordingly promised of late a certain sum of money which is contrary to law ... [65]

Admittedly an assertion like that is proof of nothing, but the government party essentially added a strong presumption of accuracy to Grange's charge when they replied that even if the story were true, while admitting nothing, the money was asked before the writ of election was issued. Henry Cunningham indeed did not content himself with that singularly inept response but went on to insist that no such objection was valid without proof, which invited Grange's retort that that was what he had been saying all along.

Finally it was the turn of the delegate of Queensferry, Bailie Archibald Stewart, who was again subjected to a barrage of specious objections from Cunningham who again alleged undue influence, which may very well have been true, but without offering any evidence to support his charges. A defect in the commission was again suggested, even though the burgh was not in the county of Fife, for the sheriff of Linlithgowshire who signed the precept was the sheriff-principal rather than the sheriff-depute, which was surely quite adequate.

The outcome of this manipulation by the provost of Inverkeithing was that there were only two votes sustained without objection, those of Stirling and Inverkeithing. That, according to Henry Cunningham's interpretation of procedure, allowed him to control the meeting by use of a casting vote, and undeterred by the opposition of the Stirling delegate, Cunningham rejected the commission of Dunfermline, sustained that of Culross and then, as there was no reason to refuse the vote of Queensferry any longer, admitted Bailie Stewart to the election.

Not surprisingly, when the votes were called for the member of parliament, Captain Peter Halkett was declared duly elected by three votes to two, but Halkett's third vote was in fact the casting vote assumed by the new governor of Jamaica as his last political service to the Administration, for Grange's vote as delegate for Dunfermline was not included. In fact Grange had the support of three towns in a five-burgh district, but he was not returned, and Peter Halkett was named in his place. This was a particularly bad return, and it was thought worthwhile trying to overturn it in the House of Commons, but Grange's petition was rejected and he had to content himself with the county seat for Clackmannan for the remainder of the 1734 parliament. The election of 1741, however, saw Grange chosen without difficulty for the towns he had already won in 1734, still hostile to the politicians who had so abused him.

The 1734 election in the Dunfermline district was fought mainly on issues of moment to the people of the communities, and, although bribery was, as usual, well to the fore in some of the burghs, corruption of the voters was secondary to the questions which mattered to the people of the district from the Excise Bill, the Triennial Parliament and other parliamentary questions to the strictly local question of the fate of Ebenezer Erskine. Erskine himself became directly involved in burgh politics, travelling from his own town to make an unsuccessful bid to turn things around in Culross, and having to concede that money would carry that town. The clergy, aided by Grange's printed propaganda, mobilised public opinion to the point where it came to have a decisive influence in some of the towns. Many of the burgh councillors were acting against their own interests by supporting an opposition candidate — something they would rarely do — and there can be no question that Government was disposed to be generous to those who went against the tide of public opinion, but it was all to no avail and it came down to a rigged return before the Court could claim a victory. Burgh oligarchies were self-electing for the most part, but they were more dependent upon the ordinary people of their towns than is often allowed. The self-election written into the burgh constitutions is not the whole story, for those involved in trade were dependent to some extent upon their customers, and even the landed proprietors in council were subject to pressure of the kind which could be exerted by Ebenezer and Ralph Erskine and their colleagues.

The election also suggests the influence still possessed by the holders of a regality court in the third decade of the eighteenth century, for this was clearly a matter of concern in Dunfermline where, in spite of the efforts of the clergy, public opinion, and a desire to maintain good relations with the Marquis of Tweeddale, the issue was long in doubt because councillors hesitated to incur Captain Halkett's enmity without a demonstration that he had broken with the marquis and would cease to be a bailie-depute. It is not necessary to suggest fear of any particularly dramatic acts of oppression by Halkett in the regality court to explain the councillors' apprehension that Halkett would take his revenge if crossed. The regality court of Dunfermline was very active, hearing many commercial cases, and there was an extensive backlog. It would be quite easy for a bailie-depute to allow an action brought by someone out of favour to languish for a year or two at considerable expense to the litigant. Probably anything more dramatic in a court located so close to Edinburgh would have been redressed by the Court of Session, and although it was in criminal matters that the regality courts were most independent, there is little evidence that Dunfermline regality made much use of its criminal jurisdiction. The conclusion of the contest for the burghs, however, was obtained by one of the oldest political expedients open to Administration when strongly entrenched, a false return in favour of their own candidate.

NOTES

1. SRO. Seafield, GD248/97/1, Lord Lovat to the Laird of Luss, 27 Aug., 1733.
2. HMC. Polwarth, v, 103, the Marquis of Tweeddale to the Earl of Marchmont, 26 Sep., 1733.

3. NLS. Saltoun MS.16551, G. Vaughan to Lord Milton, 15 Apr., 1732.

4. NLS. Yester MS.7044, James Erskine of Grange to Lord Tweeddale, 26 Aug., 1733.

5. Robert Wodrow, *Correspondence*, ed. T. McCrie [Edinburgh 1844-5]

6. NLS. Yester MS.7044, James Erskine of Grange to Lord Tweeddale, 26 Aug., 1733.

7. Ibid.

8. NLS. Saltoun MS.16552, Mrs. Mary Campbell to Lord Milton, 11 Dec., 1733.

9. Ibid., Lord Milton to Lord Ilay, undated draft to Ilay's letter of Nov., 1733.

10. NLS. Erskine-Murray MS.5074, 'Memorandum for Mr. E[rski]ne S[olici]tor G[enera]11 for Scotland,' 3 Apr., 1732.

11. NLS. Yester MS.7044, James Erskine of Grange to Lord Tweeddale, 9 Jan., 1734.

12. Ibid.

13. Ibid.

14. Ibid.

15. SRO. RH11/27/13, Court book of the Regality of Dunfermline, 1730–40.

16. Ibid. 'Act for two Court Days in the Week,' 8 Aug., 1735.

17. NLS. Yester MS.7044, James Erskine of Grange to Lord Tweeddale, 9 Jan., 1734.

18. Ibid.

19. Ibid.

20. Ibid.

21. SRO. Montrose, GD220/5/1286, James Erskine of Grange to Mungo Graeme of Gorthie, 7 Jan., 1734.

22. NLS. Saltoun MS.16555, Lord Milton to the Earl of Ilay, Jan., 1734.

23. SRO. Montrose, GD220/5/1286, James Erskine of Grange to Mungo Graeme of Gorthie, 7 Jan., 1734.

24. Ibid.

25. NLS. Yester MS.7044, James Erskine of Grange to Lord Tweeddale, 28 Jan., 1734.

26. Ibid.

27. Ibid.

28. Ibid.

29. SRO. Mar & Kellie, GD124/25/2053–4, Lord Tweeddale to James Erskine of Grange, 23 Feb., 1734.

30. NLS. Yester MS.7044, James Erskine of Grange to Lord Tweeddale, 28 Jan., 1734.

31. Ibid., from James Erskine of Grange, 9 Jan., 1734.

32. Ibid.

33. Ibid.

34. Ibid.

35. SRO. Montrose, GD220/5/1286, James Erskine of Grange to Mungo Graeme of Gorthie, 7 Jan., 1734.

36. Ibid.

37. NLS. Yester MS.7044, James Erskine of Grange to Lord Tweeddale, 10 Jan., 1734.

38. Ibid., James Erskine of Grange to Lord Tweeddale, 11 Mar., 1734.

39. SRO. Montrose, GD220/5/1286, James Erskine of Grange to Mungo Graeme of Gorthie, 21 Mar., 1734.

40. NLS. Yester MS.7044, James Erskine of Grange to Lord Tweeddale, 29 Mar., 1734.

41. Ibid., James Erskine of Grange to Lord Tweeddale, 11 Mar., 1734.

42. A son of Colonel James Campbell, cousin of the Duke of Argyll, and through his mother, a cousin of Lord Milton.

43. NLS. Yester MS.7044, James Erskine of Grange to Lord Tweeddale, 11 Mar., 1734.

44. Ibid.

45. Ibid., James Erskine of Grange to Lord Tweeddale, 18 Mar., 1734.

46. NLS. Saltoun MS.16555, Capt. Charles Campbell to Lord Milton, 11 May, 1734.

47. NLS. Yester MS.7044, James Erskine of Grange to Lord Tweeddale, 29 Mar., 1734.

48. Ibid.

49. Ibid.

50. Ibid.
51. SRO. Montrose, GD22/5/1286, James Erskine of Grange to Mungo Graeme of Gorthie, 21 Mar., 1734.
52. Ibid., James Erskine of Grange to Mungo Graeme of Gorthie, 5 Apr., 1734.
53. Ibid.
54. Ibid., James Erskine of Grange to Mungo Graeme of Gorthie, 21 Mar., 1734.
55. Ibid., James Erskine of Grange to Mungo Graeme of Gorthie, 5 Apr., 1734.
56. NLS. Saltoun MS.16555, Capt. Charles Campbell to Lord Milton, 10 May, 1734.
57. Ibid., from Capt. Charles Campbell, 11 May, 1734.
58. NLS. Yester MS.7044, James Erskine of Grange to Lord Tweeddale, 29 Mar., 1734.
59. NLS. Saltoun MS.16555, Capt. Charles Campbell to Lord Milton, 11 May, 1734.
60. SRO. Mar & Kellie, GD124/25/2071/2, 'Minutes of the election of a delegate, Dunfermline, 16th May, 1734.'
61. Ibid., GD124/25/2071/1, 'Minutes of the election at Inverkeithing, 18 May, 1734.'
62. Act 7 Geo. II, c.16.
63. SRO. Mar & Kellie, GD124/67/G784, Election account.
64. Ibid., GD124/25/2071/1, Minutes of Inverkeithing election.
65. Ibid.

Conclusion

The analysis of eighteenth-century Scottish politics in terms of minister-managers mustering their loyal cohorts of members of parliament, through the manager's dominance of a corrupt electorate, may be conventional, but it does not provide an accurate picture of political activity and creates a misleading view of the extent of ministerial dominance. Elaborate, and superficially convincing, schemes designed to arrange for the victory of Administration in a general election are frequently found among the papers of politicians, but closer investigation of the actual management of political interests at the constituency level suggests that the complicated structures were often built on sand. Henry Dundas, who by common consent must be regarded as one of the ablest political manipulators to be concerned in Scottish politics, could still suffer a humiliating defeat at the hands of the Angus freeholders who rejected a candidate whose services were of value to the Government in general and to Dundas in particular. An established interest, like that of the Duke of Montrose in the city of Glasgow, could be overthrown largely by the efforts of an ambitious bailie, while the efforts of Lord Ilay and Lord Milton could not prevent a county election in Peebles from being fought to a very close finish. Elections in eighteenth-century Scotland were won or lost, not in London or Edinburgh, but in the constituencies, and the successful politician was the one who could best manage such difficult voters as burgh councillors and county freeholders.

The corruption which was found so often in burgh elections is not itself an explanation of why one politician was chosen to represent a district and another was rejected, for in the Scottish burghs it was common for every candidate in the field to spend money freely and for all of them to claim that they had the support of Administration, or at least that they would, if elected, be acceptable to the Government and thus able to ensure a constant flow of patronage appointments and other favours. The Linlithgow district of burghs was notoriously venal, and bribery was part and parcel of every politician's plans for these towns, but victory and defeat turned not on the actual gifts to councillors but on the managerial skills of the candidates. Lawrence Dundas may have been more generous with his money than his rival, but it would be a distortion of the facts to suggest that this was why the voters of this district rejected a candidate who was supported by the leading figures in Scottish political life and chose a man who was quite unacceptable to them. Lawrence Dundas won his election by his abilities as a political manager, and this is as true of all the successful burgh or county politicians.

Management demanded abilities, and if an interest could command the necessary degree of talent, it could resist a strong attack. The ability of the interest of Sir Thomas Dundas to sustain itself in face of the attacks of Henry Dundas and Administration, even when the member of parliament was less than active, is a

233

demonstration of the durability of a strong interest consisting of a number of gentlemen in alliance. Conversely, if the leader of an interest made the wrong managerial decisions, his interest could collapse as completely as did that of the Earl of Marchmont, who so effectively alienated the freeholders of Berwickshire. Faced with a political contest, burgh politicians could, and did, involve that element of the community which was constitutionally excluded from a voice in political affairs, and the experienced local politician did not lose sight of the power of public opinion, which could sway venal councillors to vote in a way contrary to their own inclinations. Politics, in short, involved much more than drawing up plans and handing out patronage.

In eighteenth-century Scotland patronage appointments were essential to the economic wellbeing of most freeholders and burgh councillors, and politicians required access to such places in order to strengthen their relations with their constituents. Patronage, however, had to be managed effectively. An inadequate manager, like David Scott, could have the most extensive resources in his hands, yet he could still be rejected by the voters of his county and forced to retire to a burgh seat. The provision of patronage was a tool of the politician, but it demanded skill from its user. Its purpose in effective management was to cement ties of friendship between politician and voter, and the fact that there was never enough patronage to satisfy all the demands made upon the politician made it a dangerous tool. The true key to managing a Scottish county in the eighteenth century was the ability of the politician to make and retain friends, and the manner in which this was accomplished owed more to social contacts than to the mere distribution of places. Established ties of mutual regard and friendship could survive a freeholder's disappointment at failing to secure an appointment for a son or other dependent, but a politician whose contacts with his constituents were restricted to patronage letters was never strongly entrenched and would be vulnerable to any attack by a rival interest.

One of the facts of eighteenth-century life which should not be ignored was the attitude of the Scottish voter to his representative. The member of parliament was chosen to serve the interests of his electors, and in a century in which almost every form of employment which might interest a gentleman was obtainable only through the intervention of a politician, the provision of patronage was much less an attempt to bribe electors than it was a duty expected of a representative. Obviously, since so much of the available patronage was carefully controlled by the Treasury and its delegates, this goes a long way towards explaining why so many of the Scottish members of parliament voted with Administration. On the other hand, there were opposition members of parliament chosen for Scottish constituencies, and in their case the patronage distributed was commonly non-government aid, such as estate patronage, Indian appointments, commercial favours and places in mercantile houses, or even, in special circumstances, naval patronage. The ability to provide places was a requirement in eighteenth-century Scotland, and the success or failure of a county or burgh politician was determined by his skill in using the various forms of this commodity available to him. A wrong choice could damage an interest much more easily than a good choice would strengthen it, notably in the area of church patronage. But in any type of patronage appointment, where many would be disappointed for one whose gratitude might be anticipated, the personal qualities and manner of the politician were important. A politician who offended his constituents, in whatever manner, was likely to retire abruptly from political life, and it was always very easy to give offence to Scottish freeholders, who could discover a deliberate slight in any neglect; resentment, once aroused, weakened any interest and left it open to attack.

Freeholders, and to a lesser extent burgh voters, should not be seen as merely a handful of venal men manipulated by professional politicians. Most of them had a strong sense of their own social rank and constitutional powers, and if their view of politics tended to be largely restricted to their own communities and their own self-interest, that did not make them the docile creatures of the politicians. The detailed instructions given to the members of parliament, requiring them to give an account of their parliamentary conduct and to perform certain defined tasks, does not suggest that the politician was in complete command of his voters. Freeholders and councillors had to be managed to create a durable political interest, and a politician who began to take their support for granted was likely to encounter serious difficulties.

APPENDIX
Scottish Counties and Burghs represented in Parliament, 1707–1832

Counties
Aberdeen
Angus, or Forfarshire
Argyll
Ayr
Banff
Berwick
Dumfries
Dunbarton
Moray, or Elgin
Fife
Inverness
Kincardine
Kirkcudbright
Lanark
Linlithgow
East Lothian, or Haddingtonshire
Midlothian, or Edinburghshire
Orkney and Shetland
Peebles
Perth
Renfrew
Ross
Roxburgh
Selkirk
Stirling
Sutherland
Wigtown

Bute, alternating with the county of Caithness
Clackmannan, alternating with the county of Kinross
Cromarty, alternating with the county of Nairn

In all, thirty members of parliament

Burghs
Aberdeen, Inverbervie, Montrose, Brechin and Arbroath

Anstruther Easter, Anstruther Wester, Kilrenny, Crail and Pittenweem
Ayr, Campbeltown, Irvine, Rothesay and Inveraray
Dumfries, Kirkcudbright, Sanquhar, Annan and Lochmaben
Dysart, Kirkcaldy, Burntisland and Kinghorn
Edinburgh
Elgin, Inverurie, Banff, Cullen and Kintore
Glasgow, Dumbarton, Renfrew and Rutherglen
Haddington, Lauder, Dunbar, North Berwick and Jedburgh
Inverness, Nairn, Forres and Fortrose
Linlithgow, Peebles, Selkirk and Lanark
Perth, Forfar, Dundee, St. Andrews and Cupar
Stirling, Queensferry, Inverkeithing, Dunfermline and Culross
Tain, Kirkwall, Dingwall, Dornoch and Wick
Wigtown, Stranraer, Whithorn and New Galloway

In all, fifteen members of parliament

Sources and Bibliography

Unpublished
National Library of Scotland
Airth Papers
Culloden Papers
Erskine Murray Papers
Lauriston Castle, Delvine Papers
Melville Papers
Saltoun Papers
Yester Papers

Scottish Record Office
Sheriff Court Records, Freeholders Records
Agnew of Lochnaw Papers
Balngown Castle Papers
John C. Brodie, W.S. Papers
Cunninghame Graham Papers
Dalhousie Papers
Dalquharran Papers
Duntreath Papers
Elphinstone Papers
Forbes of Callendar Papers
Home of Wedderburn Muniments
Mar and Kellie Muniments
Melville Castle Papers
Montrose Muniments
Moray of Abercairney Muniments
Ochtertyre Papers
Rose of Kilravock Papers
Ross Estate Muniments
Scott of Ancrum Papers
Scott of Harden Papers
Seafield Papers
Messrs Todd, Murray and Jamieson, W.S. Papers

India Office
Letter Books of David Scott of Dunninald

National Maritime Museum
Keith Papers

North Riding Record Office, Northallerton
Zetland Papers

Theses
William Ferguson, Electoral Law and Procedure in Eighteenth and Early Nineteenth Century Scotland, University of Glasgow Ph.D. 1957
Ronald Sunter, Stirlingshire Politics, 1707–1832, University of Edinburgh Ph.D. 1971

Contemporary Periodicals

The Glasgow Courier
The Scots Magazine
The Scotsman

Published Primary Sources

Sir Charles E. Adam, *The Political State of Scotland in 1788* [Edinburgh, 1887]
The Duke of Argyll, *Intimate Society Letters of the Eighteenth Century* [London, 1910]
G.R. Barnes and G.H Owens [eds.], *The Sandwich Papers* [London, 1932–39]
R. Bell, *Treatise on the Election Laws* [Edinburgh, 1812]
James Bridges, *View of the Political State of Scotland at Michaelmas 1811* [Edinburgh, 1812]
Henry Cockburn, *Memorials of His Time* [Edinburgh, 1856]
Henry Cockburn, *Letters on the Affairs of Scotland* [London, 1874]
A. Connell, *Treatise on the Election Laws of Scotland* [Edinburgh, 1827]
J.G. Dunlop, *The Dunlop Papers*, Vol.3 [Frome, 1953]
'An Explanation of the Election Laws', *Scots Magazine*, 52, May 1790
 The Faculty Collection of Decisions [Edinburgh, 1752–1825]
Sir James Fergusson, *Letters of George Dempster to Sir Adam Fergusson, 1756–1813* [London, 1934]
John Murray Graham, *Annals and Correspondence of the Viscount and first and second Earls of Stair* [Edinburgh, 1875]
Edward Hughes [ed.], *The Private Correspondence of Admiral Lord Collingwood* [London, 1957]
The Journal of the House of Commons
Sir John Knox Laughton [ed.], *Letters and Papers of Charles, Lord Barham* [London, 1907–11]
C. Lloyd [ed.], *The Keith Papers*, Vols. 2 and 3 [London, 1951–55]
H.D. Macwilliam, *The Letters of Lord Elchies* [Aberdeen, 1927]
Memorials of the Public Life and Character of the Right Honourable James Oswald of Dunnikier [Edinburgh, 1825]
Alexander Mundell, *Considerations upon the Situation of the Elective Franchise as it Respects Counties in Scotland* [London, 1821]

John Murray, 7th Duke of Atholl, *Chronicles of the Atholl and Tullibardine Families*, 5 vols., privately printed

'Papers relating to the Royal Burghs of Scotland', *Parliamentary Papers* 1823, XV

W.G. Perrin, *The Keith Papers*, Vol.1 [London, 1927]

W.G. Philips [ed.], *The Correspondence of David Scott, Director and Chairman of the East India Company, 1787–1805* [London, 1951]

John Ramsay of Ochtertyre, *Scotland and Scotsmen in the Eighteenth Century* [Edinburgh, 1888]

R. Renwick [ed.], *Extracts from the Records of the Royal Burgh of Stirlingm 1667–1752* [Glasgow, 1889]

Sir G.H. Rose, *Selections from the Papers of the Earls of Marchmont* [London, 1831]

Royal Commission on Historical Manuscripts, Report 21, *Calendar of the Manuscripts of the Duke of Hamilton* [London, 1932]

Royal Commission on Historical Manuscripts, Report 67, *Report on the Manuscripts of the Right Honourable Lord Polwarth* [Edinburgh, 1911–61]

Charles Ryscamp and Frederick Pottle [eds.], *The Private Papers of James Boswell: The Ominous Years, 1774–1776* [London, 1963]

John Stuart [ed.], *Letters of Lord Grange, 1731–41*, in *Spalding Club Miscellany III* [Aberdeen, 1846]

Matthew Symson, *The Present State of Scotland* [London, 1738]

Thomas Thomson, *Memorial on Old Extent*, ed. J.D. Mackie [Edinburgh, 1946]

Duncan Warand [ed.], *More Culloden Papers*, 5 vols. [Inverness, 1923–30]

Robert Wodrow, *Correspondence*, ed. T. McCrie [Edinburgh, 1842–3]

Secondary Sources

George Bain, *History of Nairnshire* [Nairn, 1898]

Edward Pelham Brenton, *Life and Correspondence of John, Earl of St. Vincent* [London, 1838]

G. Brunton and D. Haig, *An Historical Account of the Senators of the College of Justice from its Institution in 1532* [Edinburgh, 1832]

W.L. Burn, 'The General Election of 1761 at Ayr', *English Historical Review*, LII

Ian R. Christie, *The end of North's Ministry, 1780–82* [London, 1958]

James Cleland, *Annals of Glasgow* [Glasgow, 1816]

William Cramond, *Records of Elgin* [Aberdeen, 1903]

Patricia Dickson, *Red John of the Battles* [London, 1973]

Robert Douglas. *Annals of the Royal Burgh of Forres* [Elgin, 1934]

E. Dunbar Dunbar, *Social Life in Former Days*, second series [Edinburgh, 1866]

William Ferguson, 'Dingwall Burgh Politics and the Parliamentary Franchise in the Eighteenth Century', *Scottish Historical Review* 38 [1959]

William Ferguson, 'The Reform Act [Scotland] of 1832: Intention and Effect', *Scottish Historical Review* 45 [1966]

William Ferguson, *Scotland, 1689 to the Present* [Edinburgh, 1968]

William Ferguson, *Scotland's Relations with England: a Survey to 1707* [Edinburgh, 1977]

Alexander Fergusson, *The Honourable Henry Erskine, Lord Advocate of Scotland, with Notices of his Kinsfolk and of his Times* [Edinburgh, 1882]

Sir James Fergusson, 'Making Interest in Scottish County Elections ', *Scottish Historical Review* 26 [1947]

Archibald Foord, *His Majesty's Opposition, 1714–1830* [London, 1975]

Joseph Foster, *Members of Parliament, Scotland, 1357–1882* [1882]

Sir William Fraser, *Memorials of the Family of Wemyss of Wemyss* [Edinburgh, 1888]

Holden Furber, *Henry Dundas, first Viscount Melville, 1742–1811* [Oxford, 1931]

George Gay, *The History of Arbroath* [Arbroath, 1876]

Donald Ginter, *Whig Organization in the General Election of 1790* [Berkeley, 1967]

T. Crouther Gordon, *Anstruther, or Illustrations of Scottish Burgh Life* [Anstruther, 1888]

Sir J.A. Haldane, *The Haldanes of Gleneagles* [Edinburgh, 1929]

James Hayes, 'Scottish Officers in the British Army, 1714–63' *Scottish Historical Review* 37 [1958]

Geoffrey Holmes, *British Politics in the Age of Anne* [London, 1967]

Joseph Irving, *A History of Dumbartonshire* [Dumbarton, 1857]

G.P. Judd, *Members of Parliament, 1734–1832*, 2nd ed. [Hamden, Connecticut. 1972]

Bruce Lenman, *Integration, Enlightenment and Industrialization: Scotland 1746–1832* [London, 1981]

George MacGregor, *The History of Glasgow* [Glasgow, 1881]

T.H. McGuffie, 'The Significance of Military Rank in the British Army, 1790–1820', *Bulletin of the Institute of Historical Research* 30 [1957]

John Marshall, *Royal Naval Biography* [London, 1823–35]

R. Montgomery Martin, *East Indies*, Vol.2 [London, 1837]

Cyril Matheson, *The Life of Henry Dundas, first Viscount Melville, 1742–1811* [London, 1933]

William Law Mathieson, *Scotland and the Union: A History of Scotland from 1695–1747* [Glasgow, 1905]

William Law Mathieson, *The Awakening of Scotland: A History from 1747–1811* [Glasgow, 1910]

George Menary, *The Life and Letters of Duncan Forbes of Culloden* [London, 1936]

James Miller, *The History of Dunbar* [Dunbar, 1855]

Alexander Murdoch, *'The People Above': Politics and Administration in Mid-Eighteenth Century Scotland* [Edinburgh, 1980]

Sir Lewis Namier and John Brooke [eds.], *The History of Parliament: The House of Commons, 1754–1790* [London, 1964]

W. Nimmo, *The History of Stirlingshire*, 3rd ed. [London, 1880]

George Omond, *The Lord Advocates of Scotland* [Edinburgh, 1880]

George Omond, *Arniston Memoirs* [Edinburgh, 1887]

S

The Oriental Herald, July 1827, 'Debate at the East India House, 20th June 1827, on the Patronage of Directors'

C. Northcote Parkinson, *Trade in the Eastern Seas, 1793–1813* [Cambridge, 1937]

Sir James Balfour Paul, *The Scots Peerage*, 9 vols. [Edinburgh, 1904–14]

C.H. and D. Philips, 'Alphabetical List of the Directors of the East India Company', *Journal of the Royal Asiatic Society* [1941]

J.H. Plumb, *Sir Robert Walpole*, 2 vols. [London, 1956–60]

E. and A. Porritt, *The Unreformed House of Commons* [London, 1903]

Charles Rampini, *A History of Moray and Nairn* [Edinburgh, 1898]

Charles Rogers [ed.], *Boswelliana* [London, 1874]

P.W.J. Riley, *The English Ministers and Scotland* [London, 1964]

P.W.J. Riley, 'The Structure of Scottish Politics and the Union of 1707', in *The Union of 1707*, ed. T.I. Rae [Glasgow, 1974]

P.W.J. Riley, *The Union of England and Scotland* [Manchester, 1978]

P.W.J. Riley, *King William and the Scottish Politicians* [Edinburgh, 1979]

Hew Scott, *Fasti Ecclesiae Scoticanae*, 9 vols. [1915–1961]

Romney Sedgwick [ed.], *The History of Parliament: the House of Commons, 1715–54* [London, 1970]

Henry R. Sefton, 'Lord Ilay and Patrick Cuming: a Study in Eighteenth Century Ecclesiastical Management', *Records of the Scottish Church History Society*, xix [1977]

J.S. Shaw, *The Management of Scottish Society, 1707–1764* [Edinburgh, 1983]

John M. Simpson, 'who Steered the Gravy Train, 1707–1766?', in *Scotland in the Age of Improvement*, ed. N.T. Phillipson and R. Mitchison [Edinburgh, 1970]

Annie Steel, *Records of Annan, 1678–1833* [Annan, 1933]

William Stephen, *History of Inverkeithing and Rosyth* [Aberdeen, 1921]

John Struthers, *The History of Scotland from the Union to the Abolition of the Heritable Jurisdictions* [Glasgow, 1827]

A. Wight, *The Rise and Progress of Parliament* [Edinburgh, 1806]

Robert Young, *Annals of the Parish and Burgh of Elgin* [Elgin, 1879]

Index